A MIDLIFE JOURNEY

A MIDLIFE JOURNEY

Gerald O'Collins SJ

GRACEWING

Originally published in 2012
by Connor Court Publishing Pty Ltd, Australia

This edition 2012

Gracewing
2 Southern Avenue
Leominster
Herefordshire HR6 0QF

www.gracewing.co.uk

The right of Gerald O'Collins to be identified as the author of this work
has been asserted in accordance with the Copyright, Designs and
Patents Act 1988.

ISBN 978 0 85244 803 8

Foreword

In his magnificent book, *Fundamental Theology*, Gerald O'Collins writes: 'All experience has meaning ... all experience bears with it a certain purposefulness or finality' (p. 39). This statement captures for me the essence of volume one of his autobiography, which traces the journey from his childhood to his taking up a post of Professor of Fundamental Theology at the Gregorian University in Rome.

My first meeting with Gerald occurred in the autumn of 1978 when I was one of the delegates at the Anglican Centre in Rome. I had been chosen to represent the Church of England, and there were some thirty or so delegates from other parts of the Anglican Communion. This unusual event aimed at introducing young Anglicans to the Roman Catholic Church. Lectures from experts filled part of our three week stay. The lecturers were all outstanding, but the one I most remember was Gerald O'Collins himself—a cheerful Australian with a mop of curly, dishevelled hair. His Australian accent was very distinctive, and added extra depth to an impression of a warm human being who seemed focused on people and not in the least solely concerned with representing an institution. Gerald made a hit with each of us; his honesty and transparency marked him out even then as a very special person. For myself, as a young evangelical clergyman who had been brought up to be sceptical of Roman Catholicism--the Church, its teaching and its priests—the three weeks in Rome turned out to be a 'conversion' moment. Gerry played an important part in my development.

Mind you, it could have turned out differently as far as our friendship was concerned because, as I left Rome at the end of my 'Roman' experience, Gerry entrusted me with a manuscript for a new book and I promised I would post it to the publishers on my return to London. On reaching my parish I forgot that commitment completely, because I was immersed in all the preparations for Christmas. I found the ms in my briefcase several weeks later! Even that ghastly mistake was forgiven by a man who became a great friend and fellow Christian.

If all experience has meaning, then an individual's encounter with life cannot be separated from family and, possibly more importantly, from the Church which for many of us is the greatest environment for meaning. So it is that Gerald O'Collins's journey coincided with all the dramatic events of the post-war European reconstruction, the demise of the British Empire, May 1968 in France, the Beatles generation and, perhaps as significant as any of them, the revolution in world Christianity caused by the Second Vatican Council. With remarkable honesty and lucidity Gerry describes the impact of Vatican II on his generation of young priests. This first part of his autobiography pulls no punches as he narrates the challenge to his thinking as well as to his calling to celibacy. Yet this story could so easily have been 'sanitised', trivialised and made inoffensive for the sake of readers who might have desired a description of clerical life devoid of real challenges. Thankfully Gerry has not given in to that temptation. With considerable and deep insight he has presented us with a fascinating and detailed autobiography of a fruitful and fulfilled life. I marvel how he managed to keep such detailed diaries, just as I marvel how he has found the time to produce works of scholarship that have blessed Christians of all denominations.

In a real sense *A Midlife Journey* sums up a journey of faith that overlaps with many Christians today. Through Gerry and others like him, my own spiritual journey has been formed and shaped. I am no longer the same evangelical Anglican who defines Christianity by the history of my church. The ecumenical journey is pointless without Rome, and I am grateful for the generous, inclusive faith of Gerry which recognises that the Spirit has been working in non-Roman

Churches, as it has within the Catholic Church. As Archbishop of Canterbury in the 90s it was my joy to meet Pope John Paul II on many occasions for personal talks and prayer. I always left his presence aware of what we shared in common. This always gave me hope that, one day, our churches will be surprised to find that we no longer have solid reasons to remain apart. People like Gerald O'Collins with their joyful enthusiasm and gift of friendship will remain prophetic figures until that time comes.

George Carey
The Most Rev. and Rt. Hon. Lord Carey of Clifton
(Archbishop of Canterbury, 1991-2002)

4

Introduction

The day President John Fitzgerald Kennedy died my midlife journey and path to Rome began. In a quiet, Jesuit seminary outside Sydney I faced my final examination in theology and philosophy—a two-hour oral conducted in Latin and with questions from four professors—and I decided, for the first time in my life, to keep a diary. Seven months later I left for Europe. An outer journey had started and would take me around the globe six times in ten years. That decade led me to live in Germany, England, the United States, Australia and, finally, Italy. It was largely a tale of three cities: the original Cambridge in East Anglia, the new Cambridge in Massachusetts, and Melbourne in Australia.

An inner journey accompanied the outer journey, yet keeping a pace of its own. The shift from a fixed place in my country, my family, and my society to series of temporary places raised and helped settle questions about myself and the wider world. Identity involved making sense of the road that was taken.

On re-reading my diary, I found it served mainly as a log for the journey. Often I recorded only outer landmarks, movements of external history. It required an effort to mark the stages of inner progress and correlate the public experience with any spiritual change. If the diary mostly reflected the surface, I had to answer the question: was there any depth and meaning in all that?

If this account of a midlife journey is to make full sense, I need to tell the story of my origins and life until November 1963 when that journey started. The first half of this book might stand in its own right. It describes the progress of an Irish-Australian family, and records what life was like in Jesuit seminaries during the Cold War, the papacy of Pius XII, and the aggiornamento initiated by Blessed John XXIII.

The second half of the book—quite apart from its journey theme—traces the ways in which I had to rethink the foundations of my faith during and after the Second Vatican Council (1962–65), and charts the tumultuous events of 1968 and their aftermath. With October 2012 marking fifty years since Vatican II opened, scholarly and popular books and articles have already begun re-considering the story and teaching of the Council. This memoir differs by offering a personal focus on the episodes and changes currently being re-explored.

I would like to express my sincere thanks to the Master and Fellows of Pembroke College, who not only supplied the financial support for a year (1973/74) but also welcomed me back to Cambridge with warm friendliness. My gratitude is owed to the late Judith O'Neill, who encouraged me to write this book during that final year of my path to Rome. She was wonderfully generous in her thorough and creative criticism of the text. My memoir is dedicated to the memory of two remarkable friends, Judith and her husband John. With grateful love I remember also my sister Professor Maev O'Collins, Fr Michael Ryan, s.j. (who read and corrected my text), and all those relatives, friends and strangers who supported me on this journey. I wish to thank most warmly the Most Rev. and Rt. Hon. Lord Carey of Clifton for contributing an inspiring foreword to this memoir.

Australian Catholic University, Melbourne,
Christmas 2011.

1

Origins

The end is in the beginning and yet you go on.
Samuel Beckett, *Endgame*

I never knew my mother's parents, Patrick and Abigail McMahon Glynn. Grandmother (1869-1930) died before I was born in Melbourne on 2 June 1931. Grandfather (1855-1931) survived my birth by less than six months. Both grandparents died hundreds of miles away in Adelaide, the South Australian state capital where they had lived since the end of the nineteenth century.

At home there were three visible heirlooms from grandmother: a regal photograph of her in London taken on the occasion of her being presented at court in 1925, an ornamental piece of white Worcester ware covered with gold leaf, and a large Royal Doulton vase. Unseen she passed on to me through my mother tendencies to thrift and travel. Her own parents, John and Abigail Dynon, who had migrated from Ireland to Australia in 1854, established a prosperous china business. It supported a home in Melbourne, numerous trips back to Europe, and education for two of their five sons at Stonyhurst College, a Jesuit public school in Lancashire. When the two boys sailed for England in early 1881, their parents equipped the ship with a cow to ensure a supply a fresh milk for the voyage around the Horn.

Too much money spoiled a few of the Dynon children. Grandmother grew up nourished by family wealth and surrounded by other *nouveaux riches*. A contemporary historian did not exaggerate wildly when he described this class as turning the 'Marvellous

Melbourne' of the 1880s into a 'carnival of extravagance and luxurious living'. Grandmother herself reacted against these antics and never cared to spend money like water. But she did indulge a taste for travel. Before her marriage in 1897, she had joined her mother on several trips to Europe. That included at least one stay in Rome and half an hour's conversation in French with Pope Leo XIII. In 1916 she shared with her husband a wartime visit to England, Ireland and North America. After the war she took her youngest daughter Mary on a European tour.

When my mother inherited his large private library, grandfather's lasting effect on my life was assured. He had helped to write the Australian constitution. Mother could show me the volumes recording debates from the 1897-99 conventions which had created that basic document for our country's life. As a spokesman for many Christian bodies, he succeeded in altering its preamble so as to include the words 'humbly relying on the blessing of Almighty God'. He had been a member of the Federal House of Representatives from 1901 to 1919, a minister in three Commonwealth governments, and the last of the Founding Fathers to sit in the national parliament. On our library shelves black rows of Commonwealth *Parliamentary Debates* preserved the record. He enjoyed broad tastes in English, French, German and classical literature. Our library held his copies of Shakespeare, the works of Voltaire, Rousseau and Newman, first editions of Dickens, an early seventeenth-century edition of Catullus, and the rest. His volumes of diaries, newspaper cuttings and cabinet files lay tucked away in cupboards. I grew up knowing that this grandfather had shaped and shared Australian history—even to the point of lunching with Sir Redmond Barry on the day in 1880 when that judge sentenced to death the legendary bushranger, Ned Kelly.

Mother determined that like her father I would learn Greek and Latin, engage in public speaking, learn to ride a horse well, and escape the narrow world of tribal Catholics. More of that determination later.

Grandfather had studied classics with the Anglo-Irish ascendancy at Trinity College Dublin. He became and remained a fearless, if ungainly, rider to hounds. He refused to allow his religious adherence dictate his friendships. If few in number, his close friends included men as different as the radical South Australian premier, Charles Cameron Kingston, and Lord Novar, a Scottish-born Governor-General of Australia.

The eldest of six surviving children, mother never enjoyed deeply happy relationships with her three sisters, Ellie, Dympna and Mary. The role of their parents focused that problem. She cherished the memory of her father and mother. They had married late, were other-worldly, and did not show their affection with natural ease, but provided their children with a secure, happy, and free upbringing. Unlike her sisters, mother did not leave home to board at the Sacred Heart convent in Melbourne, but received all her education from the English Dominican sisters in North Adelaide. As a child she contracted rheumatic fever, and suffered a long period of illness. Both during her convalescence and at other times she liked to listen to her father reading poetry—something her sisters did not care for.

My grandparents lived frugally enough to send their four daughters on trips to Europe in the 1920s and to leave all their children some inheritance. When grandfather died, mother preferred to take his library rather than accept a substantial sum of money. Rightly or wrongly, she always felt that her sisters blamed their parents for various disappointments. I never heard mother take pleasure in her sisters' sorrows, or suggest that she had 'done better' than they had. But she remained genuinely grieved that, even many years after their parents' death, her sisters failed to share her affectionate memory of Paddy and Abbie Glynn.

My reaction to this tension was twofold. Both as a Jesuit and before my entry into the Society of Jesus, I sought out the company of my aunts, partly because I spontaneously liked them and partly because

I hoped to improve family relationships. Then in 1958 I decided to write grandfather's life—wanting, I suppose, to vindicate mother's memory of his worth. That work resulted in *Patrick McMahon Glynn* (Melbourne University Press, 1965) and an edition of his family correspondence, *Patrick McMahon Glynn: Letters to His Family* (Polding Press, 1974). He became more real and dear to me than most people with whom I have shared a home. I will return to grandfather in a later chapter.

My father's parents, Patrick James and Ellen O'Collins both came from Ireland, lived most of their lives in Melbourne, and had some direct contact with me as a child and teenager. Grandfather (1856-1940) was born outside the village of Glin in Country Limerick, was baptized 'Patrick James Collins', and added an 'O' to his surname around the time he sailed for Australia. As a child he lost both his parents, first his father and then two years later his mother, through cholera or typhoid. At the age of seven he returned from his mother's funeral with his sister Brigid to find that they had been evicted and that the roof was already off their cabin. The land was wanted for cattle. Relatives looked after the two orphans. Brigid migrated to New York, married and raised a family. Pat, nicknamed 'the holy one' by some neighbours, entered the Patrician Brothers.

Grandfather was teaching trades at an industrial school when his institute adopted new constitutions that introduced two classes, teaching- and lay-brothers, with status to be determined by one's standard of studies and knowledge of Latin. As he had no Latin, if he wished to remain a Patrician, it could not be as a teaching-brother. Two others on the staff at this school, faced with the same choice, left at once and died shortly afterwards, one by drowning! Pat agreed, however, to give the life of a lay-brother a six-month trial, but found it unbearable and sought release from his vows of poverty, chastity and obedience. One photograph that survives from his period in the Patricians shows his strong jaw, brush hair and dark eyes. In the original snap he wore a clerical collar. This was turned into a bow-tie, when one of his family reproduced the photograph years later.

Now into his thirties and with more than ten years as a religious brother behind him, grandfather became a victim of his institute's reorganization and was flung on his own resources. Wherever he lived in Ireland or even England, his Catholic neighbours would sooner or later hear, 'he's an ex-brother, you know'. Rather than risk being treated like a second-rate drop-out, he decided to use the money he received when he left the Patricians to pay for the passage to Australia. He had read that Tommy Bent, the premier of Victoria, wanted a manager for a new industrial school. When he arrived in Melbourne, grandfather found that the actual terms failed to fit the advertisement and withdrew his application. He then visited Frankston, a small town twenty-five miles down Port Phillip Bay from the centre of Melbourne. He had been asked to manage the newly opened gasworks. Religious considerations stopped him from accepting the post. At Frankston he could attend Mass only once a month. A few years earlier, Michael Mornane, a wealthy Catholic lawyer with a holiday home in Mornington, had persuaded the cathedral authorities to shift the headquarters of the sprawling parish from Frankston to Mornington, a town around ten miles further down the bay. Grandfather returned to Melbourne, took a job as a meter-maker at the South Melbourne gasworks, and stayed there until his retirement in 1921. He was not, however, done with the Mornanes. His third son and my father, Frank, would marry a grand-niece of Michael Mornane, live at Frankston, and send his three sons to Xavier College, a public school built on land sold by the Mornanes to the Jesuit order.

In Melbourne grandfather became engaged to Ellen Fitzgerald (1864-1947), who had left her home near Glin on the banks of the Shannon and sailed in 1887 for Australia. By his first wife her father had nine surviving children, most of whom migrated to the Australian colonies. After his wife's death he married again and Ellen was the eldest of the nine children born from the second marriage. The majority of the second family also left Ireland. Michael inherited the family home. Joe became a parish priest in Manchester, Alice was a nun in England, Will drowned on the Gold Coast (the British colony in west Africa that became Ghana in 1957), Dan was a Christian Brother in Dublin and New York (where he died), Lizzie married a Limerick farmer, one child died in infancy, while Ellen and her brother Tom sailed for Australia. As she put matters, 'I had the choice of staying in Ireland and rearing a family who would migrate or migrating myself and having a family in Australia. I migrated myself.'

According to family tradition, her Fitzgerald ancestors had crossed the Shannon from the northern (Clare) shore in the early seventeenth century and went on to establish themselves as prosperous farmers near Glin. My home at Frankston, Rock Lodge, drew its name from the two-storey Fitzgerald house in Ireland where Ellen grew up. The crossing of the Shannon lingered on in our family memory as an exodus-event, an escape from poverty in Clare to land, homes and plentiful offspring in Limerick. The far longer journey in the late nineteenth century to Australia became a minor extension of the earlier crossing. Almost inevitably my father called his house on the shores of Port Phillip Bay after the ancestral home on the banks of the Shannon.

If grandfather and grandmother had stayed in Ireland, they could hardly have married. It was not simply that Pat O'Collins was 'a spoiled brother'. He knew the Fitzgeralds in Limerick, but ranked lower in local society. An evicted orphan could not have married a daughter from Rock Lodge. Grandmother recalled going as a small child to visit the cabin of Jeremiah Collins, her future husband's grandfather. It was an act of charity for a Fitzgerald to call on the dying old man. Apart from the fact that the living conditions of these poor peasants were different from her own, all that grandmother could remember was old Jeremiah saying to his wife: 'Sally, pass the po.' Life in Australia gave grandmother the freedom to marry grandfather, as well as liberating her energetic ambition to see her children achieve great things.

During their short engagement Pat took his fiancé once to evening devotions. She felt so shy about walking home with him that halfway through the service she slipped out of the church and went home by herself. They married in February 1890. It was Friday the thirteenth and a wet, miserable morning too. What with squalls of rain, it took some time to find a cab around seven in the morning to take them to St Brigid's, North Fitzroy. When they clattered up to the church, the priest abused them for being late. He might have been kinder, even out of respect for their piety. Although he had been working in the ministry for eighteen years in Australia, Pat and Ellen were the first couple to want more than a mere marriage ceremony and ask him for a nuptial Mass. The honeymoon was as unpretentious as their wedding—a trip the following day down Port Phillip Bay on an old steamer.

In Port Melbourne they built a house that stood on the edge of Fisherman's Bend. They looked out their backdoor onto sand hills, dumps of ash and large patches of long, rank grass which stretched across flats to the Yarra river. It was a popular place for early motorists to try out primitive motor-cars, and a decade later for madcap airmen to thrill crowds as they hurled their nightmares of canvas and wire forward and coaxed them off the ground. The area offered unlimited space to kick a football or level a pitch. Cricketers quarried ash from the railway dumps, brought it back, and fashioned fine pitches on which future Test cricketers like the McLeod brothers and J. J. Kelly played.

Grandmother's eight children were all born at home: William (1890-1970), James Patrick (1892-1983), Patrick Francis (1893-1961), Mary Margaret (Mollie, 1895-1985), Margaret Ellen (Madge, 1897-1981), Michael Fitzgerald (called 'Gerald', 1899-1983), Alice Dorothy (1901-1943), and Joseph Bernard (1902-1988). The first Sunday after they were born grandfather took each of them to be baptized at St Joseph's, Port Melbourne.

After Madge was born, grandmother remained unwell and her brother, Tom Fitzgerald, bought Dolly, a Devon cow, to provide milk for the baby. Dolly promptly tore open his prize greyhound. But she was a good milker and gave grandmother the idea of buying more cows and building up a dairy herd, which enjoyed free grazing on the unfenced areas of Fisherman's Bend. Grandfather put up milking sheds and made some of the deliveries on his way to morning Mass a mile away at St Joseph's. Two of his sons, Jim and Frank, took care of the remaining deliveries. But grandmother saw to the bulk of the business herself. Her family in Ireland would never have dreamt of letting her do the work of a dairy-maid. Now she did most of the milking, made cream and butter, and handled the accounts. She traded under the name of E.M. Collins, as the 'O' of O'Collins caused more spelling mistakes than it was worth. With a herd of 14 to 25 cows, she made about £10 a week. She kept the dairy going until early 1910 when Frank took a day off from high school to drive the last cows away for sale at a market.

Grandmother devoted herself to her family with prodigal energy. She cut down her husband's suits for the boys and made dresses for the girls. She kept a cauldron of soup simmering on the stove, and always had plenty of other food for the friends her five sons and three daughters brought home. Her husband's life ran like clockwork. He took a little tobacco money from his weekly pay and handed her the rest. Every morning grandfather attended Mass and on Sunday two Masses. He read a daily chapter of the Bible and joined his family for the evening rosary, from which he always rose to wind the mantelpiece clock.

Grandmother would jokingly say to her children: 'You've got your brains from me and your piety from your father.' He let her know that he had married in order to 'have a son a priest standing at the altar'. In fact three sons became priests (Will, Jim and Gerald) and two daughters nuns (Mollie and Alice). This pious man with his trim beard and the manners of a French aristocrat (except when a grim, silent mood took hold of him) was more than a simple-minded meter-maker. He enjoyed extraordinary powers of calculating figures in his head, whether distances or quantities, and he was a first-class chess player. The night Frank was born he was out taking part in a competition at the Melbourne Chess Club. As the baby arrived some days early, grandmother did not blame her husband for leaving her alone at home for the birth. But he never went out again to play chess. Two members of the Port Melbourne Chess Club would visit his home for a game. In the 1930s Fr Dom Kelly, the dean of Newman College within the University of Melbourne, used to cycle down once or twice a week. Grandfather would take some of his own pieces off the board to give Fr Kelly a chance, and eventually let him win one game. But the priest felt so mortified at being given a victory that he never returned to play again.

Grandfather wanted nothing more for recreation than his chess, his pipe, and occasional afternoons at cricket and football matches. During some early years of his married life, he used to send his second son, Jim, off in the evening to fetch a can of beer from a nearby pub. Grandmother would have a glass and grandfather would drink the rest. But when Jim was about eight years old, they became afraid that he was turning into a problem child. To cut off any possible avenue of bad example, they dropped the evening drink. Tom Fitzgerald, grandmother's brother and the popular lessee of the Cricket Club Hotel (later the Ritz) in St Kilda, had no children of his own and wanted Jim as his heir. He would sit the child up on the bar and show him off with a 'listen how he answers all your questions'. When Tom died, grandfather said to grandmother, 'A good thing for all of us, Ellie.' She took a long time to forgive him for that remark.

When he retired from work in 1920, grandfather went with his

daughter Madge to Europe and the United States, so that they could
visit Jim and Gerald, then students at Propaganda College in Rome,
and numerous relatives in the British Isles and the USA. He sailed
from Melbourne wearing a belt of gold sovereigns. He told his son
Frank: 'People think nothing of dashing off a cheque for a large sum
of money. But if you had to roll someone the sovereigns one by one
across the street, you would think twice about spending your money.'

Grandfather died when I was nine years of age. I remember him
appearing out of a workshop at the bottom of his garden. Towards
the end, time eluded him and he would rise hours before the dawn to
wander off to morning Mass. In trying to recapture his presence, I
am largely pulling at broken strings. But he did transmit to me a sense
of how enriching the Eucharist and the Bible might be. The rosary
was to some extent an exercise of good example for his children.
But his daily Mass and chapter from the Bible were the pillars of
his life. When he died in 1940, the old bishop of Bendigo wrote to
grandfather's eldest son, Fr Will O'Collins:

> My dear Father O'Collins, accept my sincere sympathy on the
> death of your dear father, who, in my estimation, was the best
> Catholic in Melbourne. I have no doubt that he is now enjoying the
> beatific vision. Only yesterday a visitor informed me of his death
> and funeral. I have been confined to bed for about ten days with
> the patriotic 'Pucka' throat and chest trouble, now so prevalent
> among troops and civilians in these parts. Had I known of the
> death and had I been able, I would have been at the requiem Mass
> and funeral, and I would have expressed my sympathy personally
> to the bishop, yourself, the barrister and other members of the
> family. With congratulations on so saintly a father, I remain, Very
> sincerely yours, + John McCarthy.[1]

Let me turn now from my grandparents to sketch my parents' lives

---

1 The 'bishop' was Bishop Jim O'Collins and the 'barrister' my father, Frank O'Collins. The
'Pucka'' throat drew its name from Puckapunyal, the name of an army base established in
November 1940 north of Melbourne.

up to 1931, the year of my birth. My father, Patrick Francis O'Collins, was born on 28 October 1893, in the midst of a general economic depression. That year governments slashed expenditure, banks closed their doors, and wanton land speculation plus exuberant building programmes brought ruin to many Victorian families. 'Marvellous Melbourne' lost its leadership to Sydney. But the crash of '93 hardly touched Pat and Ellen O'Collins, who now enjoyed three sons in their working-class home on the edge of Fisherman's Bend.

From his earliest years my father remained particularly close to his elder brother Jim. In their games, fights and entertainments they became inseparable. They watched (and then attempted to imitate on their own clothes-line) the exploits of a legendary tight-rope walker, called 'the Great Blondin', when he visited Melbourne shortly before his death in 1897.[2] They went down to the beach together to farewell the Victorian soldiers sailing on the troopship Metic to fight in the Anglo-Boer War. When the Duke and Duchess of Cornwall and York (later King George V and Queen Mary) arrived to open the first Commonwealth Parliament in May 1901, Jim and Frank climbed a tree to watch the royal party come ashore at St Kilda pier.

When he was not quite five and still sported long, curly hair, Frank joined Jim at St Joseph's Primary School, Port Melbourne. His diminutive godmother, Mary Keogh, taught him in the infant class. (She lived long enough to shake my hand at his funeral in 1961.) In charge of the school was William Hoy, a middle-aged man with a goatee beard, practical teaching methods, and a taste for liquor. Thereby hung two tales. In his second last year, when Frank had reached the sixth class, the prize for dux of the school should have gone to one of the three pupils in the top class, the upper sixth: Power who died in the First World War, Brennan who became a policeman, and Frank's brother Jim. Hoy, however, passed over the top class in naming the

---

2 Jean François Gravelot, nicknamed 'the Great Blondin', had become in 1859 the first tight-rope walker to cross the Niagara Falls..

dux, awarded the main prize to Harry Harman, a member of the sixth, and gave Frank a silver cross for second place. As Harman's father ran a hotel in Bay Street where Hoy could get free drinks, the choice stirred suspicion among the boys. Jim assumed the fighting leadership of a protest movement. He refused to sit for an examination, had a first-class row with Hoy, and cleared off to St Kilda to stay with Tom Fitzgerald, his uncle. When he came back to school, Jim merely got a lecture, as Fitzgerald had warned Hoy that he would 'knock his head off' if he touched the boy. Jim picked up a copy of the papers he had failed to sit for. One question in religious knowledge asked for an explanation of the letters set at the top of Christ's cross, INRI. Jim remarked: 'I would have answered, "I'm nailed right in".'

The following year, when Jim had left school to earn six shillings a week at the Port Melbourne gas works, Frank (now thirteen) was the only pupil in the upper sixth. In the mid-year exams conducted by a visiting inspector for Roman Catholic schools, he won full marks in every subject. But Hoy had another boy in mind for the top prize. He arranged that Frank should leave school before the end of the year, and take a job for seven shillings and sixpence a week as office boy with a new firm of produce merchants at the lower end of Collins Street. Hoy chose for dux a student of the sixth class, Harry Hodgens, whose father was the captain of the paddle steamer *Hygeia* and gave Hoy free trips on Sundays. Outside the three mile limit the bar could be opened. There was no examination for the prize that would have given Frank's sister, Mollie, or someone else a chance. This annoyed Ellen O'Collins so much that she took Mollie away from St Joseph's and sent her to Graham Street State School for the final year of her primary education. Grandmother discovered afterwards that Hoy himself had left St Joseph's that year, and that the Brigidine nuns had taken over the school. Later Mollie and her youngest sister, Alice, were themselves to become Brigidines.

Hoy's effectiveness as a teacher offset his taste for drink and favouritism. Frank received a first-class education in 'the three Rs', reading, writing, and arithmetic. The job Hoy recommended proved a fiasco. It took only six months for the produce firm of Ryan, Goulding and Lawrence to collapse and go into liquidation. Frank then stayed home to deliver milk, clean the sheds, bring in the cows and peel potatoes.

In those days he watched and shared in some of Jim's brawls. A lanky boy called Joe Ryan who had a good straight left gave Jim a tremendous hiding in a fight on the beach. As a consequence Jim and Frank exercised with skipping ropes, dumb-bells, and punching bags. When Jim was about fifteen and Frank a year younger, they nearly killed a big fellow in his early twenties called Michaelson. The Michaelson family, who lived in a drill-hall on Fisherman's Bend, were always leaving the gate to their garden open. Three fine heifers from the O'Collins herd kept wandering in. Eventually young Michaelson thrashed the heifers, and chased them so far away that they were impounded and sold before grandmother heard of it. When they found out, Jim and Frank determined to take Michaelson on. Their mother locked the back gate to keep them at home. Jim climbed the fence to confront Michaelson on his way home from work. Frank tried but failed to get over. By the time he had slipped out the front and arrived, Michaelson was sitting on top of Jim punching him. 'Grab that', Jim shouted and pointed to a brick. As Frank went for the brick, Jim grabbed another and 'let Michaelson have it'. The head wound needed a lot of stitches. Michaelson's family threatened to sue, but desisted when grandmother warned that she would retaliate by bringing a case against them for the loss of the three heifers.

Father continued schooling by attending night school, where the headmaster of Graham Street State School coached him. At the end of 1909 with his sister Mollie he passed the Merit Certificate and applied for the Melbourne Continuation School, which would be renamed the Melbourne High School in 1911. On Spring Street in

the heart of Melbourne they took their entrance examinations at the
school, which occupied a site now used by the Royal Australasian
College of Surgeons. After all the examinations were over the
students assembled in the hall to hear the names of the successful
candidates read out: 'First, Patrick Francis O'Collins; second, Mary
Margaret O'Collins.' Father attended Melbourne High School from
1910 to 1912, winning the Rix Prize in 1911 and being elected by
staff and fellow students head prefect for 1912. The Rix Prize went
to the boy 'who in the judgement of the staff has shown the best
character, asserted the strongest influence for good, and made the
greatest progress in his studies'. The three years at the school gave
father the chance to establish friendships beyond Irish-Catholic
circles, to register high academic achievements, and prove successful
as leader and sportsman.

From the first term his desk mate in class was Alan Ramsay, later
State Director of Education, Major General Sir Alan Ramsay, and
the first 'old boy' to become (in 1944) the principal of the school.
Father became and remained a lifelong friend of Walter ('Bill')
Cawthorn (1896-1970), who won the Rix Prize for 1913 and went on
to become a major general, an intelligence chief, and Australian High
Commissioner in Pakistan.

Bill Woodfull, the son of a Methodist minister and a future captain
of the Australian eleven, came to the school in 1912. During lunch-
hour practice at the cricket nets, Woodfull, who was too small to bowl
himself, would give father the ball to get the batsman out. It was
impossible to dismiss Woodfull, even if he did not hit the ball very far.
He had four brothers, all of whom played district cricket and for four
different clubs. As boys they played at home in their backyard, where
the rule was: 'Hit the fence on the full and you are out.' Woodfull
learned early to keep the ball along the ground. When he went to
the Teachers College, he could not get a game with the Melbourne
University first eleven. He was once selected for the seconds, because

he said he could keep wickets. He batted last and was not out when the innings closed. As he still had the pads on, he opened the second innings when his side had to follow on. He carried his bat, but he was never again selected even for the seconds. At Melbourne University only cricketers from the public schools were wanted. Later Woodfull became famous as a batsman for a country town and then for South Melbourne. He captained the Australian side in the 1932/33 bodyline series. But at Melbourne High School in 1912 father decided against giving him a game in the eleven, because he was still too small.

Ramsay, Cawthorn and Woodfull were some of father's non-Catholic friends. But his most notable friendship across the frontiers of creed and culture grew with the headmaster himself, Joseph Hocking. Father's obituary in the 1961 issue of the school magazine, *The Echo*, recalled that Hocking's narrow religious outlook and deeply seated nonconformist conscience opposed anything and everything Roman. His letters to the press directed to various Christian Brothers and priests of the day who said anything against the boys or girls of Melbourne High School make interesting reading. It was between this essentially Catholic schoolboy and this equally devout Protestant headmaster that an affinity developed. Not that Joseph Hocking, as he often said himself, could develop an enthusiastic and hearty friendship. However, we find Frank O'Collins and Joseph Hocking corresponding as friends in those dark days of World War I. Some of those letters were published in *Ours*, the school magazine of the day.

In the Senior Public examinations of 1912, father won the state exhibition for geography and geology. His first-class honours in history put him close to the top place, occupied by Robert Gordon Menzies, a future prime minister of Australia. Father also won an exhibition at Trinity College within the University of Melbourne, as well as one of the ten studentships given for the Teachers College. The studentship offered payment of fees and residence for three years, together with a further living allowance. That year father was vice-captain of the school's outstanding football team, which included five boys already playing for teams in the Victorian Football League. The Collingwood Club invited him to train. He played in the first practice match, but then stopped when Hocking pointed to his responsibilities as head prefect and asked him to quit.

The surroundings of Melbourne High School suggested two possible careers to my father: work for the government or in the church. From the school one glimpsed the spires of St Patrick's, the bluestone, neo-Gothic Catholic cathedral dominating Melbourne's skyline. Two blocks down Spring Street one came to the Victorian Houses of Parliament, where from 1901 the Commonwealth Parliament sat until the opening of Canberra as the national capital in 1927. The school itself represented a third option, a career in education. Initially Frank chose teaching rather than pursue other possibilities open to the talented but poor sons of Irish migrant families. His brother Will, who had decided to study for the priesthood, was now close to ordination at Propaganda College, Rome. Friends like Edwin (later Sir Edwin) McCarthy and Frank Murphy entered the Commonwealth public service. McCarthy rose to such posts as Deputy Australian High Commissioner in London and Australian Ambassador to the Hague. Murphy headed the Australian wool board. Another friend, Les Coleman, moved towards the hotel trade and politics, eventually becoming a member of the Victorian Legislative Council and Minister for Transport. Coleman, McCarthy and Murphy all played for the Port Melbourne Catholic Young Men's Society football team, which my uncle Jim organized and which won the premiership in their division from 1910 to 1913. Father was a member of that team from 1910 to 1912. Over forty years later he still remembered in astonishing detail the games, teams and scores from these and other competitions he played in.

In 1913, father began his three years at the Teachers College, located on the edge of Melbourne University's campus. His first two years of study took him through a range of mathematics, science, and the humanities. He was active in student politics, drafting a constitution for the student body and introducing a medallion bearing a gryphon for members of the college to wear. Sport kept its hold on him. He played as vice-captain in the college's 1913 cricket eleven and football eighteen (Australian rules). In 1914 he captained the eighteen and also led the rugby side. Professor John Smyth of the Teachers College, a fanatic for rugby, taught the game ('Go low, go hard and complete the tackle'), and made his students the first to play rugby at Melbourne University. When father went into residence at Teachers College, his parents feared that he might 'lose the faith'. So he promised to say the rosary each night. On the first night some other students noticed him praying and objected. 'It's a free country', he retorted and continued. In those first weeks at the college he practised at the university's cricket nets, but was not invited to play even for the seconds or the thirds. The old boys of the public schools kept others out. When the 1913 football season came, the captain of the university's eighteen asked him to join the team. Father declined: 'if I'm not good enough for cricket, I won't play football either.'

In August 1914 my grandparents moved to 40 Beaconsfield Parade, Albert Park. To put a railway line through to Princes Pier, the state government compulsorily acquired five brick houses which grandfather had built close to his original home in Port Melbourne. The writing was on the wall for that home; so grandfather sold up and moved to '40B' and a home facing the beach. A few weeks earlier Jim and Will returned from Rome, where Jim had gone to attend his brother's ordination to the priesthood. When in Rome, Jim made up his mind to resume secondary school studies and prepare for the ministry. (By early 1916 he would pass his Senior Public examinations and begin church studies at a seminary in New South Wales.) For the month of August father had arranged a trip to Sydney for teams of athletes, debaters and footballers from the Teachers College.

He was in Sydney when the German armies marched into Belgium and northern France. Within months he had decided to enlist in the Australian army, and took a short course for his Diploma of Education to allow him to sit for the examinations by August 1915. But when playing football (Port Melbourne against Essendon in early July), he received a nasty kick in the ankle and finished up in bed back at the Teachers College. He sat for the examinations at the end of the year, and before enlisting in May 1916 taught for three months at Geelong High School. From one former student I learned how sad the students were on the day they heard he was joining the army.

At Geelong High School father formed a friendship with a woman in her thirties. She claimed to be a Belgian and won sympathy as stories (true or merely fabricated) spread about German atrocities in Belgium. He became convinced she was a spy after she disappeared. But before that she altered the course of his military career and perhaps saved his life by delaying his departure for the front. Just as father was due to sail with a batch of reinforcements for France, she not only suggested that he take an officers training course at the Royal Military College, Duntroon, but also spoke with a major at the Melbourne Barracks about the matter. Almost at the last minute father received orders to spend some weeks at a camp in Geelong and then several months at Duntroon. He became a 'Duntroon sergeant', a soldier who had completed a course of officer training but had not yet received his commission. To fill in the time father served as an instructor in a camp outside Melbourne. The weeks slipped by. Some friends among the Duntroon sergeants left for France without waiting for their commissions. A week before another Duntroon sergeant named Ballard was to sail in the troopship *Ballarat* with reinforcements for the 38th battalion, he gave his place to my father. As Ballard wanted to go to France as a commissioned officer, he paid a warrant officer to arrange the swop.

Grandfather came down to the wharf to farewell his son when the

Ballarat left Port Melbourne at 5 a.m. on 17 February 1917. Earlier he had shown a rigid opposition to my father's decision to 'take the king's penny'. 'Go to war', he said, 'but never darken my door again.' His dislike for the English had led him to insist on the 'O' in 'O'Collins. Even in Ireland itself I have come across only one other example of the prefix being retained when *Ó'Coileain*, a descendant of *Coileain* (meaning 'Holly' or 'Fairheaded'), has been anglicized. His baptismal entry calls grandfather 'Patrick Collins, the son of James Collins and Mary Stackpoole of the Glin townland of Turraree'. Today most people in Glin still call my family 'Collins'. But that could pass for an English as well as an Irish surname. About the time he sailed for Australia in August 1888, grandfather inserted the prefix to exclude the possibility of being taken for an Englishman. Subsequent events had kept his antipathy burning. At Easter 1916 over three thousand people died in the Dublin rising, the first step towards the independence treaty of 1921. The new Catholic archbishop of Melbourne, Irish-born Dr Daniel Mannix, led the opposition to a nation-wide referendum on compulsory military service. The referendum failed and split the governing Labor Party in November 1916. Grandmother offered not the slightest opposition when father decided to enlist. Grandfather himself eventually came around. All was forgiven when father returned from Duntroon College qualified for an officer's commission.

By an odd coincidence my father's future father-in-law took office as Commonwealth Minister for Home and Territories on the day the *Ballarat* sailed. The ship called at Durban and Cape Town, taking two months for the wartime voyage to England. At night lights out was strictly enforced. 'You would almost have been court-martialled for lighting a cigarette on deck', father recalled. But the poor-grade coal sent up a great glare of fire from the tunnel. Another soldier had just declared a grand slam in a game of bridge father was playing, when a torpedo hit the ship on the afternoon of 25 April. The Ballarat slowed to a dead stop in the calm sea about seventy miles off Land's End. The crew had given the troops boat drill, but left first when the order came to abandon ship. On some of the lifeboats the tackle proved so rusty that the soldiers could not launch them. Father helped to get the boats off, and then waited with Corporal Purcell (who later won the M.C. and survived World War I to enter the Melbourne police force) for a destroyer to pull alongside. Purcell slipped down to fetch his gear from the corporals' quarters, before father also went below to pick up his own kit from the sergeants' quarters. They jumped onto the deck of the destroyer, the last two to leave the *Ballarat*. The ship took an hour more to sink. There had been no casualties; all of the 1600 soldiers and crew were rescued.

They came ashore at Portsmouth. Father was soon sent for a six-weeks course in a school for N.C.O.s, and topped the course. In July he joined D Company of the 38th battalion soon after the battle of Messines. He reverted to private's rank in France. When the company came out of the frontline to camp at Neuve Eglise, he heard a corporal make 'some very disparaging remarks' about several French nuns who had remained in the town. Father hit him and, when brought before Captain Bill Orchard, explained: 'I know it's wrong striking an inferior superior.' He knew Orchard, who played cricket for Geelong when father played for Port Melbourne. Promoted to corporal at the end of July, father had another spell in the frontline and rose to sergeant's rank. Just before the frightful battle of Passchendaele, he left for an officers' course in Oxford. Orchard had submitted his name.

During Michaelmas term father lived in Magdalen College, where the dons treated the cadets as normal undergraduates and kept up the usual formalities, including dinner with full silver. Bathtubs were still the rule at Magdalen. But the college agreed to install outside showers for the Australians. Father quickly struck up a friendship with Colonel Cox, an ex-Indian army officer and now commander of the 6th battalion cadets. One Sunday Cox took him to dine with the English critic, Sir Walter Raleigh (1861-1922), and Raleigh's only daughter. One of Raleigh's sons was a prisoner of war in Germany, and had written to his father saying that he was being treated well. Colonel Cox objected: 'It's wrong to praise the Germans.' 'One must tell the truth', retorted Raleigh. That evening father enjoyed his first taste of venison. Six foot six inches tall and a fellow of Magdalen, Raleigh spoke enthusiastically of India, where he had taught for two years at the beginning of his academic career.

In Oxford father began a lifelong friendship with Fr C.C. Martindale, an English Jesuit under whom he made a weekend retreat at Campion Hall. Father played a good deal of rugby. The highpoint came when he captained the 6th battalion to victory over the hitherto unbeaten 4th battalion, which included some members of New Zealand's invincible All Blacks. After the dinner which followed that win, he took four glasses of port and ceased to be a teetotaller. He took charge of his battalion when Viscount French, the first commander-in-chief of the British Expeditionary Force in World War I, visited Oxford to review the cadets. In the final examinations father won first place in both theoretical and practical subjects, and enjoyed a final report that recommended him as 'the best type of Australian cadet' and 'a rare leader of men'. Colonel Cox talked of the German threat to India and urged him to join the Indian army there and then. But father felt obliged to return to his company in France. All the same, he promised, 'If I am alive in six months time, I will go to India.'

At the end of January 1918 he left Magdalen College, half intending to switch from education to law if he survived the war. The term in Oxford had joined culture, religion, military training and sport to form one of the richest experiences of his life. It also offered the chance of a first trip to Ireland where he visited his uncles, Dan Fitzgerald, a Christian Brother at an industrial school in Dublin, and Michael Fitzgerald, the lord of the old family home on the banks of the Shannon, Rock Lodge. Uncle Mick kept an underground

room filled with ships in bottles, blunderbusses and old rifles. Later
he would be arrested as a Sinn Feiner for possessing guns. When
father asked him, Mick denied all knowledge of the Collinses. Father
insisted that he would go on foot to find his relatives. That made
Mick get out his buggy, as it would have been a dreadful disgrace for
the visitor to walk. Uncle Mick sat up in the buggy, while father went
from cottage to cottage searching for Collins relatives. My own uncle
Jim had visited County Limerick in 1914, and chatted with an old lady
whom he felt sure was a relative on his father's side. But she too knew
nothing. On that occasion Jim did meet his granduncle, John Collins,
a tiny old man whose five or six daughters had all become school
teachers. This seems to have been the only Collins relative any of my
family ever discovered on their many visits to Ireland.

In February 1918 father rejoined the 4th platoon, D Company,
38th battalion. By the time he left France later that year, he would
have served as private, corporal, sergeant, second lieutenant and
lieutenant in the same platoon, same company, same battalion. When
he returned to the front near Warneton, he found his unit suffering
from the endless mud and persistent enemy shelling. Every four or
five hours, forty or fifty mortar shells would rain down on them.
Father crept out into no-man's-land to fix the precise positions of the
German mortar emplacements, and gave them all women's names,
commencing with E: Edith, Elsie, Emma, and so forth. The artillery
were given exact targets and asked to stand ready for the next burst
of mortaring. As soon as it started, Captain Orchard called for fire:
'Give Edith a f…; give Elsie a f….In fact, f…the whole lot of them.'

The long-range German gun Big Bertha was shelling Paris, when
father took ten-days leave there with Captain Bill Symons, who had
won a V.C. at Gallipoli and was now serving with the Australian army
in France and Belgium.. A habitué of Paris, Symons booked rooms
for Frank and himself at the Hotel Regina in the Bois de Boulogne,
gathered two other Australian soldiers and headed for a night at the

follies. At one point in the show a girl trapeze-artist swung across their part of the audience. If anyone could catch her shoe, she could take his friends to a back-stage party. When the moment came father helped hoist Symons into the air to intercept the girl. The subsequent back-stage celebration, which moved on to Montmartre, made for the wildest party he ever saw in his life. Leave was cut short when the Germans launched their offensive on the Somme in late March.

Then six months to the day from the time Frank received his commission, order came in July 1918 to report to divisional headquarters and from there to proceed to the India office in London. Colonel Cox had carried out his side of the bargain. Father was glad to get away from fighting with hungry and dispirited enemy soldiers. An incident when his unit caught some Germans in a cutting haunted him for the rest of his life. He spoke of it obliquely, as he always believed it wrong for a soldier to admit killing anyone, let alone boast about it. But I gathered that father killed a number of Germans with automatic fire from his Lewis gun. His appointment with the A.I.F. (Australian Imperial Force) ended and he accepted a commission in the Indian Army.

He carried away two trophies from the front in Belgium and France: a silver cup and a large fragment from the plane of the legendary German pilot, Baron Manfred von Richthofen. He took the cup from a chateau in Treux, where his battalion went into action at the end of March 1918. Three weeks later he rushed to the Bray/Corbie road with other Australians, all of them anxious to secure their souvenir when the German ace was shot down. Father often joked about revisiting the village of Treux and returning the cup. But it still remains in the possession of my family. To his annoyance mother gave away the piece of von Richthofen's plane during a metal drive in the Second World War.

The late summer of 1918 drifted by without any orders coming

Rock Lodge, Frankston, in 1932

to sail for India. The delay allowed father to visit Ireland again and to see Scotland for the first time. On the train to Edinburgh he shared a compartment with a middle-aged lady who invited him to join her in visiting midshipman John Collins, later Admiral Collins of the Australian navy. They were taken out by launch to the battleship *Canada*, and shown to the captain's quarters while the midshipman was sent for. The woman, a friend of Collins's mother, gave young Collins £500 there and then and left him a further £500 in her will. The incident may have contributed to father's lifelong conviction and practice that well-timed gifts to the young could encourage them towards successful careers. With Ted Mattner,[3] a fellow Australian soldier, he visited 'Rob Roy' (Sir Walter Scott's home) and Inverness. There Mattner won a bet to speak to ten girls within a quarter of an hour. They arrived in Glasgow on a Sunday, and found the city so

---

3 Mattner had captained Adelaide High School in a football game against Melbourne High School, when father captained the latter team. In World War I, Mattner was awarded the M.M., D.C.M., and M.C.; he later became a senator in the Australian parliament and for two years served as President of the Senate.

dead that they pushed on at once to the Lake District.

On Christmas Day 1918 father was back at Rock Lodge on the banks of the Shannon, where uncle Mick cured his shocking cold with a dose of poteen. Uncle Mick wanted father to change his name to Fitzgerald and stay in Ireland, promising, 'I'll hide you.' On Boxing Day they went out together by horse and trap to visit dozens of Fitzgerald relatives. Father caught the train across from Limerick to Cork, 'rebel Cork', which would lose many of its buildings to bombing and burning before independence came in 1921. There the boys in the streets called out, 'Up the Kaiser', when they saw father in his army uniform. He had enough time for a quick visit to Wigan and his uncle Fr Joe Fitzgerald, who took him across to play bowls at Douglas on the Isle of Man.

On 13 April 1919 father joined his regiment in the Punjab Province, a day of infamy for the British raj. During World War I the demand for home rule in India had gathered momentum. The emergency legislation of March 1919, the Anarchical and Revolutionary Crimes Act, initiated Mahatma Gandhi's civil disobedience and passive resistance campaign. At the end of the month riots spread from Delhi throughout the Punjab, as nationalist feelings flared into the most violent incidents since the mutiny of 1857. The climax of civil disorder came on 13 April, when Brigadier General Reginald Dyer ordered the fifty Gurkhas under his command to fire on unarmed citizens at Amritsar and killed at least 379 people.[4] Dyer's soldiers were not under threat; it seemed that the general aimed at intimidating the populace.

When news of Dyer's murderous action arrived, father was with Major Piercey John McQueen Mottram, a member of an old Scottish Catholic family who 'despised those who received titles after 1745',

---

4 'The Amritsar Riots', a lecture father gave to the Newman Society of Victoria, appeared in the *Austral Light* for 1 August 1920.

when the uprising led by Bonnie Prince Charlie, the Stuart pretender
to the British throne, failed. Before World War I, Mottram had served
with the Carlists in Spain. Now with the British army in India, he
warned my father: 'Whatever you do, Frank, don't kill anyone.' Almost
at once father was sent with sixty sepoys to Malakwal near Lahore.
From there he wrote on 30 April to his brother Jim who was studying
for the priesthood at Propaganda College in Rome. Jim would soon
be joined by their brother Gerald, who had recently announced his
intention of becoming a priest.

> My dear Jim, Thanks for your very interesting letter of 6/3/19.
> I am still in India and am likely to remain here for many months
> to come. You may not have read of the serious rising in India
> which was quelled only on the severe measures taken by the
> Government. Further trouble is expected. I was sent to Malakwal
> with a detachment of sixty, and arrived in time to prevent [a] serious
> attack on 16 European women and children & on the Government
> property. Yet a train was wrecked, communication[s] cut & a strike
> set in motion. I was rather severe; order was ultimately restored...
> fondest love from your loving brother Frank. P.S. My French
> friend, L'Abbé Lorquier (23 Rue Hendricy, St Omer, France), is
> sending [you] several addresses of friends of his in Rome—it may
> relieve the monotony for you. He is a fine man.

As the situation eased in the Punjab, forays of Afghan tribesmen
began along the northwest frontier. The new ruler of Afghanistan,
Amanullah Khan, faced internal strife in the Afghan court; he saw
how the unrest in India that followed the Amritsar massacre might
offer the chance of organizing a successful diversion. He proclaimed
the country's complete independence from British rule and moved
troops into the border areas. The refusal of the British government
to accept this situation led to the outbreak of the third Anglo-Afghan
War on 3 May. Eight days later father wrote from Malakwal to his
sister Mollie, now a Brigidine nun:

> My dearest Mollie, I have just written to Mother. How are you

keeping? You were never the one to complain about your health. But will you always let me know just how you are; for on my return I wish to find you just as I left you, a fine, healthy   young girl. Perhaps I should not say this, but, Mollie dear, you were always my pal & class worker. Strange now to think of it! You so happy, quiet, pray[er]ful, building up fine character in the dear little children under your care. Me harsh, cruel, unpray[er]ful, seeking the slightest opportunity to kill—ever destroying. I do not doubt that my work is necessary & useful, yet not a day passes that some poor native, perhaps a scoundrel, suffers at my hands. I am still at Malakwal where I am looked upon as a real 'local hero', having been very opportune & useful on my arrival a month from date. Tomorrow I accompany my C.O. to the frontier across the Indus at Tank, going by special [train] via Kundian, Khalabagh etc. Trouble is brewing there but nothing is to be feared. At day time I am ever in readiness & at night a faithful servant watches over me. I shall be returning from above reconnaissance in a day or two. If the troops from Jhelum move out or if an officer is wanted, I believe I shall get into Afghanistan. What a treat! At present the tribes (Marris, Afridis, Wazirs, Mohmands etc.) are up in arms in a non-cohesive manner. The Afridis, I believe, will help us against the Afghans. This promises to be a fairly big show...Au revoir with kindest regards to Rev. Mother [and] Sisters, & fondest love to your dear self, ever your very affectionate brother Frank.

Shortly after he wrote, father moved to the area of fighting near the Khyber Pass, where his new friend, Major Mottram, died in an ambush. The war ended quickly with a peace treaty signed at Rawalpindi on 8 August. At the end of September father resigned his commission, left his regiment as a captain, and sailed home to Australia.

I always remained astonished at the speed with which he settled back into academic and civilian life. In the Melbourne University examinations at the end of 1919 he passed one or two subjects to

complete his B.A. The two years of arts at the Teachers College
in 1913 and 1914 had left his degree unfinished. In 1920 he began
his law studies and four years of residence at Newman College, the
Catholic men's college at Melbourne University designed by Walter
Burley Griffin and his wife. (This American architect also designed
Canberra, the Australian national capital.) The college had opened
in 1918 under the rectorship of Fr James O'Dwyer, an Irish Jesuit
and brother of Sir Michael O'Dwyer, the lieutenant-governor of the
Punjab whom father had recently met in India. On 13 March 1940 in
London, Sir Michael was to be assassinated by a Punjabi in retaliation
for having supported General Dyer's actions at Amritsar.

In 1920 and 1921 father captained the Newman cricket team and
was one of the college's top footballers. Besides the repertoire of
stories from the western front expected from 'ex-diggers', he had a
host of Indian experiences to draw on. In the college magazine he
wrote of Agra, Delhi, the Taj Mahal and the Moghul Empire, and
contributed a long article on Rabindrinath Tagore, the great Bengali
poet whom he had heard lecture. After finishing his L.L.B. at the end
of 1921, father remained at Newman for two more years as resident
law-tutor, and completed his Master of Law degree. He quickly
became a senior partner in a firm of Collins Street solicitors, which
he joined in 1924. That was the year he married my mother.

When she came across to Melbourne for a holiday in September
1920, they met at a tea party in Newman. A few days later they were
together at the Newman Society Ball, where Frank secured almost
every dance with her. He wrote to her after her return to Adelaide,
but she decided not to answer the letter after one of her sisters
remarked: 'Oh, Frank O'Collins! He's a real ladies man!' For two
years she did not see him. But he was forcefully reminded of her
in September 1921, when her father dined at Newman high table.
Mother met father again during a visit to Melbourne in late 1922.
Within a week they became engaged. In the overnight train going

back to Adelaide, she kept switching on the light in her sleeper to look at her engagement ring and assure herself that it was not all a dream. A few months later she left for a year in Europe with her sister Dympna. They were in Munich for Adolf Hitler's abortive rising and witnessed some disturbances in the street. But a policeman assured the two girls: 'Don't get worried. It's only a silly idiot who won't come to anything.'

After their marriage in May 1924, mother and father lived in Brighton, a pretty, sea-side suburb of Melbourne. Five years later father visited Frankston to check a block of land for a client. Three miles beyond the township he noticed a large property with a 'For Sale' sign posted. He walked in and at once fell in love with the view that stretched across Port Phillip Bay to the surrounding plains and mountains. He phoned mother who came down immediately. That same day they bought the whole property for £1200. They had wanted a place in the country, and father's discovery exceeded their dreams. The house they built there became the home in which I grew up.

36

2

Rock Lodge

Up to 1974 my life was divided into three parts. The first part, June 1931 to January 1944, was centred on Rock Lodge, my family home almost thirty miles from the heart of Melbourne. I played out the second part, February 1944 to November 1963 at several Jesuit schools and colleges in Australia. All of this formed a prelude to the third part, November 1963 to August 1974, a mid-point journey that took me from my thirties into my forties and brought me to live and teach in Rome for thirty-two years.

Rock Lodge was surrounded by twenty-four acres of land, with more than thirty-six acres of satellite blocks beyond the northern fence. As the house stood on the slopes of Mount Eliza we could look from our front lawn across Port Phillip Bay to the city of Melbourne. Far away to the left the You Yangs stood up like small markers beyond the western shore of the bay. To the east the Dandenong ranges filled the skyline across the plain. Visitors made gratifying noises when they stepped out of their cars to admire the view—'our view', as we always called it. About thirty yards down the slope a large eucalyptus tree, 'the big tree', divided the view. It was my archetypal tree by which I have always assessed all other trees. A front paddock, a top paddock and a bottom paddock meant that much of our land was cleared for cows and horses. Manna gums, pines, box gums, swamp gums, acacias, snow gums and tea-tree lined the paddocks, and started creeping back when the cows were sold around 1950. Trees and scrub covered much of the surrounding country side, which provided a home for possums, swarms of rabbits, some wallabies, echidnas and a few koala bears. The mysterious paths of bandicoots and rabbits ran through the long grass. We could drop down into gullies to follow fresh trickles in the creeks or find patches of sand, stained and bright with vegetable oils.

Occasionally around Christmas koalas came to perch in trees close to the back of our house. We considered that a special blessing on the season, even if their heavy snoring disturbed our sleep. Magpies, rosella parrots, finches, wrens, butcher birds, mopokes, Australian minahs, and scores of other birds swarmed through the area. The laughter of kookaburras often woke us in the morning. There were some years when a family of them arrived on our front lawn each evening for a meal of fresh meat. Occasionally one of them rapped its heavy beak on one of the large front windows when service proved slow.

I was born on 2 June 1931 in a St Kilda hospital and baptized in St Patrick's Cathedral, Melbourne. The previous year my parents had moved to Frankston. So I was brought home to Rock Lodge to join my three sisters, Moira (born 1925), Dympna (born 1927) and Maev (born 1929). My brother Jim was born on 20 December 1932 and the sixth and final surviving child, Glynn, arrived on 1 April 1934. My first definite memory is of peeping down into Glynn's cradle and admiring his tufts of red hair.

Our home stood seventy yards from the road at the end of a concrete drive. Two stained-glass windows picturing Pomona and Flora let one into a small entrance hall, which housed some of the books mother had inherited from her father. Through the library itself one passed into the front room, dominated by a vast, brick fireplace. The heads of two black buck that father had brought back from India looked across the leather sofa and armchairs to the great hearth. I like to think that this is where I learnt what fire and hospitality mean. It was the room to which my father brought an endless stream of visitors, the room where he poured beer for those guests and warmed them by his fire. To the right a door led directly to a large verandah, where he often sat in summer and enjoyed the view towards Melbourne and the north. Directly through the front room were my parents' rooms: mother's sitting room, their bedroom and their bathroom. Off to the left of the front room lay the kitchen, our bedrooms, a school room, and the rest of what we called 'the back of the house'. It was a single-storey building as were most country houses in Australia. Later when I realized that many houses were multi-storied, I yearned to stay in a house which enjoyed that magic region, 'upstairs'.

In 1940 my father had the 'back of the house' drastically altered. More bedrooms were added, a new kitchen constructed where the school room had been, and the old kitchen and laundry transformed into a large dining room. Only the small 'egg room' remained untouched. My brother Jim and his wife Posey, when they came to live in Rock Lodge, continued to speak of the 'egg room', although by then it housed their wines. A mahogany table that could seat twenty-four filled the dining room, which with the egg room was all that survived of the back of the house after a second reconstruction in 1973.

My father was a heavily built man, close to six feet tall, with black hair and tooth-brush moustache. His strength, correct bearing and careful courtesy suggested an officer. At times he was known as 'Captain', although later he became simply 'P.F. O'Collins'. The earliest thing I can remember him saying was 'Cowards die many times.' He was encouraging me not to be afraid of the dark and, especially, of those mysterious shadows and rustling shapes which I could see at night under the trees that lay behind the house. He battled sickness, business problems and various challenges with a fearlessness that made him stand up among us like the big tree which divided our view to the north. He stood there filling our landscape. He assured his children that he kept a revolver in a secret cupboard. Long after I ceased to think of this gun as our defence weapon against marauders from the outside world, I believed in his secret cupboard which now housed valuable documents as well. He would teasingly say, 'You are getting warm', as I wandered around the house tapping panels and searching for the cupboard.

He was a warmly affectionate man. When I grew up, I found it odd that other men's sons did not kiss their fathers but greeted them with a handshake. Very rarely he spanked Jim, Glynn or me with a soft, old slipper. I can still see the slipper, although I cannot remember any particular occasions of punishment. What I do recall are the times when I rolled on the front room floor in rages, started a fire in the grounds by playing with matches, seriously hurt Jim in a thoughtless accident, and did other things for which he might have thrashed me but never did. He was extraordinarily controlled for such a vigorous man. He imposed few rules: we were forbidden to approach the dam that lay behind the house, or to lift the cover on an underground tank that flanked our front drive and supplied us with drinking water.

Joan O'Collins as Mary Queen of Scots, University of Melbourne pageant, 1934

During the 1930s father took the train each day into the city. Occasionally business affairs or special dinners kept him overnight in Melbourne, where he stayed at the Athenaeum Club, the Menzies Hotel, or the Naval and Military Club. On those nights one of us six children could share the big, four-poster bed with mother. We fought for that privilege on the 'I asked first' principle. After a heart attack father retired from legal practice in 1939. By that time he had built up most of his business interests, principally several cinemas: the Astor in St Kilda, the Empire in Brunswick, the Plaza in Coburg, and the King's in the heart of Melbourne itself. Almost all the ventures proved successful, except for some speculation in land.

Mother was delicately beautiful, of middle size, and possessed a pleasant, gentle voice. After her hair turned prematurely grey, she dyed it light brown. She was absolutely dedicated to father, very rarely opposed him, and when necessary achieved her objectives through indirect means rather than direct discussion. Eventually the large dam behind the house was turned into a 40,000 gallon underground tank to supplement our water supply and enable mother to improve the garden. Father always thought that the scheme was his, and boasted that the concrete tank could be used as a shelter in time of nuclear war. But we knew that mother was the real author of the scheme. She worried about father's skin cancer, for which he had a serious operation on his neck and one shoulder in 1941, and subsequently radium treatment for various 'spots' on his face. Around that time we occasionally said the family rosary. After the prayers mother would dab father's face with water from the Blessed Virgin's shrine in Lourdes. She never seemed vigorously robust herself. A miscarriage cast heavy gloom over one childhood Christmas. She had five or six miscarriages and at least one still-born child. Yet she helped to teach us tennis and golf, and through the 1930s worked on our poultry farm. If she was inhibited in showing physical affection, we all picked up her language of 'pet', 'darling', and other endearments.

We felt absolutely certain of our parents' love. They left us surprisingly free to follow our own initiatives, supported us in what we attempted, and tried discreetly to provide the conditions for growth towards human and Christian maturity. I can recall very few occasions when we were forced to do something. Once mother stood beside a ladder and made me climb it to overcome my fear of heights.

Once I learned to walk and could move out of the house, I found plenty to explore. Behind Rock Lodge and along the left-hand side of the main drive stood cow sheds, ten or more large pens for the poultry, a large shed (housing grain, a motor-driven saw and wood for the fires), and a grain silo topped by a tank. Just inside the cast-iron gate was a weather-board cottage which my father bought with the property before building Rock Lodge. Besides my parents, my three sisters and two brothers, there were several other members of the household and they lived in the cottage: Mrs Gilder who cooked for us, Miss Gilder who acted as governess, Tom, Jock, and others. Jock migrated to Australia from the Glasgow shipyards. We laughed when he called a bucket a 'pail', and asked after being tormented during his first night by mosquitoes, 'where can I get something for the wee bombers?' The Gilders, mother and daughter, I remember as being good but severe people from Gippsland. We believed that Mrs Gilder took a cold bath each morning. Miss Gilder taught us in the school room in Rock Lodge or, when the weather was fine, at tables set up outside the cottage. Before I started schooling with her, I wandered up the drive one day, paused to sip a little methylated spirits I found in the main shed, and pressed on to see whether my sisters were enjoying the morning as much as I was. Miss Gilder caught sight of me and remarked disgustedly to Moira: 'Your brother is drunk!' A few years later she gave me an excellent grounding in reading, writing, and arithmetic. But I can remember very little of her teaching methods, except that she punished us by strapping our calves. She threatened me once: 'I'll put soap on your tongue for telling lies.'

Father tried the poultry business as a sideline, found it was losing almost a £1000 a year, and closed the farm down after seven or eight years. But it formed part of my sisters' education. They gathered and sorted the eggs, and occasionally threw one at each other. Work on our farm provided a living for the Gilders, Tom, Jock and others during the hungry days of the depression. For several years father played a prominent role in the National Utility Poultry Breeders' Association. My parents registered their poultry business as 'Talbot Farm'. They named it after Matt Talbot, a reformed Dublin drunkard who had led a life of ascetic holiness, died in 1925, and was soon considered a candidate for beatification. Mother's uncle, Sir Joseph Glynn, who published his *Life of Matt Talbot*, supplied us with a splinter from the holy man's bed of planks, the first relic I ever saw. My own lasting trophy from 'Talbot Farm' is a scar behind my right knee, received as a child when I sat on a hot pipe to the incubator in a chicken shed.

Beyond the sheds and across the concrete drive were gardens, then an orchard, and behind a cypress hedge the back drive. It led down to the road through flowering gums and native shrubs. We climbed the trees in the orchard to pluck yellow plums, greengages, brown pears, and the large, green apples. Loganberries tore us as we reached for their fruit. We squeezed the bearded gooseberries to find the ripe ones. In the vegetable beds I watched the miracle of asparagus thrusting up through the soil. A hedge that separated the orchard from the road offered a mysterious place under a pittosporum. There I lay on a brown mat of dead leaves, watching the light filter through the green screen, fingering the sweet, sticky pods, and breathing in the first scent I can recall—the smell of the delicate, white flowers.

As we did not play with any local children, we must have picked up our extraordinary convictions about nature from the farmhands. A bite from a goanna or a blue-tongued lizard would never heal. If a thunderstorm occurred while a hen was hatching its eggs, the chickens would die. On our property we often killed snakes, especially copperheads and brown snakes. We believed that no matter how fiercely we battered a snake to break its back in several places, the principle held good: 'Snakes die at sundown.' Artichokes we considered indestructible. One could cut them into slices and bury them deep in the ground, but they would always come up. I dreamt of excavating a pit twenty-five feet deep and entombing the immortal artichokes under rubble and clay only to find them triumphantly sending up shoots some months later.

I cannot dredge up a precise memory of my first visit to Peninsula Country Golf Club, which was situated about three miles away. This club remains intertwined with my parents, my childhood, and my family's continuing life in Frankston. Major-General Harold William Grimwade (of the Grimwade, Felton and Duerdin chemical firm) served for years as club president. He became my archetypal general and president. I am sure that years later he made it easier for me to accept General Eisenhower's election as President of the United States or General de Gaulle's emergence as President of France.

Sir Norman Brookes and Dame Mabel Brookes, whom I met as a child, were also members of the club and local residents. Norman Brookes had been a Wimbledon champion and a successful Davis Cup player, playing 39 Davis Cup matches between 1905 and 1920. Known as 'the Wizard', he became the first non-Briton (and the first left-hander) to win the men's singles at Wimbledon in 1907, a year in which he joined Tony Wilding to win the doubles and also the Davis Cup. He was back again at Wimbledon in 1914, won the singles and doubles, and sailed for the United States to join Wilding in winning once again the Davis Cup. (From 2006 to 2009 I was to live in Wimbledon, just a few hundred yards from the old tennis courts off Worple Road where Brookes had triumphed.) The great-granddaughter of William Balcombe who provided a residence for Napoleon during his first two months on St Helena, Mabel Brookes was a flamboyant, warm-hearted person, a leader in Melbourne society and charities. She worked tirelessly for the Queen Victoria Hospital, being president of its committee of management from 1923 to 1970. With my siblings I learnt the local adaptation of the Boston lines about the Cabots and the Lodges: 'Frankston is a pleasant place, full of bays and nooks. God knows the Grimwades and the Grimwades know the Brookes.'

By the time I became aware of Peninsula Golf Club, father had become one of the leading personalities and players there. He won every competition except the club championship. The year he died (1961) his youngest son, Glynn, became club champion for the first time. The only piece of autobiographical material my father left in writing was an account of his hole-in-one in 1939. He entitled the story 'Called to the Bar':

'This story was given to the *Herald* by the club professional, Bill Clifford. The facts are as follows. On Sunday 12 March, Councillor Connelly holed out in one at the 12th hole. That evening Ray spent at our home. Next day, Monday 13 March, was Labour Day, with a four ball best ball to be played. In the morning I played with Norman Brookes; we were six up. As we came in, Stanley Bruce was on the putting green. He had arrived from London a few days earlier. He joined us for a spot. I suggested that he play with Norman in the afternoon against me and my partner. Ray was in the room and he

The family in 1936, left to right: Joan, Glynn, Moira, Jim, Maev, Gerald, Dympna, Frank

agreed to make up the four. At the 12th I mentioned that Ray had holed out in one and invited Norman 'to do the same'. He said that he had already done so on two occasions and promptly put his ball on the green. Bruce (known as 'Joe') was also invited 'to do the same'. He said that he had never holed in one nor seen anyone get an ace. He then put his ball on the green. I then said to Ray: 'Come on. Show us that yesterday's one was not a fluke.' He put his ball into the timber, where it remains today. Ray then said to me: 'You are having a lot to say. I did it on the limit (24) and you are on two and have never had a one. See what you can do today.' I then said: 'They say that you throw it down like this, and you hit in like that.' To our amazement, the ball dropped and rolled an inch or two into the cup. Ray and I went on to win the competition eight up. But we would not have done so, if Bruce had not missed at least four putts of less than two feet. Today the four players are: Lord Bruce of Melbourne, Sir Norman Brookes, the late Sir Raymond Connelly (former Lord Mayor of Melbourne), and the Knight of Rock Lodge.'

Bruce was Prime Minister of Australia (1925-1929) and Australian High Commissioner in London (1933-1945). Connelly helped to secure the 1956 Olympic Games for Melbourne, but died before they were held.

Almost inevitably the first recorded literary composition from any of my brothers and sisters concerned Peninsula Golf Club. About the age of nine Moira wrote:

> My father's a golfer; he goes to the links.
> He calls at the bar and has a few drinks.
> He hits a long drive, and wins a new ball.
> His opponent, the General, doesn't like it at all.
> He plays in mixed foursomes, himself and his wife.
> She makes a bad stroke, and she clears for her life.

The poem ended proudly: 'My father, he plays in hail, rain or shine.' These must have been among the earliest verses I learned. We all looked back with pride to Moira's precocious judgement in picking the proper subject for her first venture into poetry.

I have only shadowy recollections of the routine for my first eight years. Nor can I remember much of the steady stream of visitors who enriched life at Rock Lodge. One of them was Hartley Grattan, a left-wing historian and leading American authority on Australia who helped to encourage research into our history and society. Over dinner one evening Grattan began to explain how to stage a Communist revolution but pulled himself up short with a plea to another guest, Sir Herbert Gepp: 'Stop me, Sir Herbert!'[1] When they were crossing Sydney harbour by ferry, father fell into a debate over our human nature and destiny, tossed a coin for Grattan's immortal soul, and won. Grattan, who spent the last years of his life in Texas, left instructions in his will for his ashes to be scattered over Sydney harbour.

C.C. Martindale, the Jesuit preacher and writer who had befriended father in Oxford during World War I, also visited us. When he came before my birth for a lecture and sermon tour in 1928, father took him to the family home in Brighton and then on to lunch at a Frankston hotel. Martindale described that occasion: 'There was another delightful, though tiring, day when my old friend, O'C., and his brother, a missionary priest in China, drove out through long distances of tea-tree in bloom to a town called Frankston.... The sense of irresponsibility was good in itself, for, actually, till the night there were no engagements.'[2] Martindale returned to Australia for

---

1 A very successful mining industrialist and public servant, Gepp had strong American ties and persistent concerns to improve conditions for workers in Broken Hill and elsewhere. The *Australian Dictionary of Biography* contains excellent entries on Grattan and Gepp.
2 *The Risen Sun* (London, 1929), 174.

the Catholic celebration timed to occur during the 1934 centenary of
Victoria. He wrote of another day spent with my father, now called
'F.' rather than 'O'C'.

> It was F., met during the war as a cadet, who six years ago took
> me to his house and then on to Frankston…This time we again
> went to Frankston, to F.'s new house on the hill above it. This gave
> me a perfect day in what I like to believe is a true Australian home.
> The house and estate are in process of development, furnishing
> thus an infinity of new interests on the spot. Drives are being
> built; trees of all sorts planted; a bathing-pool is foreseen; about
> 2,000 fowls fuss and flourish in wide spaces and most scientific
> bedrooms. Last time there were three children; now there are six,
> all very friendly (including the youngest, eight months), and two of
> them able to catch delinquent chickens at a moment's notice. Two
> young men, both most suitably if confusingly called Tom, were
> doing the hard work, though F.'s girl-like wife is perfectly prepared
> to do it too. The house, for once, is full of books; and Mrs. F. is
> also prepared to plan towns and show how her system would keep
> rents low, houses sufficiently large and spaced out, and the whole
> remunerative. Her system…takes full account of railways and the
> whereabouts of factories. Here, then, in the hot afternoon…I slept
> peacefully under the verandah looking down on the blue, curving
> bay, and was brought back in the evening in time for I forget what
> speech.[3]

If my memory has let slip much of Grattan, Gepp, Martindale and
other individuals, I can still recall the large parties which my parents
held. The following day I would stand the empty bottles in a row, and
solemnly fill up one bottle with the dregs from the others. I still see
one group of visitors, some Russian ballerinas wearing white furs and
carrying Pekinese dogs. They danced across our front lawn like a flock
of warm, exotic seagulls.

---

3 *Athens, Argentine, Australia* (London, 1939), 229

Only a handful of events hover in the memory from those pre-war years. At the age of seven I made my first Holy Communion in the Catholic church in Frankston. Someone, perhaps my mother, told me that during his last days on St Helena Napoleon looked back at his first Communion as 'the happiest day of my life'. I recall the pleasure of receiving a gaudy certificate to hang in my bedroom. A few months later I was confirmed by my uncle, Bishop James O'Collins. This involved learning by heart answers from 'the penny catechism', which by that time, I think, cost three pence. After a mild quiz by the parish priest I joined the boys and girls from the Catholic primary school for the ceremony. After confirming us, uncle Jim encouraged the whole group to 'take the pledge', that is to say, promise to abstain from alcoholic drink until at least the age of twenty-one. In fact, I abstained until thirty-three.

Two further events remain: the 'Black Friday' bushfires and the arrival of Sonny Boy, our first and most loved pony. After two critical days of fire, on Friday, 13 January 1939, the temperature rose to 114 degrees Fahrenheit and humidity dropped to 7%. Terrifying bushfires raged through the state of Victoria, destroying whole townships, over 1,300 homes, and over five million acres of forest. Seventy-one people died. A few days before a quick fire had swept through the tea-tree scrub that lined the left of our road into Frankston. Many houses were destroyed. My father drove me there to look with horror at the devastation. On Black Friday we changed from spectators into participants. A column of smoke suddenly rose in the scrub to the south of our property. The fire ran through the trees and the grass towards Rock Lodge. Fireman in breeches stood tall in the smoke alongside our farmhands and family. With water-packs on their backs and flailing beaters in their hands, they looked invincible alongside us, as we lashed at the flames with bags and branches. The human line held. The front of the fire swung away, circled our property, and roared off to the north to die out when it met the area swept by an earlier fire. Burning tree trunks and fence posts lit up the evening. Across the fields smouldering pats of cow dung sent up tiny columns of smoke. Black Friday left me with a permanent fear that one day fire would return to destroy Rock Lodge. For years whenever we drove back in the summer from Melbourne and topped the last rise, 400 yards short of the house, I half expected to see only charred ruins facing us. But bushfires never returned to threaten us again as in January 1939.

Some time that year our first ponies arrived, headed by a three-year-old, pot-bellied Shetland whom we named Sonny Boy and treasured until he was hit by a car and died in 1955. He came in a furniture van. We continued the spirit of his arrival by bringing him once or twice into the house. We were proud of his half-human blend of positive and negative qualities. He would never kick, but took special pleasure in biting us when our backs were turned. He blew himself up to prevent the girth and belly-band being tied too tightly. Although he sometimes tried to bump his rider against trees or posts, he would automatically increase pace when we turned for home, and needed no directing on the run back. Both then and later we had more ponies and horses: Sam who galloped away never to be found again, Sparkle who was dogged by mysterious ailments, and others. But shaggy, robust Sonny Boy always remained *the* horse at Rock Lodge.

The first years of the war saw an exodus from Rock Lodge. Tom and Jock enlisted in the forces. I can still hear our fox terrier Sempie (called after the 19th Baron Sempill, a notable aviator who visited Australia to advise our government on creating their air force) standing outside the front gate and howling down the road that had taken Tom off to the war. I don't know what happened to Tom. Jock served both as an army driver in the Middle East and in the navy. After a visit to Jerusalem, he sent me a leaflet containing some prayers and a leaf plucked from one of the very ancient olive trees in the garden of Gethsemane. I treasured it for years in my missal. Father had most of the sheds pulled down, auctioned various items, and over the years planted trees and shrubs where the poultry pens had been. Moira and Dympna went off to board at a Sacred Heart convent in Melbourne, where Maev later joined them. After the outbreak of the war, Miss Gilder and her mother stayed on for a year or so at Rock Lodge. During 1940 I often used to walk to a neighbouring poultry farm and pick up our mail. Frequently there was a letter for Miss Gilder from her future husband. They married and left to live in Queensland. She was in a Townsville hospital for the birth of her child in 1942 when Japanese planes attempted to bomb the airfield and railway. The patients were all put under their beds. The shock killed her. Poor Miss Gilder had always looked the plain school mistress, with her glasses and her straight hair cut to hang in a neat line behind her neck. All that remained of her short life, it seemed, was the sound primary education she gave us.

During the war years I took over the farming jobs with Jim and Glynn. My parents looked on all that as part of our education. It also ensured a fresh supply of some basic foods. We milked the cows, separated the cream, made butter, fed the poultry, collected the eggs, raised chickens, killed and dressed the poultry, took our Jersey cows three miles away to be serviced by a bull, cared for our ponies, collected fruit from the orchard, trapped rabbits, and occasionally grew some vegetables. At times the hens produced far too many eggs for our needs. So we smeared the eggs with a special paste, or packed them in four-gallon tins of water to which a preservative had been added. We stored them in the original pantry, which we renamed 'the egg room'. I am sure most of these eggs went rotten before use.

We were left free in our decisions about getting cows into calf, selecting poultry for the table, ordering food for the hens and the cattle, and treating the ripped teats of one or two recalcitrant cows. They insisted on trying to jump over barbed-wire and caught their udders in the process. I recommend trying to milk a cow with torn teats if anyone wants a ticklish task. I tried keeping dogs: first an Irish setter which died from snakebite, and then a Queensland healer which we gave away after it began systematically killing our hens. When Dan, our giant draught horse, grew old and feeble, a man came from the knackers. I stood stunned as he brought down that huge body with a bullet through the forehead. Mostly our farm work seemed like a chore, in which we fulfilled our responsibilities towards the animals, the poultry, and the trees. It was simply not fair to leave some cows unmilked, hens unfed, or fruit hanging on the trees. At times the work prepared one for the harder face of life. In 1942 I had an ingrowing toenail removed in the Frankston hospital, while my mother was a patient there. When I returned home in the afternoon with my bandaged toe sticking out of my sandal, it seemed harsh that I had to limp off and milk the cows.

In 1942 or 1943 my father engaged a farm-hand who had been discharged from the army for supposed deafness and real lack of intelligence. Wiry and willing, Albert milked the cows, dug the garden, cut timber, and took over work on the property during the week. Jim, Glynn and I had to milk the cows, feed the poultry, and collect the eggs only at weekends. Illiterate and incapable of reflecting on any topic beyond his immediate experience, Albert possessed his own special wisdom and innocent goodness. He acted as the loyal bread-winner for a family in which crime was not unknown. When I joined the Jesuits in 1950 and mother explained to Albert that I was permitted visitors only once a month, he nodded knowingly, 'just like my brother Fred.' At the time Fred was serving a sentence for housebreaking. Occasionally Albert drank too much and got into a fight in a pub. It was easy for father to ensure that the local police treated Albert gently, as the sergeant in charge had sailed with father on the *Ballarat* in 1917 to fight in France. Albert never left his head uncovered. I sometimes wondered whether he slept wearing that battered, grey hat which he kept turned down all round. On one memorable day in 1943, when Albert and I were left alone at Rock Lodge, we spent hours dismembering a petrol engine. It had served to drive a saw and to pump water from the underground tank up to the overhead tank. Father had just replaced it with an electric motor. In a fine orgy of destruction, Albert and I removed piston, rings, the carburettor, plugs, and all the other detachable parts. After ten years or so with us, he moved on to another job. Albert left me with an enduring admiration for the simple of this earth.

To offset the exodus of people from Rock Lodge, the outbreak of World War II brought the excitement of following real war games. I scrutinized aircraft recognition charts and learnt the shapes of Gloucester Gladiators, Spitfires, Hurricanes, Blenheims, Messerschmidt 109s and 110s, Heinkels, and Dorniers or 'flying pencils'. I could pour out the figures on the engines, speed, range and performance of various planes. We cheered soldiers and gave them the 'thumbs-up' sign when they roared past in trucks. Sometimes they held manoeuvres in the surrounding countryside, tearing tracks through the scrub with their twenty-five pounders, eighteen pounders, and howitzers. Jim and Glynn joined me 'digging for victory', though not by growing vegetables! I inspected plans for air-raid shelters and decided to build one at the top of the back drive. We gave up after digging a trench over three feet deep in the clay. Later some soil was dumped into the trench and a row of agapanthus planted there. We learned to sing songs like 'Hang out your washing on the Siegfried Line, if the Siegfried line is there'. I never dreamed that a quarter of a century later I was to serve in a German parish close to the French border and often see some shattered and abandoned pill-boxes that once formed part of the Siegfried Line.

The war introduced some mild rationing of food and clothing. Father stored a bottle of Tokay that was not be drunk before the war ended. When I met him carrying the bottle out of the pantry in 1943, he explained: 'The war is as good as over.' Petrol rationing posed problems, but father received some additional coupons for being a primary producer, although the eggs, cream and butter we produced were, as far as I can recall, only for ourselves. In the late winter of 1940 or 1941 father, mother and I drove north to Sydney in our grey Nash on what was my longest childhood trip.

With others in the family we had been on previous caravan holidays, which took us as far away as Mallacoota Inlet in eastern Victoria. In that wild and distant country we were told of German raiders who secretly refueled near there during the First World War. We met a minor writer who lived in a camp on the shore of the inlet and infected me with an instant interest in Australian literature. When a bush fire swept along the shore, we crossed at once by boat to inspect the burnt-out area. A five-foot goanna startled us, as it suddenly scuttled across the hot and blackened earth to climb a smouldering tree trunk. Father proved a little less than omnipotent and omniscient on those caravanning trips. He shot cormorants, mistaking them for ducks. His skill at fishing was deficient, even if he did once land a thirty-inch flathead. Even then I felt annoyed that he had failed to weigh the fish. I understood that to be the correct way of recording a notable catch.

On our visit to Sydney we stayed at the old Wentworth Hotel, tried the oysters (which made me sick), and saw *The Student Prince* (starring Nelson Eddy and Jeanette McDonald) in a private cinema, which struck me as the epitome of cosy luxury. We also took a trip across the Blue Mountains to the Jenolan Caves, where father had been the day he heard that the First World War had started. I can still see the dark wallabies hopping around the rocks at the entrance to the caves. We had the large chalet or hotel almost to ourselves. A guide helped to accentuate for me the spooky loneliness of that holiday centre in wartime. One evening after dinner, mother took me underground to wonder at the stalactites, stalagmites, shining pools, and all the eery beauty of that hidden world. We came to the 'skeleton cave', where limestone encased the remains of an aboriginal. He had fallen into the caves and died there centuries before. The guide horrified me as he spelled out the circumstances of that lonely death which had become a tourist attraction.

We drove home from Sydney along the east coast of New South Wales, stopping a few nights at Narooma. Local inhabitants still felt aggrieved that Zane Grey had chosen to stay at nearby Bermagui when he came to catch sword-fish. Bermagui prospered by being linked with the fishing exploits of that classical American writer of westerns. (Over thirty years later I recalled the laments from Narooma when I stopped overnight near Zanesville, Ohio. Across the road from our motel stood the new Zane Grey museum, which records the life and achievements of the local man whose ancestor, Ebenezer Zane, had given the city its name.) From Narooma we drove south along the coast and then cut inland across the lower slopes of the Australian Alps. For miles we followed streams that rushed down from the melting snow-fields to boil and froth along under the golden wattle. The whole trip was a typical interruption in what passed for my formal schooling. But my father always dismissed any scruple by declaring: 'Travel is the best form of education.'

One morning in December 1941 father walked into my room and announced gravely: 'The Japanese have bombed Pearl Harbour.' The following February, Jim, Glynn and I started at the Catholic primary school in Frankston staffed by several sisters of St Joseph, the institute founded by St Mary MacKillop. The school was nearly three miles away on the edge of the town. Sometimes we were driven there, but mostly we cycled, walked, or rode horses. During the day we could leave the horses tied up at the blacksmith's establishment in the centre of Frankston. The arrival of our first bicycles sent Jim, Glynn and me into a flurry of excitement over our new skills.

It did not come easily to relate happily to Jim, who was quiet, intelligent and represented a threat to my status as the favourite son. One story illustrates that status. I took the train from Frankston to Melbourne, with instructions to wait on the platform at Flinders Street, one the busiest suburban stations in the world. The train pulled into a platform that was not normal for the Frankston line. I waited there until my anxious parents found me and my mother remarked: 'We thought we had lost *our* Prince of Wales. (The news had just broken that the Japanese had sunk the British battleships *Prince of Wales* and *Repulse*.)

We all loved Glynn spontaneously. A freckled, affectionate redhead, he was often sickly but grew up to be a fine athlete and a champion golfer. He followed Jim in studying medicine, but, unlike Jim who became an outstanding surgeon, Glynn specialized in radiology. Although the youngest of the six of us, sadly he was the first one to die—of cancer in 2003.

When we began at St Francis Xavier's School, I was aged ten, Jim nine, and Glynn not quite eight. In what was our initiation into regular schooling and our first prolonged contact with other boys and girls, we supported each other well. Together we also grew to hate the jam sandwiches and peanut butter sandwiches that mother regularly supplied for our lunch. Our transition from home to school went remarkably smoothly. We had seen many of the hundred or so pupils at Mass, where some of them occupied the front pews. The place itself was familiar to us, as the school was in fact held in the church building—the ultimate in identification between Catholicism and education. During the week sliding screens cut off the sanctuary and formed two large class rooms out of the nave. A glass-enclosed verandah added two further class rooms for the top grades. Boys and girls could continue at the school until they finished the eighth grade around the age of thirteen. As far as I remember, some sat for the merit certificate, a state examination. A few went on to high school. There were no fees, but the children brought a shilling or so each week from their parents.

Apart from the occasional appearance of a cane, detailed memories of class techniques elude me. I can just remember following the fortunes of Anglo-Saxon kingdoms. The old, dreamy words still echo in my head: Wessex, Canute, Northumbria, woad. We learned to thunder out 'Hail, Queen of heaven' and 'Faith of our Fathers', to feel sentimental over 'Sweet Sacrament Divine', and to cope with 'O Salutaris Hostia' and 'Tantum Ergo', which we sang at benediction of the Blessed Sacrament. Encased in their voluminous habits, Sisters Laurentia, Baptista and Rosa seemed hard-working and cheerful. Only two things ever disappointed me about them. They seemed to have no refrigerator in their convent, which stood next to the school. When I collected my milk there, it was never cold. During part of the lunch-hour break they did not supervise the playground. Open homo-sexual acts would flare up sometimes among the older boys. They left me alone. I viewed it all as an anthropologist might view the customs of a strange tribe.

A few non-Catholics attended the school, one of them becoming my best friend for the year. The much larger state school faced us across the street, but we could have been miles away. We had little to do with the boys and girls there, and refrained from cultivating the hostility that led in other places to clashes between 'the micks' and 'the proddy dogs'.

Our building (erected in 1899) and small playground had a battered, dusty look. The boys fought over a few footballs and cricket bats that parents supplied. One parent was a naval commander, but nearly all the others belonged to the working class or the very bottom of the middle class. Yet it was not a 'tough' school. The son of an Italian greengrocer occasionally had to put his fists up.

But we picked up from the general public very little of that vicious hostility to enemy aliens that disfigured Australian life during and after the First World War. If German sausage was officially renamed

'Austral sausage', General Erwin Rommel, popularly known as 'the Desert Fox', became a legend to many Australians at home and overseas. In North Africa our troops had already captured thousands of Italian soldiers, who now provided much of the labour on Australian farms. We giggled over cartoons like the one which showed a solitary Australian soldier guarding an endless column of prisoners. He said to the Italian who walked beside him: 'Antonio, if you don't stop dragging that rifle in the sand, I won't let you carry it for me.' The public taught us a benign contempt for the army of prisoners-of-war, who enjoyed a comparative freedom in return for their work. For me real prejudice was ruled out by early experiences of lunching at the Café Latin, run by the Triaca brothers. I can still taste the sucking-pig and feel the grissini snap in my fingers. I believed that escaped Italian prisoners-of-war lived upstairs, helped cook the meals, and enjoyed an unwritten amnesty on condition that they went out only after dark.

The war hardly touched our lives at school. Once or twice we took part in air-raid drill, and marched fifty yards to a vacant allotment where the present Catholic church stands. We were told to crouch down in the slit trenches with 'rubbers' or pencil erasers clenched between our teeth. The Japanese victories affected life at home for a short time. The Australian government decided, if an invasion came, to abandon the north and defend 'the Brisbane line'. In early 1942 Margaret O'Sullivan and her two sons, Michael and Patrick, came down from Queensland to live at Rock Lodge. Michael attended Frankston High School, while Patrick who is my age came to the Catholic primary school. Jim, Glynn and I fought with these larger boys, envied their skill at marbles, and were glad to inherit some of their marbles when, after a few months, they went home to Brisbane. Their father, Neil (later Sir Neil) O'Sullivan, was to be elected a senator and become minister for trade and customs. In later life I saw a great deal of Patrick, who entered the Society of Jesus a year after I did and became my spiritual father for a number of years. We still chuckle over the circumstances in which we first met.

The year (1942) at St Francis Xavier's school brought me into close contact with the parish priest, Father Gerald Fitzpatrick, whom I remember as a reasonably tall, red-faced, tubercular-looking man. I had, of course, seen a good deal of him before. On Saturday evenings we frequently went on our knees and confessed our sins to him in the sacristy, where he sat behind a small screen, with his face turned away, and wearing a thin purple stole over his ankle-length black cassock. On Sunday mornings we attended one of his two services. Until he acquired a curate and the parish was divided, we went to Mass either in Frankston or in Chelsea, a bayside town about eight miles away in the direction of Melbourne. Fr Fitzpatrick fixed the Mass times for eight and ten o'clock, celebrating the earlier one alternately in Chelsea or Frankston. If we wished to receive Holy Communion, we went to 'the eight o'clock', as the strict Eucharistic fast prohibiting any food or drink whatsoever between midnight and the time of communion was still in force. We regarded the people who occasionally received communion at 'the ten o'clock' as heroic. In the hot summer months, waiting so late for even a glass of water must have left them nauseous and dizzy, as they sat, stood, or knelt through the stuffy, sweaty hour of Mass.

In his sermons Fr Fitzpatrick ran the same stories year after year. He emphasized the importance and rewards of fidelity to Sunday Mass by telling us of a young man in a country town who refused to leave early on a Sunday morning with the rest of his cricket team. He first attended Mass, then rushed off to the game, and scored a century. The necessity of having babies baptized without delay was inculcated by an example drawn flatteringly from my own grandfather's practice. I first learned from the Frankston pulpit that Pat O'Collins had taken every one of his children to be baptized the Sunday after they were born. Fr Fitzpatrick allowed that baptism within a month of birth would do.

He read out in complete detail not only the Christmas and Easter dues but also, I think, the results of some special monthly collection. 'Mr and Mrs P. F. O'Collins' competed for top place on those lists with Mrs Gavan Duffy, a lady who, after marrying into that prominent family of Irish-Australian politicians and lawyers, now lived locally. At times Fr Fitzpatrick would descend from the pulpit, lay aside his chasuble and, with his long, white alb gathered at the waist by a cincture or cord, walk down the church taking up the collection himself. Mrs Gavan Duffy ran a fête at her home to raise money for the parish, and so did we at Rock Lodge. The manager of one of father's cinemas staged a boxing exhibition. There were the usual wheels and stalls, and Sonny Boy provided pony rides. After one fête the parent of a child who had fallen off the pony wrote threatening a court action unless some damages were paid. Father disregarded the letter.

Over the summer a Catholic surgeon from Melbourne sometimes stayed in Frankston. I can still glimpse him through the windows pacing up and down outside the church, until the sermon was over. He offered me my first, delicious taste of lay protest movements. On occasions father himself eased the pain of the service by reading some literature from a series in our library. At first glance, but only at first glance, those slim, dark-coloured volumes could have passed for prayer books. From about 1940 I proudly owned a chunky, black 'Daily Missal', as did each of my brothers and sisters. It provided in Latin with parallel English translations the fixed texts of the Mass, all the variable texts for each day of the year, the Holy Week ceremonies, and many other items. Uncle Jim provided our missals and gave them the official approval by telling us, 'I could say Mass with one of them'. We used the slim ribbons in our missals to keep up with the priest, as he moved from the 'ordinary' of the Mass to the 'propers' and back again. I started to delight in the Mass regularly only when the vernacular was introduced and other changes began in the late 1960s.

From my childhood until then, the Mass normally conveyed the sense of a solemn endurance test, during which I tried to keep my mind on the sacred business in hand, and wait for the highpoints of the service, the words of consecration and the moments of communion. Rather than being a community *action*, the Mass gave me an overwhelming sense of the Eucharistic *presence* of the risen Christ. As for most Catholics at the time, it was the machinery for effecting this presence and required full concentration on private prayer. The only reproof I can recall my mother passing on my conduct in church was, 'You were looking around when you went up to communion.'

On Sundays I sometimes rose early to milk the cows before we went to Mass. But if the cows were left to be milked later in the morning, Jim, Glynn and I occasionally quarrelled on the way home from church, as we tried to avoid the chore on the 'I did it last Sunday' basis.

By 1942 I had learned to 'serve Mass'. That involved memorizing all the fixed Latin responses, and knowing when to shift 'the book' from the epistle to the gospel side of the altar and back again, when to bring up the wine and water, and when to thump the brass gong to warn the congregation that 'the canon' had begun, that the consecration was impending, or that they should come forward for receive Holy Communion. Normally four boys served Mass, wearing red soutanes, white surplices, and special red slippers. Three shared tasks through an intricate demarcation process, while the fourth simply knelt or sat there for the sake of symmetry. The careful ceremonial, the flowers, the candles, and the special vestments all attracted me.

Inevitably I volunteered to serve Fr Fitzpatrick during the Holy Week ceremonies. Only a very few people attended the long, Latin services on Holy Thursday or the 'Mass of the Presanctified' on Good Friday morning. At three o'clock on Good Friday afternoon people packed the church for the stations of the cross, the sermon, a collection for the upkeep of the 'holy places' in Palestine, and the adoration or kissing of the cross. Fr Fitzpatrick normally told his story of a young Russian soldier, who took on himself someone else's punishment and died under the lash. I was surprised to find the pubs open for drinking on Good Friday. It was the one day in the year when my father refused to play golf. By far the longest and dullest Holy Week service came on Holy Saturday morning. On one occasion we began around 7.30 a.m. while rain rushed down outside. The total congregation consisted of one middle-aged woman, who arrived dripping and late for the lighting of the Easter fire in the porch.

Our parish priest communicated a sense of holy other-worldliness but proved in some way too timid to be frightening. In May 1940 I sat in our car outside his presbytery, while he argued with father about the outcome of the war. France was about to fall; Hitler must win. Father felt his own optimism vindicated a few days later when the *Warspite* sank seven German ships near Narvik in Norway. Once Fr Fitzpatrick summoned me around to the presbytery and asked, 'Would you kill that sick chicken for me please?' He kept a small poultry shed behind his house, and could not bring himself to dispatch the ailing bird.

In 1943 Jim and Glynn continued at St Francis Xavier's school, but there was no point in my returning as I had already completed the top year. My parents planned to send me as a day student to a Catholic high school, and had even bought my uniform. At the last minute they dropped the scheme and kept me at home for the year. Allegedly I took a correspondence course with a Melbourne school, but in fact I pleased myself about the number of assignments I finished. Until 1973-74, that was my only sabbatical year, and I used it for reading: the works of Henry Lawson, Banjo Paterson and other Australian writers, books already coming out on the Second World War, the novels of Charles Dickens, and works in classical mythology. Stories like Anne of Green Gables filled my head with pre-adolescence fantasies. It was about this time that I first met Sir Edward McTiernan, a Labor politician who was appointed to the High Court in 1930 and became the longest serving judge in the history of the court, finally retiring in 1976. With my parents' encouragement (or connivance?), he asked me to read the speeches of Edmund Burke, a notable Whig politician (1729-97). Later I had to recite for him by heart Burke's famous speech to the electors of Bristol.

Playing chess, billiards, cards, and ping-ping with my father filled up many hours of my sabbatical. I became sufficiently expert in billiards to be a top player at my next school. The flexible routine of that year enabled me to play golf at Peninsula Golf Club and to caddy for father. The only game that remains in my memory was one with Norman Brookes and Gerald Patterson. Like Brookes, Patterson had been twice the men's singles champion at Wimbledon and a very successful Davis Cup player; he was known as 'the Human Catapult' for his powerful serves that even top players had trouble in returning. The fourth in that golf match was Harry Hopman, a good tennis player who was on the way to becoming a legendary Davis Cup coach. A nephew of Dame Nellie Melba and Brookes's former partner in doubles, Patterson thumped his drive as hard as he was supposed to have hit his serve. Courteous and careful, Brookes was the first left-handed golfer I had ever seen. With fascinating accuracy he directed his ball down the middle of the fairway. As caddy I had the job of providing the club asked for, putting clubs back into the bag, carrying the bag, holding the pin on the green, helping to find balls that had strayed into the undergrowth, and generally being as quiet, unobtrusive, and helpful as possible It was tiring work following the game around the course for three hours or more, but encouraging, since father won far more often than he lost. Afterwards the chance came to hit some balls down the practice fairway, while the players showered, changed, and had their drinks.

The sabbatical year removed me from regular contacts with other boys and girls of my own age. I became friendly with Joy Stevens, whose father lived as a recluse in the bush half a mile south of us. In a shed next to his weirdly dilapidated house he kept (but never drove) an ancient car. I marvelled at this arrangement of old brass, strange fenders, and narrow wheels, as if it were a dinosaur that had survived from an earlier stage of mechanical evolution. Years later I heard that Joy ran a multi-storey car park. The dinosaur had its long-term effect. I felt hurt when my parents cut short my quietly innocent friendship with her. I was not to visit Stevens or his daughter again. They differed from most our neighbours by failing to have a name beginning with 'M'. To the north the Mentiplays had their poultry farm. In the other direction were Mrs Minton, the Mathers, and the Morgans, a gentle, grey-haired couple who had lived on Mount Eliza since the 1880s.

Mr Morgan, a trim, little patriarch whom we called 'Dorgie', had helped lay out our garden. He told us of the days when Cobb & Co. coaches ran down the Mornington peninsula. Behind his small weather-board house was an old well with a cement top and beyond that a shed built of wattle and daub. When I knelt by the well or fingered with fascination the hard clay packed into the walls of the shed, I felt in touch with the pioneer generations and their achievements. We were only city-dwellers, amateur farmers who had come later to Mount Eliza and the peninsula. 'Dorgie' stood for those who had put through the roads, cleared the land, battled with drought and fire, and kept life going in the wilderness. He and his wife did not wait indoors when we called, but in the manner of bush-people stepped out to greet us before we crossed their neat garden to the front verandah. After their death, it was discovered that they had no formal title to the land. They had simply built and lived there without bothering anyone.

During the winter of 1943 I spent a week with some family friends who owned a property in the ranges of central Victoria. It was my first holiday away from my family. I learned to shoot rabbits, climbed up an aircraft-spotting tower which was still being manned, and suffered my first attack of scruples. My hosts, although Catholics, did not drive into town for the Sunday Mass. I said nothing, but was horrified by the fear of having lapsed into mortal sin. For that, as the nuns has taught us, three requirements had to be met: grave matter, full knowledge and full consent. I had no doubts about my full knowledge and full consent. I should have asked my hosts to take me to Mass. But was the matter really grave? My hosts lived about fifteen miles out of town. Was that distance a sufficient excuse to miss Mass even if one had a motor car? A distance of three or more miles could excuse those who had to walk. My tormented conscience tried to transpose that principle to the situation of country people with a car. On my return home I shuffled anxiously around the kitchen, and in the most normal voice I could muster raised the matter as a hypothetical question. My mother gave me some reassurance, although I cannot recall whether she answered legalism with legalism or, seeing through my screen to what actually happened, dismissed the whole business as not my responsibility.

The arrival of American marines in the mid-years of the war helped to round off the first stage of my life. Shortly after the bombing of Pearl Harbour, my father had met a couple of American army officers in the lounge of the Menzies Hotel, Melbourne. Delighted by their southern charm, he asked: 'Are all American servicemen like you?' One of them warned with a laugh, 'Just wait for the marines!' In late 1942 the seventh Marine Regiment was withdrawn from fighting in the Solomon Islands, and arrived for rest and recreation at a camp about twelve miles south of our home on the Mornington peninsula. Father met Colonel Herman Henry Hanneken, who brought a group of his junior officers for several parties at Rock Lodge. Moira had just finished her schooling at the Sacred Heart convent. She mustered her friends to help in the entertainment. They fluttered across our lawn all legs and laughter, lovely, elusive creatures from a grown-up world. Josie Filippini, the daughter of Contessa Filippini who taught Italian at Moira's school, charmed Hanneken with her vivacious beauty. A permanent marine, he was friendly, fatherly, and steely— clearly a different stamp of soldier from the cheerful young officers he brought with him. He was known as 'Herman the Vermin' and 'Horrible Hanneken'. Momentarily the tough fighter seemed softened by the innocent loveliness of a girl just out of convent school. Years later I read how he had won the Medal of Honor, the US military's highest decoration, for what he did in 1919 when putting down a 'rebellion' in Haiti. He made his way at night to the headquarters of the resistance, killed the leader, Charlemagne Pêralte, and allegedly brought his head back in a bag. Josie was to marry a South Australian lawyer, the brother of Fr Peter Kelly who would teach me moral theology and then be my 'provincial' superior from 1968 to 1973.

Some of the marines we met died later in the war in battles at Cape Gloucester and Peleliu. Ed Kirby survived and remained in lasting contact with my family. For five years I was to enjoy Thanksgiving Day dinner at his home in New Jersey. During the wartime parties at Rock Lodge, however, I spent much of my time outside with Colonel Hanneken's driver. I read his comics, chewed his gum, and chatted with him in the cabin of his utility truck.

When Hanneken and his unit moved back to the fighting, we met Lemuel C. Shepherd, Jr., then a brigadier-general and later the 20th Commandant of the Marine Corps. In 1943 I experienced some of his lively concern for personal welfare, which I learnt afterwards helped to bind the marines together. At his invitation, I lunched in a mess with the soldiers, wondered at the long line of sauce bottles which stood on the table, and enjoyed a ride out into the bay on a amphibious landing-craft. Mrs Eleanor Roosevelt came once to visit the camp. I stood by the roadside in Frankston to glimpse her as the official car whisked her by.

Both at Frankston and in Melbourne, Dame Mabel Brookes far outstripped us in her open-handed hospitality to American servicemen, who included Lyndon Johnson, the future president. For some months during 1942 she entertained General Douglas MacArthur when he had his headquarters in Melbourne. One memorable evening she slipped over to Rock Lodge, dismayed that he was moving north as the tide of war turned. To a degree father played the role of unofficial confessor-spiritual advisor towards her and some other members of the Peninsula Golf Club. He dissuaded her from following MacArthur by saying, 'Mabel, it wouldn't be good for the war effort.'

In February 1944 I left home to begin five years at a Melbourne boarding school, Xavier College. Since then I never lived again at Rock Lodge for more than a month or two at a time. But the house had given me a lasting sense of rootedness, as well as establishing the basic pattern of relationship with other members of my immediate family. I have already spoken of my parents and my younger brothers. As for my three sisters, I looked up to Moira and Dympna, whose age set them with the adults when I first became aware of them as separate characters. Small, red-haired, energetic and vivacious, Moira tackled study, singing, acting, social life and everything else with practical and wise enthusiasm. If I didn't imitate her by concentrating on modern languages (French, German, Italian, and Japanese), her excellent results set a standard for me in other subjects. She took Japanese, because mother thought it would be useful to have one member of the family fluent in that language, in case the Japanese overran our country. Moira and I rode horses and played tennis and golf together. I enjoyed her bursts of temper when she hit a bad shot at golf or found the horses difficult to catch. One winter evening Moira and I were alone at Rock Lodge when we heard noises coming from the shed halfway up the front drive. I grabbed an unloaded shotgun and Moira armed herself with a heavy iron bar, which we used as a poker for our central fireplace. We crept close to the shed and with shaky voices called out, 'Who's there?' It was a truck driver making a late delivery of food for our cows and poultry. We slipped our weapons behind some lavender bushes and tried to chat in normal voices. Moira and I have never felt the slightest barrier in understanding and helping each other. Dark-haired and lovely, Dympna was always very affectionate and generous to me. At times her face could light up with a radiant beauty, which I saw again in 1965 when visiting our Fitzgerald relations on the banks of the Shannon.

With Maev I fought frequently as a child, but have never felt the slightest guilt about it. The fighting changed into a deep comradeship and a loving admiration that grew with the years. Maev has always put back into life much more than she has taken from it. When she was born in 1929, mother and father very much wanted a son. From China uncle Gerald sent a telegram urging them to accept 'God's holy will'. Sometimes we jokingly called Maev 'God's holy will'. Father's disappointment at her not being a boy meant that it was only late in his life that they settled down to be 'good friends', as he put it. An enduring picture from my childhood is her reacting at being sent off to bed early. After some misdemeanor, father told her to leave without the evening meal and go to bed in the cottage. As she started up the drive, she suddenly spun around, stuck out her tongue and shouted back at him, 'Yair, I didn't want to eat anyway.' Maev and I have always shared a great deal, not least mid-point journeys that took us to new destinations in adult life.

Those early years at Rock Lodge (1931-44) provided an education which, if often informal, delivered me from the normal years of class-room oppression. It was a strangely privileged childhood. Wide reading offered an immense start over my peers, even if books had left me with romantic expectations that overlooked the dull and sordid aspects of life. I mixed easily and courteously with older people, but had to learn how to relate to boys and girls of my own age. I felt that great things were about to start. The gun of life was about to go off. I left for Xavier College a serious and self-confident twelve-year-old, doting upon my family and proud of their accomplishments. Coming to terms with them would eventually form part of my midlife journey. But there could never be any question of loosening that rock-hard unity with one another which childhood gave me.

3
Xavier and Newman (1944-50)

The next slice of my life took me through five years of secondary
school and one year of university studies, until in February 1950
I entered the Jesuit novitiate in Watsonia, Victoria. I spent all that time
under the Jesuits, first at Xavier College and then at Newman College
within the University of Melbourne.

In 1944 the only Catholic member of the six Victorian associated
public schools, Xavier stood on a hill that offered a broad view across
Melbourne. On the highest ground, grey-faced buildings housed class
rooms, dormitories, the great hall, libraries, offices, quarters for the
Jesuit community, and the boys' refectory. A large chapel, built of
honey-coloured stone and topped by a copper dome, stood by itself
above playing fields, pavilions, and tennis courts that stretched away
in the direction of the city.

I started in the sub-intermediate A class, and proceeded through
intermediate and leaving to matriculation which I took twice. In my
final year I studied English expression, English literature, European
history, Greek, and Latin. Mother was determined that like her father
I should steep myself in the classics and often maintained, 'You can
always tell a man who has studied Greek.' After intermediate I gave
up mathematics (at which I excelled), since boys had to choose at
that stage whether to concentrate on the humanities or on the natural
sciences and mathematics. I hurled myself into my studies, filled my
bedroom at Rock Lodge with the books I won as prizes, and in my
final year carried off every available award except the prize for dux

of the school. That was won by Ian Howells, who became a fellow in mathematics at Trinity College, Cambridge, before entering the Society of Jesus in 1960.

My spiritual life resembled my educational progress in being strenuously dedicated to clarity and success. In the morning all the boarders, one hundred and twenty or so, were gathered in the chapel for a seven o'clock Mass; in the evening they went there for the rosary. I found this regular pattern of prayer congenial. During our pre-breakfast Mass, Father Paddy Stephenson sat in a confessional box in the right transept. During the early weeks of my life at Xavier, I used to confess my 'sins' each morning to him, receiving always the same penance of 'three Hail Marys'. Did my practice spring from that widespread, if unauthorized, conviction of Catholics that confession should invariably precede communion? Or did I simply want to do something to break the monotony of the service? When some boys commented on my practice, I abandoned it in favour of confession every Saturday evening. I used to follow the Mass (which, of course, was still totally in Latin) by using either my *Daily Missal* or a small collection of readings from the *Imitation of Christ*, the New Testament, and Jeremy Taylor's devotional writings. This Anglican divine impressed me when he pointed to the serious consequences that one's choice of marriage partner carried for eternal salvation. Many years later I felt deep satisfaction at preaching during the week of prayer for Christian unity at Uppingham in East Anglia (where Taylor had been rector), and some years later, also for that week of prayer, in the Anglican cathedral of Belfast (where he had presided as bishop of Down and Connor).

Along with the day boys, the boarders attended benediction of the Blessed Sacrament and a High Mass on major feast days. On Sunday evenings, we heard a sermon, followed by benediction. At all these services participation by the congregation was minimal, apart from a little singing. The five decades of the rosary were led by different boys, but at Mass the servers made the Latin responses on our behalf. We shared the opportunities to serve Mass in the main chapel, in a tiny chapel off the main hall, or in the 'domestic chapel' which was reserved for the Jesuit community. Each morning all the priests, accompanied perhaps by a single server, celebrated alone their own Mass, apart from those who went out to say Mass at neighbouring convents. Priests concelebrating Mass together was a change that would come only in the late 1960s. The wonder is that being forced to rise every morning for Mass in a chapel that left one freezing in winter failed to make atheists or at least agnostics of us all. But by 1945 I knew I wanted to be a priest—either a Jesuit or a Columban missionary like the uncle after whom I had been named.

Life at a boarding school took some time to become attractive to me. Initially I suffered from a sharp attack of home-sickness and for a while opted for the status of a weekly boarder, which allowed me to spend Saturday night at Rock Lodge. Green potatoes, stale bread and sago pudding left me yearning for the delights of home cooking, even for mother's restricted range of dishes. My parents supplied pocket money in sparing amounts, so that I could not join the big spenders at the school tuck-shop. No rooms were heated, except that there could be fires in the first and second division libraries—for senior and junior boarders, respectively. When working in the vast study hall, we wrapped ourselves in rugs. Chilblains tormented me for one or two winters, until I remembered to wear gloves regularly.

Friends at Xavier

Friends and a wide variety of extracurricular activities made my time at Xavier increasingly pleasant as the five years went on. I played games, went fishing, saw films, engaged in debates, attended VFL football matches, and did a host of other things with friends like Jim Copeland, Greg Dening, Laurie Drake, Jim Gobbo, Phil Kennedy,

Peter Kirchner, David McCarthy, and Norman O'Bryan. Copeland and his brother were the only non-Catholics in the school, apart from several Jewish youngsters. Dening became a Jesuit, studied with me for many years, left the order, and became a professor of history at the University of Melbourne. Drake also entered the Society of Jesus, took his doctorate in seismology at the University of California, Berkeley, and taught at Macquarie University, Sydney. Gobbo won a Rhodes Scholarship, rowed in the 100th Oxford/Cambridge boat race (won by Oxford), was President of the Oxford University Boat Club, and became an outstanding barrister, a Supreme Court judge and, finally, Governor of the State of Victoria. Kennedy and McCarthy formed with me the matriculation Greek class of 1947. Kennedy had some differences with the rector of Xavier, left the college at the end of the year, took degrees in arts and law, tried his vocation as a Cistercian, became a priest in the archdiocese of Adelaide, and served as an auxiliary bishop until his premature death from a brain tumour in 1983. McCarthy and I stayed on for a second year of matriculation and constituted the entire top Greek class. He then sailed for England, entered a Carthusian monastery near London, became a priest, left the order around the late 1960s, and returned to Melbourne. O'Bryan studied law at Melbourne University and followed his father by becoming a Supreme Court judge.

During the first term holidays in 1945, Kirchner took me to Adelaide, where I stayed with his parents in a damp, decaying mansion surrounded by gardens that had run wild. It was the old Lewis home; the property was later turned into a Catholic boys school. I read some Biggles books,[1] attended a race meeting, visited a nearby Dominican convent to meet an old nun who had taught mother, and heard much about the Lewis family. John Lewis had worked as a stockman with the cattle king, Sidney (later Sir Sidney) Kidman, before making his own

1 'Biggles', a nickname for James Bigglesworth, was a pilot and the central hero in a series of youth-oriented adventure books written by W.E. Johns.

fortune as a pastoralist. One daughter had married Peter Kirchner's father; another was the deceased mother of Bob Britten-Jones, an Adelaide boy who boarded with me at Xavier and later became a distinguished surgeon. One of the Lewis sons married my aunt Mary, but the marriage broke up in the 1930s. The faded magnificence of the Lewis home mournfully recalled the first decades of the twentieth century, when mother's family came there for parties, and death and divorce had not yet taken their toll. Instinctively I saw the decline as a warning of what might happen to Rock Lodge and my own family.

When I returned to Melbourne from those May holidays, my parents enquired whether I had visited the Catholic archbishop, Dr Matthew Beovich, as they had asked me to do. I had to sit down and at the age of not quite fourteen write an apology to the archbishop for having failed to call on him when I visited his city. On the one hand, I judged the apology unnecessary. On the other hand, my parents' insistence made me feel that my family's prominence as Catholics was such that we could scarcely travel interstate without being expected to pay a courtesy call on the local church leaders.

Out of all the Xavier friends, Dening, Gobbo and O'Bryan proved the closest at school and later. We moved together through second division, in which boys remained up the age of fifteen and were fairly strictly segregated from the senior boys in the first division. Especially in the last two or three years, I worked with these friends and others in all kind of school activities: debating societies, sodalities of Our Lady, a special group collecting food and clothing for the needy in Germany, literary groups, societies for the foreign missions, and the YCS (Young Christians Students), a state-wide association for Catholic high school students. With Jim Gobbo I produced a comic play (*The Crimson Coconut*) in the crypt of the school chapel. When the audience rioted at the end, they were fiercely castigated for their irreverent behaviour in a sacred building by one of the sons of the deceased Joseph Lyons (Australian prime minister 1932-39) and

Dame Enid Lyons (who had become in 1943 the first woman elected to the House of Representatives).

At games I was fiercely keen, but a place in the sporting sun eluded me. Throughout my five years at Xavier I played for B football teams, ending as full back for the second eighteen which, I think, had an unbroken season of defeats. In athletics I won a handicap 880 yards race as a junior, spiked myself when trying the high jump at home, and finished second in the 1948 open mile. I played for the A cricket teams, in 1945 won a medal for the under-fourteen bowling average, made 86 not out in a house match that year, but ended my career with 'a pair' in the first eleven's final match for 1948. Two years earlier father had a concrete pitch laid in our top paddock at Rock Lodge, and over the summers I often played cricket there with my brothers and others. Father joined us for one match and made a century, even though we forced him to run between wickets. He tried to hit as many fours and sixes as possible, but finished up stiff for days. For teenagers it was humiliating to have their bowling hammered by a man in his fifties.

The only social activity I loathed was the weekly afternoon in the cadet corps. We learnt drill, were instructed in the use of rifles, Bren guns and machine guns, and occasionally went to ranges for practice shoots. Although serving in the cadets was compulsory, one could at least avoid attending the camps scheduled for the holidays. In June 1946, along with cadets from other schools, we marched in the victory parade through the streets of Melbourne. I found it embarrassing to add our adolescent ranks alongside men and women who had served through the war. Besides, we had to march twenty abreast and we did it badly. All in all, after two years I was glad to drop being in the cadets.

Membership in the St Vincent de Paul Society took me on occasional visits to Caritas Christi, a nearby hospice for the dying. There I met 'the last of the Austrian Jesuits', Father Johannes Peifer, who died in 1948. In 1848 Jesuits from the Austrian province came to Australia, nearly twenty years before the first Irish Jesuits arrived. Eventually the Irish took over the entire mission, and the Austrians were offered the choice of remaining in Australia or returning home. Fr Peifer opted to stay, but he was no more Austrian than I am. He came from the Mosel valley, and decided to become a Jesuit at the time when Bismarck's 'Kulturkampf' had driven the Jesuits out of Germany. So young Peifer entered the Austrian province, only to be sent to Australia in 1898. A trim old man, he explained his small bottle of wine as medicinal, and gave me a story typed on a dog-eared sheet which expounded the importance of the sacrament of extreme unction (or, as it called now, the anointing of the sick). In 1965 I was to meet some of his relatives when I worked in a parish in Trier, drank their excellent white wine, and read some of the letters he had written home from the Australian mission. He deplored the scandalous fashions of the Sydney girls around the start of the twentieth century.

Irish Priests on the Staff

At Xavier College, Irish priests, like Fathers Tom Costelloe, Tom Montague, Paddy Stephenson, William Hackett and Bill ('Gerry') Owens, predominated over the Australian Jesuits and non-Jesuits on the staff and put their stamp on the college. A tall, cheery and eloquent man, Fr Costelloe served as rector of Xavier and superior of other Jesuit communities for at least thirty consecutive years. Such offences as smoking, failure to wear the school cap or, for boarders, being out of bounds without permission normally carried a severe ration of cuts, if not worse. But the rector showed himself consistently fair and witty with the boys, and for those pre-permissive days sometimes astonishingly mild. One boarder operated as a starting-price bookmaker, and after a successful race-meeting would contribute generously to the St Vincent de Paul collection that I made at the Sunday morning line-up. At a school assembly Fr Costelloe amused his audience by deft references to betting, and concluded by looking in the direction of the culprit and declaring, 'Mr McNamara, the book is now closed.'

An excellent mathematician and strict disciplinarian, Fr Montague served as minister or second-in-charge at Xavier. For nearly forty years he produced with monotonous success the cultural highpoint of the year, a Gilbert and Sullivan opera.

Fr Stephenson both acted as spiritual father to the students and kept in touch with an extraordinary number of old boys. This diminutive, infectiously cheerful, and not too intelligent priest was everybody's friend. He showed unquestioning kindness in finding jobs for those who left school and needed work. In his simplicity, 'Stevo' would recommend anybody, even the worst qualified or least promising, and his protégés would rarely, if ever, let him down. For

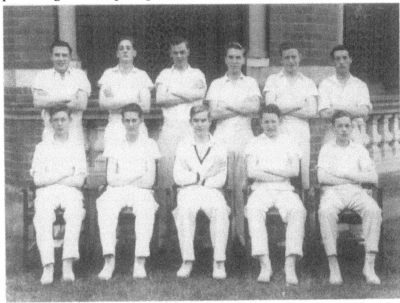

Xavier College Under-16 cricket team 1946: Greg Dening (captain) seated in middle; Gerald standing second from right.

decades he edited the college's annual, *The Xaverian*. After supper he would invite boys up to his office and with a disarming stammer enquire about their general well-being, as well as putting the question to any likely candidate, 'Ever think of becoming a priest?' One evening that question slipped out inadvertently when he was talking with the most notorious roué in the school. The boy replied with a straight face, 'Yes, Father.' Startled, Stevo urged him, 'Man, man, think about it!'

Once or twice I spoke to Stevo about my own interest in the priesthood. But I felt dismayed when in 1947 he took it upon himself to arrange an interview with the Australian-born Jesuit provincial, Fr John Meagher. I went down nervously to the provincial's office in the neighbouring suburb of Hawthorn. Although I later came to appreciate Fr Meagher's dedication, honesty, and sense of fun, that evening he left me in turmoil. With a lamp hanging over the table and dropping a pool of light between us, he sat there facing me: thin, bright-eyed, and wearing a tennis shade. Looking like a sporting inquisitor, he spoke about the novitiate out in Watsonia and warned me, 'It won't be all cake and skittles at Loyola.' When he asked, 'Will you be able to keep the sixth commandment?', I had no idea what to say. How could I know then whether I would be capable of leading a chaste and celibate life? The following year an Irishman, Fr Austin Kelly, succeeded him as provincial. When Fr Kelly visited Xavier, I was trotted out to meet him as a 'prospect'. I felt annoyed at this, since I had not yet fully committed myself to the notion of entering the Jesuits.

Fr William Hackett had been rector of Xavier, but was known much more for his work in the late 1920s when he founded the Central Catholic Library and then helped to gather in the Campion Society a remarkable group of young Catholic intellectuals. Bob Santamaria and his associates finished up doctrinaire right-wingers, while the *Catholic*

Worker group remained on the left, where the original Campion Society stood. With a brush of white hair over his twinkling eyes, Fr Hackett was almost the only Jesuit who conveyed a sense of the larger world of politics and culture. The rest, if mostly highly educated men, seemed to live in a political vacuum, and deal only with those ideas or works that had established themselves as classics. We all believed that this gentlemanly, slightly stooped priest had to leave his native Ireland in the early 1920s because of his connections with rebel leaders.[2] We heard too that his brother Francis had migrated to the United States, abandoned Catholicism, and become a celebrated writer not least for his best-selling book on King Henry VIII. We noted that sometimes a large car called at Xavier to take Fr Hackett off to Raheen, the home of the Catholic archbishop of Melbourne, Dr Daniel Mannix. Fr Hackett was his confessor and part time companion. It was this gentlemanly old priest who gathered many of us in the Bellarmine Room for political and cultural discussions, encouraged wide reading through a special collection of books kept in that room, and effected what later jargon called a 'raising of consciousness'.

By the end of the Second World War, Communists had acquired a wide and threatening control over top positions in Australian trade unions. Harassing strikes contributed to the problems of post-war recovery. Catholics organized with other non-Communists to form 'industrial groups' and win back power in the Australian Council of Trade Unions. Behind the scenes Catholics had their own organization, 'the movement', which Bob Santamaria led and a number of priests encouraged by their stress on the religious nature of the fight against Communism. The editor of the movement's paper, *News Weekly*, warned us boys against the dangers both within and beyond Australia.

---

2 In *The Riddle of Father Hackett* (Canberra: National Library of Australia, 2009), Brenda Niall tells the story of Fr Hackett's involvement with Michael Collins, Erskine Childers, and other leaders committed to the independence of Ireland and then caught up in the tragic civil war (1921-22) that followed the Anglo-Irish Treaty.

A contemporary of mine at Xavier joined a movement man on a weekend trip to Lake Boga in western Victoria. They had heard that Communists landed Catalina flying boats there to pick up arms for guerilla forces in Malaya (now part of Malaysia). My contemporary, a lieutenant in the school cadets, and his older friend contemplated blowing up any Catalinas they discovered at Lake Boga.

But it would be untrue to represent Fr Hackett's impact as simply inspiring us to rally to some militant crusade against Communism. He wanted to lead others through reading, debate, thought, discussion, and prayer to share his own ideal of being a gentleman, a scholar, and a saint. He lived by those words he loved to quote from Léon Bloy: 'The only sadness is not to love God, not to be a saint'. Like some other holy men, Fr Hackett could be forgetful. When he was still rector of Xavier, Lord Huntingfield, the governor of Victoria from 1934 to 1939, visited the college for the solemn opening of some new gates. After being welcomed by Fr Hackett, the governor looked around and asked, 'Where's Frank?' Fr Hackett had forgotten to invite my father, who knew the governor and had arranged for his visit. The rector sent a runner to make an urgent phone call; father took a taxi from his Collins Street office and, when he arrived at Xavier, said to the governor, 'I was held up.' It was a way of saving the rector's face.[3]

The last Irish priest I wish to recall was Fr Bill ('Gerry') Owens, a slim, grey-haired non-conformist with whom I studied Greek, Latin, and European history. We never knew that he had inherited the 'Gerry' from his brother, who had taught at Xavier, returned to Ireland, and as priest left the Jesuit order. In those pre-Pope John XXIII days, church authorities offered no dispensations to regularize

---

3 Brenda Niall describes Fr Hackett's major contribution through founding the Central Catholic Library (*The Riddle of Father Hackett*, 167-89). After two temporary homes, the library moved to its permanent location in the Orient Line Building on Collins Street. My father's office was in that building, and he was instrumental in making the basement available at a reasonable rent for Fr Hackett.

the situation of married ex-priests but left them to live 'in a state of sin'. However, Fr James Brodrick, the biographer of several Jesuit saints, kept in touch with Gerry Owens in London. Eventually, when he was dying, Owens sent for Brodrick who was on the point of leaving for Spain to do some research for one of his books. 'I felt like cursing him', said Brodrick, a spirited Irishman who had never been quite tamed through belonging to the English province of the Society of Jesus. 'And I did', he added. However, he delayed his departure to visit Gerry Owens and 'fix him up at the end'.

But to return to our 'Gerry' Owens. Charming and elusive, he controlled us by the power of his personality and the degree of his expectations. Individuals cringed when Gerry told them how contemptible he found their conduct, but that was extremely rare. Nothing was allowed to interfere with the one afternoon in the week when he played at Kew Golf Club. Nor did any boy dream of robbing the patch of strawberries, which he cultivated behind a hedge just beyond the junior class rooms. He made no secret of his occasional disagreements with the rector. He thought it disgraceful when Jim Gobbo was not appointed a prefect in 1948. He felt that Phil Kennedy had been under unfair pressure to leave school at the end of 1947.

In my last two years he gave me private tuition in reading Greek and Latin texts. I rewarded his interest by receiving first-class honours in both subjects, sharing the state Greek exhibition in 1947 and, on the basis of my papers in Latin and Greek, winning a Newman College scholarship in 1948. I felt privileged when he invited me once or twice to play golf with him at Kew. In my final year he agreed after much persuasion to break his rule of never visiting the parents of boys and spent a day at Frankston. Father turned on a dazzling display of golf to beat Gerry. That evening we enjoyed the blazing logs in the great fire-place at Rock Lodge, while red-haired Stewart Peters tumbled about on the floor showing off in the front of the visitor.

Not yet two years of age, my eldest nephew was to learn Greek from Gerry at Xavier, win a state exhibition in the subject, and make the third generation of our family to study with this Jesuit Mr Chips. In the early 1920s my mother's brother, Patrick McMahon Glynn, had boarded at Xavier, although he distinguished himself much more on the playing fields than in the class room.

What explained the enduring impact Gerry made on generations of Xavier boys? Perhaps it was his combination of secular and religious values. When he was growing up in Dublin, James Joyce was one of the older boys at Belvedere College, the day school Gerry attended before being sent to board at Stonyhurst College in England. Like Joyce, Gerry loved the classics and the full sweep of European culture. With teasing amusement he followed all our activities at Xavier and beyond. Yet every now and then we glimpsed a prayerful dedication to his chosen way of life.

Shortly before my ordination to the priesthood, he was to write to me in December 1962:

> Many thanks for yours. I should in any case have been writing to you, despite the increasing horror of lifting a pen! I wish & pray for every blessing on yourself & the family on this longed-for day. You will be plagued with letters; so I'll be brief...More or less on the lines of Père Godin's private litany...'From getting *used* to the Holy Mass, deliver me, O Lord. From getting used to the reception of Thy precious Body & Blood, deliver me, O Lord. From getting used to Your Divine Presence on the altar, deliver me, O Lord.' I'll be looking forward to receiving your blessing. As I explained to your mother, I'm more or less house-bound...So may His great gift come to you with holy joy. Yours as ever in Christ, W. V. Owens, SJ.

Gerry had been delighted when I entered the Jesuits, but he never dreamt of pushing me in that direction. One evening in 1948 he brought me back to earth with his gently ironical question: 'So you want to be a contemplative?' I had just returned from Valda Creed's clothing ceremony at the nearby Carmelite monastery. A close friend of my sister Maev, Valda had broken off her studies at Melbourne University to join the order. The wits in the Newman Society suggested that she had done so, because she had lost money in running their latest ball. Those wits, as well as other friends, were there in Carmel chapel to see her appear first in bridal dress, before she disappeared behind the grill to change into the brown habit and sandals of the Carmelites. One of her friends, a Communist, kept muttering, 'What a waste!', although a Newman Society member, who was enter the Jesuits with me, always insisted that he had said, 'What a waist!' I walked back to Xavier starry-eyed over Valda's heroic step, and feeling the force of the maxims I had read along the corridors in the public sections of the monastery: 'No cross, no crown', and 'A moment of sorrow an eternity of joy'.

Australians on the Staff

Besides the Irishmen there were Australians, both Jesuits and non-Jesuits, who made up the staff at Xavier. John Moore, who served as second division prefect, was still a scholastic or Jesuit who had not yet completed his studies and been ordained to the priesthood. This tough and trusting son of a Gippsland farmer enjoyed the affectionate support of the boys in his division. Some of them corresponded with him, when he went north to make his theological studies in Sydney. He believed in will-power and encouraged the boys to take cold showers in the morning. Even at the evening showers he would call for 'cold water' before giving the signal 'all out'. A first cousin of my mother, Fr James Dynon, succeeded him as second division prefect in 1946. Jim had taken a world trip after leaving school (at Xavier) and before entering the Jesuits. We found it highly amusing when we could prompt him into blurting out once again the information:

'I saw Adolf Hitler.' A deeply kind person, he encouraged some of us to visit a nearby orphanage to bring the toddlers sweets and play with them. The picture of their sadly deprived life has remained in my mind, ever since I saw those four and five year-olds surging across their playground towards me and crying out, 'Mannie'.

Two lay-masters taught the senior English classes, Lud and Joe. Lud wore a pince-nez; his dark blue suit shone with use; and he had tufts of hair sprouting from his nostrils. In a discreet corner of one class room, generations had recorded the dates under a heading: 'Lud wore a new tie.' He prepared us for examinations with conscientious thoroughness, but lacked the skill to provoke and inspire. Joe had a red nose, a thick lock of hair cutting across his forehead, and a developing paunch. He contributed mildly left-wing ideas, an insider's concern for Australian literature, and a feeling for happy married life. Most of us supported the conservatives (who had masqueraded under the name of the Liberal Party since 1944), and were to cheer when Robert Menzies led them to victory in 1949. Joe's support for the governing Labor Party led one Jesuit to mutter ominously in class: 'Pinkos are invading the school.' Joe published poetry, encouraged us to read Christopher Brennan and other Australian poets, and sat through the proceedings when our literature club moved on from George Eliot to discuss his own volume, *The Four Seasons*. He feared some of the directions taken by advanced industrial societies, warning us that we might one day have to wear lead trousers as we drove our nuclear-powered cars. He owned several acres of hilly land for his house, farm, orchard, children, and brightly attractive wife. We were always welcome at that home. Lud had a larger family, but must have been twenty years older than Joe whose married life conveyed to us a cheerful glow. During the midday break, Lud and Joe ate their lunch not with the Jesuit community but in the boys' refectory. Nothing expressed more clearly how at that time lay-masters were deemed second-class extras, made necessary because the Jesuits could not provide the entire staff.

My Family

In my own family much changed during my five years at Xavier. Jim came as a boarder to the school in 1945 and Glynn in 1947. Jim did very well at studies and remained a voracious reader. In his first term Glynn hurt a knee that had already proved troublesome. While watching the public schools' boat race on the Yarra, he was caught by a crowd of boys surging up and down the bank. I felt guilty at having failed to stay with my little brother to protect him. Later that year he burst into tears when I slipped down one evening to second division to break the news that our grandmother, Ellen O'Collins, had died.

A few weeks earlier I had visited her in Albert Park and sat with her in front of a glimmering coal fire. One strong old hand grasped my arm, as if she were trying to draw vitality from my youth. She gave me ten shillings and her parting views on many of the family. Glynn was 'a nice little boy'. She went back to her dairying days to describe another relative as being 'like a good cow that gives a lot of milk and then kicks the bucket over'. At a time when few predicted the scope of the boom that came to Victoria in the fifties, grandmother told me, 'I'm sorry I won't be alive to see the great expansion that's coming.' Her son Gerald had shortly before left to resume his missionary work in China. She kept asking, 'Has Gerald gone?' Her death followed when it came home to her that she would never see her favourite child again.

Bishops, priests, nuns, religious brothers, and lay Catholics crowded the funeral Mass celebrated by Bishop O'Collins. The occasion strengthened my conviction that we were 'the' Catholic family of Victoria, and brought a wave of religious seriousness to Jim, Glynn, and me. We asked our parents to buy us copies of the New Testament. Afterwards I made little use of the ugly Australian edition of Ronald Knox's new translation that I received. What lasted for years was the sense that grandmother still presided over all her descendants, and could take credit for the successful direction of their lives.

At Xavier College itself Jim, Glynn, and I rarely had the chance of being together much. We were too segregated by our division, our class, or our team. But we sometimes went into the city to see a film or lunch with our parents. Father ran the King's Theatre, which occasionally staged live shows like *The Desert Song*, but mostly showed films. We went back repeatedly to see a long-running success, Humphrey Bogart's *Casablanca*. Through the manager of the King's we could get free tickets to a number of other city cinemas. In a building off Collins Street we took a few lessons in voice production with a dapper little man, who taught me to spit out 'my dear people'. Did he guess that I would enter the ministry? A year or two later at the end of an opera, I was startled to see him come forward to take a bow on the stage of His Majesty's Theatre. He had trained the chorus for a visiting Italian company. With my parents we lunched in the stately Windsor Hotel (where my grandfather had stayed during sessions of the Commonwealth Parliament) or, more frequently, in the Menzies Hotel at the far end of the city. My memory reaches back to final years of the war to see father wearing his dark, striped suit and Returned Soldiers League badge and filling the Menzies lounge with his presence. From there I would walk a few steps to the dining room, often trail after him when he crossed to chat with friends already seated, and then move on to our table for a lunch of oysters, steak, sole, or more complex dishes. Its lofty ceiling, great pillars, and elegant mirrors made this dining room my archetypal place for eating out. During my year at Newman College, I occasionally took a girl friend there and signed for the meal on father's account.

In our earlier years at Xavier my two brothers and I spent some holidays with our uncle Jim in his massive, bluestone house at Ballarat, the former gold-mining town about seventy miles from Melbourne. The first native-born Victorian to become a Catholic bishop, he had completed his theological education at Propaganda College in Rome, where he was ordained to the priesthood on Christmas Eve, 1924. His

Australian contemporaries there included Matthew Beovich, Norman Gilroy and Alfred Gummer, all future bishops. In 1930 he was consecrated a bishop by Dr Daniel Mannix and took over the West Australian diocese of Geraldton, which covered over 300,000 square miles of mostly desert country. In 1941 he was translated to the see of Ballarat and served there for thirty years until his retirement at the age of seventy-nine. He proved himself the most relentless traveller of the family. Between 1914 and 1970 he travelled eleven times from Australia to Europe and back, not to mention visits to Asia, South America, and the United States.

A short, thick-set man with dark hair, uncle Jim enjoyed excellent health, worked hard, and always seemed imperturbable. In a part of Victoria where it occasionally snows in winter, he slept out on a verandah, exposed to the winds and night frosts. To fit in his daily routine of prayers he would sometimes recite the rosary when driving, and on one hair-raising trip read part of his breviary while driving down a ten-mile stretch of straight country road. 'Tell me if you see another car coming', he asked me. He never seemed upset when we broke things, damaged the bikes he provided, or even when we once smashed the rear door of his car. He distrusted theories, resembled his contemporaries at Propaganda in being unswervingly faithful to Vatican policies, never failed in sympathetic help to people in distress, could work well with tools, and never lost the common touch. He could have been a great trade union leader or even Labor Party leader—this loyal and loving man who summed up for me his philosophy of life as, 'Keep your nose dry, your mouth shut and your bowels open.' He and father were extraordinarily fond of each other, and that made us instantly at home with him.

Many stories about his eleven years there had drifted back from Western Australia. On one occasion his car broke down on a desert road, and a passing motorist stopped to see what the trouble was. Uncle Jim crawled dusty, and in one version swearing, from under his

car, accepted some help, and chatted with the stranger, who eventually
asked him what he did for a living. 'I'm the Bishop of Geraldton', uncle
Jim explained. 'Pig's bloody arse', retorted the astonished stranger. In
Ballarat on Saturday evenings uncle Jim used to cross Sturt Street to
see films in the boarding section of St Patrick's College. One evening,
when a love scene drew some whistles from the audience, the brother
in charge interrupted the film to reproach the boys for their conduct
and threatened to stop proceedings altogether. Some boys claimed
that they heard a voice from the back urging, 'Get on with the bloody
film!'

We enjoyed the run of his mansion with its high ceilings,
nineteenth-century bathrooms, brass-knobbed beds, and bounteous
food. He had inherited from his predecessor a fine cook, who felt it her
duty to fatten uncle Jim's nephews, nieces, and all the other relatives
who came to stay. The bishop's property, although surrounded by
suburban housing, was large enough to provide grazing for several
cows. Gradually uncle Jim replaced a potato field with lawns, put in
fish ponds, and built aviaries. Lake Wendouree, on which the rowing
events of the 1956 Olympic Games were held, lay a few yards beyond
the back fence. Around the shores stretched botanical gardens, where
we chased squirrels and tried our luck in getting in and out of a
maze. We took rides on the quaint Ballarat trams, went to cinemas,
and visited the Eureka Stockade, the scene in 1854 of Australia's
only 'revolution', a brief and bloody stand by gold-miners against
oppressive taxes. Once at an orphanage on the edge of town I went
into the ring and was, to my embarrassment, awarded the fight. The
orphans' champion had clearly won out-boxed me, but the referee felt
it his duty to crown the bishop's nephew.

Sometimes uncle Jim took me on trips around his diocese, which
covered the western half of Victoria. Right through his thirty years as
bishop, diocesan affairs reflected the general stability and conservatism
of that part of the state. In most areas Catholics reached at least the

national average, and in a few towns enjoyed a majority. We happened
to visit one parish on the occasion of a marriage between a Catholic
and a Protestant. I plumped myself in the very front pew, doubtless
dislodging some close relative, and was astonished to note that the
priest not only failed to celebrate a nuptial Mass but also conducted
the bridal pair through the sanctuary and out into the sacristy for
the actual ceremony. With regard to mixed marriages and other inter-
church issues, ecumenism came slow to uncle Jim and most Catholic
bishops. He insisted that his priests should give the non-Catholic party
a thorough instruction 'in the faith' before the wedding, recognized
that many of the non-Catholics became converts and often better
Catholics than their Catholic spouses, but opposed admission of non-
Catholic children to Catholic schools. In the 1930s he had seen how
many Anglican and Protestant children attended at Catholic schools
in West Australia. He concluded that this policy caused too much
leakage among Catholic students.

According to one story from the 1960s, a young curate in the Ballarat
diocese told uncle Jim how he had arranged an ecumenical service
for the boys and girls at the local high school. The arrangement had
been made that the non-Catholic students would leave after the 'bible
service' (or 'liturgy of the word'), while the Catholics would remain
for the rest of the Mass. 'But they all stayed', the curate explained,
'and at the time for Holy Communion most of them started coming
up to the altar.' 'What did you do?', uncle Jim asked anxiously. 'Well',
said the curate, 'I thought to myself, what would Jesus have done?'
Uncle Jim broke in aghast: 'You didn't, did you?'

Uncle Jim hoped to see one or more of his nephews follow his
own path to Rome, Propaganda College, and the diocesan priesthood.
He arranged for the younger sons of his sister Madge to study in
Ballarat at St Patrick's College, apparently believing that, if Bill who
had begun at Xavier continued there, he would become a Jesuit.
Eventually Bill and his younger brother John studied in Rome and

became distinguished priests in the archdiocese of Melbourne.

Aunt Madge lived on Beaconsfield Parade, quite close to the wharves in Port Melbourne. Uncle Jim normally stayed there on his frequent visits to the city. In his old age he prevailed on her not to sell the house, as 'so many Masses had been said in it'. She cared for her mother until Ellen died in 1947. Aunt Madge then returned to her profession of teaching and took a post at a girls school run by Anglican nuns. They wanted her to teach religious knowledge, as well as other subjects, recognizing that she would be thoroughly 'orthodox'. But she drew a line at that, feeling that it would be somehow fraudulent. She was one of the most honest and forthright persons I have ever met, someone whose cheerful company I always enjoyed. After the sudden death of her husband Stan, the rents from grandmother's houses in Port Melbourne kept the family going, along with generous help from uncle Jim. Madge's eldest son, Jim, became a doctor, and Frank, the youngest (who was born little more than a week after Stan died from heart failure brought on by his asthmatic condition), worked as a solicitor. Her other two children, Bill and John, became diocesan priests.

A few doors along Beaconsfield Parade from Madge's home stood a convent, where we first met our aunts Mollie and Alice, both Brigidine nuns. I have only a vague memory of Alice. She died in 1943 from an abdominal cancer that the doctors failed at first to diagnose. She suffered from being treated for a while as a hypochondriac. After her death father received back a copy of the New Testament that he had given her when she entered the Brigidines. Years later I took it away with me to the Jesuit novitiate. At the back aunt Alice had written some prayers of her own. They expressed an intense love for Christ and asked for the grace to endure silently the sufferings and humiliations that came her way.

As a schoolboy I often visited aunt Mollie, who for twenty-four

years was novice mistress for the Brigidine sisters. She wrote to me
regularly on my birthday, followed with obvious interest the progress
of her nephews and nieces, and conveyed to us the feeling that she
loved us all warmly. A prayerful person and an excellent teacher, she
had inherited an Irish horror of sexual sins. She told me of her method
of checking homosexual activity among the boys in a country school
where she once taught. After lining them up, she made them stretch
out their hands, turn them over, and look at them closely before
uttering the warning: 'Boys, you will carry these hands with you to
heaven or hell.' Father sent cases of evil-looking stout to aunt Mollie
who often suffered poor health. We viewed her steady consumption
of this beer as an astonishing piece of liberality. In those days it was
unheard of that nuns should drink and smoke or even eat in public.

To come back to my brothers and sisters. At Rock Lodge, Jim,
Glynn, and I played cricket, football and tennis together. On one
occasion Jim covered himself with nets to lead us in a wild attempt
to rob a native beehive. We failed when the ladder broke that Glynn
and I were holding for him. On the beach one day we came across
two fisherman who had netted a large school of salmon. They invited
us to wade into the shallow water and help ourselves. Glynn and I
grabbed a couple of fish, but Jim systematically hunted down the
largest salmon in the catch. Glynn and I once rode our horses ten
miles across the peninsula to Hastings, then a tiny country town on
Westernport Bay. I can still taste the fresh warmth of the meat pies we
bought at a bakery. Glynn told me later that he began to suspect the
career I had in mind, when I stopped my horse to 'make a visit' in the
tin-roofed, weatherboard church at Hastings. As soon as she got her
driving licence, Maev took us on picnics up and down the peninsula.
Even though none of us were strong swimmers, we sometimes surfed
at the dangerous Portsea back beach. Over the years many people have
drowned along that stretch of coast, including an Australian Prime
Minister (Harold Holt in 1967). We also drove around Westernport to

see the penguins, mutton birds, and koalas on Phillip Island.

During the May holidays of 1948, Jim and I travelled by train over two hundred kilometers into Gippsland and then headed further east on our bikes. The sound has always remained in my ears since we stood on a headland, looked across a dreamy inlet at Lakes Entrance, and listed to dozens of wattle birds shrieking as they tumbled among the banksias under a warm sun. In the town of Lake Entrance we stayed at a guest house, where the handful of guests included a honeymoon couple who clutched each other with what I felt was an obsessive lack of restraint. 'But if you don't enjoy yourself on your honeymoon', an older guest asked, 'when will you enjoy yourself?' Father did not worry about such trips provided we kept his rule: 'Never ride your bikes at night.'

During the middle and late 1940s relatives and others often came to stay at Rock Lodge. The cottage provided extra bedrooms, and for a time we had the use of a large caravan parked down the back drive. The McCarthys (aunt Madge and her sons) and grandmother stopped with us once or twice. The four McCarthy boys helped to make up our teams for games, as well as being thoroughly pleasant companions. When uncle Jim came, he brought with him a battered suitcase containing the vestments, vessels, and missal to celebrate Mass for us at home. Jim, Glynn, and I had to remember an extra washing of the hands and the variations in the Latin responses required when serving Mass for a bishop. Deirdre and Patrick Lewis came down from Sydney, as well as their mother Mary. I was instantly attracted to aunt Mary with her gleaming blue eyes, bright personality, and devotion to daily Mass.

Beyond question, uncle Gerald was our most intriguing house guest. This legendary missionary whose name I received spent most of the war years interned by the Japanese in a Yankow camp. We waited for his return like a resurrection from the dead. He had been away from home for ten years and arrived just before Christmas 1945, a white-haired, bearded man with a face so leathery and rutted that it seemed the winds of China had driven the mud of the Yangtze Kiang into his skin. He appeared to live mainly on cigarettes, coffee and toast, and talked long into the night of floods, bandits, Communists, and strange dishes of food he had eaten in China. He told us frightening stories about demon possessions, recalled some unpleasant fellow prisoners, and predicted that the Americans would arm the Japanese to fight against the Russians. He gave me a pocket watch on the back of which a friend in the internment camp had carved a train.

Uncle Gerald's return allowed him to resume his astonishing battles of golf with his three brothers: uncle Jim, my father, and uncle Joe. A neatly built, grey-haired doctor, Joe (he preferred us not to call him 'uncle Joe') seemed in many ways a scaled-down, gentler version of my father. He married late and had two daughters, Geraldine and Josephine. Looking back, I am conscious of my meanness in thinking that the name 'O'Collins' could be transmitted only by my brothers and myself. Joe always showed himself to me as an affectionate, cheerful friend. On the course at Peninsula the four brothers fought out their games with a passion that became a legend at the club. My favourite story from those battles concerns uncle Jim. As he clambered down into a drain to play his ball out, he steadied himself on the bank with his club. 'Penalty stroke', called out one of his opponents. Technically uncle Jim had grounded his club in a hazard.

Sometimes uncle Will spent the day at Rock Lodge, while his four brothers battled on the course. In the front room he would fill a leather-covered armchair with his large frame, and looked extravagantly content as he puffed away on a cigar provided by one of his brothers. During the First World War, Will had worked as a military chaplain at a camp north of Melbourne. He collected money for Newman College and served in several parishes before sailing for Europe at the age of thirty-five to join the Society of Jesus in 1926.

After four years in Ireland he went to Rome to begin his tertianship, the final year of Jesuit training. He had been off his food and was already spitting blood, but he drove himself relentlessly. He soon collapsed with tuberculosis, and spent Christmas 1930 fighting for his life in a Naples hospital. Without writing ahead, uncle Jim took a boat from Australia to bring his invalid brother back. But uncle Will had rallied enough to drag himself on board the *Otranto* and start for home. Their ships passed in the Red Sea. After six months recuperation in a sanatorium and with a priest friend in Brisbane, Will joined Jim in Geraldton, stayed with him for three years, and regained some strength under the West Australian sun. Then for twelve years he directed the retreat house at Loyola College, Watsonia, where he was also rector 1939 to 1947. I have a vague memory of visiting the college as a child, enjoying a meal alone at a refectory table that stretched away endlessly, and climbing the tower to inspect some aboriginal axe-heads that the students had unearthed in the college grounds.

In 1947 uncle Will moved from the seminary/retreat house to work in two parishes until his death in 1970, shortly before his eightieth birthday. He took pride in having, despite his shattered health, outlived most of his fellow seminarians. So far as I know, he was one of only two diocesan priests in the twentieth century who became Jesuits in Australia. He spoke sometimes of 'the brethren' or mentioned some priest as being still 'on the mission', and one realized that he meant the diocesan clergy. In the 1930s my father used to describe with a smile the vocations of his three brothers in holy orders (Gerald in China, Jim in Geraldton and Will in the Jesuit order) by saying, 'Gerald went east, Jim went west, but Will went to the devil altogether.'

With a shiny black suit hanging on his gaunt body, uncle Will looked severe, but was in fact immensely fond of his family and a deeply compassionate priest. Once he was asked if the sexual

behaviour of his teenage contemporaries in the first decade of the
twentieth century differed from their counterparts in the permissive
sixties. 'No', he replied. 'It was only that we didn't talk about such
things in those days.' He made himself available for confessions at
any hour of the day, being brief and comforting to an endless stream
of penitents. Few priests can have heard anything like the number
of confessions he did. In the pulpit he practised his precept: 'Be
brief, be clear, be gone.' With a touch for simple illustrations and the
manner of a born teacher, he was more successful providing religious
education in parish schools or instructing converts. He 'received'
many people 'into the Church', as the old terminology put it, and
maintained that Presbyterians with their firm sense of doctrine made
the best Catholics.

A few of his convictions verged on the superstitious. When
his brother-in-law Stan died, Will went into the bathroom of the

Xavier College prefects 1948, Gerald standing at right.

McCarthy home, flushed down the toilet the contents of Stan's many bottles, and declared: 'That's what comes from taking all those medicines.' Will was once instructing a non-Catholic clergyman and hesitated about receiving him into the Catholic Church, because the would-be convert wore a ring. He always suspected men who wore rings. Reluctantly Will received him, but felt his instinct justified when the convert soon afterwards gave up Catholicism. Years later, however, the man returned to the Catholic Church and entered a religious order. When he was ordained, I wanted to pass on the news, but uncle Will had died before I could do so.

Once I visited Will's room in a cold, blue-stone presbytery. Apart from the stretcher-like bed (on which he often rested) and a cupboard, the room contained little more than family photographs, a few detective stories and dozens of pamphlets expounding points of Roman Catholic faith for interested enquirers. He constantly read the crime fiction of Agatha Christie and similar British authors, but at times his language hinted at the influence of Damon Runyon. I have forgotten every detail of one of uncle Will's stories, except for the final line, 'and then he upped and died'.[4]

Through the long and lovely summer of 1945/46 we prepared for the first break in the family circle, Moira's wedding. She had begun studying for an arts degree at Melbourne University and brought home a string of friends. They discussed the latest novels by Graham Greene and Evelyn Waugh, planned the reform of society, and debated the wisdom of Whitlands, a rural commune in the mountains, where single and married Catholics followed a life of work and prayer under the leadership of Ray Triado. After a distinguished record in studies and sport, this charming man had abandoned an obvious future in law to lead a new style of religious movement. Mother saw in it an implied

4 To those who would like to read more about uncle Will, his parents, and his seven siblings, I recommend W.J. McCarthy, *The O'Collins Story: A Melbourne Family* (Melbourne: Motion Press, 2002).

criticism of Melbourne Catholic society: 'They look on us as if were Babylon.' She knew Triado, who in 1934 had played Lord Darnley to her Mary Queen of Scots in a pageant that Catholics contributed to the centenary celebration of Victoria. Dr Mannix refused to support Whitlands, members left, and Triado himself married one of the young women (with the archbishop himself presiding at the wedding) to settle down as a country farmer. In the light of recent experiments in mixed communities, I still wonder whether Whitlands was a genuine experiment in religious living that collapsed because Melbourne Catholics assumed that following the 'evangelical counsels' could only mean entering some existing religious order or congregation. Most would have agreed with the archbishop's judgement on Whitlands: 'If they don't embrace religious life, they'll soon be embracing one another.'

Moira's circle of friends included several officers from the Royal Australian Air Force, but she married a lieutenant-colonel who had survived the siege of Tobruk and the battle of El Alamein, James ('Jim') Sturrock Peters. A dark-haired, stunningly handsome surgeon, Jim was descended from Scottish immigrants, and had been a champion footballer for the Melbourne Blacks in the 1930s. Twelve years older than Moira, he was close to my father, who advised him in business matters, played golf with him, and constantly enjoyed his company. When father died in 1961, Jim was to remark, 'I've lost my best friend.' My brothers and I stood in awe of Jim and for some years continued to address him as 'sir'. When he took Moira horse-riding, Glynn played the role of chaperone and trotted along behind on Sonny Boy. Jim slept on one of the bunks in the two bedrooms shared by my brothers and myself. Once when he and Moira went out for an evening, we sewed up the legs of his pyjamas, and kept awake to hear him quietly swear away to himself when he undressed in the dark and discovered what had happened. One morning Moira asked me what I thought of him and, resentful at the thought that we might be losing her, I replied, 'I don't like Scotsmen.' Afterwards I was embarrassed to learn that they had become engaged the night before.

At Christmas 1945 uncle Gerald came to stay, celebrated a midnight Mass at home, and insisted on singing the Mass and using incense. I was already feeling unwell, having swallowed some petrol when blowing clear a blocked fuel pipe in our utility truck. The incense sent me rushing out of the room to be violently ill. We had Christmas dinner around our vast mahogany table, the first of five post-war Christmasses that I spent at Rock Lodge. Those gatherings are among my happiest memories. There was a feeling of complete security and union among us, as we sat together in a dining room that was to be lined with family portraits. My sisters normally dominated the talk, and Jim Peters had to learn, as he put it, 'to grab a break in the conversation, if the O'Collinses ever left one'.

At Moira's wedding in April 1946 I had the job of looking after an elderly lady whom I remember as dripping jewelry over a sequined dress. Her deceased husband had made money from gold mines. Later I learnt that she had gone to spend her last years attached to a Carmelite monastery, asking for no special treatment except that her meals might be sent in. Uncle Jim celebrated the nuptial Mass in the chapel of Newman College, the first of four family weddings at which he officiated there. My two brothers and two brothers-in-law were all resident students at Newman.

Adolescent Love

It must have been shortly after Moira's wedding that I fell in love for the first time. 'Toddy' was the daughter of an American colonel serving as military attaché in Melbourne. Slim and tanned, she had an easy friendliness and did something none of my three sisters dared to do. She wore a two-piece bathing costume. I took her to

our school performance of Gilbert and Sullivan, went home with her
to eat popcorn, and left cursing myself for being too shy to kiss her
goodnight. When she asked me to a Halloween party, I chafed under
the school regulations for boarders that made it impossible for me
to accept the invitation. I asked her to the 1947 Xavier ball. When
she wrote later to say she wanted to go with someone else, I mooned
around the school humming to myself, 'You always hurt the one you
love.' It was small consolation that her father was suddenly moved to
another posting outside Australia before our ball took place.

What one can sum up as 'sex education' proved the least helpful
aspect of my time at Xavier. I took some classes in dancing (at which
boys danced with boys), just as I went to some special boxing classes.
The boxing instructor was clearly more competent in his field than
the dancing master. When John Moore, our beloved second division
prefect, asked if I needed to learn how babies were born, I protested
in fright that I knew all about that, and continued to entertain various
bizarre notions for some years. The masters in senior catechism
classes, if they raised the issue at all, isolated the physical aspects
of sex, and asked few questions about its deeper implications in
our evolving human experience. They encouraged us to judge the
morality of kissing by the stop-watch, and take a self-centred view
of sexuality. We were to ask: 'Is this making *me* passionate?' Passion,
of course, was to have no place in personal growth and commitment.
Kissing found its justification under the general heading of 'signs of
affection'.

My most wretched memory comes from one Sunday sermon. The
preacher did not switch on the electric lights, and spoke in a quiet,
chilling voice about the evil of sexual sins. As the last evening light
faded from the school chapel, he warned us that we would sin gravely
by touching others, and that in confession a penitent had to specify
whether it was a boy or a girl he had touched. On another occasion
he used the same techniques of voice and lighting for a sermon about

stealing and achieved a similar effect, a chapel full of boys with terror-stricken consciences. We could have been back with James Joyce at Clongowes Wood College (or was it in Dublin at Belvedere College to which Joyce moved?) and listening to the sermon on hell he immortalized in *A Portrait of the Artist as a Young Man*.

The school failed to give us what we needed, positive help towards growth in psycho-sexual maturity. I can recall my mother saying to my brothers and me as she saw us to bed after night prayers: 'Fold your arms like the angels.' The celibate Jansenism of Xavier did nothing to offset the somewhat otherworldly ignoring of sexuality that I experienced at home. Like so much Catholic education, my religious instruction tended to create or at least reinforce guilt feelings about sex. I sincerely believed that on several occasions after I left school I had committed mortal sin and would be damned for ever in hell if I remained in that state. I had aroused my passions by holding girls' hands, dancing cheek to cheek, or indulging in some necking. Confessors accepted my accusations and, with one cheerful exception, never queried my attitude.

Leaving Xavier for Newman

Let me complete this chapter by tracing some events in my last year at Xavier and my year at Newman College. I began 1948 by inviting Jim Gobbo and Greg Dening to a film the night before Greg entered the Jesuit order. This simple celebration was the first of three that I arranged, culminating in an elaborate party for my own group in January 1950. Several other old-Xaverians joined the novitiate in Watsonia with Greg. I knew them all well and remained conscious of their presence on the road ahead, defining the way I might decide to live.

Back at Xavier I became a prefect and enjoyed the freedom and prestige involved in that. The boy prefects had a special common

room, took responsibility for order at line-ups, enforced silence at
set times, and attended to other minor matters of discipline. Morale
ran high when we won the public schools' boat race, our first win for
eleven years. My friends, Jim Gobbo and Norman O'Bryan, rowed in
the victorious crew which was stroked by Brian Doyle. At the 1956
Olympic Games, Brian was to stroke the Australian eight that won a
bronze medal.

In 1948 we celebrated the centenary of the archdiocese of
Melbourne and also of the establishment of the Catholic hierarchy
in Australia. Many overseas church dignitaries and the Irish leader,
Eamon de Valera, came to support a show of religious strength. In
the Exhibition Building Monsignor Fulton Sheen, soon to become an
American television celebrity, spoke to a vast audience on the origins
and nature of Communism. I heard Cardinal Francis Spellman of
New York address a crowded gathering of Catholic men in the great
hall at Xavier. When he had difficulty lowering the microphone
to suit his height, he referred to industrial conflicts of the day by
remarking: 'Your iron-workers must have fixed this mike.' I served
as an altar boy at the outdoor benediction of the Blessed Sacrament
that formed part of a huge reception for the laity held at Xavier.
Overseas the Cold War was warming up, inside Australia the battle
with Communists for the control of the trade unions continued, and
within the Melbourne archdiocese Catholics found in Dr Mannix an
eloquent and imperturbable leader. Since 1848 he was only the third
bishop to occupy the see, and would remain there until his death in
1963. He towered over Xavier as he did over the whole archdiocese.
With the exception of 1945, when Dame Enid Lyons came, he
presided at the annual speech night and presented the prizes.

The school ball formed the social highlight of 1948. I invited
Barbara Coleman, a blond convent girl and only sister of four Jesuits.
Paul had already begun his novitiate, Peter would enter with me,
Gerald came a year later, and in 1959 Michael joined to die suddenly

at the end of his thirty-day retreat. In 1943 at the age of 41, their mother Alma had died from tuberculosis contracted through nursing a sick girl who worked in their home. The young house-keeper concealed her condition because she feared to lose her job during the depression. Mrs Coleman found blood on the girl's pillow, and instead of sending her away to a sanatorium took the fatal risk of caring for the patient herself. But for the need to look after her father (who died in the 1950s) and Michael, Barbara would, I suspect, have joined the Religious of the Sacred Heart. The five Coleman children were vivacious, recklessly generous and immensely attractive persons. In various ways my life was to remain intertwined with Peter and Barbara. But I hardly recognize myself at that Xavier ball, stuffed into uncle Joe's dinner jacket, holding a balloon, and mildly embarrassed by my inability to dance well.

In the middle of the year Moira returned from England ahead of her husband, as she was expecting their second child. I felt slightly heroic declining an invitation to a party, so that I could be on hand the weekend Marion was born. My first niece was so tiny that I took one glance at her and tactlessly remarked, 'a Belsen baby'. Moira took me to my first operas, *Aida* and *Madame Butterfly*. In *Aida* a diminutive Argentinian tenor comforted a huge Italian soprano, as they faced death together in a tomb. Rina Malatrasi as Madame Butterfly swept me into a world where I sensed love and death with a new intensity. Some months earlier I had joined a party of cricketers from St Ignatius College, Riverview, in seeing *Oklahoma* performed by an American company. The straw boaters worn the boys from our sister school in Sydney suggested light opera and brought an invitation to go backstage after the show. There was an easy friendliness about the company. All bright-eyed and entranced by the occasion, we clustered around the leading lady. Those months saw my own sensibility growing, just as Moira's children brought an increase of love and laughter to our family circle.

The mortality and beauty of the world came home to me in a year when I became intensely conscious of the need to settle the question of my future. At times I stood on the front lawn at Rock Lodge, smelling the eucalyptus in the air and looking down the slopes to the dreamy bay. Here and there little spirals of light brown smoke might rise through the trees where some gardener was burning leaves. Out on the water a column of white-sailed yachts sometimes slipped into view. The thought ran through my head: 'I've lived sixteen or seventeen years. One quarter of my life is already over.' I won a special English prize with a long essay on Francis Thompson's poetry. The lines from his *Hound of Heaven* haunted me: 'I fled him down the nights and down the days, I fled him down the arches of the years.' The sense grew that I *had* to become a priest. I would be running away from myself and God if I failed to do so. As I recall it, this feeling of compulsion seems to have been more insistent than another instinctive conviction: I would lose my soul if I avoided the priesthood. That conviction linked itself to the gospel question: 'What does it profit a man if he gain the whole world and suffer the loss of his immortal soul?' My sense of compulsion obviously blended other powerful strands: the pull of friends already in the Jesuit order, the example of three uncles who had become priests, my mother's wish to see one of her sons enter the priesthood, and my own fears about coping with a growing sexuality. This is not to deny that God can take and use such pressures, but to acknowledge some of the complex roots in most, if not all, vocations to the priestly ministry.

A school retreat at Loyola College, Watsonia, settled my half-formed decision. In the background I glimpsed Greg Dening and other Xavier friends busy about their novitiate duties. The director who gave us the conferences and led us in prayer left me with the overwhelming sense that nothing mattered except to discover and follow the will of God. During the retreat another priest explained how one could make an 'election' about one's vocation. The issue presented itself clearly: either (1) to become a priest and that meant for me becoming a Jesuit, or (2) to study classics and law and settle down eventually to married life. I lined up the pros and cons, and prayerfully decided that the first course constituted God's will for me. Any detailed memory of those pros and cons eludes me except for two: on the one hand, 'I have felt attracted to the priesthood for some time', and, on the other hand, 'I won't be able to live without a wife'.

My father objected to my entering the order straight from school. I had won the first Newman College Old Boys Scholarship, a scholarship awarded to the son of a former student. I decided to delay any action on the basis of my 'election' and start a classics course at Melbourne University as a resident of Newman College.

The five years at boarding school ended almost with the feeling of concluding a religious novitiate. We wrote 'A.M.D.G. (*Ad maiorem Dei gloriam*, to the greater glory of God)' on the first page of our essays, we kept a 'major silence' from eight or nine in the evening until breakfast next morning, and we followed a daily routine of Mass, the rosary, and other prayers. Those years at Xavier left me with an aversion to the notion of teaching. The life our masters led looked too dull, boring, and unrewarding. I never put to myself the question: how could I enter the Jesuits and avoid being involved in education? Nevertheless, the influence which Gerry Owens exercised over generations of school boys secretly impressed me. Years later I was to read a biography of Benjamin Jowett, which brought out into the open my belief in the unique role of a dedicated teacher at the heart of an educational institution, preferably a great one.[5]

After leaving Xavier, I eased myself into the adult world by a pre-Christmas job sorting and delivering letters for the Frankston post office. After the morning's work we had to wait an hour or so before

---

5 Benjamin Jowett (1817-93) was a notable scholar and outstanding translator of Plato, but his most significant work was done as a fellow and then Master of Balliol College; he made Balliol one of the leading Oxford colleges.

the second daily batch of mail arrived. I used to sit in a park eating
my lunch and reading books with the sun warm on my face. One day
an elderly lady walked by carrying a heavy load of meat and groceries.
I took the bag, carried it a mile or so to her home and chatted with
her along the way. She accepted my help without protest or effusive
thanks, as it it were the most obvious thing in the world for me to do.
For years I treasured the memory of that tiny incident for its simple
beauty, a wholly uncomplicated interaction of two human beings.

After Christmas I hitchhiked to Sydney with another boy to attend
John Moore's ordination to the priesthood. After a day on the road I
found myself, to my surprise, becoming peevish with my companion.
It was a small but useful introduction to the way travel tests human
relationships. I stayed in Bellevue Hill with a family friend, Don, who
gave me an overcoat. The weather remained cool and the rain fell in
torrents during my visit. I had assumed that a Sydney summer made
overcoats superfluous. Now a medical student, Don recalled the salad
days of 1945 when he visited Rock Lodge as a young RAAF officer.
He reflected on two of Moira's friends: 'They were really passionate
girls.' I felt uncomfortable with this style of description but had to
nod agreement. I visited my aunt Mary Lewis and her son Patrick,
who had just completed his studies at St Ignatius College and was
about to enter the Jesuits.

Soon after I returned to Melbourne, Patrick came down from
Sydney and I drove him out to the novitiate in Watsonia. It was a
hot evening. As we stood chatting in the entrance hall, I had the
feeling that I was with someone about to abandon normal living and
begin an existence that looked like a cross between an heroic military
adventure and a life-long gaol sentence. Patrick pressed all his loose
change into my hand. 'You take this; I don't want "them" to have it.'
And then with a 'perhaps we ought to be going', the novice master
encouraged me and the other visitors to say our final goodbyes to the
new novices. A couple of days before, I had arranged a farewell for

three old-Xaverians, who were there in the entrance hall entering with Patrick. Half a dozen other school friends had joined them and me for dinner and a film before they took the plunge.

Some weeks remained before the university year began. I continued to enjoy some minor success as batsman and bowler with a local eleven, which played against other cricket teams up and down the Mornington peninsula. We used concrete pitches, and the fields were often as bumpy as cow paddocks. Umpires showed themselves persistently partisan to their local side. One could always survive a leg-before-wicket appeal, if a team mate was umpiring. Wives and girl-friends supplied lavish afternoon tea under the gum trees. The atmosphere resembled English village cricket, except that we often played under a blazing sun and were hunted by squadrons of flies.

There were about eighty students at Newman College the year I went into residence. About half were following courses in medicine and dentistry; law was well represented. But very few residents were working for an arts degree. I caught up with Patrick O'Sullivan, who had begun a course in philosophy and Latin the previous year and shared rooms with his brother Michael, who was studying law. We had hardly glimpsed each other since we were together for a few months in 1942 at the primary school in Frankston. Patrick and I took college tutorials in Latin with the rector, Fr Jeremiah Murphy, and our group included another resident (Sid) and a non-resident (Enid Murphy, who went on to graduate studies in French). Sid already showed signs of a serious drinking problem. For college tutorials in Greek I went across to Trinity College, where we worked through Hesiod with a university lecturer who suffered from his wartime experiences and was to drink himself to death.

As my third subject I chose Ancient History for which, John Mulvaney, whose rooms were on the next staircase to mine, gave the college tutorials. Short, dark-haired and engagingly kind, John soon became a close friend. In the spring he wanted a tip for the Melbourne Cup. I mentioned a horse, backed it with John himself, and had the satisfaction of seeing it win at fourteen to one. I teased him a little about his shyness with girls and, without consulting him, invited a partner for him to the college ball. When we met again years later, he told me with glee that he had married a girl who, among other adventures, had shot crocodiles in northern rivers of Australia. In 1949 he completed his B.A. and began work on a M.A. thesis. He was to do further studies at Cambridge University, initiate professional archaeological work in Australia, and become the founding professor of archaeology at the Australian National University. John gave me my first taste of academic life. At Melbourne University he belonged to the history department and taught a course on the rise of Christianity. John opened that course by quoting a line from a current film on St Bernadette Soubirous of Lourdes: 'For those who believe no explanation is necessary, for those who do not believe no explanation is possible.'[6]

Both 'the Christian cause' and the place of Catholics in Australian society claimed some of my attention that year. I remember arguing during the Berlin airlift that the Americans would be justified in using atomic bombs against the Russians! I heard Max Charlesworth and another Catholic debate the justice of the Cardinal Mindszenty trial with two Communist opponents.[7] The audience packed the public lecture theatre to roar approval for their chosen side. Max ended his speech with a peroration that denied all good human qualities in Communists. In those days I doubt whether Catholics constituted two per cent of the Melbourne University teaching staff, even though

---

6 The film *The Song of Bernadette* was based on a book by Franz Werfel (1890-1945), a Czech-born Jewish writer who fled from Vienna to the USA and escaped the Nazis.

7 Cardinal Jozsef Mindszenty (1892-1975) was head of the Catholic Church in Hungary. Opposed to Communism and the brutal suppression of freedom, he was tortured, forced to confess and in 1949 given a life sentence for treason at a show trial that generated worldwide condemnation.

they amounted to twenty per cent of the general population. Their vastly increased participation in academic life was clearly coming fast, but the feeling of 'them' and 'us' still hung in the air. This affected areas as different as philosophy and football. At that time Max showed the influence of a rigid Thomism espoused by the circle which gathered around a Dominican priest. It annoyed 'us' that university departments could ignore the clear rationality offered by Catholic philosophy and theology. Newman College approached its annual football final against Ormond College with the ferocious determination of a religious minority. We had to prove the truth of our cause by once again defeating the Presbyterians. We lost that year, thus ending a long run of unbroken success.

I represented Newman in cricket, debating, and athletics. At the university athletics meeting for freshmen, I came second to John Landy in a mile race that he won in the mediocre time of four minutes forty seconds. Landy was to improve dramatically, just fail to be the first to break the four minute barrier for a mile, hold for a time the world record at three minutes fifty-eight seconds, and win a bronze medal for the 1500 metres at the 1956 Olympic Games.

Two Jesuits served as rector and dean at Newman, Fr Murphy and Fr Philip Gleeson, respectively. A witty and compassionate Irishman, Fr Murphy was rector from 1923 to 1953 and established himself as one of the best known and most loved figures at the University of Melbourne. My father regarded him with deep affection and often entertained him. He reciprocated by encouraging father in his one persistent educational interest, a lifelong concern with the welfare of Newman College. In 1927 father became the first old boy to join the college council, on which he remained until his death. He was elected president of the Newman College Old Boys Association in 1927 and again in 1948, when the college magazine described him as 'the perfect host' at the dinner given to celebrate Fr Murphy's twenty-five years as rector. At our home father always made Newman students and old boys very welcome. The 1944 number of the college magazine remarked how he 'graciously invites half the College down to Rock Lodge periodically', and in the 1960 number he was still the 'genial host at Rock Lodge'.

Since Fr Murphy and the college were so familiar to me, going into residence seemed like coming home. Two wings stretched away from the central dome that covered the dining hall. We took pride in the fact that the architect for our double-storeyed sandstone building was Walter Burley Griffin. An associate of Frank Lloyd Wright, with his wife he designed the new national capital, Canberra, and lived on in Australia for years after his appointment was terminated in 1920. At the city end of Newman College, Fr Murphy had added a fine, if austere, Gothic chapel built of stone matching the other buildings.

To celebrate the end of first term in 1949, the students planned to hold a dance in college and wanted permission to entertain girls in their rooms. Simply doing this without rectorial permission never occurred to them. They presented their request with the slogan, 'no rooms, no social'. Fr Murphy addressed the student body, and with his special combination of wit and authority swept aside all the students' objections. We had to hold the social outside the college at some commercial establishment for parties.

When I told Fr Murphy at the end of 1949 that I would be entering the Jesuits and would not return the following year, he replied with his indirect way of putting things: 'Oh, so you are moving out to one of the suburbs. Well, you should be back here as rector one day.' As it happened, I was to be back at the University of Melbourne for four years but never as rector of Newman College.

Around 9.30 on several nights a week, Fr Gleeson held a roll call together with prayers in a small, upstairs chapel. Freshmen and, I think, second year students were obliged to attend or pay a small fine. Many stayed on for the rosary which followed the roll call. An energetic man, Fr Gleeson always impressed me with his priestly devotion and a lifelong concern with contemplative prayer. But a touch of puritanism and insensitivity stopped him from enjoying the full influence his other qualities deserved. He encouraged me in the practice of morning Mass, and provided me with a tiny daily office he had put together. His collection of scriptural texts, psalms and other prayers anticipated the wave of new prayer books which swept through the Christian churches. He had himself been an outstanding footballer and he coached the college eighteen expertly. Towards the end of 1949 he left for philosophical studies in Oxford, but some health problems meant he had to be satisfied with a B.Litt.

Besides being dean of Newman College, he had acted as chaplain to all the Catholic students at the University of Melbourne. They were all deemed to belong to their denominational society, the Newman Society. Before the academic year began, I froze at a 'freshers camp' Fr Gleeson ran by the ocean. During 1949, I spasmodically attended group meetings and dances, as well as the annual ball arranged by the Newman Society. That year, for the third time, my father acted as president of the Newman Society.

The students club submitted freshmen at Newman College to a fortnight or so of initiation at the hands of a committee headed by a medical student, who was later to be a competitor with my brother-in-law (Jim Peters) and my brother Jim in the field of urology. We heard dramatic stories of initiation ceremonies in earlier years when, for instance, fully clothed freshmen had to line the college's swimming pool with orders to dive in at the count of three. Someone called out, 'one, two, two and a half'. When most of the freshmen dived in, they were fished out and beaten with knotted towels for their disobedience. When my father entered the college after World War I, the students already in residence planned to impose initiation on the newcomers. But the returned soldiers, headed by Jack Clareborough, put a stop to that. Tradition recalled that Clareborough, later a prominent

Melbourne dentist, mounted the first-storey parapet, drew his service revolver, fired a shot in the air, and announced, 'Come and initiate me, if you want to.'

Our initiation consisted in memorizing the college song ('Man of Newman' sung to the tune of 'Men of Harlech'), learning significant facts about present and past college residents, and demonstrating that we did not keep to narrow circles of school friends but were actively mixing with everyone in the college. It was most important to show 'college spirit', as well as to turn up for phone duty. Once a month or so each freshman answered incoming calls for an evening. Fr Murphy had civilized initiation ceremonies some years before I arrived at Newman.

During the evening we slipped off our jackets and wore dressing gowns as we studied, attended roll call, or took supper. Jim Peters presented me with the bright red dressing gown he had worn at Newman in the 1930s. Eventually I was to pass it on to his eldest son, Stewart, when he became a resident at the college.

Sometimes after the roll call, I was invited to coffee by two older friends I had inherited from my sisters Moira and Dympna. Tony and Frank took me to St Patrick's Cathedral for *Tenebrae*, the matins and lauds of the last three days of Holy Week, that service during which all the candles were successively extinguished and the lights turned out. I found the final moments of darkness in the great cathedral deeply moving. Tony had completed an arts course before moving on to law, while Frank had studied with the Jesuits for several years before leaving the order to take a law degree. Both proved a cultured relief from the monotonous talk of sport, horse racing, drinking, girls, and one's own subject, in which a fair section of the college indulged. During my year in college I went to many films, plays and concerts. I remember especially one performance in the Melbourne Town Hall by a visiting Polish pianist. His interpretation of Chopin left the huge audience ecstatic. We clapped our hands sore and milled around his car to wave him goodbye.

Third term brought the need to settle my future. I had found life at Newman liberating and enjoyable. One day in the kitchen at Rock Lodge I raised the matter with my mother, and suggested that I might continue at Melbourne University for two more years to complete my arts degree. 'If you don't try to become a priest', she replied, 'the thought of priesthood will haunt you all your life.' I decided to write a formal letter to Fr Austin Kelly, the provincial, and apply to enter the Society of Jesus the following year. He sent back various forms, and indicated the need for several interviews and references before I could be accepted. One form listing the personal effects that novices should bring with them had been drawn up in Ireland perhaps fifty years earlier. Even though I took everything extremely seriously, I found the old-fashioned names for some articles of clothing rather comical. Uncle Joe gave me the required medical examination, noted that I had inflamed tonsils, and sent me off to an ear, nose and throat specialist. The specialist considered an operation, but I lied vigorously to assure him that I was never troubled by sore throats. I had no desire to spend part of my last 'free' summer in hospital.

Around that time I drove Greg Dening's parents out to see him at Loyola College. His father remarked when we left the novitiate's grounds, 'A lot of good boys are out here.' I felt torn between indulging myself or making some heroically generous gesture. I toyed with the idea of spending my last, pre-Jesuit days working as a male nurse at Caritas Christi, a hospice for the terminally ill. The thought even crossed my mind of cutting all my natural ties by sailing for Ireland and joining the Society of Jesus there. Instead I gave the final frantic months over to playing golf and going to as many parties as possible.

To celebrate the end of the academic year I bought a supply of firecrackers with which Pat O'Sullivan and I disturbed our final lecture (on the fall of the Roman Empire). Afterwards we wandered out into the corridors of the old arts building, spotted some girls we knew, and threw a cracker in their direction. At the crucial moment the diminutive and fragile professor of French emerged from his office and nearly collapsed when the cracker exploded at his feet.

In the examinations that followed a few weeks later, I got a IIA in Ancient History, and shared the exhibitions in Greek and Latin with firsts in both subjects. If I had continued, I must have stood a good chance of winning a Rhodes Scholarship—something my father very much wanted to see me do. In the event he encouraged Jim Gobbo to become a resident at Newman, suggested other helpful moves, and had the satisfaction of seeing him win a Rhodes in 1951, the second Catholic ever to do so at the University of Melbourne.[1] Before that happened, father attended some function at Xavier College and, pointing towards Jim's photo in the 1948 head of the river crew, remarked to the rector, 'Your first Rhodes Scholar.' 'No! No!', exclaimed Fr Costelloe, who had never warmed to Jim. Father heard the news of Jim's success from one of the Rhodes selection committee, who was not entirely pleased that a Catholic had been chosen, and telephoned to say, 'Your cult has won.' 'What was that?', father asked. 'Your colt', the man said. 'You know, your young horse.'

Before I departed for the novitiate, I gave my father some satisfaction by bolting home in a tournament at Peninsula Golf Club with a sixty-one net. He had hoped that I would follow him by studying law, inheriting the family home, and becoming like him a prominent figure at the club. When I visited aunt Mollie in her convent, she compared father's readiness to let me go with Abraham's obedience to God's will in being ready to sacrifice Isaac! But in leaving Rock Lodge I felt slightly like an Abraham going forth from the land

1 The first Victorian Catholic Rhodes Scholar, a future Nobel Prize winner, was the neurophysiologist Sir John Eccles (1903-97) who won his Rhodes in 1925.

I loved so much. All the buildings, trees, bushes, and even patches of grass were intimately familiar to me. No other place has ever given me such a sense of communion with the earth and what grows out of it or stands upon it. To surrender the chance of spending my life there cut deeply.

Just before the novitiate began on 1 February 1950, I orchestrated an elaborate farewell for the old-Xaverians about to enter the Jesuits. There were six others and five of them were available for a dinner together with our school friends and girl friends. After the meal we saw Mario Lanza in That Midnight Kiss, and then went for a late supper at the home of one of the parents. The host embarrassed me by making a speech about 'these young men who are sacrificing themselves for us'.

A couple of days later my sister Maev drove me up from Frankston through steady rain to begin my life as a Jesuit. Confused fears struggled with the sense that I was coming home at last to my destiny.

4

Seven Years Hard (1950-56)

Merely to have survived is not an index of excellence.

Anthony Hecht, *Rites and Ceremonies*

Loyola College stood on a small hill around twelve miles north of
Melbourne, and looked across rolling countryside to the Kinglake
Ranges. A central tower and some half-hearted battlements gave the
three-storey building the slight air of a Spanish castle. The 'retreat
house' took up the front of the building. Boys, laymen, or groups of
priests stayed there for weekends and longer periods when making
retreats or adapted forms of St Ignatius's Spiritual Exercises. Novices
occupied the wing at the Melbourne end, and scholastics (who were
mostly studying philosophy in the college or following courses at the
University of Melbourne) the wing at the opposite end. A chapel ran
out between these two wings to make the overall structure resemble
the letter E on its back.

The front door faced a central lawn planted with trees. Off to
both sides of this lawn more trees dotted the areas of rank grass.
Behind the college lay vegetable gardens, a large orchard, a decrepit
vineyard, poultry sheds, three tennis courts, a football oval, and two
large paddocks. In the warm weather dust rose from the gravel and
cinder paths that criss-crossed the property. In the rain the grey
stucco made the building another 'Bleak House', as one of my
contemporaries called it. In 1973 the Victorian government paid nearly
one million dollars for the college and twenty acres of surrounding

land. It seemed dismally appropriate that it would become the Social
Welfare Department's training centre for jail, youth, social welfare,
and probation officers. One friend offered me a prediction before
I arrived there: 'You are sure to hope the place will burn down.'
But more often my fantasy took the form of pressing a plunger to
detonate an explosion and blow the building up for the closing scene
of some film.

The Novitiate

Twenty-nine others joined the Society of Jesus with me, ranging
in age from sixteen to twenty-seven. Two or three held university
degrees, well over half came straight from secondary school, less
than half had been students at Jesuit colleges. Eight of our group
remain working as Jesuits today and three have died in the order. By
comparison eleven out of thirty remains a good record. Some of the
subsequent groups were to suffer a higher percentage of departures
either in the novitiate or later. Out of the twenty who entered with
Ian Howells in 1960, only he and three others are still Jesuits today.
We joined a group of eighteen second-year novices, which included
my cousin Patrick Lewis and several friends from Xavier. Pat was
now the 'porter' or head novice, a job held for three or four months
at a time. In the role of *'angelus'* helping me as his *'anima'*, to use that
terminology of 'angel' and 'soul', one novice guided me and a 'co-
anima' through the fortnight of 'first probation' that introduced us to
novitiate life. Normally new novices arrived on 1 February, but a few
entered at other times in the year. At one point during my novitiate
our total numbers rose to over fifty.

A vow ceremony took place the morning after our arrival, and
vividly presented to us the immediate goal of the two-year novitiate.
Eight novices, who included some friends from Xavier (Greg Dening
and three others), took their first vows of poverty, chastity, and

obedience, and promised to 'enter' (in the final, canonical sense) the Society of Jesus at the end of their fifteen years or more of training. Despite their name, these first vows were perpetual or deemed binding for life unless one received an official dispensation. Wearing new black suits and clerical collars, the eight novices pronounced their vows at Mass just before they received Holy Communion. The ceremony recalled the vows taken by St Ignatius Loyola (the founder of our order) and his earliest companions at Montmartre (Paris) in 1534.

In the novitiate we wore lay clothes over which hung a sleeveless, loosely fitting black gown, a quasi-habit worn by Jesuits in the British Isles, Australia, and New Zealand. On the second floor we slept eight to a dormitory, pulling the light curtains at night to form separate cubicles. On the first floor we occupied corresponding *cameratas*, study rooms in which only our desks, chairs, a handful of books from the novitiate library, and our prayer stools relieved the total bareness. Every few months the novice master, Fr Edward Riordan, announced a change of quarters and we all shifted to different dormitories and *cameratas*. Normally on these occasions the porter, sub-porter, prefect of outdoor manuals, prefect of indoor manuals, sacristans, and other office-holders were also changed.[2]

A thin, ascetic Irishman then aged forty-five, Fr Riordan had known Fr Michael Browne and Fr John Sullivan, two saintly members of the Irish province whose lives encouraged a world-denying pursuit of mystical prayer. Fr Riordan showed himself utterly dedicated to his novices, occasionally absent-minded, and rigidly poor. When a cousin of his was getting married, she invited him to officiate at the wedding. He refused to allow a car to be sent, but insisted on riding his bike over twelve miles through the summer heat to the church. He lost his way and arrived late. Naturally witty and deeply sympathetic, he

2 'Manuals' was the term used to designate work in the garden or cleaning jobs in the house.

could sometimes astonish us by his insight into problems we found it difficult to discuss with him. He imposed on us a system of religious life, which was rigid, ancient, and alien to our culture. If many were to look back on the novitiate and, even more, the later years of training with grief and anger, 'Ned' or the 'Mag. Nov.' (short for *magister novitiorum*), as we called him, retained his hold on the affections of his ex-novices. Quite a few even managed to visit him in Lahore, where he worked for years on the Pakistan mission. His old, severe attitudes towards religious life had in any case undergone a drastic transformation.

The *socius* or assistant to the master of novices was a tubby Australian of forty-one, whose streak of fussiness tempered his smiling nature. He took charge of discipline, assigned us penances in the refectory, taught Latin and catechism classes, gave us new razor blades, and shared the task of correcting our reading in the refectory. I can recall studying Horace's odes with him. He also took us through some sections of *The Catholic Catechism* by Cardinal Pietro Gasparri (1852-1934), and led discussions that have vanished from my memory except for some questions about the Eucharistic fast: Did flavoured tooth-paste break the fast? What if one suffered a cut lip or bleeding nose and swallowed some of the blood?

The morning programme ran as follows: we rose at 5.25, recited the *Te Deum* with the other members of our dormitories, and by 5.50 were expected to be kneeling in the small novices chapel for a brief period of prayer called 'morning oblation'. At ten to six the porter who knelt at the back put out a holy picture portraying St Patrick driving the snakes out of Ireland. (Those who 'saw St Patrick' had to request a penance, which normally took the form of asking pardon from the 'holy fathers and loving brothers' in the refectory for 'being late for morning oblation'.) Meditation in the *cameratas* followed from six to six fifty-five. The porter gave the signal for changes in posture during that hour. We knelt, stood, sat, and knelt again. After attending

Mass with the scholastics in the main chapel, we took breakfast at 7.45. We filled in the rest of the morning with periods of spiritual reading, conferences on the Jesuit rules and constitutions, Latin classes (or in the second year Greek classes), and indoor manuals during which we cleaned the house.

'Rod' provided our staple spiritual reading, as he did in other Jesuit novitiates around the world. The three volumes of *The Practice of Perfection and Christian Virtue* by Alfonso Rodriguez (1538-1616), which had been fully or partly translated into twenty-three languages, drew on scriptures, church fathers, mediaeval theologians, and the history of the Jesuits. Special chapters in which 'the above' is 'confirmed by sundry examples' piled up exotic stories often taken from the desert fathers and the origins of monasticism. This work by a Spanish Jesuit, who was himself twenty-two years master of novices, could almost have been simply entitled *The Practice of Perfection and Virtue*. Pelagianism and Stoicism never seemed far under the surface of this approach to the spiritual life, which stressed ascetic achievement, measurable progress in prayer, and human determination on the road to sanctity. After my novitiate several French writers, Jean Pierre de Caussade, Jean Nicholas Grou and, above all, St Francis de Sales, helped to undo some of the damage done to me by Rodriguez. The saint's *Introduction of a Devout Life*, which combines the highest ideals with a deep regard for a healthy human life, liberated me when I found that my pre-Christian passion for self-perfection would not work.

At the morning conferences Fr Riordan dictated commentaries on the Jesuit rules and constitutions which we copied into exercise books. Next day we would be expected to have memorized the rules and be able to offer an accurate account of the commentary. Some mornings we also faced 'quarters of charity', in which one novice was called to kneel on the floor and the others were asked in turn to point out his faults. Mainly external matters were mentioned: 'Brother puts his elbows on the chapel benches', 'Brother does not keep good

custody of the eyes', or 'Brother chews with his mouth open'. We
were supposed to kneel bolt upright with only our hands resting on
the bench in front of us. The 'Rules of Modesty' proscribed free and
easy looking around.

In my second year a graduate in classics from Sydney University
joined the novitiate. While the other second-year novices began the
study of Greek, he gave three of us who already knew the language
a superb course in Greek history, art, and literature. He suggested
reading that took us beyond the Euripides, Herodotus, Plato, and
Thucydides that had been my staple diet at school. I remember with
special pleasure the idylls of Theocritus. Even though the morning
programme allowed us only an hour or so for this study, I enjoyed
the liberating sense of reading the classics and, for the first time since
1945, facing no examinations on the texts covered.

At the signal for indoor manuals we would line up to receive an
assignment from the prefect: *latrinas nostras, balneas, via maxima,* or
whatever else needed attention. We would clean toilets and bathrooms,
prepare bedrooms for retreatants, lay tables for dinner, and polish
floors. The *via maxima* or front corridor ran almost the full length of
the college. We would smear wax on the dark red Australian wood, rub
it in, and then polish it with instruments that looked like giant brooms.
At manuals, just as at other times outside formal recreation, our brief
communications with each other had to be in Latin. During reading
periods in the *cameratas,* if we went out to the toilet, we whispered
to the novice in charge '*statim venio*' and on our return '*necessitas*'. We
called each other '*frater*' and during the time of recreation 'brother'.
The use of first-names was forbidden.

A fifteen minute examination of conscience preceded dinner at
1.30. This Irish and European custom of taking the main meal in
the middle of the day died hard in the Australian Jesuit province.
Twice a week we would perform penances at meals. We would say

the Latin grace on our knees with arms outstretched, ask pardon for some fault, kiss the feet of whatever novice or scholastic happened to be sitting at the end of a table, or take the entire meal kneeling on a prayer stool. Except for 'villa' days (normally Thursday),[3] when the main meal would be postponed to the evening and we talked at table, there was reading at almost all meals. We heard the scriptures in Latin, the various Jesuit rules in Latin or English, the *Imitation of Christ* by Thomas à Kempis in English, selections from the Jesuit *Epitome of the Constitutions* in Latin, and then in English either lives of the saints or, occasionally, more exciting reading like Paul Brickhill's *The Dam Busters*, the story of a May 1943 raid when the RAF used a 'bouncing bomb' to destroy two dams in the Ruhr valley. Dinner ended with the reading of the Roman martyrology in Latin.

At meals the priests sat at the top of the refectory, the scholastics at long tables that ran along one side of the refectory and the novices at similar tables on the other side. Up to 1951 both the fathers and the scholastics wore black birettas or priests' caps during the meals, often perching them rakishly on the back of their heads. The handful of brothers in the community took their place at the kitchen end of the refectory. They wore the same university-type gown as the rest of us, except for the 'wings' or vestigial sleeves being removed.

Once a year every scholastic and novice had to preach a sermon during dinner or supper, almost the only sermons we ever heard, as there were none at Mass. Many of the preachers chose basic themes like sin, death, judgement, heaven, and hell. It seemed bizarre to be forking down beef and mashed potatoes, while being warned against sinful pleasures, reminded that death could strike us at any moment, or

3 From the sixteenth century Jesuit communities in cities often owned houses in the nearby countryside. Members of the order would go there for recreation, generally on Thursdays. Originally a place for one's day off, 'villa' was applied in the terminology that I inherited both to the weekly free day as such and to the annual two weeks vacation. In later years I took this vacation at the Jesuit 'villa houses' in Anglesea (Victoria) and Gerroa (New South Wales).

assured that at the last day Jesus, whose presence among us remained hidden, 'will suddenly be in the sky'. The novices shared the work of serving at table with the scholastics, but did all the washing up. The food was good, if plain, and there was plenty of it. Most novices put on weight during their two years.

After dinner the porter assigned us to 'companies' of three or four for recreation. Except on such 'experiments' as working in a hospice for the dying, we were forbidden to do things in pairs. That might lead to 'particular friendships', which I realized years later was a traditional term for homosexual attachments. At 3 p.m. conversation ended abruptly when the community bell rang. We went to the *cameratas* to read Abbé Constant Fouard's life of Christ (first published in 1880) or sometimes to doze off at our desks. Twice a week we played games, baseball in summer and Australian rules football in the winter. We had to wear long trousers for both sports and, what was troublesome, play football while keeping the '*ne tangas*' rule which prohibited physical contact. On other afternoons we had outdoor manuals, which included digging in the vegetable garden, chipping grass off the paths, and cutting lawns. Parties of four or five pushed or pulled a horse mower, those at the back being showered with the grass flung up by the blades. The cry of '*insula*' would go up, if an 'island' or patch of uncut grass was left behind. At times Fr Riordan took his place with digging parties in the garden and, even though hampered by the coat and collar he still wore, set a furious pace. The work of chipping the paths recalled the devotion of that desert father who for years watered a dry stick out of obedience to his superior's command. Onion grass sprouted everywhere, and quickly grew again after we had chopped off the heads.

Ten minutes spent reading Thomas à Kempis' *Imitation of Christ* preceded the meditation that we made together in the novices chapel from 5.45 to 6.15. That 'evening med.' remains my most peaceful memory of the novitiate years: the Eucharistic presence, the light slipping away from us, sometimes a blackbird singing in the cypress hedge outside, and Jesus' farewell discourse in John's Gospel providing an unfailing basis for quiet prayer. Often benediction of the Blessed Sacrament took up the quarter hour before supper at 6.30. Evening recreation began with a period of Latin conversation, in which words counted for everything and endings for nothing at all.

At 8.30 we made 'points' or prepared for the morning meditation, before doing a fifteen minute examination of conscience. Normally one of the 'scholastic novices' gave these meditation points to the brother novices. The latter did not intend to be ordained priests and were often, but by no means always, less well educated than the average 'scholastic novice'. I hope three Jesuit brothers, who later did exceptional good work which included one of them being an outstanding wine maker at Sevenhill, forgave me for the boring platitudes I offered them when I had the job of providing 'points' for meditation. At 9 p.m. the whole community of Loyola College gathered in the main chapel to recite in Latin the litany of Loreto and the litany of the saints (to which we added a full list of canonized and beatified Jesuit saints). Apart from occasional additions for novenas, these prayers remained unchanged every night. The responses from one hundred voices rolled through the chapel like waves of sound rather than accurately articulated prayers. 'Ora pro nobis' often came across as if we were saying 'Hurrah for Moses'. The novices stayed on after the community litanies to be led by their porter in some prayers of their own. When he added the 'Memorare' or 'Remember, O most loving Virgin Mary', this indicated that the following day would be a villa day.

On Mondays and Fridays there were 'penances for all', which meant doing a penance in the refectory and 'taking the discipline' before retiring to bed. The porter rang a small ball (the 'tocco'), and behind the curtains in their dormitories the members of each group would beat their backs with a small whip of cords while rapidly reciting in

Latin the psalm '*De profundis*'. On two mornings a week we wore the
'chain', a thin band of steel wire with a mass of blunt endings pointing
inwards. We wore it next to the skin wrapped around an ankle or a
thigh, putting it on when we rose and taking if off after breakfast.
Those who tied it too tight would limp around awkwardly. Those
who tied it too loose could find it coming adrift and falling down their
trouser leg as they went in line to Mass. By mistake one new novice
wrapped the chain around his middle, bent over at Mass to recite the
'*Confiteor*', and straightened up with a sharp cry when the points cut
into his soft stomach. (In case some reader is curious, let me add that I
have never seen a hair shirt in my life.) One of the novices whose job
bore the bland name of 'trades' learnt the craft from a predecessor,
and spent the time of indoor manuals manufacturing chains and
disciplines. His production had to rise beyond local demands when
some outsider or some other religious community put in a request for
these instruments of penance.

Most, if not all, novices asked Fr Riordan to approve of their
taking the discipline or wearing the chain on an extra day or so each
week. We made that request as part of the application for 'monthly
permissions', which always had to include drinking glasses of water
outside meal times and 'the use of ordinary things'.

All in all, the novitiate programme encouraged a competitive spirit
in the pursuit of a life of prayer and sanctity. We thought little of
Christian ministry, let alone of the priesthood to which we aspired.
Sometimes this holy rivalry took amusing forms as when we did
refectory penances for breaking plates and other pieces of household
property. One novice raised an audible gasp of admiration when he
accused himself of breaking a crowbar. The porter rang dozens of
bells each day to teach us to throw ourselves into periods of prayer,
study, and work—only to give them up at the first sound of the next
bell. In the long term this obedience to bells has perhaps made Jesuits
(and ex-Jesuits) more punctual than other people. But I doubt if

the difference is great. The whole exercise was too artificial to be genuinely effective.

We lived a hard life, symbolized by our heavily patched gowns and tattered clothes. Electric razors were forbidden, and for the duration of the novitiate we surrendered our watches to Fr Riordan. We had, of course, no money of our own, not that the opportunity to visit a shop or see a film ever arose. We never used the telephone or received the daily papers. On villa days we wrapped our sandwiches in old newspapers, but even such newspapers fell under the prohibition against 'reading waste paper'. We may have seen *The Advocate*, then the Catholic weekly for the Melbourne archdiocese, but I cannot remember that we did. Along with other major events in world history, the Korean War passed us by. The only time I can recall being permitted to listen to the radio was to hear a sermon preached by a Jesuit on the occasion of the canonization of Pope Pius X.

In winter, central heating kept the college warm, although the main chapel always remained rather cold. At night the heating was switched off, and around 5 a.m. came on again with a thunder of expanding pipes. Sticky flies swarmed everywhere in summer. As the refectory windows lacked wire screens, we had to keep them shut, as well as destroy the flies that somehow made their way in. The priest who acted as 'procurator' or bursar refused to buy fly wire on the grounds that it would stop the flies getting out once they got in. One of my fellow-novices felt what he took to be another blow-fly land on his upper lip. Rather than brush it off, he left it there as an act of mortification. The bee rode around quietly for a while, but eventually stung him. The swelling almost blocked the novice's nostrils.

Once a month we were allowed family visitors for an hour or perhaps an hour and a half. We sat with them in the front parlour, on a lawn-bench, or in a car, and we could eat the afternoon tea they brought. But we could not provide hot water from our kitchen to make their tea or coffee. In January 1951 when my sister Dympna married Kevin Coleman (a Melbourne barrister and the only son of an old friend of my father), it was out of the question that I would attend the wedding, even less the reception that followed. We took for granted such rigorous separation from our families. I felt surprised and touched by Fr Riordan's kindness the following day. He called me into his room to show me some wedding photographs that had appeared in the daily papers.

As there were very few brothers and no lay employees, the novices often had to work very hard to keep the college running, especially when groups of diocesan priests filled the retreat house for weeks on end. We cleaned rooms, made beds, emptied a few chamber pots, served the retreatants in their own refectory, read spiritual books to them during meals, and in general supported the ministry of retreats by our physical labour. It was never suggested that we could share directly in this work even by leading school boy retreatants in prayer and discussion.

Our conversation was controlled almost as much as our use of time. Rules and customs encouraged us to speak of the lives of saints, 'the sayings and doings of ours', spiritual insights that had occurred to us, and similar edifying subjects. A list of 'forbidden topics' excluded talking about school experiences, our families, and the practices of penance. It was taken for granted that we would never talk about former girl friends or use coarse language. The novitiate was an astonishingly sex-less environment. It came a shock a couple of years later to hear a visiting speaker use the word 'sex'. While still in the novitiate, I felt mildly horrified when I heard a scholastic exclaim 'bugger' when he missed a shot on the tennis court. Andy Zerafa, a plump Maltese ex-sailor, when he first heard of forbidden topics, found the notion so extraordinary that he went out and carved on a tree 'AZ loves FT.'

Andy's action catches the happy hilarity that filled our lives. Before I entered the novitiate, one Jesuit recommended to me the practice of 'high ideals and a sense of humour'. His advice caught the mood of the novices. We put our hearts into the programme, and for the most part experienced deep contentment and joyful peace. A Jesuit scientist from Paris, who visited us on his way home from a French expedition to Antarctica, caught the atmosphere by remarking with a look of existential anxiety, 'You Australians have no tragic sense of life.'

Every Thursday and on some major feasts of the Church we went on 'villa' into the surrounding countryside, no matter how bad the weather was. We had to wear coats and ties, hitch-hiking was forbidden, but we often covered up to thirty kilometers in the seven hours at our disposal. Provided there were at least three in the group, we could choose where we went, except when a 'general villa' meant that all had to gather at the same spot for lunch. Returning after five o'clock involved a refectory penance, at least for the leader of the group. We swam in the Yarra river or in a foul dam on the Plenty, explored old gold mines, and learned to cook wild quinces in our blackened 'billies' We cut thick slices of bread for our jam sandwiches. Once I was taking a snack on a park bench when a man wandered up who had the look of a recently released convict. My short hair and lunch packet wrapped in newspaper may have attracted him. When I offered him a sandwich, he stared in astonishment at the vast slices held together by jam, and exclaimed, 'A bit thick, isn't it!'

We never spent a night away from the novitiate, unless we had to go to hospital. After Christmas there was a short holiday, when a 'late call' allowed us to sleep until six. We could play more games, and read some literature not normally available to us. This reading did not, however, include any novels or plays, except perhaps the works of Shakespeare. We went on one or two day-long excursions to a seminary or a seaside school, where we played tennis or handball, swam, and consumed huge quantities of food. Those wildly noisy trips by van or truck looked and sounded like picnics for prisoners.

We formed a tightly knit group with its own special jargon. If we had not heard it before, we learnt to use standard Jesuit terminology for the main officials of the college: rector, minister, and procurator. We spoke of the head novice as the 'porter' and the head scholastic as the 'beadle'. The scholastics were divided into juniors and philosophers, and we called the wing in which they lived the 'monk-house'. We had meals with the scholastics on 'long table days', the ten or so major feast days of the year when we enjoyed a special dinner at which the rector gave the '*Deo gratias*' or permission to talk. Otherwise we spoke with the scholastics only on the few occasions each year when the superiors allowed 'fusion'. We gave our own name to several places to which we walked along two river valleys: Faber (after Blessed Peter Faber), Bobola (after St Andrew Bobola whom Cossacks had flayed alive), and St Anthony's (presumably after St Anthony of Padua). We divided the human race into 'externs' and 'ours'. From basic Jesuit texts we picked up phrases and terms like 'watering a dry stick', 'going in or out by the ordinary door', 'deso' (short for spiritual desolation), and 'the eleventh'. The eleventh rule from the Jesuit constitutions encouraged us, for the sake of Christ crucified, to suffer patiently even undeserved offences and injustices. Hence 'giving someone the eleventh' meant humiliating him. Under our gowns we wore 'examen beads', a string of ten beads with which we could register lapses into faults that we were attempting to eradicate with our 'particular examen'. At the midday and evening examinations of conscience we marked down our score on a particular examen card. 'Pulling a bead' signified acknowledging that we had spoken uncharitably or committed some other common failing, even if we did not go through the physical motion of shifting a bead along the string. We even had our special pronunciations: 'We ate in a refectory' and accented that word on the first syllable.

We called speech training 'tones'. Everyone had to memorize the 'ordinary tone', a brief sermon that incorporated verses from the prophet Joel and demanded repentance from a sinful congregation. Sometimes at tones (which occurred on Sunday mornings) we had to preach a brief homily after only half an hour's notice. We learnt speeches from Shakespeare that we delivered with appropriate gestures and emotions. Tones and refectory reading served to correct false pronunciations, as well as forcing us to speak up and to speak clearly. It was presumed that the laws of classical rhetoric governed the composition of sermons. We never discussed the theological aims of preaching and contemporary ways for achieving those aims.

The Long Retreat, Experiments, and 1950

The long retreat was the outstanding landmark in the first year of novitiate. A week after Easter we went into this period of complete silence and intense prayer that lasted until Ascension Thursday. We gave eight, ten, six, and four days, respectively to the four 'weeks' of St Ignatius's Spiritual Exercises. We spoke with each other only on 'repose days', which we took between the first and second, the second and third, and the third and fourth weeks. On those three days we lunched in the countryside, but remained segregated from the second-year novices, who took over all the house work during the month. We entered into the long retreat with some curiosity about what was to happen, as we had not been permitted to read beforehand the book, *The Spiritual Exercises*. We found that St Ignatius confronted the retreatants with a series of meditations and contemplations, mainly concerned with Christ and essentially designed to help them reach major decisions about the future shape of their lives. In our retreat it was presumed that we had already decided on our vocation through joining the Jesuits.

Four times a day Fr Riordan brought us all together in the novices chapel to give us points for meditation and explain the text of *The Spiritual Exercises*. He also saw us individually every couple of days. Reluctantly he allowed me to make a second general confession to him during the retreat. (Shortly after I arrived in the novitiate I had made such a confession of all my past sins.) He encouraged us by his whole-hearted commitment to his own role as director, helped us interpret what we experienced, and tolerated the general giggling which strain brought on during the last 'week'. Each day we read the scriptures, the *Imitation of Christ*, and the appointed sections of *The Spiritual Exercises*. We took our meals apart from the community, listening at table to books that included *A Christian Directory* by Robert Parsons (1546-1610), a sombre spiritual classic by a great friend of St Edmund Campion who, like him, served on a mission in England, but, unlike him, evaded capture and being hung, drawn, and quartered.

The long retreat had three main effects on me: it renewed my shame at the sins of my past life; it encouraged in me a single-minded dedication to religious life; and it left me with an abiding sense of God's presence. One entry in my notes can illustrate the sense of shame: 'How utterly degraded my past life has been! How could I possibly avoid sinning against God, if in things not sinful I paid not the slightest attention to His will...always ready to exercise the body in golf & tennis, but never the soul in spiritual exercises?' After meditating on Jesus' life at Nazareth, I wrote: 'How can I do great things for Christ, unless I learn to do little things for Him perfectly? [I must] become a perfect novice...How can I...preach, teach etc, move a single soul, unless I prepare [and] make my own soul as secure as it can be?' Throughout the month brilliant sunshine poured down on us. After the midday dinner I normally sat on a log-seat under a cypress hedge looking at the immense sky. Often white puffs of clouds drifted across the distant mountains, and moved over the river red-gum that spread its branches down the slope of our orchard. Now and then a train whistle sounded from the suburban line almost a mile away. In the quiet warmth of those autumn afternoons God was there. My sense of sin and expressions of devotion have changed, but I am grateful that the divine presence has always remained just as real.

Besides the long retreat we were also assigned to do several 'experiments' during our novitiate. For many weeks I was supposed to teach catechism at a home for intellectually disabled boys. Instructing our group of Catholics seemed hopeless and hilarious. Mostly I would bring with me another novice who played the piano expertly. We often filled in the time singing hymns and songs. During the month of the 'kitchen experiment', I lived with the brother novices in their separate dormitory, rose with them at five to five, and spent my days working in the scullery or helping the brother cook.

The 'hospital experiment' took to me Caritas Christi, where we washed, fed, and prayed with dying men, mainly terminal cases of cancer. We worked with trained nurses, both nuns and lay women, including a certain Miss Smith. One day a brawny New Zealand novice decided that the easiest way to bring a small patient back from the bath was to dry him, wrap him in a blanket, and carry him to his bed. The novice arrived at the ward, nudged the door open with his foot, and with the little old man in his arms announced in a loud voice, 'Miss Smith, it's a boy.' Another novice collected a heap of false teeth on a tray, carried them away to clean them, and, having thoroughly mixed them up, had to go around the ward trying out the dentures on various mouths. The patients were amused by our amateur mistakes and liked our cheerful gaiety. For our part we needed to joke and laugh, if we were going to cope with the work of comforting the dying, laying out corpses, and dealing with grieving relatives.

I spent about five weeks at Caritas Christi, travelling there and back each day by train. In the morning we joined the rush hour crowd. Some of our fellow passengers must have been astonished at us. When they looked over our shoulders, they found that the book in brown paper covers that these quiet young men read so avidly was entitled *The Practice of Perfection and Christian Virtues*. We used Latin if we had to say something that we did not wish the other passengers to understand.

In the novitiate we had little to do with the rector of the college. A kindly old man, he treasured Latin literature, hated to see any trees cut down, and encouraged young Jesuits with axioms like '*non progredi est retrogredi* (not to advance is to fall back)'. On 31 October 1950 he summoned the whole community to the main chapel for the only 'domestic exhortation' I ever heard from him. He announced 'three reasons for rejoicing', which all came as surprising news to the novices: the following day Pope Pius XII was to proclaim the assumption of the Blessed Virgin Mary into heaven as a dogma of faith; the Australian Jesuit vice-province had been raised to the status of a province; and we had undertaken to staff a mission in India.

Pius XII did not want the Holy Year of 1950 to pass without honouring the Virgin Mary in some special way. Belief in her assumption into heaven had enjoyed undisturbed assent among Catholics and Orthodox from the earliest centuries. Renewed Marian devotion would strengthen the Catholic faithful against the inroads of materialism and atheist Communism. In August that year the Pope had issued *Humani Generis*, an encyclical aimed at 'correcting' new ideas coming, especially from French Dominicans and Jesuits, and at recalling wanderers to the truths of neo-Thomism and the theology of the traditional 'manuals'.[4] Melbourne Catholics responded to the Pope's initiatives by two mass events. A quarter of a million people gathered in the Botanical Gardens to recite the rosary. Tom Daly (later Chief of the General Staff), Jack Purtell (a highly successful jockey),

---

4 Those interested in what was at stake in theology in 1950 and how it played itself out at the Second Vatican Council (1962-65) could consult G. Flynn and P. Murray (eds.), *Ressourcement Theology and Vatican II: A Movement for Renewal in 20th Century Catholic Theology* (Oxford: Oxford University Press, 2011).

Patricia Kennedy (a well known radio actress), Arthur Calwell (then the deputy leader of the Parliamentary Labor Party), and Fr Patrick Peyton each led the huge crowd in one decade of the rosary. The gathering was also part of the family rosary crusade that Fr Peyton had launched in the United States and taken to other parts of the world. He preached a sermon that went beyond the theme of 'the family that prays together stays together'. Parents, he assured us, could not rise from their knees to offend God. In plain terms, he meant that the family rosary would help couples to avoid practising artificial birth control. Around that time Catholics expressed their devotion to Mary by another large religious gathering, this time at the Melbourne Cricket Ground. We saw a performance of *Everyman* on a stage erected in the middle of the ground. Choirs sang new compositions, 'Mother of Mercy, Mother of Grace' and a new setting of the *Magnificat*. During my novitiate these two big Catholic gatherings were the only public occasions I attended.

In 1933 what had been a 'mission' of the Irish province of the Jesuits became the Australian vice-province under a 'vice-provincial', who was in fact normally called 'the provincial'. Some Irish Jesuits continued to come to Australia until a big influx of Australian novices in the post-World War II years allowed us to dispense with this support, become a full province, and take on our own foreign mission.

A few months after the October 1950 domestic exhortation, Fr John Moore and some other priests left Australia to begin their work in the province of Bihar. Until visa problems arose in the 1960s, groups of scholastics and occasionally a priest sailed for India each year. In those days Jesuits on foreign missions normally stayed there for life. Our missionary 'send-offs' became moving farewells to heroic friends, whom we never expected to see again unless we joined them in India itself.

Fr Kelly revelled in these farewells, which he staged at the big Jesuit

churches in Richmond or Hawthorn. Wearing the white cassocks
that would be their everyday clothes, the scholastics about to leave
for Bihar received mission crosses from him. He preached stirring
sermons to large congregations of friends, relatives, and well-wishers.
Enthusiastic optimism for the cause of Christ came through. In the
pulpit and elsewhere 'splendid' was one of his favourite words. But
particular sentences could defy analysis, as did some of the logic
connecting his thoughts. A very well read and courteous Irishman, he
held his head on one side as he moved his portly body along at a brisk
rate. He worked extremely hard, could be autocratic in his methods of
government, and so obviously wanted the whole province to create
a perfect public impression that we nicknamed him 'Austintatious'.
He liked to dramatize the religious life. When I volunteered to go
on the mission in 1954, he answered with utter seriousness, 'Gerald,
you will find your India in Melbourne University.' Towards the end
of his term as provincial, he fussily insisted that Jesuit houses should
carefully indicate the *clausura* or enclosure, which women could enter.
He had plastic signs reading 'private' erected at the provincial curia or
headquarters in Hawthorn. With a perfectly straight face, one visiting
Jesuit told him, 'I like your plastic privates.' The priest knew full well
that Fr Kelly was far too proper to catch the double meaning.

Fr Kelly could not resist accepting invitations to put Jesuits into
new works. The number of our houses and commitments rose rapidly
during his years in office. Besides the Indian mission, he agreed to
run one seminary and four university colleges, as well as taking on
a secondary school and some other apostolates. All these ministries
drew off some of the best young priests who might otherwise have
been available to offer spiritual leadership to the scholastics. Fr Kelly
seemed to believe that if the province generously supplied missionaries
to India, God would supply an increase at home. Undoubtedly he was
too ready to admit novices into the order. He should have rejected
some candidates or postponed their admission until they could make

a more mature decision. When he ceased to be Australian provincial in 1956, he moved to be superior of our Indian mission. He had scarcely gone before scholastics began to leave the order in numbers. Hitherto we had suffered only an occasional departure, but nothing like this exodus that led to our community in South Australia being called 'the launching pad' or 'the rocket range'. The new provincial, Fr Jeremiah ('Dermot') Hogan, continued the habit of sending there scholastics who were 'on the way out'.

When Dermot took over, he complained to a few friends about the need to 'clean up the mess that Austin had left behind'. In fairness to Fr Kelly it should be pointed out that his term as provincial began in the Cold War at the height of Pius XII's reign, and ended shortly before the Kennedy era and Pope John's revolution. Changes were not only sweeping through the world and many sections of the Catholic Church, but were also altering the position of Australian Catholics. From being largely a working-class minority of Irish background, they were climbing the socio-economic scale and increasing in numbers through an influx of Italian, Dutch, Croatian, and other European migrants. All these transformations affected the decisions of young men about entering and remaining in the Jesuit order, as well as calling into question some of the traditional Jesuit ministries.

End of the Novitiate

On 2 February 1952 I pronounced in Latin my vows of poverty, chastity and obedience with twenty-five others. A few days later came the vow ceremony for two more novices, who had arrived a little late in 1950 and had to complete the full two years of novitiate. We felt proud that twenty-eight out of the original thirty were still there to take vows. A tailor had made for us new gowns and heavy, old-fashioned suits. I was to receive my next new suit and gown eleven years later at ordination. Wearing our clerical collars and black suits for the first time, we knelt in a great circle at Mass, and in an order determined by our age each read the vow formula before receiving Holy Communion. We experienced deep joy at dedicating ourselves, being accepted provisionally into the Jesuit order, and moving on to the next stage of our training. We each received a copy of the *Thesaurus Spiritualis* (which contained *The Spiritual Exercises*, rules of the order, and some other basic Jesuit texts). I was allowed to keep a hollow metal crucifix blessed by both Pope Benedict XV and Pope Pius XI, which uncle Jim had given my father in the 1920s. To mark my vow-taking, uncle Jim inserted inside this crucifix relics from three fairly recent saints (St John Berchmans, St Gabriel of the Sorrowing Virgin, and St Paul of the Cross), plus a supposed relic of the second-century martyr, St Justin.

Two letters that I kept catch the feelings of that occasion. Uncle Gerald wrote:

> I wish you every joy and happiness your heart desires and God's most abundant blessings on the occasion of your taking your vows. My Mass on Saturday morning, one of the most memorable days in your life, will be offered in honour of the Our Blessed Lady for you, my fond nephew and namesake. Two years ago…this great day seemed far off, but how quickly has the time passed, and you now enter into the life of a Jesuit scholastic with the priesthood your desired goal. The years until that great day will pass quickly as did those in the novitiate. My good wishes, prayers and frequent Masses, so long as God spares us, shall be offered that when that holiest day in a man's life arrives you will go forth a worthy soldier and minister of Christ. All at home in Frankston are very well. Your father is well, happy and proud of you. He does not say much, but his quiet (for your father!) joy and pride were very noticeable.

Gerry Owens wrote to me from Xavier College:

> While I lazily let this great day pass in silence for my friends, somehow I cannot do so this time. It is a wonderful day of

consecration: so for you I am praying that its high aspirations may meet no waning. High adventures for God through what years He grants and may they be many in His service. May no veil ever come between your soul and God's will, and may each year see you make, no matter how small, ascent to union with Him.

We made our final preparation for the vow ceremony through the annual, eight-day retreat, which we did together with the scholastics. This always came in January, the hottest month of the year. For a long time no one thought of suggesting a more suitable time, when the retreat need not assume the character of a spiritual endurance test, as it did during heat waves. The retreat master that year gave me the parting advice, 'Don't change.' I took this so much to heart that in retrospect my life until 1965 looked very much like an extension of the novitiate. The rules, the daily timetable and the fixed round of prayer formed an objective standard to which I clung tightly. When I went through the yearly eight-day retreats, I forced them to be briefer re-enactments of the sentiments of sorrow, gratitude, and dedication which I had experienced in the novitiate's long retreat.

Four words gather together some general impressions of the novitiate I was leaving and the three years of philosophy I was facing: (1) Roman, (2) Irish, (3) memory-oriented, and (4) monastic.

(1) We never forgot that we were a highly centralized order with a tradition of special obedience to the pope. We took for granted that our rules (including specific rules for rectors, ministers, scholastics, brothers, cooks, sacristans, and other officials) offered the fixed guidelines we needed. Letters from our father general in Rome and various Vatican documents fed our thinking on contemporary Jesuit life and emerging issues. In those years I never heard anyone seriously ask: what do present conditions in Australia suggest about adapting our community life and work? We listened to Rome for our answers and our questions. I heard

one rector praised for keeping on his desk the back numbers of the *Acta Romana*, the annual collection of letters from our general and other official documents from our headquarters. If a new issue arose in his community or someone asked for an unusual permission, this rector simply checked the *Acta Romana* for his appropriate response.

(2) The Irish influence went beyond the sheer fact that our master of novices, provincial and many other priests in the province were born and educated in Ireland. Up to the Second World War, many Australian Jesuits had continued to do most of their studies there. We wore the gown of the Irish province, followed their customs in such matters as eating and drinking, and listened to stories from Milltown Park, Rathfarnham Castle, and University College Dublin. It was sometimes a relief when those who had studied in Europe invited us to sing German songs, or told us about the illegitimate sons of a Spanish parish priest fighting for first places in a procession of the Blessed Sacrament, about the excessive demands of Karl Rahner (some would say the greatest theologian of the twentieth century) when he began teaching at Innsbruck, and about the depressing skies of a Belgian winter. Some Australians had studied on the island of Jersey with French Jesuits in exile from their own country. As they were allowed to use the bathing facilities only once a week, several of them climbed over the partitions to have extra showers or baths, or slipped down to the beach for a swim. A French provincial came on 'visitation', heard of these practices, and made them one of the chief themes of his exhortation to the scholastics. He reached his rhetorical climax: 'And what did you enter the Society of Jesus for? Was it to wash?' From the back an Australian was heard to mutter, 'No, you dirty bugger.'

(3) In the novitiate we trained our memories through learning by heart the Jesuit rules, our sermons, and Latin prayers like the *Te*

Deum. Our subsequent study of philosophy involved memorizing definitions of terms, summaries of false views held by the 'adversaries', and proofs for our own positions. Success in regular 'repetitions' and 'circles', as well as in the annual examinations largely (but not wholly) depended on one's ability to recall what had been taught. This stress on memory hampered the proper development of our sense of independent criticism. Old lives of Jesuit saints and blesseds crammed our novitiate library and suggested models for us to remember and imitate. I read how Blessed Antonio Baldinucci flogged himself in front of country crowds to encourage their repentance, how St Aloysius would not look at any women including his own mother, and how St Francis Xavier refused to visit his family home, even though he passed very close to it on his way to live and die on mission in Asia. I took far too seriously such strange and inhuman stories, which in some cases were sheer legends. In our first struggles with philosophy, it became clear that we were to learn approved doctrine rather than engage in independent thought. One of my class suggested that we could approach the problem of knowledge by attempting to doubt everything. But our professor of epistemology ruled out such a methodological, universal doubt, since it disagreed with the position taken by the Roman author of our Latin textbook.

(4) Almost from its beginning the Jesuit order had let slip something of the flexible freedom for the apostolate envisaged by St Ignatius and his first companions, and assumed features of the already existing orders. We looked thoroughly monastic at Loyola College. Priests, scholastics, brothers, and novices took their appointed places in the refectory and main chapel. We filed to meals and community prayers in disciplined columns. Once the novitiate ended, very little apostolic work took the scholastics away from their regular hours of prayer and study.

I went to Pentridge, the forbidding Melbourne gaol, for two debates

against excellent teams of inmates. But I looked on those evenings
as chances to debate in unusual surroundings rather than exercises
in pastoral ministry. We wore black gowns, as though Jesuits really
did have a religious habit like Dominicans and Franciscans. Superiors
persistently emphasized the rule of silence and the sacrosanct nature
of 'major silence', which ran from the evening litanies until after
breakfast the following morning. Exact punctuality was inculcated.
In another community a few years later, the superior addressed to the
scholastics a four-thousand word letter on the importance of bells
in religious life. We kept chickens and bees, grew vegetables, ate fruit
from our orchard and (occasionally) from our run-down vineyard,
and cut the timber that we burned in one of our boilers. Today all that
might suggest a rural commune. But in the early 1950s it represented
the efforts of monks to live from the produce of their own hands.

Our monastic existence stood for a withdrawal from the wicked
world that we partly identified with the city life from which most of us
had come. We spoke of going 'in mundo [sic!]' on those rare occasions
when we visited Melbourne. I shared with many of my contemporaries
the sense that our world was threatened from without by the menace
of Communism and from within by drunkenness, gambling, sexual
sins, and the selfish pursuit of pleasure. We withdrew to pray and do
penance for such massive evil. We 'sacrificed ourselves', to echo the
language I heard at my last pre-Jesuit party. The Catholic community
understood and approved our vocation in those terms, just as some
other Christian denominations have expected their ministers to atone
for the sins of others by abstaining from drinking, smoking, and
dancing.

The Scholasticate

In the scholasticate we had three hours of prayer each day: an hour's
meditation before Morning Mass, two examinations of conscience, a
period of spiritual reading, the rosary, and the community litanies. We

rose at 5.25, except during the summer, May, and September vacations when a 'late call' allowed us to sleep until six. For my first two years of philosophy I studied and slept in one of the 'cubicles'. These lined a long corridor, and were separated from each other by fixed partitions which did not reach up to the ceiling. During meditation and examination of conscience, a 'visitor' put his head in the door to check whether we were at our prayers. I remained fiercely loyal to the appointed programme, and respected the advice one scholastic gave me when I joined him in the 'monkhouse': 'The battle is fought out on your knees.' Those who lived in cubicles normally took the discipline on Friday nights, and some kept up this practice when they moved into their rooms. Most scholastics said grace on their knees at dinner on Fridays.

In the three years of philosophy we studied epistemology (or the theory of knowledge), general metaphysics, theodicy, philosophical psychology, cosmology, and natural ethics, as well as several 'minors' like biology, physics, chemistry, and some history of philosophy. In the major subjects the professors lectured in Latin, usually keeping close to the textbooks published in that language by Jesuits who taught at the Gregorian University in Rome: Arnou, Dezza, Hoenen, Morandini, and Siwek. We learnt their neo-Thomism by tirelessly copying and summarizing our notes, being called on to outline and defend theses in regular class 'repetitions' and in 'circles'. For a circle one of us would be appointed beforehand to expound a particular thesis, and then meet the difficulties raised by two 'objicients'. After these three had completed their task with sporadic interventions from the presiding professor, members of the class could also put objections—'ex corona', as we called it. We conducted the entire operation in Latin, used syllogisms to make our objections and distinctions, and often restricted our debates to a word-play that would have delighted late mediaeval nominalists.

Twice a year we staged a 'disputation', to which all the fathers and

scholastics were invited. In both of the two major subjects being
taught, a scholastic prepared to defend half a dozen theses, and learnt
after breakfast on the morning itself at which thesis the two objectors
had decided to aim their fire. The disputation began with a fifteen-
minute paper in a Latin, followed by two 'circles' of thirty minutes
each, in which the chosen thesis would be presented and debated.
Proceedings ended with a fifteen-minute paper in English. A further
paper (in English) would be read at dinner in the refectory. I recall
delivering one paper on Henri Bergson's argument for God's existence
and another on the value of intelligence tests. None of us ever noticed
how astonishing it was to find Latin circles and disputations held in
a semi-rural, Australian seminary in the 1950s. The scenes and the
language could have come straight out of a sixteenth-century or even
a mediaeval European university.

What did I learn from these three years of philosophical studies?
I became very familiar with a branch of neo-Thomist philosophy in
which Maurice de la Taille and Joseph Maréchal were strong influences.
I had to exercise my memory constantly and sharpen my capacity to
argue logically. In one way or another we became acquainted with
all western philosophy, from Thales to the early twentieth century.
We heard very little of analytic philosophy and Marxism, even
though they heavily influenced the contemporary academic scene in
Australia. We busied ourselves with age-old controversies about the
distinction between essence and existence, the nature of universal
concepts, and the reconciliation of true human freedom with divine
fore-knowledge and sovereign activity. In cosmology, questions of
space and location led us to discuss the nature of the Eucharistic
presence. Our treatment sounded more like essays in supernatural
physics than reflections shaped by the New Testament and the liturgy
of the Church.

The works of Hume, Kant, Locke, and other 'adversaries' were
not available to us, or if they stood on the library shelves they bore

the sign 'NSL (*ne sine licentia*)'. Few of us ever went to the trouble of seeking permission from the prefect of studies to read them. The system oriented us towards textbooks rather than the original classics of western philosophy. We took our textbooks' word for what Kant was about rather than explore for ourselves *The Critique of Pure Reason*. In epistemology we did study some writings by Descartes, but any other direct contact with original texts I had to acquire for myself. I read two volumes of Maréchal's *Le point de départ de la métaphysique*, Thomas Aquinas' *De Veritate*, some Bergson, and (in Greek) a number of Plato's dialogues.

I found a copy of Plato's *Republic* which had belonged to Fr Albert Power, a tiny Irish Jesuit nicknamed 'the mighty atom'. He had known my father at Newman College, taught for many years at the Melbourne diocesan seminary, and lived in retirement at Xavier College. At school I stood chatting with him one early summer evening as we waited for a comet to appear in the western sky. He had read the *Republic* sailing between Australia and Ireland around 1900, and left interleaved notes in the volume. When I noticed that he had kept hard at his Plato even while the ship was steaming through the heat of the Red Sea, I reflected that the least I could do was to persevere with text under conditions that were considerably less trying.

As a break from philosophy I worked through some of Shakespeare's comedies, novels by Dickens and various biographies, including *Edmund Campion* by Evelyn Waugh. That exquisitely written life dazzled me with its picture of the martyr's dedication both to religious life and to scholarly excellence. For years Campion's words inspired my efforts to study until commitment became second nature: 'Only persevere, do not degenerate from what you are, nor suffer the keen eye of your mind to grow dark and rusty.' Superiors considered that the novels of Waugh and Graham Greene should be kept from us, as well as standard weeklies like *Time* magazine. Any books that had been 'put on the index' were, of course, unavailable. Once or twice a week the scholastics could read the front page of a Melbourne daily. We saw the diocesan weekly, the *Advocate*, and the very conservative *News Weekly*.

During those three years of philosophy I took my first steps in writing for publication. The philosophers issued in roneoed form a slim journal called *The Canisian*, which they circulated among the Jesuit houses in Australia. Greg Dening began *Nostra*, an annual illustrated with photographs and cartoons which covered almost every aspect of life in the scholasticate. *The Canisian* folded in the middle 1960s, *Nostra* lasted until 1969. I cannot recall writing for *Nostra*, but I contributed at least one article to *The Canisian*, 'Four Ways to the Natural Law'. I also published in the *Madonna* (a Catholic monthly for sodalities of Our Lady), brief articles on Geoffrey Chaucer, St Robert Southwell, and other poets who had taken the Virgin Mary as one of their themes. The editor of the Madonna persuaded me and some other scholastics to begin a series of short daily meditations which he continued to run into the 1970s. On the occasion of the 1956 Olympic Games (held in Melbourne), the quarterly *The Twentieth Century* carried an article by me on the ancient Olympic Games.

Fr Pat McEvoy, our prefect of studies, towered over the other professors of philosophy. So far as I know, he failed to publish a single article. He certainly avoided philosophical discussions with outsiders, and remained imprisoned by the system of teaching he had inherited. He issued—in Latin, of course—his own *codices* on psychology and theodicy, keeping his lectures close to them, but with an occasional nod towards the textbook. He had a first rate philosophical mind, communicated a sense of genuine issues, could lead us through highly complex arguments in fluent Latin, and was always relentlessly honest.

A bulky, bald priest in his forties, Pat looked after the college's Bedford truck with which he collected the laundry and did other jobs. He delighted in thundering through gates with only inches to spare on either side. His clothes normally looked squalid, and his hands were often greasy from working on the truck or on an old motorcycle he rode. From time to time he took parties of scholastics to the mountain ranges where he used a mobile saw to cut timber that could then be split and loaded on the truck. The company that manufactured the saw used for advertising purposes a photograph which, from behind, showed Pat felling a tree. Bolder scholastics teased him for having his backside known all over Australia. Those were glorious, long days in the mountains when we drove hammers down on wedges, loaded the timber on the Bedford, and smelt the damp earth enriched by centuries of leaves and rain. The trips endangered our lives as we swung down the twisting road perched precariously on top of towering loads of logs, but they saved some of us from breakdowns caused by the strain of our intense religious existence.

On one occasion some bad meat gave the timber-cutting crew mild food poisoning. It hit Pat harder than the others. He clung to the wheel, and somehow got his truck down the mountain and home to the college, where he collapsed into bed. Around nine p.m. a breezy scholastic dropped in to cheer Pat up by reporting a discussion with Max Charlesworth, who was being treated for tuberculosis in a nearby sanatorium. Max had taken a rigidly traditional view on Thomas Aquinas's 'five ways' for establishing the existence of God. The scholastic had expounded a faulty version of Pat's reduction of the five ways to two arguments: one from physical causality and the main argument from the finality of the human intellect. 'And I told Mr Charlesworth', the scholastic concluded, 'that this was your view.' 'Oh, my God', Pat groaned from his bed of pain.

Until the provincial stopped him, Pat used to sell some of the timber we cut to house-holders. He would bring out an annual statement showing how much it cost the college to run the truck and what it brought in. He anticipated what has become standard practice in many religious houses: common responsibility for the finances.

Apart from Pat's small gesture in one sector of our community life, we never learnt what our total expenses came to or how much we derived from the seminary foundation, our own earnings, and gifts from benefactors.

Apart from the timber-cutting trips, we could go on villa every Thursday and there was no prohibition against going in pairs, as in the novitiate. During the vacations there were 'banger days' when we took sausages (or 'bangers') and chops for our lunch in the bush. The May and September vacations each brought an excursion day, when with a few shillings in our pockets we could leave the house as early as we wished and return late in the night. A small fleet of old bikes was patched up for the occasion and, whether we were walking or riding a bike, we also hitch-hiked to increase our range. One pair once made it across the state border into New South Wales and back in a day.

I contented myself with visiting nearby places, and always spending some of my money on copies of the daily papers. I can still hear our billy boiling and a mountain stream hissing by one day in 1953, when I squatted by the fire luxuriating in the chance to read about Queen Elizabeth's coronation and Edmund Hillary's ascent of Mount Everest. Flat tires and breakdowns were regular hazards, but the scholastic who crashed into a wombat undoubtedly suffered the most unusual accident of my time. He was riding fast down a hill, when at a bend in the road he hit the beast in the dark. He spun into the air, flew over a fence, and still clinging to the handlebars splashed down in a conveniently placed dam. In the freezing water he let the bike go and struck out for the bank. At a neighbouring farmhouse he met with stunned silence, when he knocked dripping at the door, told his story, and asked for a pole to recover his bike from the depths.

The fact that he was dressed exactly like a priest partly accounted for the silence. Except for the timber-cutting trips, we always had to wear both clerical collars and tattered black trousers and jackets whenever we went out. If we kept off the roads, we sometimes looked for a convenient tree, dumped our collars and jackets there, and on the way home put them on again. Once the local police found the clothes of a scholastic who was collecting ants in the hills. While he was still happily hunting down a new species of ant, they noted the 'S.J.' on his name tag and contacted the provincial's office, thinking that some Jesuit priest had chosen the middle of the bush to abandon his collar, coat, and vocation.

At home in Loyola College, various games, the stage, and the choir provided outlets for us. We flung ourselves into football, tennis, and cricket with a passion for success that could have been found in most English-speaking seminaries of that period. Almost everywhere both diocesan seminarians and students of religious institutes led secluded lives in colleges, some of which lay much further out into the countryside than Loyola did. I think here of such American theological colleges as Alma in California, St Mary's in Kansas, West Baden in Indiana, and Woodstock in Maryland. Sport could readily possess the imagination of students, although we did not go as far as some seminaries in the United States and England, which—often with immense labour from the students themselves—kept up their own golf courses. One of our scholastics introduced the art of spear throwing, as well as inventing a new kind of super-boomerang that looked like three boomerangs joined together. We were lucky that no one was impaled or decapitated.

When playing football, I slipped a disc in my back, damaged it again at tennis, and finished up in hospital. In the room next to me an old priest had his own method of dealing with an aged nun who insisted on visiting us too frequently. From beneath his reading shade he would catch sight of her gliding down the verandah towards his room. I could hear him groan, 'Oh, go away! I'm asleep.'

Besides doing some Gilbert and Sullivan, we staged elaborate productions of plays like *The Alchemist* (by Ben Jonson), *The Moon is Down* (by John Steinbeck), *Sport of Kings* (by Ian Hay), and *Fire on the Snow* (by Douglas Stewart). Jesuits from other houses in Melbourne came in large numbers for the evenings, and there would be a second performance in an institution for 'delinquent girls'. As well as these major productions, there were occasional evenings of entertainment for the scholastics only, when we indulged in some first rate imitations of the priests. Both in public and in private, mimicry was a highly developed art. Later I discovered how this passion for drama was shared by other seminary students as far away as Ireland and the English College in Rome. We also shared with most of our counterparts overseas a veto against female parts. We had to adapt for an all-male cast both Gilbert and Sullivan and some plays—sometimes with unintended comical results. Many forces lay behind our passion for drama. We had to provide our own entertainment. From 1950 to 1958 inclusive, I never went to the theatre or to a public concert, let alone to opera or ballet. Suppressed sexuality doubtless played a part. The stage also offered scope for our independent creativity. Once superiors gave permission to produce a certain play, scholastics took charge. Superiors believed, of course, that acting would prepare us to be effective preachers and teachers. They may have dimly remembered that Jesuits can claim a special link with the stage. At a time when the order's tastes in art, architecture, and music often failed to rise above a deplorably low level, our stake in drama kept alive a traditional Jesuit concern for the arts.

Mainly thanks to several scholastics, the standard of music and liturgy gradually improved during my time of training as a Jesuit. In the earlier years one still heard those interested in liturgical renewal being sometimes dismissed as 'litur-bugs'. Occasionally the old quip about 'being as helpless as a Jesuit in Holy Week' was quoted to justify a policy of neglect, as if one could be a genuine Catholic and member of a religious order, but remain uninterested even in the major events

of the Church's liturgy. Dialogue Masses came in very slowly. We
left the responses to the two servers and much of the singing to the
choir. In the early 1950s we heard Masses by nineteenth- and early-
twentieth-century composers, but a reform movement drove these
out in favour of Gregorian and the classical polyphony of Giovanni
Pierluigi da Palestrina and Tomás Luis de Victoria. I was never in the
choir and did very little acting. I achieved my most notable 'success'
by once singing an easy lesson at *Tenebrae* and taking a minor role in
The Alchemist.

What was happening to me during those seven years at Loyola?
Rigidly intent upon doing God's will and following Christ, I never
doubted that this meant anything other than persistent commitment
to the programme the Society of Jesus set before me. Two maxims
attributed to St John Berchmans (1599-1621) summed it up for me:
'*age quod agis* (do what you are doing)' and '*serio attendam quid agendum
sit* (I will seriously attend to what must be done).' I wrote on the cover
of my 'Communion and Mass Book' some words of St Paul's 'for me
to live is Christ' (Philippians 1: 21) in the original Greek, and added
the gloss: 'Fidelity to Christ in my daily life'. External observances
preoccupied me, so that breaches of silence and occasional episodes
of horse play by other scholastics shocked me. 'Going the whole
hog' led me to volunteer for our Indian mission and enroll in the
Pioneers, a total abstinence society honouring the Sacred Heart of
Jesus and designed to make reparation for sins of drunkenness. A
Spanish scholastic (who had come to study philosophy with us)
gathered around him a group of other scholastics who consecrated
themselves in a special way to the Sacred Heart and met for prayerful
discussions of the spiritual life. I joined this group which, in fact,
encouraged a 'holier than thou' attitude towards others. Our leader
preached the finest sermon I ever heard in the refectory, and
combined an attractive friendliness with a fervent devotion to the
Sacred Heart. He went to the Philippines, left the order, and returned

to work as a married man in Australia.

Every January we had the opportunity of refurbishing our spiritual lives through the annual retreat. Almost without exception, they were given by competent, interesting, and dedicated priests. We did not speak of 'preached' retreats, but that term describes the external structure of those eight days of silence and prayer. We went to the chapel for four talks a day, followed by our own personal meditations. Most of the retreatants visited the director only once. In recent years Jesuits have turned to 'directed' retreats, which correspond more faithfully to the original practice of our founder, St Ignatius. There is perhaps one talk a day for the whole group, or the director might content himself with an appropriate homily at the Eucharist. The retreatants visit him every day or so, discuss their progress and experience, and allow him, as far as possible, to help them in their individual needs.

Twice a year we renewed our vows after a '*triduum*'. The original vow-taking had committed us. This repetition of vows after three days of silence and some extra periods of prayer was an exercise of devotion. Most of us found the external structure of these '*tridua*' boringly repetitive. In the refectory we listened to a letter written by a seventeenth-century Jesuit general, Fr Vincent Carafa. In the prescribed Latin formulas we submitted a list of external faults we wished to accuse ourselves of. The minister (the priest second-in-charge to the rector) gathered our slips of paper, spent part of dinner reading them out at maximum speed to the entire community, and gave us the common penance of a visit to the Blessed Sacrament. In what we called the '*concio*' (Latin for an assembly) the rector addressed the scholastics on matters of discipline, and inevitably included an exhortation to practise silence more strictly. The priests appointed to direct the '*triduum*' often seemed puzzled as to what they should present in the two talks they gave each day. Sometimes we heard what one of my contemporaries described as 'horror stories from the Irish province'. One old priest offered us rhymed recipes for our studies. His recommendation for the notes we took at lectures ran: 'Churn 'em and learn 'em. Otherwise burn 'em.' He encouraged me to use my mediocre talents by saying, 'Do what you can, being what you are. Shine like a glow-worm, if you cannot be a star.' Wartime searchlights made him think of death: 'Flash in, flash out. Without doubt we must out.' I can recall another rhyme inspired by the development of aircraft, but have forgotten the point of it all: 'From Jenny to jet, simplicity set. And on to greater simplicity yet.'

As a scholastic I saw a little more of my family than had been allowed in the novitiate. We could secure permission from the rector to spend a day at home three or four times a year. Our parents spent an afternoon with us at Loyola once a month, and relatives from interstate could also visit us when they came to Melbourne. Permission was always granted to visit my married sisters, Moira and Dympna, when they were in hospital having a baby. But I never dreamt of asking permission to attend the christenings. Uncle Will baptized nearly all my nephews and nieces, just as uncle Jim officiated at the weddings. Maev had completed her arts degree at the University of Melbourne, studied social work at Sydney University, and began a fifteen-year stint at the Catholic Family Welfare Bureau in Melbourne—'doing the work of a nun', as aunt Mollie put it. Jim and Glynn went into residence at Newman College to study medicine. I joined them at the University of Melbourne when I resumed my arts course in 1955.

The three years of philosophy had ended with the one hour '*de universa*' examination, in which we defended (in Latin) theses drawn from six major fields covered during the whole course. I finished with a mark of nine, a *magna cum laude*, a result that I first learnt twelve years later. We had to repeat examinations if we failed. Otherwise we received no official indication of our results in philosophy.

Back to the University of Melbourne

Jesuit terminology used to distinguish between philosophers and 'juniors' (who did university studies or their equivalent). 'Home juniors' did such studies for a year or two at Loyola College itself before going on to philosophy. Logically those studying at the University of Melbourne should have been called 'university juniors', but we were known as 'university scholastics'. Through 1955 and 1956 I continued to live at Loyola, travelling in to the university either by train and bus or by a Volkswagen minibus.

There were fourteen of us altogether, too many for one bus load. Our prefect of studies, Fr Noel Ryan, decreed that those studying science and mathematics should always have a place on the bus. He agreed with the commonly held view that the study of philosophy had left them behind in their subjects, whereas in many branches of the humanities that study had helped us. As beadle for the year I allotted places on the morning run to the University of Melbourne, and occasionally had to put up with snubs from those who disliked travelling by train. More serious friction arose over meals, since some arrived home too late from lectures to eat with the community. 'The university scholastics are a pest', the minister once informed me. But no tensions really mattered, as it felt thoroughly liberating to spend the day away from Loyola and continue university studies.

Brother Maurice Joyce drove the bus, since scholastics were then forbidden to drive. Besides being dressed in black clothes and clerical collars, we carried black hats. In the late 1960s the Volkswagen minibus became a symbol for permissive American youth, but the University of Melbourne students nicknamed our early model 'the chastity chariot'. When we left the house we said a Hail Mary with the invocation, 'Our Lady of the way, pray for us.' As novices we had recited in Latin and by memory the Litany of Loreto whenever we went out. I sometimes thought that we should have said this longer prayer as scholastics, since many of the priests who had driving licences drove badly even by clerical standards. When he could, one priest used to drive down the wrong side of the road 'to wear the tyres evenly'. Maurie Joyce, however, was just as expert at driving as he was at being a generous, affectionate friend of us all.

Noel Ryan was thirty-eight years old when I came under his direction as prefect of studies. He looked clever and ill. His sickly face and habit of twitching one leg when seated made this highly gifted and compulsive scholar seem like the epitome of a healthy mind in an unhealthy body. About practical matters he could be astonishingly absent-minded. For months one of the brothers secretly filled the tank of Noel's motorbike, and claimed to have led him to believe that he got a miraculous mileage per gallon. A priest in the community borrowed the bike one afternoon and died in a tragic accident. Noel happened to be the person who opened the front door, when a grim-faced policeman arrived to report the death of 'Noel Ryan', the name under which the bike had been registered. 'It can't possibly be me', Noel is supposed to have blurted out. 'I've been home all afternoon.'

Noel revolutionized Jesuit university studies by widening enormously the choice of subjects. Our predecessors had confined themselves to English, French, Greek, history, and Latin, with a few scholastics taking courses in physics, chemistry, and mathematics. Noel secured permission for us to take courses in biology, fine arts, music, philosophy, Russian, and other subjects. He suggested that, as well as majoring in Greek and Latin, I study Hebrew. But the provincial vetoed this on the grounds that I would be studying the Old Testament with a Jew. Noel encouraged us to buy books for the library on a generous scale. When I became librarian in 1956, I sent off a steady stream of orders to Blackwell's for many standard works and basic reference books that the juniors' library lacked. He saw to it that we bought the Melbourne *Age*, and authorized subscriptions to journals like the *Economist* and *Nature*. He had taken his M.A. in

English, but his range of interests was prodigious. During philosophy, Noel had lectured to us on education and modern psychology. He treated Freud's views with fairness, although he never suggested that theories about the super-ego, repression, or reaction formation might throw some light on our lives. When we brought questions about our studies to Noel, he usually had sound and even brilliantly helpful advice to offer. Without fussing or bullying, he effectively encouraged us to aim at the highest academic excellence, even if we laughed when he talked of creating 'another Oxford'.

Noel warned against forming any friendships with girls, lest that lead to what he described as 'spitting on the collar'. He discouraged us from becoming involved with student affairs or even with the Newman Society. Since he exempted departmental societies, it was open to me to play a full role in the Classics Club and serve for a time as secretary. I helped to produce Euripides' *Bacchae*, ran a group which read Greek legal speeches, organized dinners, and arranged talks. These included a wildly successful talk on ancient Greek music by Dr Percy Jones, a jovial Catholic priest who taught in the Conservatorium of Music. Noel made a number of gaudy and effective posters. I can still see the beaming face of Dr Jones as he prepared to play a record by first dusting it on the shiny seat of his black trousers.

Fr Austin Ryan had helped me to resume my interrupted classical studies very smoothly. In his fifties he lived with us at Loyola before joining the staff of Corpus Christi College, the diocesan seminary in Werribee. A large, untidy and deeply caring priest, he enjoyed a dazzling mastery of Greek and Latin literature. He took a number of us through Latin 'unseens'. We read among other texts some satires of Persius, a writer whose style seemed as contorted and unpleasant as his character. Austin believed that if we could read Persius, no Latin writer would defeat us. Austin himself combined a warm sense of humour with a relentless capacity to worry. There was still a thread of pain in the horror stories he recalled from some years of study in

Spain. After he arrived at one Spanish religious house, he wanted to have a bath or a shower, and was taken to a bathroom where he was handed what looked like swimming trunks. When he asked what they were for, he was told: '*Por los angeles*'. I can still hear his accents of astonished dismay over that confrontation with prudery. At Loyola he had to go into hospital for an operation on his haemorrhoids, and left the house quoting Shakespeare's *Hamlet*: 'There's a divinity that shapes our ends,/ rough-hew them how we will.'

At the University of Melbourne the scholastics took their lunch in the Newman College dining hall, but at a separate table from the other students. Apart from those we studied with, we kept fairly aloof from all students. We were looked on as an exotic adjunct to university life. Our astonishingly good academic results reassured some Catholics that members of 'the Church' could perform as well or even better than anyone else. But we were not capable of plunging into a full range of university activities. My own five depersonalizing years at Loyola College produced an innocent immaturity. I had fallen behind my own contemporaries in the power to cope with aggression, sexual attraction, and the other realities of ordinary living. A sheltered all-male environment had left me both afraid of showing anger, and automatically disposed to deny any reactions to the sweatered bodies and rounded thighs that drifted past my desk in the university library.

The University of Melbourne in 1949 had still been thronged with returned servicemen, as well as being possessed with the debate about Communism. In 1954 Dr Herbert Evatt, the leader of the Labor Party in the federal parliament, precipitated a split in his party by attacking the industrial groups and exposing Bob Santamaria's 'movement', which formed a Catholic underground behind the groups. The split brought down the Victorian Labor government in which my brother-in-law's father, Patrick Leslie Coleman, had been Minister for Transport. Les lost his seat in the 1955 state elections, when he helped to lead the Anti-Communist (later Democratic)

Labor Party. I felt deeply saddened in 1962 when I wanted to invite another Catholic politician, Jack Galbally, to my ordination, but was told that both Les and my brother-in-law would refuse to attend if I did so. Les maintained at that at some key point Jack had gone back on his pledged word of support, in order to stay with the Labor Party and remain in the state parliament.

Uncle Jim had worked hand in glove with Santamaria, and was furious when Cardinal Norman Gilroy withdrew any official Catholic support for the 'movement' in Sydney. That helped the New South Wales Labor Party to stay in power. In Victoria Bishop Arthur Fox, an auxiliary to Dr Mannix, told Catholics it would be a sin to vote for the Labor Party because of its softness on Communism. The Jesuits who staffed the Institute of Social Order in Kew gave strong support to Santamaria and to what became the Democratic Labor Party. A few Jesuits passed on stories about Dr Evatt and Dr Jim Cairns (also a prominent Labor Party parliamentarian) being secret members of

The five O'Collins brothers in 1946: Standing from left, Joe and Frank, seated, Will, Jim and Gerald.

the Communist Party. Pat McEvoy, however, made no secret of his opposition to Santamaria's 'movement'.

Within my immediate family my sister Maev worked for the Anti-Communist Labor Party in the 1955 elections. Mother complained about the way Santamaria and his associates had turned Catholics into 'second-class citizens', even if opposition to Communism had sunk deep into her since the 1930s. She had studied *Das Kapital* and further Marxist and anti-Marxist literature, as well as following the Spanish Civil War in great detail. She often insisted: 'Communism is wrong, even if everyone in the Soviet Union eats off gold plate.'

I cannot recall my father, however, expressing strong feelings against Communism, although he used to note that his American friend Hartley Grattan had been rightly called before a commission to be questioned about his Marxist views. Father expressed to uncle Jim his unqualified disapproval of the way Santamaria's attempt to mobilize opposition to Communism led Catholics to treat other non-Communists unfairly and grab too much for themselves. He put this point to me through some episodes drawn from the past history of football politics in Melbourne University. Catholics from Newman and Presbyterians from Ormond College had on occasions packed meetings to advance the cause of their own representatives. Father held that such denominationally based actions were improper in an open society and inevitably provoked reactions.

Before the First World War father had nursed Jack Galbally on his knee, and then years later employed him in his law office. In the circumstances of 1954 and 1955, however, father did not believe that Jack 'had done the right thing'. Not long before his own death in 1961, father met him at a party and Jack observed, 'Frank, you don't approve of me these days.' 'I approve of your golf', father replied. Then a week or two before he died, father was entertaining uncle Jim at Rock Lodge. In the summer Santamaria used to bring his family on holidays to Frankston. One afternoon he came up to sit on the front verandah and chat with uncle Jim. From his bedroom father caught sight of Santamaria and, rather than come out the normal way and meet him, laboriously climbed out a back window to escape. Just before I left Australia in 1973, I ran into Jack Galbally at a golf club. We chatted and I recalled how he bought me a bottle of lemonade when he saw me fishing off a bridge as child. 'At least you approve of my lemonade', he remarked sadly, and left before I could protest that old quarrels did not count with me.

I have dwelt on these events from the Labor Party history, partly because I found it surprising how non-political the student body had become by the mid-1950s. Interest had shifted to religious societies and questions, and remained there. Among Catholics, Vincent Buckley and his friends (who mainly opposed Santamaria and his 'movement') were developing their ideas on Christ, culture, and academic life. On the side of unbelief, an ex-convent girl with bright red hair and a stunning upper-class accent organized a series of lunch-time lectures entitled 'The Case Against Religion'. The audiences packed the public lecture theatre in the old arts building. Various members of the philosophy department demolished proofs for the existence of God, explained away religious experience, rejected Christ's resurrection, and maintained that the reality of evil could not be reconciled with the notion of an all-good and all-powerful God. Christians rose to argue against these unbelievers and arranged subsequent talks by their own speakers, of whom Davis McCaughey of Ormond College was undoubtedly the most impressive. I wrote an article that reported the series, rebutted— as I hoped—some of the major arguments from the agnostics and atheists, and pointed out how their versions of theist positions were drawn from eighteenth- and nineteenth-century writers. How could it be otherwise? The university library contained hardly any recent works of Catholic philosophy and theology. When I submitted my piece for the usual Jesuit censorship, Fr Jim Dynon, my cousin who had become Fr Austin Kelly's 'socius' or secretary, rejected it for publication in the quarterly *Twentieth Century*. 'It would cause controversy', he explained. To strike some blow for the cause, I asked my mother to donate some appropriate books to the university library. She agreed to present them as long as it was in memory of her father. I chose several volumes by Monsignor Ronald Knox, Canon George Smith's *Teaching of the Catholic Church*, a book on Jewish-Christian relations, and some other works.

My first two years back at the University of Melbourne sped past, although my group grew impatient to move out of Loyola into a house for university scholastics. Noel Ryan pressed for this, but the outgoing provincial, Austin Kelly, procrastinated. Finally, action came with the new provincial, 'Dermot' Hogan. We could move into a new house, which would be called Campion Hall after the Jesuit hall of residence in Oxford.

With the rest of Melbourne we enjoyed a gala conclusion to 1956, the Olympic Games, which took place from 22 November to 8 December. My family took me to the opening ceremony, at which the recent Hungarian revolution prompted loud cheers for the Hungarian team. Being Australian, the crowd loudly whistled at the tight-skirted, high-stepping girl who led a team from a South American country. I attended another day to see American sprinters assert their usual supremacy and massive Russian women dominate the shot-put.

Finally 1957 arrived to end seven years of living at Loyola College. It was good to get away from the grey 'monastery' to life in a small community of our own.

In this chapter I have tried to tell the story fairly and perhaps too dispassionately. Conceivably the discipline of those seven years has proved so effective that, even in retrospect, I find difficulty in giving away what it was like. After more than five decades the time at Loyola rises up in my memory like an unpleasant but anaesthetized dream that swept me through my early twenties. I accepted the programme without question, felt content, pushed ahead relentlessly with my quest for perfection, and experienced astonishingly little loneliness or sadness. I can honestly recall only one occasion when I fleetingly asked myself whether I was in the right place. Some mild disregard for silence and external rules on the part of other scholastics upset me to the point that I let the thought of becoming a Cistercian run through my mind. For some moments one evening I thought longingly of the strict observance of that contemplative order.

If superiors hurt my feelings, I usually succeeded in repressing my emotional reactions. When I was confined to bed, first at Loyola and then in hospital, with a slipped disc, it pained me to find that some of the scholastics I expected to do so failed to visit me. (That experience made me resolve never to neglect the sick, a resolution I have generally managed to keep.) One or two of my companions made me miserable by their sharp remarks, when I helped another scholastic get rid of two dogs that had made the night hideous with their barking.

I puzzled over my reaction when my cousin Vivienne visited me. She had left school in Sydney, came to live interstate, and was thinking of becoming a nun. Her extraordinary beauty hit me and left me feeling giddy. It was hardly surprising. For years I had never chatted face to face with any girls of about my age, and Vivienne was stunningly lovely.

Below the surface of my admissible feelings I kept down a good deal of anger, generated by the inhuman side of life at Loyola. 'Getting out of the place' meant escaping from a programme that went far beyond dedicated Christian discipleship to deny much that is normal and healthy. When I reached Campion Hall, I astonished myself by suddenly bursting into rage at a superior over some trifling misunderstanding. Any expressions of aggression I had identified with sin and consistently blocked off. This eruption of anger simply rose from the depths of an outraged nature. But normally religious motivation proved so strong that such human feelings remained repressed.

5

The Path to Priesthood (1957-63)

*I should call anything a real fall which made us hate the road
that had led us to so great a blessing.*

St Teresa of Avila, *Life*.

Campion Hall belonged to that section of Melbourne sometimes called 'Vatican Hill'. When you climbed Studley Park Road from a bridge over the Yarra, the first buildings you reached as the ground levelled out on the left were a Catholic hospice for the dying (Caritas Christi) and Raheen, the mansion that was the home of Archbishop Daniel Mannix. Across the busy road stood Burke Hall (a preparatory school for Xavier College), Campion Hall, and—two hundred metres further along—a residence of the Pallotine Fathers. A grey-walled Carmelite monastery lay down a side street just below Campion Hall.

Built at the beginning of the twentieth century in Queen Anne revival style, my new home had been bought in the late 1940s by Xavier College and used to house boarders from Burke Hall. The masters secured astonishing cooperation from the boys, who left no marks on the panelled walls and the timbered staircase that swept down into the entrance hall. We needed to eradicate a dozen possums, who lived above the elaborate ceilings and prowled around our stately home. When a friend of mine surprised a large possum in the old-fashioned, downstairs bathroom, it leapt for the toilet chain. The possum then swung to and fro, staring down in disbelief as the water flushed through the bowl below. Some fine cedars, oaks, and other trees filled the spacious grounds. During my two years at Campion, I worked away cutting off dead branches, clearing rank undergrowth, laying two brick paths, planting shrubs, and helping to restore the neglected gardens. In 1957 a new wing was added at the back to provide sufficient rooms for the rising numbers of scholastics who began university studies.

During our first year only seven or eight scholastics, two priests and one brother lived at Campion. Noel Ryan and Maurie Joyce came with us from Loyola; Noel continued as prefect of studies and Maurie became our cook. Noel ate his breakfast so fast that Maurie decided to set up a domestic imitation of Roger Bannister's recent achievement in breaking the four-minute barrier for the mile. Under Maurie's direction and without a word to Noel, we served the cereals, coffee, toast and eggs as rapidly as possible, and had the satisfaction of seeing Noel complete his breakfast in three minutes fifty-five seconds.

Life in our small community allowed us to invite to dinner some professors and other teachers from Melbourne University. I started again to keep dogs: first, a great Dane bitch and, after she was killed by a car, a beagle called 'Pop'. Impossible to tie up and utterly safe in traffic, Pop roamed freely over a broad sweep of Melbourne suburbs and made friends everywhere. We gradually drifted apart. Eventually he would return home only once a week, when he made great efforts to greet me effusively. The last time I saw him, he was riding around in a car, delighted no doubt at his new method for increasing the range of his wanderings. Our surroundings at Campion encouraged a feeling for human contacts that seven years at Loyola had inhibited. As the evening light faded out of the sky over Melbourne and we sat studying at our desks, gusts of laughter would sometimes drift up from the Carmelite garden. Apart from a couple of 'extern' sisters, we never met any of the Carmelites, but they always seemed a comforting, joyful presence to me. We lived close to Burke Hall, Xavier College, and other Jesuit communities. We appreciated their hospitality and the chance to use the Xavier swimming pool in hot weather. Occasionally we slipped across the road to help at Caritas Christi. I recall one procession led by the nuns through the wards. Grasping a candle in one hand and trying to conceal my distaste for the sentimental hymns we sang, I heard one dying patient exclaim: 'Ah, it's so beautiful.' Many people I knew lived in neighbouring suburbs and, even though I could not visit them, their presence contributed to the sense of returning to normal human activity. My two married sisters had their homes nearby. Reasons for seeing them cropped up, and in a small community superiors did not maintain the strict standards that had regulated contacts with 'externs' at Loyola.

Bill Daniel and Greg Dening

Through 1957 and 1958 friendships flourished with other Jesuit scholastics like Bill Daniel and Greg Dening. A plump old-boy of St Ignatius College, Riverview, Bill was a year ahead of me in classics, a relationship that lasted for some time. He wrote his M.A. thesis in 1957; I wrote mine in 1958. He taught at St Louis School (Western Australia) in 1958; I taught there in 1959 before joining him for theology in Sydney. He directed the 'spiritual semester' at Corpus Christi College (Victoria) in 1963; I did the same in 1964. He made his tertianship or second novitiate at Münster (West Germany) in 1963/64; I went there for tertianship in 1964. My 'one-year-behind-Bill' relationship ended at that point, since I did not go to Rome in 1965 to join him at the Gregorian University, as we had originally planned. During our classics course we did some subjects together, including comparative philology, a vast subject in which it was clearly impossible to cover adequately the material relevant to any topic. Before we went into the examination (in which there was to be some choice), I asked Bill whether he would pick a particular question if it came up. He assured me that he would and mentioned the points he intended to make. The question was on the paper. After writing as much as I could in the time allotted, I ended by listing further points that the examiner would find in Bill's answer. The examiner was not amused. Bill won the gold medal in classics and went off to be games master at St Louis School. We laughed over that in the light of what happened to the other honours students in his class. Of the two who shared second place, one was accepted for the diplomatic service and the other won a Shell Scholarship, which took him to Cambridge University. The student who came fourth won a Rhodes Scholarship and left for Oxford.

Once or twice Bill and I spent February tutoring for the Greek summer school at the University of Melbourne. Professor Harold Hunt, the head of the classics department, offered beginners an intensive course which enabled them to take Greek I at the pass level and, in some cases, move to honours Greek in subsequent years. Bill and I showed no reluctance in speaking out for Catholic truth. I remember some Anglican theological students in one summer school being upset at the emergence of the Church of South India. This union of episcopal and non-episcopal churches threatened their belief about apostolic succession. I supported their doubts. Such a merger rendered invalid what they held: a ministry transmitted from the apostles through a line of validly consecrated bishops. Professor Hunt's habit of using passages from the New Testament, as well as texts from Greek philosophers, allowed other issues like church unity to arise. It seemed quite clear to me that the scriptures expressed an unambiguous message about organizing the Christian community and that the unified Catholic Church lived the truth of the message. At Loyola one professor had expressed and reinforced prejudices by assuring me: 'I think most Protestant ministers are in bad faith.'

Two experiences shook my uncritical and bigoted version of

Christianity. I heard a lunch-hour symposium presented by three speakers: an Anglican, a Roman Catholic, and a Presbyterian. The occasion, I think, was the week of prayer for Christian unity. Davis McCaughey, then professor of New Testament at Ormond College, spoke eloquently and movingly about the work of Abbé Paul Couturier, who had promoted this movement of ecumenical prayer. It surprised me to hear a Presbyterian endorse the Apostles' Creed with its profession of belief in 'the holy, Catholic Church'. Fr Jerry Golden (the chaplain of the Newman Society), 'as a Jesuit supporting a Protestant from Northern Ireland', endorsed Davis' invitation to prayer. The Anglican speaker, Dr Stuart Barton Babbage, showed himself astonishingly at odds with the other two speakers and the occasion itself. He called on his audience to safeguard 'the precious Protestant liberties' for which their ancestors had fought. A current adaptation of a music hall song ran through my mind: 'Barton Babbage is my name. Carting cabbage is my game. I'm the idol of the barmaids and Barton Babbage is my name.' If this Anglican's prejudices proved satisfying to my own prejudices, Davis' genuine Christianity helped to shift me almost unawares to new attitudes. In fairness to Dr Babbage, let me add that, during a subsequent career in the United States, he encouraged the enrolment of Catholic nuns at the strongly evangelical Gordon-Conwell Theological Seminary, and as dean led this seminary into an ecumenical union within the Boston Theological Institute.

In 1958 the Catholic Church celebrated the centenary of the Virgin Mary's appearances to St Bernadette Soubirous at Lourdes. I wrote two articles for the February issue of the *Sacred Heart Messenger*, and became interested both in St Bernadette herself and in the question of miraculous cures at Lourdes. At the University of Melbourne, under the auspices of the Newman Society, I gave a lunch-hour lecture on those miracles. In preparation for that lecture I read D. J. West's *Eleven Miraculous Cures*, a detailed examination of the documentary evidence for eleven miracles preserved in the medical bureau at Lourdes. West's negative conclusions not only shook my belief in the exact standards of that bureau, but also sent slight ripples of doubt across the surface of my faith. He briefly depressed me by forcing me to raise my first real questions about the Catholic Church's concern for truth. In a meeting at Campion Hall I read a paper on St Bernadette, and was taken aback when Greg Dening asked what role the psychological states of an adolescent girl might have played in her visions of the Virgin Mary.

Charming, highly intelligent, and a little intense, Greg was beadle (or head scholastic) in 1957, and our happy beginning at Campion Hall owed much to his powers of leadership. During his history courses he seemed to win every prize within sight, except when John Eddy (who majored in politics) took one or two exhibitions away from him. Greg joined John Mulvaney's early expeditions to aboriginal sites in South Australia and Victoria. The three of us once drove out of Melbourne into the countryside and spent the day inspecting a diacrite outcrop, where an early nineteenth-century aboriginal manufactured axe-heads, and exchanged them for kangaroo skins and other goods. While questions were gathering darkly in my brain, Greg now and then challenged commonly held Catholic positions. I remember him one day arguing that a variety of moral codes around the world threw doubt on the absoluteness of ethical principles. As librarian I asked superiors whether Samuel Richardson's *Pamela*, Karl Marx's writings, and similar books 'on the index' (a forbidden list that the Second Vatican Council abolished less then ten years later) should be on the open stacks. I was fussily scrupulous about Church law, superiors vacillated, and Greg was rightly furious at the nonsensical proceedings.

We received insufficient help to integrate our academic growth and our religious life. Every week or so a priest from another Jesuit community visited Campion Hall as our spiritual father. He had little to offer, apart from his cheerful kindness. In his exhortations we waited for him to drag in yet once again his favourite biblical text: 'Your ways are not my ways", says the Lord.' A priest who led us in one triduum talked about sexuality and our spiritual life with a refreshing honesty that I welcomed. But he lessened his overall impact by building one talk around what I knew to be a mistranslation from St Paul.

I felt very much at home with the new provincial, Fr Hogan. But he exuded imperturbable common sense rather than inspiring reflections on our life as religious. He assured us one day, 'I'm no starry-eyed enthusiast, but you need ideals.' What we needed were creative insights rather than generalities. He thought our problems resembled closely those of his own student days at University College Dublin. Such Irish comparisons aroused resentment among Australian scholastics.

The prevailing Irish influence in our province drove me into a phase of extra loyalty to Queen Elizabeth II. In 1954 I had walked for miles to see her drive past on her first visit to Australia. At Campion Hall I ordered a print of Pietro Annigoni's portrait of her and planned to have it autographed through the services of Commander Michael Parker, an old-boy of my school who served as equerry and then private secretary to Prince Philip. My sister Maev had become a friend of Commander Parker's sister Mary, who worked for the media in England. Via the United States, Maev travelled back to Australia with Mary, who then became a presenter when Melbourne television started in time for the 1956 Olympic Games. I bought some fine writing paper, studied the correct form of address, and had gone as far as composing a letter to the Queen when Commander Parker lost his job at court. I had to be content with hanging the print in a gilded frame over the fireplace in our common room. 'What's she doing up there?', one old Irish priest asked when visiting Campion Hall. The picture surprised a few non-Catholic visitors from Melbourne University. My blatantly displayed symbol of patriotism was also aimed, I suppose, at proving to doubters that even Jesuits could be loyal subjects after all.

The University of Melbourne

In the 1950s the University of Melbourne enjoyed an unusually high standard of academic staff. Monash, La Trobe and other future Australian universities had not yet drained off some of the young scholars and teachers, who gave great strength to the history, philosophy, and other departments. A former teacher at Melbourne Grammar School, Harold Hunt ran a small and friendly classics department. We read intensively some prescribed texts, composed Greek and Latin prose and poetry, learnt to translate 'unseens' and, in general, followed the existing pattern of an Oxbridge classics course. George Gellie communicated a fine literary appreciation of Greek drama, and Kenneth Quinn did the same for Latin lyric poetry. In 1949 I had already studied with George, and enjoyed warm relations with this elegant scholar who had played intercollegiate football against my brother-in-law, Jim Peters. I found Quinn cooler and made him laugh only once. For a course on Propertius we used a commentary by a Dutch classicist called Enk, who had so far covered only one or two books of Propertius's odes. When we moved on to the later books, I remarked to Quinn, 'We have run out of Enk.'

Overseas scholars came to lecture, notably two from Cambridge: W.K.C. Guthrie and Sir John Sheppard, a former provost of King's College. Sheppard perched on the rostrum, swung his legs to and fro, and charmed us with his reflections on Homer. King Priam asking Helen to name the Greek warriors outside the walls of Troy sounded like an old don asking a research student's wife to identify for him partners at a Cambridge May Ball. I enjoyed working with Guthrie on my B.A. thesis, a study of Plato's use of myths. In his area of classics Guthrie ranked with the best in the world. Receiving his high approval cured my unconscious sense of academic inferiority, that cultural cringe which made many Australians feel that in some or even many fields they fell below the standards of that great, mythological world we called 'overseas'.

Professor Hunt encouraged his students to enjoy effective contact with other departments. John O'Brien, a history lecturer whose incorrigibly dry humour only Jesuits appeared to enjoy, took us for courses on Latin inscriptions. As part of a course on the pre-Socratics I attended a seminar run by a philosophy lecturer, David Armstrong.

In the 1957 finals I won the gold medal for classics, and stayed on for another year to write an M.A. thesis. Professor Hunt secured a grant, provided me with an office, and gave me a temporary post as a part-time tutor. This involved little more than taking a Latin I class for prose composition. Officially Professor Hunt supervised my research on a particular aspect of Aristotle's theory of matter and form, but I derived much more help from frequent meetings with Armstrong.

David was a tall, darkly handsome, and pleasantly argumentative agnostic. I chuckled a few years later when I read a letter to an Australian paper that accused him of showing prejudice against believers. In 1958, as far as I recall, he gave research supervision only to me and a final-year B.A. student, who played a prominent role in the Student Christian Movement and subsequently became a Catholic. David showed genuine interest in religious questions, and no desire to penalize or subvert believers. It gradually dawned on me that the version of Christianity which he would endorse, if ever he came to believe, was curiously conservative. In Cambridge I was to encounter further examples of modern British philosophers entertaining remarkably old-fashioned notions of religion, irrespective of whether they personally accepted them or not. On BBC television in 1973 I watched a debate between Professor Bernard Williams and Cardinal John Carmel Heenan, the Archbishop of Westminster. They stuck on the topic of birth control and the Catholic Church. The Cambridge philosopher's remarks revealed how in such matters he interpreted papal authority in a strong fashion, which made him at one with his conservative opponent. The only difference was that the philosopher did not happen to accept this authority (so understood), whereas the cardinal did.

My thesis filled two volumes, the first containing my text with numerous quotations (in Greek) from Aristotle and the second containing the footnotes, bibliographies and translations of the passages cited in Greek. I had chosen to do research on Aristotle, because so far I lacked any direct acquaintance with his work. I believed that I could profit from spending a year on a central theme in his philosophical writings. In the event this prolonged grappling with one of the sharpest minds in western civilization proved stimulating and enriching. David encouraged me to concentrate on the best passages rather than clutter up my thesis with exhaustive historical detail. I attempted to expound and critically evaluate Aristotle's main arguments for his theory of matter and form. My background in Thomist philosophy led me to treat him somewhat too leniently, but the thesis earned its keep by some technical controversies with Sir David Ross, a standard authority on Aristotle. The examiners of the thesis, David himself and Max Charlesworth, awarded it a first. David took an agreeably generous view of my capacity as a philosopher and suggested that I should go on to a B.Phil. at Oxford.

I rewrote one chapter of the thesis as an article for an American philosophical journal, which failed to reply for a year or two and then rejected my piece. In 1960 I trimmed down the notes, shortened some sections, and turned the whole thesis into a book. Publication seemed the correct way of bringing a large and successful research project to its proper conclusion. I also wanted to change a long-standing situation in Australia. For decades Jesuits had failed to produce any scholarly works. I tried a university press in the United States, which returned my manuscript so fast that I doubt whether it was ever read. The Australian Humanities Research Council agreed to publish it, provided I put up a guarantee of two or three hundred pounds.

Graduation at University of Melbourne, 1958.

But I felt reluctant to ask either the Society of Jesus or my family to back the venture. The effort to publish my insights into Aristotle ended there. In any case another project had deeply engaged me, the biography of my grandfather, Patrick McMahon Glynn.

Mother had kept her father's diaries, other private papers, and his library, while my sister Moira had collected from relatives in Ireland eighty of his letters. In late 1957, I sounded out Greg Dening to see whether he might be interested in doing research on Glynn. When it became clear that his historical concerns lay elsewhere, I decided to take on the task myself. Various academic and personal interests came into play. The powerful history department attracted me not only by the success enjoyed by Greg (and John Eddy) but also through friends like John Mulvaney and John O'Brien. Work on my B.A. thesis and the initial stages of my research into Aristotle convinced me that I could handle a large and long-range project. Half unawares, I also wanted to justify my mother's loving admiration for her father—an attitude that her sisters did not fully share. Perhaps too I wanted to establish his rightful place in an Australian Catholic tradition, which seemed to pay excessive attention to republican, Labor Party, and working-class figures. During 1958 I had grandfather's diaries typed out, a necessary preliminary to any further research. Professor John La Nauze secured a grant to cover the costs of the typing, encouraged the whole project, and impressed me deeply by the impeccable standards he exemplified in his own work on a leading colleague of my grandfather in federal politics, Alfred Deakin. My father took La Nauze and myself to lunch at the Menzies Hotel—my first visit there for nearly nine years. A sense of change struck me when I returned to the dignified opulence of the old hotel. I was back but in the company of an academic perfectionist, who fed my desire to succeed in research and writing.

At tea one morning Kenneth Quinn breezed into the classics department, caught sight of me, and remarked teasingly, 'I see you have a peasant for a pope.' Angelo Giuseppe Roncalli had just been elected and took the name of Pope John XXIII. Shortly before the papal election a Melbourne photographer had urgently contacted my family, hoping for a scoop. Years earlier he had taken photographs of us with Cardinal Agagianian (the Patriarch of 'All the Armenians'), when uncle Jim brought us together for a meal with this visitor from Rome. The cardinal went into the 1958 conclave a highly favoured candidate, but supposedly was not elected when he would give no guarantees about his choice for secretary of state. He had studied at Propaganda College with uncle Will, and later showed himself a good friend to uncle Jim and uncle Gerald. They had three stories to tell about him. He was so young when he arrived from Armenia to study in Rome that he travelled 'as a parcel'. His ticket and a note indicating his destination were attached to his coat. At one meeting with the members of Propaganda College, Pope Pius X stood in front of the ranks of assembled students. He wanted to meet the brilliant young Armenian and, using his Christian name, cried out, 'Lazarus, come forth!' Uncle Jim after his own ordination stayed on at the college for a short time as a sub-prefect. This enabled him to check the examination records. Agagianian had scored the top mark of ten in all but one subject. A later hand had altered the solitary nine into a ten, to give Agagianian a perfect record.

Uncle Jim had sometimes recommended to me the value of studying in Rome. There, he argued, one learnt 'the mind of the men who run the Church'. His friend Agagianian had become Prefect of the Sacred Congregation for the Propagation of the Faith (now the Congregation for the Evangelization of Peoples) and one of the most powerful Vatican officials. This was the man we met face to face in aunt Madge's home. He exuded an air of quiet piety, and made encouraging remarks about 'a great family' when he saw over twenty of uncle Jim's relatives assembled to greet him. It amused me to notice how uncle Joe, generous and lovable man that he always was, reacted when the cardinal remarked that Dr Mannix, nearly in his nineties, could still truly pray (in Latin) at the beginning of Mass: 'I will go unto the altar of God, to God who gives joy to my *youth*.' Uncle Joe, even if he was still a fulltime doctor in his Balaclava practice, felt himself well into middle age and could not enthuse over any spiritual significance of 'youth'.

Leaving Melbourne

My two years at Campion Hall closed with a two-week vacation at Werribee and the annual eight-day retreat. On both occasions we joined the scholastics at Loyola College. From 1952 to 1958 I took my annual vacation at Corpus Christi College, the former home of the Chirnside family which was built around 1877, bought by the Catholic archdiocese of Melbourne, and became after the First World War the nucleus building for a large seminary. Andrew Chirnside had chosen honey-coloured stone to make Werribee Park the loveliest stately home in the Australian countryside. The long entrance hall stretching to a broad, central staircase, the chandeliers, and the elegant ground-floor rooms conjured up Victorian days of lordly, pastoral wealth. The house looked out on lawns lined with cedars, flowering gums, golden cypresses, oaks, jacarandas and other trees laid out by the botanist and explorer, Baron Ferdinand von Mueller. He also designed the botanical gardens that surround government house in Melbourne.

Grey-faced buildings were added to the back and sides of Werribee Park to house the refectory, chapel, hall, class rooms, and bedrooms. A few hundred yards beyond these new buildings the Werribee River flowed past into Port Phillip Bay. Beyond the river lay the main Melbourne sewage farm. One warm afternoon when a wind from that quarter carried a sickening smell across the college, I met an older member of the staff who had been walking up and down on a balcony and 'saying his office' or daily prayer. 'Father', I asked, 'aren't you picking up a bad smell?' 'No', he replied, 'but I'm beginning to get a dirty taste in my mouth.'

Werribee was a deadly dull place. A pervasive dust rose from the flat plains to increase the incidence of respiratory complaints in the area. Irrigation channels cut across the landscape to bring fertility to the red soil, and a livelihood to vegetable and dairy farmers. We heard whispered stories about an Italian woman who had the evil eye. A farmer with whom I chatted one day guessed at once that I was at the seminary, even if he had trouble with the name: 'You must be at Corpus Crispies College.' I never heard of anyone but Jesuits taking their holidays at Werribee. A truck-driver who picked up a scholastic on his way there colourfully expressed his astonishment: 'What do you want to go to Werribee for? It's the arse-hole of the world.' But we found it a welcome break, above all during our years at Loyola. In any case renting a guesthouse for fifty or sixty scholastics would have been very expensive. Werribee offered a holiday on the cheap.

Within the college grounds we could swim in the river, read, or play tennis and handball. I used to ride a bike to play golf on courses twelve or more miles away. Hitchhiking was forbidden and clerical dress had to be worn outside the college. God knows what motorists thought when they saw me and other scholastics pedalling along the busy road, wearing black suits and Roman collars and carrying a bag of golf-clubs slung across our backs.

What I particularly enjoyed about the vacations at Werribee was the chance of meeting the Jesuits who staffed the seminary. Until his death in an accident, Fr Hackett came with us as 'spiritual father'. A picnic with him has stayed fast in my mind. The college owned a jinker and a black mare who could trot for hours. Another scholastic and I invited him to join us on a trip to the You Yangs, the only hills that stuck up from the Werribee plains. Fr Hackett sat between us, telling us story after story of the Irish 'troubles' and suddenly stopping to ask, 'I'm not boring you, am I?' He enthralled us, even if I cannot remember precisely a single story from that day of blazing sunshine. He sat in the shade at the foot of Flinders Peak, while we scrambled up through rocks and stunted gum trees to the top of the You Yangs.

Fr Hackett met death in Kew one bleak evening, when he went out to give Benediction of the Blessed Sacrament at a nearby convent He had declined the offer of a younger priest to take his place. Under his umbrella in the drizzling rain he failed to see a car coming. He lay on the road too broken to be moved until an ambulance arrived. In hospital he lingered on and gradually recovered consciousness. 'I've had a bit of an upset', he observed. After a week death came to this lovely man, who used to say with perfect sincerity, 'The love of God is the greatest adventure in life.'[1]

A Year in the West

In January 1959 I left Melbourne and travelled west by train across the continent to spend a year's teaching at St Louis School, Claremont (a suburb of Perth). Six priests and six scholastics provided nearly all the teaching staff. There were around eighty boarders and over three hundred boys all told. I had an extraordinarily competent group of scholastics to work with. But the good-natured quip (from one of the priests) that the school was 'conducted by the Jesuit fathers and run by the Jesuit scholastics' did much less than justice to the hard-working team of priests.

We used the strap far too freely and the boys had to 'line up' far too often. This involved forming orderly lines and standing in silence for a few moments before going into class or chapel. Perhaps some of us succumbed to the feeling that the easy-going 'sand-gropers' needed more discipline. I came to loathe using the strap, but almost all the boys preferred to receive some 'cuts' on their hands rather than face detention periods, which we called 'penals'. All in all, it was a happy school that still preserved the family spirit inculcated by Fr

---

1 Brenda Niall has a moving account of his death in *The Riddle of Father Hackett* (Canberra: National Library of Australia, 2009), 267-69.

Austin Kelly, who had founded St Louis in 1938. He had also decreed the traditional Jesuit names for classes, which ran from Rhetoric and Poetry down through Syntax and Grammar classes to Rudiments and Elements. I taught some highly gifted boys, like Robert French, who in September 2008 was appointed the Chief Justice of the High Court of Australia, and several descendants of the Duracks, a pioneer cattle family of Queensland and Western Australia. The less gifted included one boy who could produce astonishing answers in history and other subjects. Questioned about Sir Isaac Newton, he explained: 'Newton was sitting under a tree one day when an apple fell on his head. He said, "It must be the season for apples."' The same boy began his comments on a Portuguese explorer by noting: 'Magellan circumcised the globe with a forty-foot cutter.' The poor lad entered the army and was killed in Vietnam, the first old-boy of St Louis to die in war.

I taught English and Latin to Poetry and Syntax II, a light load of four classes a day since I was first division prefect. That job entailed organizing games, looking after the older boarders, and maintaining discipline around the school. Once they moved into Grammar I at the age of twelve or so, the boys left the junior school and came under my charge. I enjoyed all the work, even if it left me physically tired and meant sleeping in a corner of the boys' dormitory. On Saturday evenings the boys watched a film, before another scholastic took the juniors to bed and I followed with the senior boys. Just as I was going upstairs one night, I glimpsed a school cleaner slipping back to his quarters with a woman on his arm. Being unsure whether it was school policy to turn a blind eye to such activities, I mentioned the matter to an older scholastic, the one in charge of the juniors. He disappeared downstairs at once. He took the woman the whole length of the school property down to Stirling Highway, put her on a bus going back into the city, and was drenched in a snap thunderstorm. Meantime I had seen all the boarders to bed, had switched out the lights, and was doing a circuit of the dormitories to discourage talking or pillow-fights. The other scholastic padded up to me in the dark, and dripping with water whispered in my ear, 'Next time there is a prostitute to be shown off the property, please do it yourself.'

The elderly matron occasionally came looking for someone in the dormitories—much to the consternation of the older boys. She insisted that the small boys cut their fingernails and toenails properly before they went home on holidays. One day she pursued two of them into the shower-room where I was on duty keeping silence and order. As the older boys stared in disbelief from under their showers, she planted herself in the middle of the room, slung a small boy's leg across her knee, and trimmed his toenails like a blacksmith shoeing a horse.

In the late 1950s the big economic boom had not yet affected life in Perth, which still conveyed the feeling of large and friendly country town. Jesuits enjoyed easy relationships with the bishops and diocesan priests. When Archbishop Redmond Prendiville called one day at the school, he looked at me and commented, 'You have a real O'Collins chin.' After his secretary became an auxiliary bishop and was assigned the 'titular see' of Antipatris, the new bishop phoned the school to discover where his 'see' was located. I suggested that a Vatican official had probably wanted to make a reference to the Australian forces who served in North Africa during World War II. Tobruk had taken the place of the ancient city of Antipatris. Staff members at the University of Western Australia welcomed us and offered helpful advice about preparing boys for examinations and future studies. One of our scholastics conducted the school choir in performances at the university, as well as giving piano recitals for the local branch of the national radio. In the city I heard a concert given by the visiting Viennese Boys Choir and saw a production of *A Midsummer's Night Dream* by John Alden's Australian Shakespearian Company. Those evenings broke a drought of nearly ten years, since I had not been to public plays or concerts after entering the Jesuits. Alden's production enthralled me, although it probably fell well below the performances of *Othello*, *Richard III*, and other works by Shakespeare, in which I had seen Anew McMaster, Laurence Olivier, Anthony Quayle, and Diana Wynyard when they visited Australia in the late 1940s.

Later I regretted not having taken the opportunity of that year in Perth to make trips down to the forests in the South-West and up to Geraldton. Uncle Jim had served for eleven years as bishop of Geraldton, where he encouraged the priest-architect John Hawes to build a remarkable series of stone churches, including the cathedral itself. To the north of Perth, I did, however, visit New Norcia, a village built around a nineteenth-century Spanish Benedictine monastery. We did not find the Vatican and the Spanish flags flying together, as legend sometimes asserted. The museum contained various objects dating back to the earliest efforts made by the Spanish monks to help the Australian indigenous peoples. Under a small square of cloth one read: 'This is the cloth with which Bishop Salvado began his work of civilizing the natives by clothing the nakedness of a native woman. It was shortly afterwards found up a gum tree.' My only other major trip was down to Boyup Brook for the funeral of my uncle Patrick.

Mother's two brothers, Patrick and Gerard, had both settled on the land in Western Australia, married, and raised families. In early 1958 uncle Patrick's eldest child and only son died in a car accident. Eighteen months later uncle Patrick suddenly collapsed and died himself, having never really adjusted to the loss of the son who was to take over his property. When news of his death came, the rector of St Louis bundled me into his car and at once drove me two hundred miles down to Boyup Brook, driving back alone that same afternoon. It felt strange staying for a few days in a private house, something I had not done for close on ten years. Sympathetic presence was all I could offer aunt Eileen, who was shattered by this second fierce blow in less than two years. The simple country style of Mass and funeral touched me. During the Mass a farmer offered his tribute by singing with fair competence the long Gregorian offertory. Afterwards I wondered whether he had learnt the Latin chant years before at some Benedictine school in England.

One sensed the English influence in that part of Western Australia. The local bishop, Lancelot Goody, was the only English-born Catholic bishop in Australia. Some notable people from the United Kingdom had taken up properties after World War II. At the funeral I met Lord and Lady Byron[2] and Air Vice Marshal Sir Ranald MacFarlane Reid, an air ace from World War, and his wife. An even more distinguished airman from World War II, Air Chief Marshal Sir Basil Embry, lived nearby on his sheep station.

During the rest of 1959 I saw something of the MacFarlane Reids and their two children, a boy in his early twenties and a teenage daughter. Their son had studied with the Benedictines at Ampleforth and then took, I think, a year or two at Cambridge University before migrating to Australia. Initially he worked as a jackeroo 'back of Bourke' before moving to more hospitable country in the South-West of Western Australia. His parents and sister followed him out. For a time he was friendly with uncle Patrick's eldest daughter, but eventually married someone else. Lady MacFarlane Reid was American, about fifty years of age, and had attended a convent school in Paris. I enjoyed her liveliness and stories. When the archbishop of Paris visited her school, the nuns made a special point of presenting to him the daughters of a Russian nobleman, who in December 1916 joined others in killing Rasputin, who was considered anything from a saintly healer to a religious charlatan but who certainly exercised a strong influence over the Russian imperial family. Was it because the girls belonged to an aristocratic family in exile that they met the archbishop? Or had their father's deed given them a special aura in the eyes of the nuns? I was never clear about that. Now in his middle

2 Like MacFarlane Reid and Embry, Rupert Frederick George Byron, the 11th Baron Byron, had a farming property, but, unlike them, he had been born in Western Australia.

sixties, Sir Ranald was enthusiastic about the mild rigours of country life, slightly deaf and, as far as I remember, not a Catholic. He seemed to annoy his wife slightly by recalling a time when they lived near Oxford and he met Hilaire Belloc's granddaughters. 'Gad, they were beautiful', he remarked, as if his standard of beauty could never again be met once he had seen them. Quite unawares the MacFarlane Reids drew me towards England and the two old universities.

Back at St Louis an important Jesuit from Rome, Fr John Swain, stayed with us for a holiday during his official visit to Australia. This Canadian Jesuit, who enjoyed a remarkable memory for names, had become vicar-general to the head of our order, the Belgian Fr John Baptist Janssens. During a stopover in Sydney, Swain, accompanied by the Australian provincial (Fr Dermot Hogan), went on a courtesy call to Cardinal Norman Gilroy, who vigorously protested, 'Your men are not loyal to me.' The cardinal had in mind above all the staff of the Institute of Social Order and their journal, *Social Survey*. They favoured the Democratic Labor Party and Santamaria's movement (later known as the National Civic Council), while the cardinal lent his support to the Australian Labor Party. But he was so partisan in his angry criticism that he saved Fr Hogan the need to defend the Jesuits at the Institute of Social Order.

We took Fr Swain out for a picnic in the hills above Perth, showed him the first kangaroo he had ever seen, and let him take one or two religious knowledge periods. I met him as he emerged from one class with handclaps still rippling around the room. 'They gave me an *acclamatio*', he observed with a smile. I only hoped he had not heard me shouting angrily at a boy in Syntax II. Among the significant changes that followed Fr Swain's visit to Australia was the right of scholastics to begin theological studies after ten years in the order. Every Christmas Eve the superiors of all our houses in Australia posted the status, a document from the provincial that announced new assignments for the coming year. I was delighted to find that, in accordance with the new 'ten year regulation', my name was 'on the *status*' to begin theology at Canisius College, situated in the Sydney suburb of Pymble.

The year of teaching in a hard working and happy community fed my sense of Jesuit family spirit. Fr Austin Kelly was supposed to have described St Louis School as 'the Duntroon of the province'.[3] Apart from one Jesuit in a Perth parish and two at St Thomas More College at the University of Western Australia, we lived two thousand miles from the nearest Jesuit community (in Adelaide). Normally the most competent scholastics were sent to St Louis (as budding officers posted to their 'Duntroon'). We found it agreeable to live for a time so far from the provincial's headquarters in Melbourne, and enjoy a few minor relaxations (like frequent surfing at a nearby ocean beach) that the stricter regime in Jesuit houses 'back east' did not allow. The first resolution I made at the end of the annual retreat in December 1959 called for 'kindness towards and interest in every member of the Company. To give up time entertaining another Jesuit should not be considered time lost, but a joy and privilege. I should go out of my way to meet, write to, and pray for other Jesuits.' I concluded that resolution by noting that that I must 'pray for vocations'.

Over the next two or three years about ten boys from St Louis School entered our novitiate, most of them, I suppose, influenced in their decisions by the scholastics they knew and admired. Only one has remained a Jesuit. All the rest left as novices. I puzzled over that series of departures, since I still took our harsh system for granted but knew them to be generous-hearted boys. Had they, with one exception, all become lonely and capitulated to a longing for the sun and surf of Western Australia? Or were they signalling the fact that in the 1960s the system of Jesuit training needed a drastic overhaul?

---

3 The Royal Military College for training officers was situated at Duntroon, on the outskirts of Canberra.

The Move to Pymble

In January 1960 I travelled 'back east' by train, reading half a dozen novels by Evelyn Waugh to relieve the tedium of the journey across the desert. Its miles of surf beaches, months of winter sunshine, and harbour of unsurpassed beauty made and make life in Sydney physically most attractive. Canisius College stood on twenty acres of prime land in one of the opulent north-shore suburbs. Thirty years earlier, the Society of Jesus bought the property from an orchardist, who left the property after he shot a policeman and was acquitted on a technicality. Crowded with roses, camellias, jacarandas, magnolias, oaks, and gum trees, our garden spread around an unobtrusive, double-storey, brick building, which stretched away in two wings towards 'the forest', a stand of gum trees seventy feet high or more. Beyond the forest you reached an oval, one or two tennis courts, and paddocks for several cows. In the other direction, the college looked across a busy road to reserves, through which we wandered for miles to take our 'villa' at inlets of Middle Harbour or on sandstone outcrops among the flourishing gum trees.

Four years of theological studies faced me. About thirty-five scholastics, half a dozen priests, and three or four brothers made up the community. Greg Dening and John Eddy joined me in the first year, as well as Peter Coleman who had returned from seven years in India, weakened by an attack of polio. Bill Daniel and my cousin, Patrick Lewis, were a year ahead of me in the course.

We rose at 5.25, did an hour's meditation before Mass, performed the usual daily round of two examinations of conscience, spiritual reading and the rosary, and met for community litanies in the evening. I made my meditation and said my prayers in business-like fashion, but can recall very little detail, except for the haunting impact on me of a prayer from John Henry Newman. It begins: 'O Lord, support me all the day long.' After the novitiate I had gradually abandoned exercises of penance, and finally parted with my chain and discipline on the Nullarbor Plain. After I left Perth on the transcontinental train, several articles disappeared from one suitcase: a couple of Evelyn Waugh's novels, a pair of shoes, and my chain and discipline. When I discovered the loss, I imagined a guard limping along the train's long corridors with my chain around his thigh, stopping to read a further chapter of *Scoop*, and returning to his compartment to atone for his misdeeds by a few strokes of the discipline.

At Canisius the liturgical services were still in Latin. The celebrant never preached a homily at Mass. The only sermons we ever heard were over dinner (at which each scholastic had to preach once a year), or at occasional meetings for 'tones' or practice sermons. In an Australian Jesuit house of formation I never heard a homily at Mass before 1969. In all the chapel services we had to follow the rubrics and prescribed texts meticulously. One newly ordained priest altered an invocation at benediction by calling on 'St Teresa of the Child Jesus', instead of 'St Teresa of the Infant Jesus', to pray for us. He was reprimanded for this and, without waiting for his normal turn to come up again, had to give benediction again and say the prayer correctly. With competent precision we often sang the office of Compline and, on some Sundays, Vespers. I belonged to the choir, did singing exercises regularly, and learnt to sing a High Mass exactly.

Our Professors

Nearly all our classes came in the long and crowded morning. Major subjects involved up to five periods a week. Fr Val Moran, our rector and a large Irishman in his late forties, drew on immense learning to delight us with ironical judgments and illuminating stories for his courses in church history. 'Pius IX', he once observed, 'was both surprised and pleased to hear that his secretary of state, Cardinal Giacomo Antonelli, had asked for the last sacraments when he was dying.' Regrettably no one ever recorded the two or three exhortations that Val delivered to us each year in his role as rector. This genre of address blended spiritual instruction with disciplinary admonition. He made them finely phrased, superbly delivered, and witty masterpieces—like his everyday conversation. Someone from a government agency for artificial insemination came one day to service one of our cows. When Val heard that the cow had kicked the man into a ditch, he commented, 'I suppose she doesn't care for a bull in a bowler hat.'

We enjoyed first-rate scripture teachers in Bill Dalton and John Scullion. Both graduates of the University of Melbourne and the Biblical Institute in Rome, they were young, professionally qualified, concerned to publish, and ecumenical in outlook. Thanks to them, I read W.F. Albright, C.H. Dodd and Vincent Taylor. One could put together a more radical team of non-Catholic authors, but by contrast in dogmatic theology we had no access to Barth, Calvin, Luther, Tillich and other classical figures in Protestant theology. Bill and John also took me regularly to an inter-denominational biblical fellowship that met at Sydney University. At those meetings I came into contact for the first time with rabbis (one of whom showed me over his synagogue), made some new non-Catholic friends, and learnt to shed more of my prejudices, even if I provocatively chose James 5:14-15 as the topic for the one paper I read to the fellowship. (Catholics have traditionally cited that passage to justify the sacrament of extreme unction, as we still called it then.) There was no departure from my assured vision of the Church. I saw no reason to query Pius XII's encyclical of 1943, *Mystici Corporis*, which taught that those who did not 'profess the true faith' could not 'be accounted really members of the Church'. Through the biblical fellowship I first came to recognize how extremely 'evangelical' many Sydney Anglicans could be, once they moved from 'mere' scripture to theology. The principal of Moore College, their seminary at Sydney University, like some Calvinists used the mnemonic 'Tulip' to list his essential doctrines. T stood for 'the total depravity of human nature', U for 'unconditional election', L for 'limited atonement' (since Christ was not believed to have died for all human beings), and I for 'irresistible grace'. After all that 'perseverance' (for which P stood) hardly seemed necessary.

Unlike scripture and church history, dogmatic theology was taught in Latin. A tall, swarthy Australian in his mid-forties, Fr Peter ('Pedro') Kenny offered us courses in such areas as grace, original sin, and the Eucharist. After postgraduate studies in Europe, he brought back Karl Rahner's ideas, and from the 1950s spread them among Australian Catholics. One (American) seminary dubbed him 'Concupiscence Kenny', as he clearly and forcibly expounded Rahner's ideas on that topic, and went on to write the relevant article in the *New Catholic Encyclopedia*. Pedro gave retreats, contributed to the *Australasian Catholic Record*, the *Clergy Monthly*, *Heythrop Journal*, and *Sursum Corda*, and in other ways acted like a normal, if superior, professor of dogmatic theology in those days, except for one thing: his interest in religious art. Until he resigned over some disagreement, he belonged to the committee that awarded the annual Blake Prize for Religious Art. Pedro indulged a taste for colourful language and vestments. In one article in *Quadrant*, he complained of some artists 'being locked in the airless hole of their own egoism'. Although not yet in orders, I occasionally took the part of sub-deacon at High Masses that he sang at a nearby convent. Pedro looked particularly fine in red vestments, as he sat there in the marble-floored sanctuary on a large cushion, letting the silk chasuble flow down across his feet and waiting for the choir to finish the *Gloria* and the *Credo*. The breakfasts of strawberries and chicken that followed were fit for oriental potentates.

Pedro read the Greek and Latin fathers with deep affection, appealed to the scriptures (sometimes in a startlingly uncritical fashion), linked theology with liturgy, and governed his own statements by constant reference to the authoritative pronouncements of popes and church councils. Very occasionally he lapsed into empty speculation, as when he spent one or two classes discussing whether the blessed can eat in the next life. Half joking at himself, he observed, 'You might put the question this way: Will there be sewers in heaven?' In wooden receptacles that looked exactly like a bricklayer's hod, we carried each day a set of books to dogma classes: Denzinger's collection of official definitions and doctrines, Rouet de Journel's selection from the fathers, Merk's or Bover's edition of the Greek New Testament, a copy of the Vulgate (Latin) Bible, and usually one volume from a series of Latin textbooks produced by Spanish Jesuits and published by the *Biblioteca de Autores Cristianos*. For almost every thesis Pedro could find appropriate documents in Denzinger that established the main lines of our position. Behind our wall of books we could escape from note-taking to non-theological reading when lectures became too tiresome. Sometimes for several days on end, Pedro used the entire period to talk at us, without allowing any time for questions or discussion.

By 1960 he had abandoned some excessive claims he had made earlier for the authority of papal encyclicals, but still insisted on the importance of 'theological notes', which graded the degree of certainty or probability attaching to theological propositions. He normally settled the question by examining the nature of negative judgments that church pronouncements had passed on opposing errors. These judgments ran all the way from anathematizing heresy to declaring that some teaching was 'dangerous, temerarious, and offensive to pious ears'. Early in our first year Greg Dening brilliantly expounded some thesis on grace at an official class repetition. Pedro's only reaction was regret that Greg had failed to announce the theological note of the thesis.

At that time Pedro was probably the best Catholic teacher of dogmatic theology in Australia, far superior to his opposite number at St Patrick's College in the Sydney suburb of Manly, T.W. ('Bull') Muldoon, who in 1960 became an auxiliary bishop for the Sydney

archdiocese. During a class Muldoon was examining one day the
views of several classical theologians on some issue. He would lift up
a volume, discuss the author briefly, and then drop the volume on the
floor with the comment 'Suarez', or whoever it was, '*nescit* (does not
know), using the church pronunciation of 'sh' for 'sc' in *nescit*. And
so it went on: 'Suarez *nescit*, Cano *nescit*, and Bellarmine *nescit*', until a
student murmured half-aloud, 'Muldoon, bull shit'.

After well over ten years of continuous teaching, Pedro returned
to Europe for a sabbatical, developed a taste of the thought of Pierre
Teilhard de Chardin, and published books on the notion of the
supernatural, non-Christian religions, and anonymous Christianity.
He gave strong support to the Catholic Family Movement,[4] and
continued to be an excellent retreat director, although now handling
the role in a more flexible fashion. From 1969 I was to enjoy working
with him, not least because of his shift away from a somewhat sterile
'orthodoxy' to a tolerant peace with theological diversity.

I have dwelt at length on Pedro, because he stood head and
shoulders above the other priests who taught us dogmatic theology
for all or part of my four years at Pymble. A word about two of
them: Joe and Hank. A towering, kindly American, Joe had been a
close friend of Daniel Berrigan, who was to be gaoled because of his
opposition to the Vietnam War. Joe's uncritical enthusiasm alienated
me for life from the thought of Bernard Lonergan and nearly did
the same for Thomas Aquinas. Hank, an angular Irishman, dictated
summaries at us, required that we memorize them, and once summed
up the ecumenical movement as follows: 'You listen to their questions
first, and then you give them all the answers.'

Peter Kelly taught us canon law (a minor subject in which we
covered selected sections from the 1917 code), and moral theology

---

4 In this and similar movements, groups of married couples would meet for discussion,
prayer, the Mass, and a meal in the home of two of the members.

in which we spent two years studying two large volumes, Genicot's *Theologiae Moralis Institutiones*. We learnt a traditional Catholic system of morality, dominated by (1) the decisions of popes, councils and synods, and (2) the opinions of authoritative moral theologians of the past and present. We respected dead authorities like Arregui, Liguori, Noldin and Vermeersch and such living authorities as John Ford and Gerald Kelly, but dissociated ourselves from 'laxists' like the seventeenth-century moralist Antonino Diana, nicknamed 'the lamb of God' because he took away the sins of the world. On the good side, those two years trained us to reach moral decisions on the basis of reasoned principles rather than hasty and shallow judgments. On the bad side, Genicot represented a legalism that effectively divided human actions into sinful and non-sinful, bypassed the scriptures, and entertained us with relatively minor questions. What precisely constituted genuine *vinum de vite* (wine from the grape) that could validly serve for the Eucharist? Could one use rosewater for baptism? What broke the Eucharistic fast? Originally published in the nineteenth century, Genicot had undergone several revisions and we used the 1953 edition. But a few ancient oddities lingered on. I read that a wife had the right to refuse intercourse with her drunken husband, on the grounds that a conception which might take place could lead to the baby being born a deaf-mute. When I drew Bill Daniel's attention to this curious piece of biology, he nodded wisely and asked: 'Don't you realize that all the humours go to the seed?'

Slim, dark-haired, and charmingly courteous, Peter Kelly had taken a law degree at the University of Adelaide before entering the Society of Jesus. He educated us to respond to concrete problems with understanding and sympathy, constantly introduced us to the current literature on moral issues, and arranged a series of visiting speakers. Some psychologists, doctors, and social workers (including my aunt Mary Lewis) offered lectures and led discussions on human development, sexuality, teenage problems, and alcoholism. A complex modern man, Peter remained, nevertheless, essentially loyal to the role of transmitting an integral tradition of Catholic moral teaching. Through their key positions in seminaries, a few teachers of moral theology around the world secured an astonishing uniformity in the judgements priests offered in the confessional.

Our course in moral theology led up to an examination in hearing confessions, the '*ad auds.*', short for '*ad audiendas confessiones*'. For that we needed to know exactly the limits of our powers to hear confessions, a list of excommunications penitents might have incurred,[5] and the proper methods of procedure when only a higher church authority had the power to lift an excommunication for some rare and heinous sin. A professor at St Mary's College, Kansas, is supposed to have told his astonished class that 'perfect' sodomy committed with a pope on a 'reserved' altar would constitute the most difficult case for absolution from church censures. Our examiners normally avoided absurd and trick questions, presenting standard confessions in which they played the role of penitents who accused themselves of theft, lies, adultery, missing Mass, uncharitable gossip, and other such sins. After 'confessing his sins', one examiner did, however, go on to ask John Eddy's advice about a school to which he might send his hermaphrodite child. John reacted by asking: 'Has this happened in your family before?'

Once or twice a year the whole community met for a formal academic event, the *disputatio menstrua* or *menstruum*. It drew its name from the fact that we were given a month to prepare it. Scholastics defended theses in Latin, as in those latter-day survivals of medieval disputations that I had already experienced at Loyola College. But English was used for other items on the programme, and we dealt with contemporary topics. On different occasions I shared in a panel discussion about interpreting 'eschatological' language (or the

---

5 In nearly fifty years of priestly ministry I have never been faced with a penitent under an excommunication.

language in the Bible dealing with the last things), and read papers on church-state relations and the importance of literary criticism for understanding the New Testament.

One of my class organized an inter-seminary association, which brought Columbans, diocesan students (from St Patrick's College, Manly), Jesuits, Marists, and other seminarians together for two or three afternoon conferences a year. We chose themes like the theology of work, which cut across the normal classification of theological subjects. The speakers distributed their papers beforehand, groups met for discussion, and, after an elaborate afternoon tea, a general session concluded the afternoon. This successful student organization showed up the dismal lack of official collaboration between Catholic seminaries. Hardly any exchange of staff ever took place between the half dozen seminaries in Sydney, let alone any mergers that could have raised the level of teaching and provided larger libraries. I can recall only one occasion of official sharing by another seminary. We went across from Canisius to St Patrick's College to hear two lectures by a visiting American scripture scholar, Fr Bruce Vawter.

During my four years at Canisius, Frank Sheed called on us, and two Jesuits, Fr Bernard Leeming and Fr Robert North, came to teach for a term. Born and educated in Sydney, Sheed had established the London (and later New York) publishing house of Sheed and Ward. On his visit to Australia he stopped first in Brisbane, where the Catholic archbishop, Sir James Duhig, had as his coadjutor Dr Patrick Mary O'Donnell. Sheed later called on Dr Mannix, still the legendary Catholic archbishop of Melbourne, who slyly asked: 'What news of Sir James? And how is Lady Mary?' In 1961 Leeming gave us a good course on sacramental theology, but his most significant effect in Australia was to give the ecumenical movement a remarkable nudge through his blend of English charm and warm enthusiasm. A wandering, American polymath based on the Biblical Institute in Rome, North took us through sections of the Old Testament. He also lectured at a milestone in Australian inter-denominational relations, the 1963 biblical conference held at Sydney University.

Dennis Nineham (then at King's College, London) and Günther Bornkamm from Heidelberg provided the keynote lectures. I marvelled at the tentativeness of Nineham (who prefaced some remarks by saying, 'May I suggest what might just possibly be the beginning of an explanation)', as much as at the critical rigour of his German friend. I felt mildly put down when, in answer to a question, Bornkamm refused to allow me to use a passage from Romans to illuminate what Paul meant in 1 Corinthians. Several years later in Cambridge I was to hear Bornkamm deliver a visiting lecture in the Divinity School. When I opened my broad-margined edition of the Greek New Testament to make a note, it seemed surprising to find the note already there. After this happened a couple of times, I realized that I had heard the same lecture before—ten thousand miles away in Sydney.

That 1963 conference enthralled me, as we clipped on our nametags and trotted around Sydney University to hear lectures, take meals, and make new friends. For me these included John O'Neill, then still teaching at Ormond College in Melbourne but soon to take a chair at Westminster College, Cambridge. It was my first professional conference, and initiated me into some of the ways in which real scholars and marginal figures behave on such occasions. A Baltic philologist read a paper that explained why women had found Jesus' tomb to be empty on the third day. His body had decayed at a remarkably rapid speed!

Surviving Canisius

I passed through the four years at Canisius College generally enjoying the community life but sometimes feeling under strain. The conditions for human and religious life surpassed what I had experienced at Loyola. In all sorts of ways we were less cut off from the outside world. We received the morning paper and could leave the college more frequently. I was able to see a stage production of *My Fair Lady*, as well as Robert Speaight playing in *A Man for All Seasons*. Greg Dening took me to watch Gary Sobers make a graceful century against the Australian Eleven on the Sydney Cricket Ground—the first test match I had seen since the 1940s. I renewed my driving licence, since scholastics were allowed to drive the one or two cars that the college owned. The staff lived in much closer and more friendly contact with the scholastics and brothers. At Loyola we might have periodically complained about the ban that was introduced on hitchhiking, but it never occurred to us to question such larger matters as the structure of philosophical studies. At Canisius, however, some scholastics seized the opportunity provided by a 1961 'visitation' of the Australian province to press for change. During such a visitation, the Jesuit who came from another province to act as visitor had wide powers to shift personnel, close houses, initiate new works, and make other far-reaching changes. Our visitor was Fr John McMahon, who had been provincial of the New York province. Thanks to him, we secured a few alterations in the curriculum: notably, I think, greater freedom about class attendance. From the end of 1962 we began to receive the results of our examinations. Previously one was notified only of failure.

As Canisius became more crowded, scholastics contributed to plans for an additional wing. Building operations were about to start, when another scheme emerged. With the aim of shifting the theological college to Melbourne, Fr McMahon authorized the purchase of some land in Narrewarren. On the outskirts of Melbourne, the property was about forty minutes by car from Corpus Christi College, Glen Waverley. At that time Jesuits staffed this seminary, to which diocesan students came after three or four years at Corpus Christi College, Werribee. The idea was that if our theological college was built at

Narrewarren, a more efficient use could be made of Jesuit staff. They could commute and teach daily in both colleges. As it was, some of the Canisius faculty sometimes spent a term at Corpus Christi, and one professor occasionally came up from there to teach at Canisius. Thank God, the Australian Jesuits never paid for a building in Narre Warren, and remained free to move their theological college in 1969 to a location in the heart of Melbourne. The only building operations I watched during my four years at Canisius were those I shared in, at our villa on the south coast of New South Wales.

For years the scholastics could spend a week of their May and September vacations working in Gerroa with a local builder, Ken Watson. He put up the main house on top of a cliff looking straight down Seven Mile Beach. During my time at Canisius, Ken added a smaller house across the street. We worked hard under his direction, cooked for ourselves, enjoyed a plunge in the surf before dinner, and were constantly entertained by Ken, a classic Australian from the bush. 'A surf boat', he assured me, 'rode in here so fast one day that smoke was coming from its sides.' He told us of a skin diver who was fishing at the 'bombora', a submerged reef not far from our house. A shark swept by to snap off his mask and a piece of skin from the end of his nose. The woman who ran the local store used to keep an eye on local activities by raking the area with her field-glasses. Ken suggested that we should put up a notice in our front window: 'Mrs Pocock, if you can read this, you shouldn't be looking.' We went down in parties of seven or eight for a week at a time. I painted fences, cooked meals, and watched the line of breakers shimmer and grow dark as the last light left the sky. In 1963 those peaceful and refreshing breaks at Gerroa were stopped. Apparently superiors believed that we should (and would) do more study, if we all stayed at Canisius right through the May and September vacations.

That year we started classes in February, the May vacation was cut down to ten days, and two scholastics suffered mild nervous breakdowns. Right through my four years at Canisius there was too much tension, brought on by our collective refusal to face the need for massive change and, in particular, for eradicating some elements that suggested a disciplined boarding-school rather than the common life of dedicated Christian adults. In 1961 I was beadle for the year, a job that drove me frantic but never prompted me to seek large scale innovations. I had to ring the house bell a dozen times a day, take responsibility for a mass of domestic arrangements, and go hat in hand to the rector with requests from the scholastics. If he granted a 'coffee', that meant cake and coffee after the midday meal and free time until late in the afternoon. Woe betide me, if I failed to get a coffee on those Saturday afternoons in winter when some scholastics wanted to watch their favourite rugby team play.

We never shared our feelings sufficiently. We remained stuck in an ordered regime that failed to help individuals in their emotional needs. The upshot was that at some point in my four years of theology over fifty per cent of the scholastics were or had been visiting psychologists. Only one or two in the community openly raised questions about what was causing this. We shrank from making those who received therapy feel that they were doing anything strange or reprehensible. One priest who came to give a triduum angered us by asking: 'What kind of Jesuits are those who prefer to visit a psychologist rather than their spiritual father?' The same priest described those who left the order as 'trampling on the blood of Christ'.

During my stay at Canisius only two scholastics departed from our community, but twenty or so in other houses left the order. The groups who entered the novitiate between 1955 and 1965 seemed particularly prone to heavy casualties both as novices and as scholastics. The root cause was clear. Superiors, spiritual fathers, and others in key positions placed so much stress on external observances and the performance of one's 'spiritual duties' that they made their communities, especially Loyola College and Campion Hall, look more like military academies than houses where we supported our companions in living as disciples of Jesus. Affectionate concern for one another's real feelings, needs, and problems was widely lacking. In their university studies scholastics competed fiercely against one another. It was not good enough to do as well as one could. Only the top places really counted. This atmosphere triggered in the less brilliant a smouldering sense of inferiority. The rule, the order of time, and hard work smothered loving sensitivity. When I returned to Canisius after my father's death, I can recall only Greg Dening asking with warm sympathy, 'How are you feeling?' One scholastic staggered me with his question, 'Did you have a good time in Melbourne?' I suppose he wanted to express some sympathy, but was so inhibited that these totally inappropriate words came out.

My own reactions to departures from the order changed. When a brother left during my early years at Loyola, it felt as if he had died. One day in the mountains north of Melbourne I ran into a picnic party, a young man with his wife and children. We chatted away happily until he asked me about a former school-friend, a scholastic who had recently departed. My sense of shame at telling this friendly stranger what had happened made me wish the bush track would suddenly split open and swallow me up. Instead of feeling chill horror at someone's departure, I gradually came to accept the news in the spirit of dull resignation at another casualty. Not until the late 1960s did we receive any official notification, when a priest, scholastic, or brother was dispensed from his vows. The news travelled by word of mouth or through private letters. Some scholastics talked it over with their contemporaries before they left. Others, after making the necessary arrangements with superiors, abruptly disappeared. This could come as a complete surprise. Others departed after seeming unhappy and unsettled for some time. With the wish that we should all read it, one of my contemporaries left behind a letter from the Jesuit general approving of his departure. The two scholastics who left during my time at Canisius went around the whole community to say goodbye.

The thought of quitting never crossed my mind. Yet the strain of our intense and regimented religious life at one stage brought on a nervous twitch and burst a small blood vessel in one eye. Work on the biography of my grandfather and contacts with relations and friends helped to keep me going.

When Peter Coleman arrived at Canisius, he was still weak from the polio he had contracted in India. I cleaned his room, carried his banana bed to class (which for the first year he attended lying down), and took him swimming. He was thin, limping, and prematurely grey, but determination shone through his vivacious eyes. He had set his mind on recovering sufficient strength to be able to resume missionary work in India. Once or twice a week he swam in a rock pool on the edge of a surf beach. As the weather turned cooler, my cousin Patrick Lewis and I stood shivering on the rocks, while we watched him painfully completing yet another lap of the pool.

Mostly we used a college car for these trips to the ocean. When she was in Sydney, Barbara Coleman, Peter's only sister, took us in her car. A sense of heroic generosity hung in the air, so that her blond hair and brown body proved only mildly distracting. Barbara herself went to India in 1961 to work for Leonard Cheshire, a top pilot with the RAF, who won the Victoria Cross for his exploits in bombing Germany, was an official observer at the dropping of the atomic bomb on Nagasaki, and dedicated his later life to founding homes for the aged, hospitals for the incurables, and refuges for lepers. Barbara continued to work for Cheshire in various parts of Asia until 1973 when she married Patrick Lewis. Back in the early 1960s none of us on those trips to the surf would have dreamt that Peter Coleman and Patrick were to be ordained priests but later leave the order and marry. In those days a prominent Melbourne surgeon wanted to marry Barbara and expressed his anger at 'bloody Cheshire' who had led her astray. After the Chinese seized a high altitude plateau and initiated a war with India in October 1962, the surgeon flew to India in a vain attempt to persuade Barbara to come home. She filled her letters with gruesome details of hospital staff dying of smallpox, scorpions blinking solemnly out of the night, and other horrors. When Barbara returned to Melbourne in 1963, my sister Dympna wrote to me: 'Last week was the most fantastic lecture I have ever had the privilege of attending: Barbara Coleman on the Cheshire homes. It was enthralling. She looked so beautiful and talked so humbly about work among the destitute.'

My four years at Canisius brought me very close to Patrick. We went to the crypt of St Mary's Cathedral to see the *Play of Daniel* and to the Cell Block Theatre for the *Wakefield Cycle*. He took me to an exhibition of paintings submitted for the Blake Prize—my first visit to a gallery in over ten years. Occasionally we called on our cousin Vivienne, by now Mother Macgillicuddy in the Religious of the Sacred Heart. I helped Patrick lay out the garden for his mother's new home, a white terrace house in North Sydney that she shared with her sister Dympna and daughter Deirdre. We often had meals there and at times helped to entertain a flock of relatives. They fluttered around Patrick and me, waiting with happy pride to see us priests.

I never noticed how the Society of Jesus had failed to help Patrick grow free of his intensely lovable but strong-minded mother. Geographically he continued to live within her reach. He had been a boy at St Ignatius College, Riverview, had returned there as a scholastic, and was appointed there after his ordination to the priesthood. During the four years at Canisius he also lived close to her. In the Jesuit order he had not studied for a degree, and after failure in philosophy 'went down' to the minor course in theology. In dogmatic theology separate lectures were given to those on the minor course, from whom less was demanded in the examinations. Eventually in 1971 Patrick asked to break off his work at Riverview, and begin studies at St Louis

University in the United States. His course led to a Master of Social Work, freed him from his mother, and allowed him to leave the order and marry with the confident assurance that his midlife journey had brought him home to fulfillment at last. But in the early 1960s I failed to foresee how he would be forced one day to take a stand or else collapse as a person. His affectionate kindness and laughter distracted me.

By and large I gave little more than the minimal time to theological studies, and devoted most of the hours I saved to writing the biography of my grandfather, Patrick McMahon Glynn. I shared in one private group that studied St Matthew's Gospel, gave some free time to reading both the Bible and modern biblical commentaries, wrote for *Kerygma* (a short-lived journal produced by the scholastics at Canisius) an article evaluating the New English Bible translation of the New Testament, and had several scriptural meditations turned down by *Sursum Corda*, an Australian journal of spirituality. A good memory and the ability to speak fluent Latin helped me to success in the examinations, which in the major subjects took the form of orals. Right from the novitiate I had learnt to operate with a broken-up day. This enabled me to concentrate fast and get the most out of periods of theological study.

In 1960 I gathered a set of fruit-cases in my room, filled them with grandfather's letters, diaries, volumes of newspaper cuttings, and other private papers, and set to work organizing the material into a coherent whole. Greg Dening suggested that I should offer for publication some trial chapters. I did this and two articles (which became chapter three and part of chapter four in the completed book) appeared in *Twentieth Century*. At Canisius we had classes on Saturday morning and a villa day on Thursday. I spent many Thursdays in the Fisher Library at Sydney University or, more often, in the Mitchell Library. The Mitchell, a library specializing in Australian history, became my mecca of peaceful research, where the courteous efficiency of the staff encouraged me to forge ahead with the project. I took sandwiches for lunch in the Domain or in the botanical gardens. Any strain of life at Canisius fell away, as I sat on a park bench soaking up the sun in those warm Sydney winters.

The grandfather whom I had never known became intensely real to me. I followed his voyage to Australia, his frustrated attempts to find legal work in Melbourne, his move to South Australia, and his final success when he won a place in the political sun of his adopted country. In January 1961 I travelled by train to Adelaide, where I visited grandfather's home, met old friends and acquaintances of his, checked the records of his law firm, and received help from university staff members. A.J. ('Tacky') Hannan took me to lunch at the Adelaide Club with several aged survivors from grandfather's era. Stuffed heads of African animals shot by members looked down on us. The leather-covered chairs smelt faintly but agreeably, while my grey-haired hosts raked their memories for stories and impressions of 'Paddy' Glynn. I finished my research in Adelaide and took a train up to Kapunda, the country town where grandfather first established himself as a lawyer, politician, and writer. I felt very much at ease during those days of dusty heat. People welcomed me like a returning son and led me to sources on the history of their town to which grandfather had come as a lonely Irish migrant, nearly eighty years before.

My Father's Death

Both coming and going between Sydney and Adelaide, I broke my journey in Melbourne. My father looked peaceful and tired. When he played golf with me nearly two years before, it had been sad to see him weakly nudging the ball down the fairway. Heart failure was draining the power from his thick frame. During a visit to Sydney in 1959, he had fallen ill, but he brushed that aside when I saw him a few months later. He preferred to describe with relish a reception given at a Sydney club by Alfred Hitchcock, then a long-established director of 'thrillers'. A hearse stood outside the club when mother and father arrived. Lighting was subdued. The waitresses were dressed in black, like widows. A number of guests spotted the hearse and drove away at once, thinking that someone had died in the house. Those who came in to the reception stood around chatting nervously and being discreetly filmed by Hitchcock. They jumped and screamed when—at a prearranged moment—a waitress suddenly let a large tray of glasses crash to the ground.

Towards the end of January 1961 I left Melbourne on my way north to resume theological studies in Sydney. A few days later father played—and won—his last game of golf, a fourball with my brother Glynn and two others. On Saturday 4 February, father drove up to Melbourne from Frankston to meet an employee at one of his cinemas; the man had stolen some money. Years before a member of father's law firm had embezzled funds, become desperate when his theft was discovered, and drowned himself. This suicide haunted father. He refused to allow any proceedings against the cinema employee, and tried to help the man make a fresh start in life.

The following Tuesday father retired to bed. On Thursday he got up, put on his dressing gown and went into his study for a few minutes, saying he wanted to look for some letters. As mother discovered later, he had simply searched for his will and put it on top of his desk, so that it would be easily found. He looked gravely ill, when Glynn, then a second-year resident at St Vincent's Hospital, called. Against the wishes of the local doctor, Glynn insisted on calling an ambulance. 'Look after your mother when I'm gone', father told him, as they rushed up to the Mercy Hospital in East Melbourne. When the ambulance team carried father into the hospital, they met a priest who gave him the last sacraments. On Saturday morning Maev phoned to tell me that father was critically ill. That afternoon I flew from Sydney to Melbourne, my first airplane flight as a Jesuit. Jim

Peters, my elder brother-in-law, met me at the airport and drove me at once to the hospital. 'Frank is lying there, saying nothing but fighting back', he told me. 'It's just like when he's one down and two to play.' 'Gerald's here', Jim said when we reached the hospital room. Father's eyes flicked towards me in recognition, but he could say nothing.

Next day he was in a deep coma. His breath came in great, irregular gasps. Except for my brother Jim (who a few weeks earlier had left by ship for further surgical studies in England), all the family were there. Moira clung to her father's bedside with ferocity, as if the strength of her body could somehow ease his going. An old friend, Les Coleman, called to see father, having heard that he was in hospital but not knowing that he was dying. We knelt around the bed to recite the rosary. At three o'clock in the afternoon father's breathing stopped. The room was silent, except for the quiet hiss of the oxygen escaping from the mask. After some minutes mother said, 'I would like to go to the chapel.' Through the sun-drenched afternoon I took her across

Mother and Father around 1946.

the courtyard to the hospital chapel and prayed. 'I want to see him again for a moment', she said. We went back to the room. She pressed a kiss on his forehead and left. Uncle Jim arrived. At fierce speed he had driven down from the country and felt cheated to have come too late for the death of his brother and dearest friend. 'I'll sing a requiem for Frank in the cathedral', he told me, 'if you can find a choir.' Two nuns, old friends who had nursed father during several stays in the Mercy, took me to a room where I phoned Campion Hall. It was immensely cheering when a group of Jesuit scholastics instantly volunteered to sing the Mass. I laid down the phone and wept—the first tears I had shed since childhood. 'We all loved him so much', I murmured to the sisters as the tears poured down my cheeks. Life suddenly seemed strangely lonely. The rock on which I stood had been swept away.

In St Patrick's Cathedral uncle Jim sang the Mass, flanked by his two brothers and two nephews (Bill and John McCarthy). I knelt with mother in the front pew, saddened that I was not yet a priest and could not join my uncles and my cousins at the altar. I took my mother's arm to follow the coffin down the aisle. The cathedral bells tolled and upset me more than the sombre waves of Gregorian chant that had been sweeping across us. I felt so utterly torn with grief, that I wondered how I could support mother out of the cathedral without breaking down. I cannot recall whether mother came to the cemetery in Kew. Moira stood beside me at the graveside and gripped my hand, as the clods thumped down on the coffin. I remembered Euripides' *Alcestis* and prayed: 'May earth fall lightly on you from above.' I have never been back to my father's grave. He is alive and with me. It has always seemed irrelevant to look for him in a cemetery.

We were surprised that the congregation filled the cathedral for father's requiem. For some years he had lived a quiet life at Frankston, being actively engaged with not much more than his business interests and the affairs of Newman College. Hundreds of letters and telegrams poured in. I wrote personal replies to some of them, and arranged for a supply of cards to be printed. The most touching tributes came from 'little people' like the barman at Peninsula Golf Club or from those whom father had quietly but effectively helped at some critical point in their careers. I wrote my own tribute to him for the Melbourne Advocate and for the annual magazine of Newman College.

Ordained Priest

Father's death and my approaching ordination brought me even closer to the other members of my family. Letters came frequently from mother, Dympna, and Maev, and I began to hear from my nephews and nieces. For the first time in my life I began to keep some letters. In August 1962 one nine-year-old nephew informed me: 'Every night we say a prayer for you; I hope you are feeling well. Love, Nicholas Coleman.' Uncle Jim offered to ordain me in his own cathedral, while the other twelve due to be ordained with me would be 'priested' in St Patrick's Cathedral by Archbishop Justin Simonds, the coadjutor archbishop of Melbourne. For a time uncle Jim remained unsure whether proceedings at the Second Vatican Council would allow him to return from Rome for the ordination in early January 1963. Just before the Council had opened in October 1962, he wrote:

> You ask about the date of our homecoming, so as to print cards. So far there is nothing certain. The general opinion is that we will adjourn on 8 December and reassemble after Easter. However, we will know for sure in the first week of the Council—so Cardinal Agagianian told me. At the present all I can say is that you make the arrangements on the assumption that we adjourn on 8 December. If we go on, then you will not have Archbishop Simonds back for your companions. I will let you know as soon as possible. If you prefer it, you can make the same arrangements as the rest of the students and be done [sic] in Melbourne. I will not mind a bit. It certainly is very disconcerting to be kept up in the air on these

matters and I sympathize with all of you. All one knows here is
that the Council will open on next Thursday. I was in St Peter's
this afternoon (Sunday) with Dr Lyons [Bishop of Sale]. No one
is allowed in. However, we went in through the sacristy and found
a few men acting as watchmen. The sight is really frightening: two
long galleries of seats, about 1100 on each side—ever so high up.
I climbed to the top row and sat in one of the seats. How they
will get 2500 bishops into those seats is more than I know; they
are something like theatre seats with a small, pull-up desk. Old
men will never be able to climb up. I dread to think what will
happen. We are meeting bishops from everywhere. We have very
comfortable quarters here. I had an enjoyable time in the USA,
Ireland & England before arriving here. Successful fishing at the
Corib, in the North of Ireland. My above remarks are not for
publication. Hope you are well & with all good wishes etc.

Your affectionate uncle + Jim.

Then a letter from uncle Jim on 12 November gave me the news
I was waiting for:

> You will be pleased to learn, if you have not done so already from
> the press, that we were told yesterday that will resume on 12 May.
> I will be home on the 13 December, and so will have the great
> pleasure of giving you holy orders. The Council is moving along
> a little quicker now. With speeches of not more than ten minutes,
> I find that enough. But how did the bishops suffer speeches of
> some hours? I have seen some of the press reports of the goings
> on of the Council inside and outside [the congregations], and
> I find it hard to believe most of the stuff could be written. We
> Australians had an hour's audience with the Holy Father [John
> XXIII] on Sunday evening. We enjoyed it, & so did the H.F. He
> was in excellent form.[6]

6 Like most of the Australian bishops (with a few notable exceptions such as Archbishop
Guilford Young of Hobart and Francis Rush, newly appointed to the diocese of
Rockhampton), uncle Jim had no sense of the far reaching changes needed and of what
the Council would do in revitalizing Catholic Christianity. See my *Living Vatican II: The
21st Council for the 21st Century* (Mahwah, NJ: Paulist Press, 2006).

On 17 October Maev had assured me: 'It really will be a wonderful experience for the children to see their uncle being ordained by their granduncle, and already several little make-shift altars for practising serving [Mass] have appeared.' 'I have been going to Mass and praying for you', she added, 'and will continue to do so every day, if possible, until your ordination'. Untiringly she helped with all the preparations for what she called 'Operation Ordination', and admitted: 'We are also guilty of referring to it as Gerald's wedding or coronation, as the absent-minded spirit moves [us].' "Moira', she added, 'has caught the ordination fever, very distressing disease. Its main symptoms are looking through lists and shrieking, "You left out the O'Briens; find O'Briens" etc. etc. P.S. Justin and Leslie are very keen to serve as many Masses as possible. I think Stewart is too but a little shy. So be prepared to be followed around like a pied piper.'[7]

In December I was out at Sydney airport to greet a group of tired and unshaven Australian bishops returning from the first session of the Vatican Council. Before he left on a Melbourne flight, I chatted with uncle Jim and settled some details of the ordination. The approach of priesthood filled me with awe. I had prepared myself conscientiously to preach, hear confessions, and administer other sacraments. But it was the Mass that mattered. Long ago in the Frankston church I had learned to share Fr Fitzpatrick's intense devotion to the Eucharistic presence. With his back to the congregation, he stooped over the altar and whispered the words of consecration so softly that only the servers could hear them. With slow reverence he lifted the host high above his head, and for some moments held it there framed by his fingers. Ordination was going to initiate me into that sacred function of standing at the altar to say: '*Hoc est enim corpus meum*' and '*Hic est enim calix sanguinis mei.*'

---

7 Stewart and Justin Peters were sons of my sister Moira, while Leslie Coleman was the eldest son of my sister Dympna.

For weeks I practised the Mass, learning when to genuflect, make signs of the cross, and perform all the other intricacies prescribed by the rubrics. We bought new Latin breviaries, and accustomed ourselves to the elaborate details of the daily office. We were obliged to recite it, once ordained sub-deacons. Just before Christmas we made our annual eight-day retreat under the direction of a visiting Irish Jesuit. He introduced a meditation on sin by suggesting: 'Take a piece of chalk and draw a circle for a mile around this college. Think of all the sins which will be committed within that circle tonight.' It was clear what kind of sins came into his mind. His Jansenism amused us. We were too happy to be disturbed. Some personal notes I made at the time take up the story when I travelled south by train after Christmas:

> On Boxing Day (a Wednesday) 1962 at 8 p.m. with ten other scholastics I left by the *Aurora* for Melbourne and ordination. Two other scholastics to be ordained drove down with Fr Peter Kelly, [now] the rector of Canisius. It was my first visit to Melbourne since my father died in February 1961. Mother & Maev met me at Spencer Street Station where [there] was quite a crowd of Jesuit relatives...Maev drove me for a cup of coffee at Glynn's newly purchased, terrace house in East Melbourne. Then to Mass at St Francis in Lonsdale Street, lunch, and down to Rock Lodge, Frankston, where Jim & Moira, Kevin & Dympna, and their children were holidaying. In the evening Maev drove me to Loyola College. Fr Will O'Collins had been at Rock Lodge and returned to Melbourne with us. As an ordination gift he presented me with a relic of the true cross that he had been given in Rome years before.

> Friday I spent at Loyola meeting the scholastics there. On Saturday morning the ceremony of ordination to the sub-diaconate began. Dr Simonds was the ordaining prelate, and thirteen Jesuits and one Redemptorist were ordained. On Monday morning at nine Dr Simonds ordained all these sub-deacons to the diaconate. Around eleven Maev, my generous chauffeur during the ordination period, was there to run me into the city, and in the afternoon Bishop

O'Collins drove me up to Ballarat. It was the first time I had visited his house since I called in late January 1959 on the way to doing a year's teaching in Perth.

On the Tuesday I said one last practice Mass, in the oratory of the bishop's house & clad in the bishop's alb. That day at the cathedral Fr John Molony, the master of ceremonies and a nephew of Bill Molony of Donald,[8] took me through the ceremonies. Back at the bishop's house, Dr Joe O'Collins, his wife Frieda and their two daughters arrived with Fr Will O'Collins to stay for the night. That evening Frieda ironed any creases out of the beautiful, Gothic vestments of French make which mother and Maev had provided) and the lovely alb with an inset band of lace (which Dympna and Kevin had provided).

Relatives, friends and well wishers crowded the cathedral for the ordination at ten o'clock. During the Mass and the ordination ceremony, a pale altar boy and John Molony distracted me frequently. Eventually the altar boy fainted into the bishop's lap. John seemed extraordinarily nervous. Later I wondered what was going through his mind that day. He was to leave the ministry shortly afterwards, marry, and teach history at the Australian National University. After the ninety-minute Mass and ordination ceremony, I came out of the sacristy to give my blessing. A newly ordained priest made a sign of the cross over the head of men and on the shoulders of women (who still often wore hats in church), and allowed them to kiss both his hands. My mother knelt there, the first in line to receive my blessing (in Latin). I felt so overwhelmed by love and gratitude towards her that I could hardly pronounce the words of blessing.

Forty relatives sat down to dinner with uncle Jim. I wrote in my personal notes: 'I suppose it was only when I arrived at the bishop's house around ten to one and little Bronwen and Joanna [daughters of my sister Moira] rushed out to claim me at the door that I realized

8 Bill had married Mona Peters, a sister of my brother-in-law, Jim Peters.

With Bishop O'Collins and Monsignor Fiscalini, after ordination in 1963.

just what a wonderful event for the family was the ordination.' Warm happiness and the laughing chatter of children filled the dining room. As he sat carving the turkeys, the bishop looked like a lovable, latter-day Abraham presiding over his tribe.

The following day I celebrated my first Mass at the convent of the Sacred Heart. When I rose in the morning, the uncomfortable thought struck me: 'I was so distracted by John Molony and the altar boy that I didn't hear the actual words of ordination.' The Mass itself swept away this absurd scruple. Apart from some English hymns, the liturgy was all in Latin and there was no sermon. I shared a sacred joy with the relatives and friends who had come for the ceremony and the breakfast provided afterwards by the nuns. A whirl of Masses (at convents and in the Frankston parish), a reception at Moira's home, and another reception at Rock Lodge filled the week that followed. I dispensed blessings, ordination cards, and a holy happiness. I felt myself surrounded everywhere by that vivid faith that the event of priestly ordination evoked in Catholics.

Uncle Jim arranged for me to visit Dr Mannix, still at ninety-eight the archbishop of Melbourne. As his legs had failed, Dr Mannix could not rise to greet me when I entered his upstairs sitting room at Raheen. He sat there in an armchair with wisps of white hair curling around the edges of his biretta and seemingly undisturbed by the cool breeze coming through the open window on the back of his neck. We talked for nearly an hour. He spoke of Frank Woods, who had visited him shortly after arriving from England to become the Anglican archbishop of Melbourne. 'I told him', Dr Mannix recalled, 'that I was glad to see him, and explained that I hadn't called on him first simply because I never visit anyone. He said he quite understood, as I was a Jesuit and Jesuits don't visit. He was wrong on both counts', Dr Mannix commented with an ironic smile. 'I'm no Jesuit, and Jesuits do visit.' I enquired about a churchman who had earned his post as auxiliary bishop by devoted work and not for any gifts of open-minded intelligence. 'He's in the Holy Land at present', Dr Mannix told me. 'Is this his first trip overseas?', I asked. 'Oh, no', came the quick answer and I caught the mischievous eyes of the old archbishop: 'He's been to Tasmania.' Uncle Will had pointed out to me that Dr Mannix had become ill shortly before his ninetieth birthday. 'He'll get nervous again', he predicted, 'when he's moving up the straight towards his century.' In fact, Dr Mannix died in November 1963, within six months of his hundredth birthday.

I spent 1963 back at Canisius College, engaged in my last year of theology and frequently taking weekend 'supplies' in parishes around Sydney. All thirteen of the 'fourth-year' fathers were available for such work. (For the sake of the record, let me say that five of us remain active in the ministry; three have died in the Society; and five left the Jesuits and the priestly ministry.) Through 1963 we heard our first confessions, preached and celebrated Mass in a variety of places: a boys' reformatory, the busy churches of newly developed suburbs, well established parishes, or in one of the two Jesuit churches in Sydney. I met my first alcoholic priest, failed to get a single offer when I once preached at five Masses in an appeal for foster parents, and learnt to admire the short and beautifully timed homilies of Fr Tom Costelloe, my former rector from Xavier College and now parish priest of St Mary's, North Sydney. At home we frequently had to say Mass alone and without a server. In those days there was no concelebration.

The year raced by. The biography of my grandfather was nearing completion. My own future work had been determined: teaching theology. During my four years in Sydney I had first been informed by the dean of studies that I was to do graduate studies in dogmatic theology. Then this was changed to scripture. Then once again I was told to prepare to teach theology: specifically, ecclesiology or the doctrine of the church. No superior ever sounded out my personal inclinations in the matter, but it never occurred to me that such decisions should arise through consultation and prayer. I was happy with my future assignment, and looked forward eagerly to finishing my stay at Canisius College with the final or '*ad grad.*' examination. That determined one's personal 'grade' in the Society of Jesus. Success in the examination almost automatically meant that one would take the 'solemn' final vows of a 'professed father': poverty, chastity, obedience, and a special vow of obedience towards the Pope. Failure led to the vows of a 'spiritual coadjutor', who normally could not hold certain posts like the office of provincial.

I was to take my examination on 23 November, a two-hour oral in Latin covering most of the material we had studied in seven years of philosophy and theology. We had the right to protest against the presence of particular priests on the examining board of four. Some of my year refused to allow Hank on their boards, but I decided not to make a fuss. His manner could be awkward, while his theology blended empty logic, isolated texts plucked from the scriptures, and 'facts' selected from church history. Yet he had usually been fair and even generous in the marks he had given me in previous examinations. So I determined not to challenge his presence on my board, take the '*ad grad.*', and leave for Melbourne as soon as possible.

6

The Road to Cambridge (1963-65)

I may be accused of laying stress on little things, of being beside the mark, of going into impertinent or ridiculous details, of sounding my own praise, of giving scandal. But this is a case above all others, in which I am bound to follow my own lights and to speak out of my own heart.

Blessed John Henry Newman, *Apologia pro Vita Sua.*

I walked out of breakfast on 23 November 1963 to learn that President John Fitzgerald Kennedy had been assassinated. He died in Dallas on 22 November, but, given the time difference between the USA and Australia, we heard the news on 23 November. The news cast a shadow over my two-hour *ad grad.* examination that morning and helped to trigger an episode with Hank, the second examiner. He continued to cut in and even stop me in the middle of a sentence, until I exploded with anger. When Peter Kelly's turn came, he pushed away at the question: can someone lose his faith through no fault of his own? I insisted that this could happen. In any case others would be to blame: for example, corrupt church officials who effectively destroyed the person in question. I pointed to a safe example, the canons in Regensburg cathedral in the sixteenth century. Their evil example went even as far as committing murder. Both Peter and I identified 'faith' with Catholic orthodoxy. Hank did not penalize me for our clash. My result was ten out of ten, a *summa cum laude*. That afternoon Hank joined me and two others for a game of golf on a nearby public links and, if I remember rightly, he and his partner won.

That day I decided to start keeping a diary. I felt as if I were emerging from a tunnel into the light of new life. Four deaths during 1963 marked the end of my beginnings. My much loved teacher at Xavier College, Gerry Owens, had died in the middle of the year, a few months before Dr Mannix, who had been Catholic archbishop of Melbourne since 1917. I felt furious when the *Sydney Morning Herald* hardly bothered to conceal its satisfaction at Dr Mannix's passing and falsely suggested that every cause espoused by him had failed. This eloquent, ironic and liberal Irishman was my archetypal archbishop. The two 'Johns', Pope John XXIII and now President John Kennedy, had represented a new world of peace, love, and youth. By the end of 1963 they were also both gone.

Back to Melbourne

By the Southern Aurora I left Sydney for Melbourne on 28 November, happy to be moving from seminary solitude into a wider existence. Uncle Gerald happened to be on the same train, going south for a holiday after preaching in a series of Sydney parishes. His presence conveyed the sense of a pre-arranged welcome home to the world of action. I was back from a place where, in many ways, I had quietly marked time and time had marked me.

If those four years at Canisius left me doggedly devoted to my spiritual duties, order of time, and work, they had also opened me up somewhat to the love of relatives and Jesuit friends. Aunt Mary Lewis wrote to me a few weeks after my departure:

> I simply want to say how much I appreciated your stay in Sydney, and you will never know what it meant to me. You were so affectionate, humble & stimulating, and I will miss you very much.

However, you will always have my prayers, and I will follow your
progress with the greatest interest. With a loving thank you, and
may God bless your endeavours. Very affectionately, Mary.

In Melbourne I met for the first time my brother Glynn's fiancée,
Stephanie Pryde. When I made a speech the previous January at my
ordination dinner in Ballarat, I had suggested that Glynn had drawn up
a list of things to be done: 'Win Peninsula Golf Club championship,
buy a house, get Gerald ordained, etc.' The 'etc.' proved to be a tall,
chatty and very pretty twenty-year-old nurse. Her dark eyes, lovely
skin and black hair hit one smartly. After father died, Glynn had been
the man on whom mother lent. He took much of the responsibility
for decisions about business affairs, while mother learnt to cope with
her changed life and Glynn began specialist work as a radiologist. Like
my three sisters and other brother Jim, I loved Glynn as the baby of
the family, and hoped that Stephanie would give him all the affection
and support we wanted for him. One middle-aged Jesuit vexed me by
asking: 'Isn't her father a Protestant?' His implication was clear. No
child of a mixed marriage could count as a *real* Catholic.

Before leaving Sydney I completed the manuscript of grandfather's
life, which Sir John ('Jack') Barry suggested submitting for publication
by the Melbourne University Press. After growing up a Catholic,
Barry became and remained an agnostic. He had been a friend of
my family for years, but it was only in the sixties that I came to know
him well. He was then a judge of the Victorian Supreme Court. We
corresponded a little. I felt touched both by the way he effectively
encouraged my scholarly work and by his concern for my personal
welfare. It was characteristic of him to begin a letter to me when
I reached Germany in 1964: 'Your time seems fully occupied, and
with the constant impact of new experiences, there will be little time
for the homesickness which, in my experience, is prompt to assail
Australians abroad.' Shortly before he died some years later, we spoke
by telephone. I was about to leave Melbourne to teach for a semester

in Boston. In tones of kind sincerity he warned me against falling victim to the silly season of theology. His blend of friendship and agnostic honesty seemed curiously comforting to my own Christian faith.

Once in Melbourne I called on Hal Gye to ask permission to use his cartoon of Patrick Glynn in my forthcoming book. I found him engaged on a coloured version of the illustrations for C.J. Dennis' *Glugs of Gosh*. Kim Bonython, who devoted a room of his Adelaide home to Dennisiana (the 'Gluggery'), had invited Gye to prepare this coloured version. In the early part of the twentieth century Gye published some short stories in *The Bulletin* under the name of James Hackston. One or two of these later appeared in an Oxford University Press collection, *Australian Short Stories*, which was subsequently translated into German. The translation added brief biographies of the authors. Gye took a copy of the German work off a shelf, and asked me to translate into English his own biographical entry. He chuckled to hear how Teutonic scholarship had thoroughly established the identification of Hal Gye with James Hackston. Along with David Low (who moved to London and became a merciless satirist of Hitler, Mussolini, and Stalin) and Norman Lindsay, he belonged to that fabled group of cartoonists who lifted their art so high in the early decades of the twentieth century. Old and grey and full of gentleness and love, Gye acted as though he were officially welcoming me to a lifetime of writing.

I spent the first half of December on 'villa' in Anglesea at a battered guest-house that the Australian Jesuit province had bought. I served as confessor to some scholastics, said Mass for them, and spent much of my free time playing golf on the local course. Mobs of half-tame kangaroos hung around the fairways and 'rough', looking like small boys hunting for balls lost in the grass. One day I hit a low drive clean through the legs of a kangaroo who in astonishment watched the ball whistle just under its pouch. For years I enjoyed golf, not least because it drew together many members of my family. Golf opens the way to the friendship of others through the highly organized system of play that takes one's mind off any concerns and worries. It calls for a wide variety of shots, offering always the possibility of instant and perfect success. Mediocre amateurs can never bowl a cricket ball as fast or kick a football as far as the top professionals. But in golf everyone can now and then play a shot that would satisfy the best in the world. Uncle Jim once remarked to me: 'Priests who play golf don't leave the ministry.' Cheekily I drew his attention to one or two who had done so. 'Well', he replied, 'at least they left quietly and without making a fuss.'

On 18 December I received the province *status*, which assigned me to begin my tertianship or second novitiate in Münster, West Germany, the following September. After that year I was to do a doctorate in ecclesiology at the Gregorian University in Rome. I sensed a certain parting of the ways with Greg Dening (who would study at Harvard) and John Eddy (who was off to Oxford). We had shared many experiences, notably the years at the University of Melbourne and then theological studies in Sydney. The day after the status appeared I saw Peter Coleman sail from Port Melbourne to resume his work as a missionary in India. Hardly enough strength had returned after his bout of polio in 1959 and subsequent recuperation during our four years together at Canisius. But he limped at life with heroic determination. My diary describes my first Christmas as a priest.

> Dec. 21. I began a summer supply at Immaculate Conception Church in Hawthorn under Fr Henry Johnston as parish priest. Trim, crowned with luxuriant white hair and infuriatingly self-assured, he gives straight answers and lives behind a cool but not intimidating shield. We enjoy playing golf together at Kew Club. Dec. 25. At the parish midnight Mass I performed as sub-deacon. Despite my brother Glynn's urgent invitation to join the family at

Rock Lodge, I decided to remain at Hawthorn for Christmas dinner with the Jesuit community. The triumph of duty over love? The dinner turned out a pleasant, sleepy affair. Nearly all the priests on the staff run to twice my age or more. Dec. 26. Glynn took me for a game of golf at Peninsula Golf Club before he drove me over to Rock Lodge. We found Bishop O'Collins, Fr Gerald O'Collins, Fr Will O'Collins, Fr Bill McCarthy and Dr Joe O'Collins already there. Father seems close when his clan gathers again in his house, which in any case remains charged with his presence.

During my seven weeks at Hawthorn, I heard confessions, said parish Masses, preached, performed my first baptism, and gave my first retreat, a weekend at the Convent of the Sacred Heart for about 75 ladies: single, married, and widowed. One middle-aged woman told me that I reminded her of the late John F. Kennedy! Several of those on the retreat talked with me about severe problems facing them. The evil with which some had to struggle frightened me. I could do little more than murmur: 'It must have been hard to come and speak about this. You seem brave and realistic in coping with your problems.'

After five years away from Melbourne, work in the parish allowed me to meet old friends again. One Sunday morning a class mate from Xavier College who had become a university lecturer in English literature served Mass for me. Beforehand he warned me that he lacked practice. Old instincts reasserted themselves, and just before the people received Holy Communion he inserted a second *Confiteor*. The congregation must have noticed. I wondered how many imagined that I had forcibly co-opted as server some long-standing sinner, a stranger to recent (minor) alterations in the Mass. He had belonged to a literature group I had run at school. Although we met rarely in later years, I always responded warmly to him.

Fr Johnston assigned me a light load of parish duties and allowed time for some theological study. He had himself taught for years in seminaries and published some works in apologetics, like *A Critic Looks at the Catholic Church* and *Plain Talks on the Catholic Religion*. When he noticed me reading Edward Schillebeeckx's *Christ the Sacrament*, he warned me against moving on to Hans Küng: 'He's young and bold and has every mark of an heresiarch.' Fr Johnston may not have known that both Schillebeeckx and Küng were currently official advisers or *periti* at the Second Vatican Council. I would drift away from my initial admiration for both of them.[1]

I went out with mother to the airport to welcome my brother Jim home after three years away, completing his FRCS (Fellow of the Royal College of Surgeons) and then giving time to enriching practice in England and the United States. In my diary I wrote:

'Jim looked haggard as he walked from the plane to meet us in the terminal. It's less, I am sure, a matter of fatigue from the journey across the Pacific than the worry about coming home to professional uncertainty. I hate to see him suffer.'

My easy childhood relationship with Moira, Dympna, and Glynn persisted and kept growing into adulthood. As a child I fought with Maev, but this never mattered. We have drawn closer together as the years passed. In the early sixties she seemed pleased when I sometimes called her 'the family cement'. She played that role by entertaining her nephews and nieces, caring for mother without allowing mother to become dependent, visiting ageing aunts and uncles, and keeping us all together by her sensitive generosity when help was needed.

Uncle Jim officiated at the ceremony and celebrated the Mass when Glynn and Stephanie married in the chapel at Newman College a few months after Glynn had won for the first time (of thirteen times) the championship at Peninsula Country Golf Club. At the reception Sir Norman O'Bryan, (a Supreme Court judge who had been with

---

1 See what I wrote on both of them: *Jesus Risen* (New York: Paulist Press, 1987), 86-94, 15-17; id., 'Newman Seven Notes: The Case of the Resurrection', in I. Ker and A.G. Hill (eds), *Newman After a Hundred Years* (Oxford: Oxford University Press, 1990), 337-52; see also my review in the *Tablet* (5 June 1993) of Küng's *Credo: The Apostles' Creed Explained for Today* (London: SCM Press, 1993).

my father in France during the First World War and who was the father of my school friend also called Norman O'Bryan), proposed the health of bride and bridegroom. The professor of obstetrics and gynaecology at Melbourne University, when proposing the toast to the parents, pointed out that any obstetrics and gynaecology that Glynn or Jim knew they had learnt from him. In his response to Sir Norman, Glynn remarked: 'I'm sorry that my father is not alive to be present here. There were three things he wanted to see: an O'Collins on the championship board at Peninsula, a son ordained a priest, and a son married.' He paused for a moment and looked at Jim: 'But that doesn't let you off the hook, Jim.' Glynn's ethereally holy look at the chapel ceremony had given way to a charmingly satisfied one. My blond-haired niece Joanna Peters, not quite eleven, danced vigorously with her father at the reception. She looked as if she could hardly wait for 'the big time' to begin.

(Retrospect casts a shadow over that wedding. Glynn and Stephanie had five children. Then she ran away with another man, divorced Glynn, and died of lung cancer a few years later.)

The impact on my family of the 1963/64 summer recalled the death of my father three years earlier and my own ordination a year before. We were drawn together in a mood of mutual admiration. Moira now had seven children, her husband ranked as one of Australia's top urological surgeons, and her eldest boy was to be 'dux' or top pupil at Xavier College for 1964. Dympna, as well as bringing up three children, worked untiringly for hospitals, the Australian Jesuit mission in India, and other good causes. Her husband had made his mark at the Victorian bar, and within a decade was to be appointed a County Court judge. Maev, who handled adoptions for the Catholic Family Welfare Bureau, had won wide respect as an effective social worker. Glynn was happily married. Jim was home with his FRCS, and the two brothers were pressing ahead in the medical profession— Jim as a urologist and Glynn as a radiologist. We fought shy of any disagreements, saw a great deal of each other, and gave support when necessary. Still in the honeymoon period of my ministry, I moved along happily as the promising young priest and writer in the family.

I wanted to arrange things smoothly for the future. In any case my boyhood education, Jesuit training and family pride seemed to guarantee that there would be no cracks in the wall of my performance. Occasionally one heard of dissident priests and angry people. But Paul VI, elected pope in July 1963, was following Pope John's lead in bringing the Catholic Church up to date. Xavier Rynne, Robert Kaiser, and other journalists kept us abreast of the progress being made at the Second Vatican Council. Cardinal Alfredo Ottaviani and other curial villains had been unmasked. The prospects for well regulated change looked green.

Corpus Christi

In early February I shifted from Hawthorn to Corpus Christi College, Werribee, where I was to conduct the 'spiritual semester', a form of novitiate for second year diocesan students. I prepared conferences, revised the previous year's bibliography of spiritual reading, and studied a little German. I was surprised to find some of the classical authors on spirituality like the Adolf Alfred Tanquerey (1854-1932) offering lifeless schemes, a kind of holiness by headings. One work—I think it was written by the co-founder of the Maryknoll missionaries—amused me by one lively exception from endless pages of dull abstractions. He stepped aside to comment fiercely on the frequency with which priests and religious could pay unjust wages, tell lies, and allow themselves to commit further basic breaches of natural morality in the name of some 'higher' cause.

The Jesuits who staffed Corpus Christi made me feel a welcome addition to the team. On some evenings the minister of the college took me out in a utility truck to shoot rabbits that infested the grounds.

He roared across the lawns to catch the rabbits in the headlights, while I stood at the back and blazed away with a shotgun over the top of the driver's cabin. At the college five or six Irish nuns took charge of the cooking, laundry, infirmary, and other domestic arrangements. They overheard me practising my German pronunciation. From across the bluestone courtyard at the back of the Chirnside mansion (which formed the core building of the college), I could occasionally hear a sweet Irish voice saying in slightly mocking tones: '*eins, zwei, drei*'.

When the students returned to Corpus Christi at the end of February, a heavy programme began for me. I taught a course on the Synoptic Gospels (Matthew, Mark, and Luke), and took a dozen first-year students in a Latin B class. I pushed them through the grammar, some Augustine, and the easiest passages I could find in classical authors. Although they were beginning their seminary studies only that year, most of the Latin B's were into their twenties, a few years older than the usual first-year seminarians. We jogged along happily together. But every now and then the unspoken question got reflected in their grins: 'Why does this slogging away at Latin *really* matter for us?'

The thirty-nine students whom I directed in the spiritual semester took up most of my time. Both as individuals and as a group I tried to help them enrich and deepen their Christian lives. Youth was on my side, our enthusiastic dedication ran high, and I established myself with them rapidly. We met frequently for conferences on such themes as: the following of Christ, grace, the Trinity in one's spiritual life, prayer, chastity, priestly holiness, devotion to the Sacred Heart, devotion to the Blessed Virgin Mary, the Mass, confession, and liturgy in general. I had worked hard in preparing my lectures, allowed time for questions and discussion, but failed to cater for individual learning processes. It seemed quite clear to me that the spiritual life of these future diocesan priests would best develop by following an adapted form of the spirituality practised by Jesuits. I gave my students the most theologically informed version of that spirituality which I could put together. The New Testament, the three volumes of Karl Rahner's *Mission and Grace*, the work of Joseph de Guibert, some encyclicals of Pius XII, and the 1963 constitution on the liturgy from Vatican II provided the most valuable sources.

The students in the spiritual semester joined the other seminarians in the regular round of daily Mass and further chapel services, including Sunday evening vespers (in Latin) and benediction of the Blessed Sacrament. It never dawned on me that a special group liturgy could have been a fruitful means for promoting spiritual development. But at that time no Australian seminary had begun the practice of shared homilies, spontaneous prayer, and common preparation of the texts for the Eucharist.

On Sundays and important feasts the seminarians sang one of the Gregorian Masses. They performed the Holy Week ceremonies with precision. I was the chief celebrant at the Palm Sunday liturgy. Our procession began under the tower at the entrance to the Chirnside mansion, and circled the buildings on our way to the chapel. The red vestments glowed in the morning sun, as we clutched our twigs of cypress and roared out the ninth- century hymn to Christ, '*Gloria, laus et honor*'.

A constant stream of visitors came to Corpus Christi to offer the students glimpses of a wider world. One evening we heard Bishop Katkoff, a bearded Russian who had left China to live in Rome, describe the progress already achieved at the first two sessions of the Council. He brought a Father George and a Father Seraphim to concelebrate with him in the rite of St John Chrysostom. I was impressed by their custom of addressing each communicant by name. This made communion in our Latin rite resemble an exercise in infantile anonymity. On other occasions we listened to Archbishop

Leonard Raymond of Nagpur and Fr Eric D'Arcy. Eric spoke of studies in Oxford where he had just completed a doctorate in philosophy. There were lay visitors like Herb Elliott, the champion runner. He had broken the world records for the mile and the 1500 metres, as well as winning the gold medal for the 1500 metres at the 1960 Olympic Games in Rome. He fitted naturally into the Corpus Christi scene. The seminarians constantly played football, tennis and handball, and trained hard for athletics. On another occasion John Mulvaney came down from Melbourne University to describe his archaeological work on indigenous sites. I was glad to see again my old friend and former teacher.

The students sometimes staged their own special evening entertainments, notably the Pentecost concert in the college hall. For that they used tunes from *West Side Story*, composed satirical texts, and stumped around the stage mimicking the 'professors' (as they called all the staff). In my case they concentrated on golf and rabbit shooting. In one skit I missed the rabbits, but shot down the rector who happened to be flying a light aircraft low across the grounds at night.

My work at Corpus Christi ended in June. The 'semestrians' invited me to a farewell picnic in a Geelong park. The 'spiritual bouquet' (or '*pneumatikos stephanos*' as they called it), which they presented to me, included 280 Masses, 275 rosaries, 2150 ejaculatory prayers, 180 meditations, and other prayers offered for my intentions. In little less than three months together I had grown to value their generous, boisterous solidarity, and felt touched by their affection.

The period at Werribee brought my first radio broadcast which I took with excessive seriousness. The religious section of the Australian Broadcasting Commission asked me to give a thirteen minute talk on St Mark. I began by insisting that this gospel is the oldest one we have. Both then and later many Catholics and some Anglicans puzzled me by their stubborn opposition to Marcan priority. Did some false quest for security keep them clinging to the view that our (Greek) Matthew comes chronologically first and derives from a primitive (Aramaic) Matthew? I detected here another case of those marginal but 'sacred' beliefs that people refuse to give up, in case all should fall. From Sydney aunt Mary wrote encouragingly: Just a line to tell you how much I enjoyed your talk on St Mark. I recognized your voice immediately and it was such a clear and lucid exposition, and thank goodness not too far above my old head. We all felt terribly proud of you.'

I was also cheered to hear from John O'Neill, then on holidays with his wife:

> I wish you could have seen Judith and me on Sunday afternoon crouched over our transistor on the beach. We disapprove of transistors on the beach, & had smuggled ours down in a shopping bag to hear your delightful talk on St Mark's Gospel. We both thought it was very good indeed: clear, thoughtful and presented at just the right pace. I was particularly glad to hear your simple opening statement that St Mark was the earliest account, & then to realize, as you went on, how closely together Protestant & Catholic scholars are now working on the Gospels. I knew [that] in theory, of course, but it was wonderful to have it demonstrated so clearly & openly in Australia.

John was soon to leave for Cambridge, to take up a chair in New Testament at Westminster College. J.A.T. Robinson, who shook many Christians in 1963 with his *Honest to God*, had supervised John for his Cambridge PhD. Now John was about to return to Cambridge, since he saw the chance in England of doing the work he wanted to do. We exchanged addresses, and looked forward to meeting in Europe. I had no idea that by the end of the year John would have helped me to be accepted for research in Cambridge.

At that time I still expected to begin doctoral studies in Rome in late 1965. I had contacted Fr Jan Witte at the Gregorian University, and he agreed to supervise my proposed thesis, a theological investigation of an ecumenical enterprise in my own country. The Congregational, Methodist, and Presbyterian churches in Australia had begun working towards a union. I planned to study the biblical and theological material that had been produced to help, hinder, or explain this projected inter-church merger. Several times I visited Davis McCaughey, one of the chief architects of the scheme and now master of Ormond College within the University of Melbourne. He provided copies of the relevant articles, position papers, and other material. His friendly courtesy, sharp theological mind, and easy connections with powerful people in academic, professional, and business life struck me. But I never dreamt that he would become one of my dearest friends.

I talked over the topic with John Eddy, then at the University of Melbourne for a few months before he began his research at Oxford. After lunch one day at University House, we strolled across the campus to Newman College to chat with Brian Fleming, a Jesuit six years older than me who had just returned from doctoral studies at Louvain to become dean of Newman. Thin as ever, his face rutted and topped with short hair turning grey, Brian refused to rustle up evidence to support dishonestly a plan he inwardly jibbed at. He evaluated my proposed thesis topic as too slight and too contemporary. John Eddy uttered sympathetic grunts in the background, but declined to offer an opinion one way or the other. Doubtless he realized that two strong and reliable voices in opposition might discourage me from making even a preliminary expedition into the topic. Brian dampened my enthusiasm but I clung to my theme. It satisfied my two theological needs—to be ecumenical and biblical.

Before leaving Australia I had one academic task to complete, my biography of Patrick McMahon Glynn. Melbourne University Press had accepted the work, but requested a few alterations and some expansion of the final chapter. The director of the press, Peter Ryan, was fascinated that grandfather had lunched with Sir Redmond Barry on the day the judge condemned to death the doyen of Australian bushrangers, Ned Kelly. Ryan was working on *Redmond Barry*, a booklet eventually published in 1972 for an Oxford University Press series *Great Australians*. I knew that Barry had four children by a Mrs Louisa Barrow, who lies next to him in Melbourne General Cemetery. Ryan confirmed all that, and assured me that (for reasons of propriety?) Barry never stayed overnight with the lady with whom he was bound by very strong love. He called on her or she called on him.[2]

En Route to Germany

I enjoyed two family gatherings before leaving for West Germany. To celebrate the fiftieth anniversary of uncle Will's ordination to the priesthood, uncle Jim gave a dinner at Ballarat for 'all the family': that is, for all the living descendants of Patrick and Ellen O'Collins and their spouses, if they were married. Jim Peters was about the only absentee. His (then) youngest son and namesake brought into action his best bellows and screams to disrupt the Mass, which uncle Will offered before we sat down to dine. A mass of red curls surrounded a face where the shifting moods ran from breath-taking innocence to spitting insolence. (Now fifty years of age and a leading barrister, Jim along with his wife Sally have become very close friends.) Uncle Will's class in Rome had turned out to be singularly undistinguished; none of them became bishops, archbishops or cardinals. One of them entered the Italian navy (as a chaplain presumably) and was blown up with his ship early in the First World War. Another, a priest from a central European country, collaborated after the Second World War with a Communist regime to the point of being personally excommunicated by the Vatican. With a sense of sad irony uncle Will pointed out that the only member of his class ever to rate a mention in the *Acta*

---

2 Years later Ann Galbally produced a full study, *Redmond Barry: An Anglo-Irish Australian* (Melbourne: Melbourne University Press, 1995).

Apostolicae Sedis was this early friend, whose excommunication that official Vatican publication recorded. Uncle Will stayed with him in 1926, when making his way across Europe to enter the Society of Jesus in Ireland.

My sister Moira gave me a going away party in her large and comfortable home. Most of the guests had come to a similar party she had held after my ordination eighteen months earlier. I remarked in my diary: 'Tonight we could relate more normally. Then many guests tended to treat me like some awesomely sacred object.' Later this sense that people, particularly Catholics, expected to see me playing a 'special', religious role was to prove oppressive and make my quest for self-identity difficult.

En Route to Germany

I left Melbourne on 17 June to stop overnight in Sydney before flying on to India and Europe. On arrival in Sydney I heard that my cousin Vivienne Macgillicuddy had just left the Religious of the Sacred Heart and was returning to Australia. I had planned to visit her at the institute's tertianship in Rome on my way to West Germany. Among my younger female relations on both sides of the family Vivienne was the only nun. It seemed sad that she had to go so far away before she could reach a decision to leave her institute. Her departure struck a slightly chilling note, but hardly dampened my enthusiasm to be visiting that magic land, 'overseas'. I was just thirty-three, my brother Jim had recently returned from three years of graduate work as a surgeon in England and the USA, and now my turn had come to complete my education in Europe. I was making a grand tour in reverse: through India, Greece and Rome, and on to northern Europe.

Aunt Mary Lewis came out to Sydney airport to farewell me when I flew out on an almost empty Boeing 707. Police ringed the terminal as they waited for the return of the Beatles from Melbourne. The group had already roused mass hysteria. The newspapers revelled in photographs of mounted police riding into crowds to snatch up fainting girls and ride out with the limp bodies slung across their saddles. But when I arrived at the airport on the morning of 18 June, there may have been more police than spectators waiting to welcome the Beatles on their second landing in Sydney. I bought a bottle of duty-free whisky for £1, stuffed my pockets with razor blades for the 'monks' in India, and went on board with John Wilcken and Norbert Olsen, fellow Jesuits also heading for a Goethe Institute course in Germany and then tertianship. Via Darwin and Hong Kong we landed in Calcutta to spend the night in locked and barred rooms at Dum Dum airport. On the flight out of Sydney I took my first alcoholic drink, a bottle of Danish beer. Goodbye to the Pioneers, the total abstinence association I had joined in 1952!

The following day John and I left on a DC3 for Ranchi, while Norbert flew north to visit Australian friends in studies at St Mary's College, Kurseong (near Darjeeling). Via Jamshedpur (where a Hindu crowd had recently killed a Belgian Jesuit trying to save some Muslim women and children), we landed at Ranchi around 10.45 a.m. to be met by an Australian Jesuit from Hazaribag. He drove us across town to Manresa House for Mass and lunch. I sat tight in the land rover bewildered by the cars, trucks, buses, cyclists, cycle-powered rickshaws, cows, and pedestrians that filled the streets with complex confusion. Ranchi had Catholic institutions galore: high schools, a university college, the cathedral, the Catholic press, and other church buildings lined one street. I sighted several aged and bearded Belgian priests strolling around in cool, white cassocks, the last of those patriarchs who built up the Ranchi mission from the end of the nineteenth century. One of those I met had arrived in India back in 1904.

Around 2 p.m. we pushed on to Hazaribag. The monsoon had just broken and low-lying areas already shimmered with the delicate green of young rice. From the fields water buffaloes slowly stared at

us. Small cows and bullocks, humped, off white or cream in colour
and with their ribs showing, shuffled along the roads. We scattered
chickens, diminutive goats and black, scavenging pigs. Everywhere
there were quiet knots of people: children watching goats or cattle;
women washing clothes at the wells or in the shallow rivers; men
walking some paces in front of women who carried bundles of fire-
wood on their heads. Men were piercing together fresh branches to
fashion enclosures for tiny vegetable or maize gardens. 'Biblical', I
kept saying to myself as my eyes took in the village wells (equipped
with wooden poles for drawing water), the mud or brick walls of
houses (through which thieves could dig), the tiled roofs (which
could be opened to lower a paralytic on a stretcher), the unfenced
fields (where seed could easily fall on the paths or the hard ridges that
separate the plots), and pairs of bullocks pulling a single-share plough
(from which a farmer cannot afford to look back). Our Jesuit driver
told us that in the villages lunatics were sometimes taken to the local
blacksmiths to be put in irons for safety's sake. Was the Gerasene
demoniac of Mark 5: 1-20 really the village lunatic?

In Hazaribag we stopped overnight at St Xavier's school, the star
institution of the Australian Jesuit mission in India. Multi-storey
dormitory and classroom blocks, several playing fields, a large hall and
a generous campus served a student body of four hundred boarders
and roughly the same number of day boys. Clumps of eucalyptus
trees shaded the school grounds on one side, a police training school
protected it on the other.

One of the priests at St Xavier's drove us to Sitagarha and a college
which served as both novitiate and tertianship. At the main entrance
I met the tertian instructor, Fr Schillebeeckx. Earlier in the year I had
learnt much from his brother's *Christ the Sacrament*. What could you
say to the Jesuit brother of a famous (and soon to be controversial)
Dominican theologian? I murmured one or two pleasantries before
ambling off to find Peter Coleman and present him with the bottle

of whisky that I had carried from Sydney. He confessed to selling it a day or so later at an exorbitant profit! Sitagarha hill dominated the college, which enjoyed huge grounds heavily planted with large trees. In fact, the whole area was well wooded and offered a home for bears and a few tigers. Peter took me around to the college cemetery, which already held the graves of two Australian Jesuits: Jim Collins and Phil MacInerney. Jim had died in 1963 when his car (or land rover?) overturned. Earlier in 1964 Phil had died after an operation for haemorrhoids. In 1950 Jim and I sat together in the chapel of Loyola College to hear the rector announce to the assembled community that the Australian province of Jesuits would begin to send missionaries to India. He went on to predict in his rumbling tones that some present would 'lay down their bones' under an Indian tree. And here was Jim fourteen years later in a shaded grave on a hillside in Bihar.

We drove back to St Xavier's past the Hazaribag reformatory and gaol. A few years before, the governor of this gaol, which once housed leaders of the Indian home-rule movement, offered to juggle the dates for an execution, so that a visiting Australian provincial could attend the hanging.

On the afternoon of 20 June we left with the superior of the mission, Fr Ted O'Connor, to spend the night at the Chandwa parish centre. This included a house for girl boarders, another for boys, quarters for the teachers at the school, a convent, the parish priest's bungalow, playing fields, an old church, an orchard, a piggery, and a shed for chickens. Walls of brick already lined the area where, with money donated by the parents of Jim Collins, a new church would be built in memory of him. We sat on the bungalow verandah. Fire-flies gleamed in the dark, and a few mosquitoes buzzed around us, but were not nearly as unpleasant about their business as their Australian cousins. The boys and girls from the boarding establishment came and knelt in front of the bungalow for the night's blessing given by Ted as mission superior.

The following morning at 5.30 I celebrated Mass and gave Communion to several bare-foot, Indian nuns. The congregation sang local hymns and chanted their own prayers during the liturgy. We drove back to lunch at St Xavier's in Hazaribag. In the afternoon John Wilcken and I were called on to give benediction at the Holy Cross convent, where rows of novices and postulants in white habits sang lovely Indian hymns.

On 22 June at a Catholic ashram in Hazaribag, I celebrated Mass at 6 a.m. for the boys and girls attending the ashram's boarding school. After breakfast Ted drove John Wilcken and myself to Bhurkunda, a growing town supported by open-cut coal mines. We visited the large school and church in the Catholic parish before heading for Ranchi. There we learnt that one of the two engines of the DC3 from Calcutta had failed on the flight up to Ranchi; we were told to wait in town until a backup aircraft arrived. We filled in the time by visiting a lace factory run by Ursuline sisters for hundreds of women. They embroidered saris, made bed covers, fashioned lace albs, and created other products. As they worked barefoot and squatting on the floor, many of the women kept their sleeping babies at their side. Then we called on the director of the Manresa Press, a cheery, fair-haired Belgian who did a lot of printing for Indian journals. We were wandering back from the press, when Ted dashed up to say that our flight was waiting for departure. Through a torrential downpour he hurried us by jeep to the Ranchi airport. It was a false alarm. On the phone an airport official had told him that the plane for Calcutta was waiting, and asked him to bring us immediately. There was a plane standing on the tarmac, the one with engine failure. The backup DC3 had not yet arrived. We waited at the terminal with a group of Czechoslovakian engineers, their wives, and children who were going home after a tour of work near Ranchi. But for them, I am sure the airline would not have bothered to fly up another plane.

Eventually the backup aircraft droned in. As soon as it taxied to a stop, we all dashed down the tarmac to it. We landed in Calcutta at 8.25 p.m. A turbaned official working for Air France hurried John and me into the terminal to snatch up the bags and coats we had cloaked there three days before. He then rushed us on board the Boeing 707, snapping a final salute at the foot of the gangway, a touch of old-fashioned, Sikh courtesy.[3] Norbert Olsen, full of stories of Kurseong and the Himalayas, had joined the aircraft at the scheduled time and long ago given John and me up for lost. Our flight for Athens took off at 8.45.

After those intensely busy three days it was goodbye to India, at least for the time being. I left dazzled by the hospitality and dedication of my friends. They walked ten feet tall. Rich benefits flowed to a Christian and non-Christian public from their missionary work in education, medicine, and agriculture. The Australians had followed the Belgians by making a shining contribution to many dimensions of life in that part of India. Over fifty years later more of those who left Australia for India have died, while Indians, from Bihar and elsewhere, have entered the Society of Jesus and carry on the work through the institutions I saw and new ones that have been subsequently founded. The Australian Jesuit province and its friends continue to support financially and in other ways the remarkable work of what is now the Hazaribag Province.

For years I continued to envy those Jesuits at their work in India, just as I used to envy my uncle Gerald, who served as a missionary in China until the Communist victory in 1949. I once saw a film in which he briefly appeared, sitting by himself at the back of a river-boat as it moved up the Yangtze Kiang. The mysterious loneliness of the silent man, seen against a broad background of swirling waters, stayed in my mind. From the late 1960s that picture remained tied to the persistent yearning that the opportunity to make some total act of

3 Seven years later and again in Calcutta, a Sikh army officer was to come to my rescue in another difficult situation, as I will explain in a later chapter.

commitment would one day come. Only that could save me from the
soft selfishness and ambiguities of my way of life.

But back to 1964 and the journey to Germany. With John Wilcken I
stopped three days in Athens. After Mass (at separate side-altars in the
Jesuit church, where I was sorry to see the local Jesuits celebrate in the
Latin rite) and breakfast, we rushed out on our first morning to stand
on the Acropolis by 7 a.m. That moment seemed a sufficient reward
for the years at school and university spent studying the classics. I had
come home at last to the glory of the Propylaea and the Parthenon.
We took a siesta before visiting the archaeological museum to marvel
at the golden jewellery from Mycenae: highly patterned signet rings,
necklaces, bracelets, and death masks. After supper I strolled along
the streets of Athens to watch children gather small piles of rubbish,
light them, and then jump through the flames. They were celebrating
St John's Eve.

John and I spent our second day on a bus tour. Through rocky
Attica we drove past olive groves and the sparkling sea to our first
stop, old Corinth. I let down a cup by string to drink cool and tasty
water from the fountain of Pirene. Then I mounted the *bema* where
a Roman proconsul once sat in judgement on St Paul. Long grass,
thistles, and other weeds sprouted everywhere to give the ruins of the
agora the look of an untidy paddock. The massive *acropolis*, once home
to Aphrodite's courtesans and now surmounted by a Frankish fort,
filled the middle distance.

Our husky and hearty driver swung the bus along fields of
tobacco, orange groves, vineyards, white-washed houses, long-tailed
sheep with shepherds attendant, mule carts, men and women riding
donkeys side-saddle, and donkeys balancing baskets on either flank
or moving underneath bales of straw larger than themselves. Every
now and then the driver played the notes of his horn to acknowledge
policemen, other drivers, or a donkey-rider who took his fancy. We

headed through rocky hills up the valley of the Argolis to Mycenae, where the *acropolis* stands on lower slopes framed by two commanding mountains. I strolled under the lion gate with one of our tour companions, a Japanese architect who had studied in Denmark with Jorn Utzon and was flying out to Sydney to work on the opera house that his teacher had designed. I feasted on the thought that I was walking under the earliest extant pieces of European sculpture, the pair of female lions that guard Agamemnon's gate, with a man who would help create one of the architectural wonders of the modern world.

From Mycenae the bus took us along an avenue of Australian gum trees, through Argos to lunch in an ultra-modern *xenia*, poised above the sea at Nauplion and guarded by a Frankish fort. I ate with a Brisbane business man and a married couple from Philadelphia. I felt the husband, a research scientist, wince when his wife informed me: 'Two things I miss in Greece are negroes and pregnant women.' At 3 p.m. we left for Epidauros, where the bus drove in past the stadium (where some of the ancient starting blocks and seating still remain intact) and the sanctuary of Aesculapius to visit the theatre. Maria, our tall Greek guide who spoke both English and French fluently, mounted the stage to drop a coin and tear a sheet of paper. Yet another bunch of tourists huddled in the back row and declared the acoustics of ancient Greece perfect.

John and I rested on our third morning in Athens, and then took a bus from the residence down to Constitution Square in the afternoon. We strolled through the Acropolis and its surroundings. In the Theatre of Dionysus I noticed that the front rows of marble seats bore inscriptions indicating reservations: 'priest of Apollo', 'priest of Demeter', and so forth. It struck me how the clergy claimed their privileges even then! I was to remember Athens for its fast and orderly traffic, its vexatious shoeshine boys, some old men selling roasted corn, the cycle-powered delivery vans, and the bearded priest who watched us closely in the sumptuous cathedral. Dusty, a little untidy, and sometimes smelly, Athens came across as a thoroughly jovial, friendly, chatty place—my first introduction to that Mediterranean world in which I had immersed myself since childhood.

We reached Rome halfway through the Second Vatican Council, with two sessions completed. In St Peter's we gazed up at the huge rows of seats that lined the nave and waited for the bishops to return for the final sessions of 1964 and 1965. I walked to some churches, museums, and the Roman Forum, but postponed visiting certain highlights like the Sistine Chapel, as I expected to be back in Rome fifteen months later. I took a bus out to the Casa del Sacro Cuore on the Via Nomentana to spend half an hour with Mother Schroen. As 'mistress of tertians' she was in charge of Vivienne Macgillicuddy until her departure a fortnight before. A highly intelligent American, Mother Schroen seemed like a nun who really believed in personal freedom, unlike a number of religious superiors I had met. 'I could easily have influenced Vivienne to stay', she told me. Behind walls over three metres high, the convent stood in grounds planted with cedars and pines, flanked on one side by the Russian Embassy and on the other by the Afghan Embassy.

John Wilcken and I made three more stops en route to southern Bavaria and a two months course in German: Geneva, Zurich, and Munich. Looking for help towards my Gregorian University thesis, I called at the new World Council of Churches headquarters in Geneva. Davis McCaughey had put me in touch with Lukas Vischer, the research secretary of the Faith and Order Commission. Unfortunately he was away, but I talked with Patrick Rodger, a Scottish Episcopalian who served as executive secretary of the commission. Warm and candid, he offered much useful advice and I left feeling greatly encouraged. John and I walked across the Rhone to gaze at the Reformation Monument. My diary records my reaction:

Behind a fishpond a wall stretches for about seventy-five yards as a backdrop to the stone figures of Calvin, Farel, Beza, and Knox. The main inscription reads: '*Post tenebras lux* (after darkness light)'. At either end stand two free blocks of stone which, though marked 'Luther' and 'Zwingli', support no figures. What happened? The grey and gloomy monument forms a cheerless contrast to bright and brisk Geneva.

We reached Zurich by train in time to join the Jesuits of the Apologetical Institute for an evening meal, a feast of cherry pie and nothing but cherry pie. Those Swiss Jesuits wore shirt and tie—the first community that I had encountered which dispensed with the clerical collar. A thin quirky member of the team that produced the fortnightly *Orientierung* pointed out to us a wild duck that had made its way up from the lake to nest for the third time in the institute's rose garden. In 1963 a hedgehog stole her eggs, one each night. But in 1962 she had successfully raised her ducklings, and paraded them around the garden to show them off to the Jesuits before leading them down to the lake.

First German Experiences

Another overnight stop followed in Munich, where we stayed right opposite the main railway station at the Europäischer Hof, a hotel run by nuns. I prayed at the tomb of Fr Rupert Mayer, a Jesuit preacher and spiritual director, who was silenced by the Nazis, died shortly after World War II, and would be beatified by Pope John Paul II in 1987. In Rome I had celebrated Mass at the tombs of St Robert Bellarmine and St Aloysius Gonzaga. It cheered me on the way to tertianship to pay my respects at the graves of notable Jesuit forerunners. Before leaving Munich for the Goethe Institute in Kochel, I dropped around to the Michaelkirche to arrange with a Jesuit mission 'procurator' to have a tractor sent (as a gift from the West German government) to our Australian mission in India. Ted O'Connor had made this last minute request to me when we stood on the tarmac at Ranchi airport.

At the beginning of July, John Wilcken and I took the train south from Munich to Kochel am See, rejoined Norbert Olsen, and began our course in German. John and I had quarters in St Annaheim, a home for about 150 girls (orphans from broken families), run by forty nuns. Many of the sisters were old, as was their sprightly Jesuit chaplain. He quickly gave us two excruciating piano recitals in his rooms. 'Does he intend', I noted, 'to threaten us with more if we disregard his request not to speak with any of the girls? We must seem uncivilized, since we pass the girls several times a day when we cross the grounds of the convent.' Our rooms were in a new wing, right underneath a hill topped by a small and tattered Schloss. The Nazi youth-leader, Baldur von Shirach, once lived in this Schloss with his wife and four children. In 1964 he was still serving a twenty-year sentence in Spandau for war crimes. At the end of the war the nuns had cared for his wife and children. The hot water was switched on only once or twice a week, but otherwise the nuns proved very hospitable. Often we returned from class to find cakes, biscuits, fruit, and soft drinks piled on our tables. The village of Kochel lay right at the foot of the Bavarian Alps. From my window I looked across the convent vegetable garden to the rugged Jochberg. Across to the right was the Kochelsee (one of those spectacularly beautiful Bavarian lakes), with another mountain, the Herzogstand, overlooking its waters. Often I stood at my window and let the words from the psalm run through my mind: 'I lift up my eyes to the mountains...'

I had reached the first temporary stopping place on a grand tour, which continued to excite my curiosity as fresh impressions poured in. I was quickly emerging from the Australian world to experience with delight European art, nature, and church life. I had left behind Australian seminaries to move happily into a wider Jesuit world and life outside seminaries.

Settling into the course, however, seemed a little threatening at first. I had to re-establish myself with new group and accept my limitations. Many of the other students already spoke better German than I did. My daily programme ran as follows: Mass, breakfast at the Goethe Institute at 7.30, class 8.30-11.30, lunch at the Restaurant zur Post, afternoon class 3.30-5.30 (with no afternoon classes on Wednesdays and Saturdays), evening meal at the Post. Sunday was free. In my class, *Grundstufe zwei*, there were two married couples from Brazil, a Greek girl from Cyprus, a Swiss student from Fribourg, a Turk, an Iraki, a Canadian priest who had been studying at the Biblical Institute in Rome, several Finns, a reserved American girl, an Australian boy with an American father, a lively French girl, a complicated Japanese doctor (who might have been as hard to understand in Japanese as he was in German), and a Japanese ski-instructor who had won a medal (bronze?) at the last winter Olympics. At least thirteen further nationalities were represented in the other classes.

I wore an open-necked shirt. It was the first time in my life as a Jesuit scholastic or priest that I had left off the clerical collar in such circumstances. But it was to be four more years before I started wearing ties. I found that a much more difficult clothing barrier to cross, mainly because of the British public. They seemed surprised when a Catholic priest wore anything else than a Roman collar, even when they saw photographs of German priests such as Professor Joseph Ratzinger wearing a dark jacket and tie at the Second Vatican Council. At first, despite practice in Germany, I lacked the self-confidence to take an independent line. By 1971 I was to realize how far I had come in such matters when I attended a meeting of priests in Rome (where I had made stopover en route to India and Australia). My tie stood out in a sea of clerical collars. The monsignor who chaired the gathering noticed me, and made an amusing but barbed comment about 'transvestites'. I felt free to join in the laughter, but knew very well that I was not going to let this Vatican official bully me into conformity.

The eight weeks in Kochel allowed me to explore a broad sweep of German countryside. Memories of war, glimpses of Bavarian history, and some Catholic customs caught my eye. In Kochel itself the walls of the parish church carried large photographs of parishioners killed in the First World War, miniature photographs of those who died in the Second World War, and the medals of those who fell in 1813, 1866, and 1870-71. That frightful reminder of militarism shrieked aloud in a romantic village, where mountains, fields, forests, and the lake lavishly suggested peace, beauty, and the presence of God. But I felt even more depressed by a visit I made to the concentration camp of Dachau, where—as I discovered later—many Jesuits had been imprisoned, including one (Anton Mruk) who survived to be my colleague and friend at the Gregorian University in Rome and confessor to Pope John Paul II.

With an American priest I went to Dachau on 15 August, the feast of Our Lady's Assumption, a public holiday in Bavaria and the only special day free during our Goethe Institute course. For the last stage of our journey we had to take a taxi. Although he lived nearby in Munich, the German taxi driver had never visited the camp and decided to come along. As a child he had seen columns of prisoners shuffling along the road to Dachau. Their destination left him and us profoundly shaken. The American army had requisitioned part of the original camp for a storage area. Homeless derelicts occupied some of the huts, thus continuing in their own way the experience of suffering inaugurated there by the Nazis. In the main part of the camp, the empty but haunted huts, the gas chambers fitted out to look like shower rooms, the 'blood ditch' where thousands fell with a bullet in their necks, and the ovens which reduced the dead to ashes untwisted the last strand of my capacity for horror. Yet an even uglier sight was provided by the neatly typed and correctly signed orders for the movement and destruction of prisoners. I was aghast that human beings could sit at tables and issue with bureaucratic thoroughness documents bringing about the murder of their brothers and sisters. As we left with our taxi driver, I thought to myself: 'If only I had some cutters, I could take away a few inches of barbed wire from the collapsing outer fence and keep alive in my memory the misery of Dachau!'

Twice I took a bus south from Kochel to Oberammergau, where the townspeople for centuries have performed a passion play every ten years. As I wandered around the theatre, it stirred my imagination to see the costumes (for the high priest, the apostles, the Virgin Mary, Mary Magdalene, and other roles), the spears, shields and helmets for the Roman soldiers, a crown of thorns, and Christ's two crosses (the one he carries and the one on which he dies). I found it very poignant and real to find these props in the empty dressing rooms. On the first Good Friday night similar reminders of the recently enacted drama hung on racks or in cupboards in various parts of Jerusalem: the weapons carried by the centurion and his troops on Calvary, the dress Mary wore when she saw her Son make his painful way out of the city, and the robes Caiaphas had donned for the proceedings against Jesus.

In Oberammergau's baroque church the *pièce de résistance* was the skeleton of St Amanda, which lay in a glass case equipped with martyr's palm and crown. Red and gold braid had been wrapped around the bones. I spotted something similar at the nearby Benedictine monastery of Ettal. There the church contained the skeletons of Felix, Bonifacius, and two other martyrs in glass-fronted reliquaries, once again with braid covering the bones. The parish church of Schlendorf, a tiny village near Kochel, preserved the most startling example of this method for honouring ancient Roman martyrs. Glass cases housed the reputed remains of St Marcus and St Constantia. Their bones had been wrapped with red and gold braid, crowns rested on their skulls, and their 'hands' grasped palm branches that lay modestly across their loins.

An excursion which the Goethe Institute arranged to the Weltenburg monastery and the city of Regensburg yielded further impressions of Bavarian Catholicism. After the lunch provided by the Benedictine monks at Weltenburg, we visited the monastery church and the finest Baroque fantasy I have ever seen. Over the tabernacle stood a statue of St George slaying the dragon on the gospel side, while the maiden shrank back on the epistle side. Light from unseen windows filled the space behind the statue. The church itself was lit with windows that remained largely out of sight. Darker on the floor, the building became flooded with light towards the gilded ceiling. On the gospel side a pulpit emerged from a painting and stood above a confessional surrounded by rocks. A vision swept before my eyes of sinners terrified out of their seats by the preacher above, and creeping into the confessional below to whisper their guilty secrets in the ear of the waiting confessor.

Exquisitely finished, the whole church had been beautifully preserved. But my diary recorded doubts about this Baroque masterpiece: 'The pulpit is not organically linked with the altar. The liturgy of the Word remains separated from the liturgy of the Deed. There is a delight in tricks and sheer human beauty and cleverness, but no sense of mystery. This style suggests the beauty of a theatre, a concert hall, or a sacred museum.' I continued and harshly contrasted it all with some of the Gothic churches I had seen: 'Baroque churches could be temples of pagan gods. In them the people enjoy no more unity than in a concert hall. These churches fail to reflect the idea that here God's people are assembled. A Gothic cathedral tells the story of God and man; so too does a Baroque church. The Trinity, the apostles, Mary, Sacred Scripture, sin, the sacraments, death etc. are all there. But how differently!'

Those eight weeks at Kochel come back in my memory with a blaze of sunshine and a babble of happy voices. I enjoyed the easy company of students from so many nations. We had to try our German out on each other, since probably less than half knew English. In any case most made an honest effort to mix with the students from other countries. I thought this mixing was going to kill me one day when I went out in a car with the Japanese Olympic skier and a French-speaking Swiss called Willi. At high and terrifying speed Herr Sugiyama drove us to Starnbergersee, celebrated in the poetry of T.S. Eliot. On the shore a memorial chapel in Byzantine style marked the place where crazy King Ludwig II drowned with the doctor he always kept in attendance. In the distance a hideous, grey Bismarck Tower rose among the trees. I thought of war and death: 'This Kamikaze driver will take Willi and me with him.'

At Kochel I met James McCaughey, the eldest son of Davis McCaughey whom I had come to know earlier in 1964. After graduating in classics from Melbourne University, James had gone to Cambridge on a Shell Scholarship and had just completed half of his two-year divinity course. I enjoyed James's company immensely, not least for the chance of lively discussions on theological questions and for his account of the state of theology in the United Kingdom. Slim, talkative, and exuding easy charm, he joined me for one memorable Sunday trip to Salzburg.

We left about 5 a.m. and arrived in time to hear a High Mass in Salzburg's enormous cathedral. It was first time that I had heard violins played in church. The organ postlude left James and myself enthralled, as we strolled across the river to the Mirabell Gardens. My eyes feasted on the beds of red, pink, and white begonias. We lunched at the Sternbräu before visiting Mozart's house, several churches, the Hohensalzburg castle, and the convent of Nonnberg. Just as we entered the brooding Gothic chapel of those contemplative sisters, we ran into two girls from South Australia. I felt happy for James in his pleasure at this unexpected encounter with one of the girls. She was completing at Cambridge her master's degree in physiology, and earlier that year had been his partner at a May ball. The unseen nuns had reached the last section of Compline. I found their *Salve Regina* simple and uplifting. Before our bus departed, there was time to slip into the Petersfriedhof to marvel at the fourth-century passages tunnelled by Christian soldiers. A thousand steps led down from the Roman fortress to two caves below. In one they celebrated Mass, and in the other they had buried their dead. Mass was still being said in the first cave, making it the oldest Catholic church still in use in Austria and Germany. When we arrived home in Kochel around 10 p.m., I invited James to come for a snack in my room at St Annaheim. We discovered that the sisters had left a meal on my table. 'The Church looks after its own', he remarked with amused respect for their kindness.

During the two months at the Goethe Institute, the divisions of Christianity pressed themselves on my attention. After the Second World War many Protestant refugees from East Germany and elsewhere settled in predominantly Catholic Bavaria. In Kochel itself the Protestant community had built a church right opposite a typically Catholic wayside shrine, a statue of the Virgin Mary at the foot of the cross. I reached Kochel just too late for the annual Corpus Christi procession honouring the Blessed Sacrament, which made one 'station' in front of this new church. With some of this flock the Protestant pastor stood at the porch to acknowledge this pause for prayer, while some of the Protestant children walked in the procession itself. Their participation in a very Catholic ceremony sounded, however, more like a cultural phenomenon than a product of the current ecumenical movement.

Towards the end of the course I delivered a class talk for an hour and quarter on 'the differences between Protestants and Catholics'. Our teacher suggested the theme and talked me out of a literary topic that I had proposed. Although himself a Protestant, he showed little sympathy for Christianity except in the Catholic version. In the evening, nine of the class continued the discussion of religious questions over beer and sausage meat in his home. I was delighted to find that persistent work had made it possible for me to speak reasonably correct German for such a long period of time.

In late August 1964 it hurt a little to say goodbye to the other students. We had come from many parts of the globe, shared an intense programme, formed a friendly community, and then parted after eight weeks. My later wandering was to accustom me to many such meetings and partings. I also had to say goodbye to my fellow Jesuits from Australia, John Wilcken and Norbert Olsen; they left to do their tertianship in Austria.

The Road to Westphalia

Tertianship began in Münster on 7 September. En route I made stops in Munich, Augsburg, Würzburg, Frankfurt, and Bonn. I stayed first at Berchmanskolleg in Pullach on the outskirts of Munich. Situated off a main road, this battered Jesuit college looked in need of some fresh paint, but was set against a pretty forest. One evening I showed seventy colour slides on Australia to the scholastics. Despite my limited German, the pictures of kookaburras, yachts on Sydney harbour, indigenous dancers, the platypus (which I described as a *Naturwitz* or 'joke of nature'), the Snowy Mountains, and the rest offered some relief from a book being read at meals, an economic history of France in the twentieth century. When I asked how they endured it, one of the scholastics replied with an ironic smile: 'We're lucky that the prefect of reading has economic rather than sociological interests. A sociologist might have prescribed the Munich telephone book for reading at table.' One evening I wandered beyond the college's swimming pool into the cemetery where I prayed at the graves of the sixteen scholastics killed in a June 1951 bus smash. A whole ordination class had been wiped out. When news of that level crossing accident reached the Jesuits in Melbourne, death surrounded me. I was working as a novice in Caritas Christi hospice for the dying.

In Munich I spent hours in the Alte Pinakothek, where the paintings of Rubens, sensational and all as they are, deeply moved me. In the Frauenkirche, the city late-Gothic cathedral where 'onion towers' rise above walls of warm, weary brickwork, I attended a High Mass. A mixed choir sang a four-part Palestrina Mass with precision. I pressed on to Augsburg to stay overnight at the Jesuit residence. It lay right behind the town hall and next door to the convent of St Maria Stern, which boasted the oldest 'onion tower' in southern Germany. The superior of the residence who spent World War II in Dublin radiated hospitality, and spoke English with an Irish accent. After a hot bath I fell into bed to be lulled to sleep by the gurgling of an old mill-stream that ran past my window.

I said a 6.30 Mass for two nuns who acted as housekeepers, and stepped out at 8 o'clock to see Augsburg. Under a flood of sunshine I sped around in an exalted mood to visit some of the principal sights: the cathedral with its stained-glass windows that looked like old tapestry; some Roman remains; the former palace of the bishop where the (Lutheran) Confession of Augsburg was proclaimed in 1530; the Carmelite monastery in which Martin Luther stayed during his 1518 conversations with Cardinal Thomas Cajetan; the graceful family residence of the banker Jacob Fugger where Luther met Cajetan; and St Ulrich's church with its three vast and exuberantly Baroque altars. I was beginning to feel as it I could reach out and touch the Reformation and the Counter-Reformation in Germany.

From Augsburg I pushed on to Würzhurg, where I stayed two nights at Leighton Barracks in the American camp. I spent my full day there tramping around the city on foot and visiting the university. I could not believe her, when one of the staff in the university library explained to me what their *numerus currens* system meant. They catalogued and shelved books solely according to the date of accession! In an inner courtyard of the Marienburg I came across an archaeologist, who had a team of young girls and boys at work with picks and shovels. He claimed to have discovered Greek remains from around 1000 BC! Before taking a taxi home to Leighton Barracks, I ducked back to the Neumünster for a second look at a statue of the crucified Christ that troubled me. His side showed a gaping wound. His eyes were open and his arms folded across his chest with the nails still in his hands.

I continued down the Main to stay three nights at Sankt Georgen, a vast Jesuit seminary across the river from Frankfurt. Diocesan seminarians occupied one half of Sankt Georgen and the Jesuit community the other half. When glass doors were installed to divide the two communities, the seminarians laid a wreath in front of these doors to honour their separated Jesuit brothers 'behind the wall'. I could not leap four years ahead to know how eight days of prayer (my annual 'retreat') was to bring me pain about what was happening in the Catholic Church and my future. In the summer of 1964 my journeying was external and aesthetic. A sense of the grand tour possessed me, as I swept through galleries, universities, churches, and monuments. I was coming alive culturally after years of artistic starvation.

In Frankfurt I visited the Goethe museum and family house. Goethe must have been one of the relatively few great poets to have come from a wealthy, well connected family. As a small boy he and his sister ran a popular puppet-theatre in their home. Around one small table, fitted with four book-rests, the parents and their two children often spent the evening reading books at point-blank range from each other. In the room where the poet was born, I was touched to see two wreaths still there. Every August some English organization honoured Goethe's birthday in that way. The Germans reciprocated by sending a wreath for Shakespeare's birthday. On my way home by tram I fell into conversation with the conductor (a German) who had lived in Sydney until 1959. 'I still own some land in the Blue Mountains', he told me. 'Should I sell it?' 'No, hang on to it', I replied, guessing and hoping that my advice was correct. After the evening meal in Sankt Georgen, three scholastics invited me upstairs for a drink. 'During your year in Westphalia', one of them urged, 'don't become a Prussian pig.'

The mood of the grand tour took over fully, when I boarded the steamer Lorelei to travel down the Rhine from Mainz to Koblenz. I revelled at the view from the front deck: vineyards festooning the banks, ruined castles, inhabited castles, and everywhere the heavy traffic of barges witnessing to West Germany's 'economic miracle'. As we slipped past Bingen, the phrase mother loved to quote from her mother ('Fair Bingen on the Rhine') ran through my head. At the Lorelei we heard over the steamer's loud-speaker the song about the bewitching maiden who lured sailors to destruction on the rocks. From Koblenz I caught a train to spend two nights at the Jesuit residence in Bonn.

I spent a Sunday visiting Fr Walter König at Aloysius-Kolleg in Bad Godesberg. Under the Nazis he was forced to leave Germany, and worked in England until the outbreak of World War II. Since he had served as an officer in the German army during World War I, he was interned and sent out to Australia for detention at a camp in New South Wales. Thanks to the chaplain general, Dr Daniel Mannix, he was soon released and went south to teach classics to the young Jesuits at Loyola College. In 1949 he returned to his native Germany, but loved to keep in touch with Australian Jesuits. We had never met before, but I gave him what he wanted—the assurance that he was affectionately remembered, as indeed he was, by those who had known him in Australia. During the 1940s my uncle Will had been his rector at Loyola. Old Fr König wished me well as I left to begin my tertianship at Haus Sentmaring in Münster.

Tertianship in Münster

My whole shift from Pymble to Cambridge would last from November 1963 until September 1965. It was a period of intense travel: from Sydney to Melbourne, from Melbourne to a village near Munich, from Munich to Münster, from Münster to Ireland, and from Ireland to Cambridge. I made many stops along the way, the longest being for tertianship in Münster (September 1964 until July 1965). Ideally tertianship should provide a period of prayerful re-assessment that comes after years of study and some experience in the priestly ministry. Its core element, the thirty-day retreat, might issue in a second conversion and some far-reaching decisions about one's lifestyle.

In fact my priestly work had not yet offered much material for reflection. I had helped at weekends in parishes around Sydney (February-November 1963), and for six weeks over Christmas and New Year in Melbourne. We called such work 'supplies'. That term suggests part of the spirit in which we approached these tasks, as breaks from other routines, when we helped out where parishes suffered from shortages of personnel. My years of study had seen me adhere fairly inflexibly to patterns of prayer, self-discipline, and daily order that the novitiate had set up. Ordination came too late to shake these patterns, let alone allow the ministerial priesthood a chance to form and fashion new attitudes. Doubtless it was because I looked a solid religious, rather than because I had already proved myself an innovative young priest, that the provincial appointed me to conduct the spiritual semester for the diocesan students at Corpus Christi College. I never dreamt of learning from or even growing with those students. I played the role of the master offering sound teaching on the spiritual life. Tertianship was to prove an extension of my theological studies, taken after a short break at Werribee. The only major decision was to be thrust suddenly upon me when I finished my long retreat.

Haus Sentmaring was a grey German mansion, to which a wing had been added for old and infirm Jesuits. Beyond that wing a separate house guarded the gate, where several Jesuits lived who were studying at the local university. A network of cinder paths criss-crossed the grounds, which enclosed an orchard, a vegetable garden, a lonely draught horse, and several acres of shrubs and trees. The twenty-five tertians occupied the main house along with a small, permanent community of priests and brothers, including the tertian instructor himself, Alois Stein. A brush of white hair topped his reddish face and stubby figure. Now into his mid-fifties, Fr Stein had worked as a missionary in South America, spent some time with tuberculosis in a sanatorium, and been rector of Aloysius-Kolleg in Bad Godesberg. Three Australian Jesuits had already done their tertianship under his direction: John Scullion, Brian Fleming, and Bill Daniel. I inherited his warm regard for them. In general he treated foreigners with a friendly and amused tolerance. His fellow Germans often seemed a little apprehensive of him. Around the house we all wore black, ankle-length cassocks, which fastened closely at the throat and were gathered at the waist by a sash.

My fellow tertians came from eight countries: Canada, England, Germany, Holland, Hungary, Italy, Portugal, and the United States. When I met them first, a sense of anonymous unimportance hit me hard. From being in charge of thirty-nine seminarians in my own country, I had arrived to join a group of strangers. In this new setting I was searching for my identity and recognition. Of course, there was no need to rediscover and re-establish myself absolutely from scratch. We were all young Jesuit priests. The sole Hungarian knew something of the Hungarian Jesuits who worked in Australia for migrants from their own country. One of the three Portuguese had formed a friendship with Bill Dalton, my former scripture professor when they met several years earlier in Spain. Several of the Germans had studied in Sankt Georgen with another Australian Jesuit. I found myself to be the senior in years spent in the order, since I had entered the novitiate six months ahead of any other tertian. At forty-six Myles Lovell, the only Englishman, was the senior in age.

A brisk, bald ex-major, Myles had turned from agnosticism to Catholicism, entered the Society of Jesus, and blended a convert's dedication with immense cheerfulness. He also felt an instinctive distaste for Germans, which he hoped the tertianship would help him overcome. As a schoolboy he had visited Germany before entering the British army and taking part in the 1940 retreat to Dunkirk. There he had shared a bottle of champagne with another officer to 'celebrate', when they blew up their artillery.

Whenever other commitments left us free, Myles and I spent the weekends at the British school in Hamm. During World War II I had listened to the BBC four o'clock news, which would report almost like a chorus, 'The RAF have bombed the marshalling yards at Hamm.' Now to my astonishment I found myself in that dull city, ministering to the hundred Catholics at the boarding school for five hundred sons of British soldiers serving with the army of the Rhine. Some Sundays I said a Mass in the Catholic chapel at 8 a.m. Then I would hear confessions before and during the 10.15 Mass that Myles celebrated. On other Sundays Myles took the earlier Mass. After the second Mass we taught classes in religious education. The Scottish matron, one of the house masters and a handful of other Catholics on the school staff supported us well. We ran a series of sermons on the commandments, experimented with techniques of religious instruction, and tried to improve the liturgy by turning the altar towards the congregation and encouraging the boys to sing hymns. It remained dull, uphill work. Schools in England seemed to have creamed off the brightest boys. But I welcomed those weekends, which not only made a break from the daily routine in Haus Sentmaring of study, conferences, prayer, and house-work, but also afforded a 'breather' in an English-speaking environment.

On 24 September all the tertians walked out through radiant sunshine to the shrine of Our Lady of Telgte, about ten kilometers from Münster. At 10 a.m. we sang a Mass at which Fr Stein preached. This was the first time I ever heard a sermon at a Mass for Jesuits. The shrine, a small seventeenth-century chapel, contained a *pietà* from the mid-fourteenth century that rested in a niche on the wall immediately behind the altar. The figure of Mary which dwarfed that of the limp Christ struck me as strong and Germanic, a real Westphalian widow. We returned by bus for the midday dinner. It happened to be the feast of St Gerald, my *Namenstag*. The Germans congratulated me in a jovial fashion, and the minister presented me with a bar of chocolate. Our thirty-day retreat began at 8.30 p.m. with benediction of the Blessed Sacrament.

Throughout four weeks of silence, intense prayer, and reflection, we followed closely the order of St Ignatius' Spiritual Exercises. We broke the routine by three 'repose days', when we took some recreation together. Fr Stein, Karl Rahner and Ernest Hemingway helped me through. I found consistent value in the questions, reflections, and stories with which Fr Stein sprinkled his talks to us. He asked whether 'the deepest reason for the present crisis in the Society of Jesus is our latent uncertainty. Are we one in our faith in Christ?' 'Temptation', he reflected, 'so shakes a man and disturbs him that it seems as if there is no firmness left.' He pushed me into challenging myself: 'What are my dreams? What really engages me?' I wanted to grow in the sense of belonging to God and allow God to be, as I put it, 'the goal of my life'. But I asked myself: 'Is life for me merely personal achievement and self-satisfaction, even though this achievement and self-satisfaction take place in the religious sphere?' Other observations from Fr Stein left me more at ease like his remark on keeping one's mouth shut: 'Absolute silence is one of the hardest tests of brotherly love.' At least there, I thought, I had been fairly consistently in the right. That was one area where my conscience would not menace me.

Fr Stein blended Germanic abstractions ('God is the hidden source of being' and 'we must correspond to the truth'[4]) with plenty

---

4 'Gott ist der verborgene Quellpunkt des Daseins', and 'wir müssen der Wahrheit entsprechen.'

of apt stories. One story which he told in connection with Christ's death concerned an SS purge during the war. A certain Willi Schmidt was listed among the persons to be executed. Only after he was shot was it discovered that the SS had murdered the wrong man. He had nothing in common with the real Willi Schmidt except his name. It all looked like some ghastly accident.. On the desk of the unfortunate victim was found a slip of paper containing a quotation from a letter that St Bernard wrote to a pope: '*Ordinatissimum est* (it is part of the highest order of things) that sometimes something apparently not in order should happen.'

In his conferences at the end of the third week Fr Stein kept talking about Christ's tomb. I found that irritating. Otherwise throughout the thirty days I welcomed his emphasis on faith, his desire to evoke in us a prayerful encounter with the living God, and his concern that we should make the Spiritual Exercises as a community, consciously praying with one another and for one another. Gathered from far-flung places for ten months together in our Westphalian tertianship, my companions generated in me a sense of life's transitoriness. 'We are always saying goodbye', I noted, 'packing up, gathering addresses, hoping to see people again one day. But life goes on—unrepeatable.'

Fr Stein began one conference with the astonishing news, almost the only news we heard during the retreat: 'Nikita Khrushchev has fallen.' On 15 October Khrushchev had resigned as First Secretary of the Communist Party in the USSR and Chairman of the Council of Ministers or Premier. Leonid Brezhnev became First Secretary and Alexei Kosygin took over as Premier. It shook me to reflect that, in little more than a year, death and political intrigue had removed the trinity who provided a reassuring horizon in my world: Pope John, President Kennedy, and now Khrushchev.

Apart from the New Testament and Thomas à Kempis' *Imitation of Christ*, I read only two books during the retreat. A small work on everyday faith by Karl Rahner comforted me, especially with its theme that the present gathers up the abiding harvest of the past. It came home to me that my outward journey did not inevitably vanish into oblivion. The results of each period need not die with the resumption of my wanderings. Several times during the retreat I rose to make a midnight meditation in the chapel. In other ways I pushed myself into a slightly intense, nervy state. To ease the strain I read Ernest Hemingway's *A Farewell to Arms*, which I happened to find stuffed away in a cupboard. It helped, despite its pessimistic message that the good die young, life is cruel, and love exposes one to suffering. I ended the retreat with various resolutions:

> Be ready for weariness, sickness, the pain of leaving people and places that I have come to like. Do all this not in a sad spirit, but in an enthusiastic desire to share Christ's cross for the salvation of the world and to preach Christ. Precisely then can I be sure that Christ's grace is with me at its strongest. Don't be too engrossed with immediate goals, the self-satisfaction of doing things well. Hold to Christ. Use the drive for success in Christ's service. Hunger to help souls. Think actively of others and of helping them.

When I picked up my mail at the end of the retreat, there was a letter from Peter Kelly, the rector of Canisius College in Pymble, asking that I should switch my doctoral plans from ecclesiology to fundamental theology (which involved study in the area of scripture and revelation). Peter proposed that I should spend three years in Rome: two years securing a licentiate from the Biblical Institute and one year completing, if possible, a doctoral dissertation at the Gregorian University. This scheme, which sprang from a desire to provide a better scriptural basis for teaching theology, had attracted a number of Jesuits, including one of my fellow tertians, an American who was to begin his Roman studies in the autumn of 1965. Without much hesitation I wrote at once to Peter telling him that I would be happy to shift to fundamental theology, but asking him to request (from his studies committee and the Australian provincial) permission for me to go rather to Cambridge University.

Various motives fed into my decision. Fr Robert North and my sister Maev had, quite independently, impressed on me the value of seizing any chance to spend some time studying in Oxford or Cambridge. A couple of my fellow tertians planned to study classics at Cambridge. A New England Jesuit, George MacRae, was already there, completing a PhD in early Christian history. I shared a conviction that had begun to lead many Jesuits (and other Catholic priests) to undertake graduate work in theology outside Rome, Louvain, the Institut Catholique in Paris, the Catholic University of America (Washington, DC), and other places to which they had traditionally gone. Some Catholic theology was sub-standard, and we could learn from non-Catholic theologians. As I saw it then, the Gregorian University and the Biblical Institute represented the past, where Bill Dalton, Peter Kelly, Peter Kenny, John Scullion, and other Australian Jesuits had inevitably gone. Finally, I wanted to support myself during my studies abroad. A decision to work at the Gregorian or some other continental university would have made it harder, perhaps much harder, to win a University of Melbourne Travelling Scholarship, the only grant genuinely open to me in Australia.

I knew John O'Neill and James McCaughey, both now in Cambridge. In Sydney I had attended lecturers from Dennis Nineham, recently appointed Regius Professor of Divinity in Cambridge, With admirable clarity John supplied me with the information I needed, and contacted Nineham, who agreed to supervise my research in the area of revelation. James helped to get me accepted as a graduate student by Pembroke College, the college which his father had also attended and to which Davis sent a steady stream of graduates from Ormond College, Melbourne.

The only alternative to Cambridge that I seriously entertained was Tübingen, to which one of my fellow tertians planned to go for doctoral studies in theology. In the middle and late sixties Ebeling, Käsemann, Küng, Moltmann, Oberman, Ratzinger, and others made the Protestant and Catholic faculties of theology in Tübingen immensely strong. However, I shrank from undertaking a doctoral programme in Germany. One had first to write a dissertation, and then a year or so later pass the *rigorosum*, a comprehensive oral examination covering all the major areas in theology. After so many years of Jesuit and university studies, I was tired of facing examinations. At Cambridge a successful dissertation was the only requirement for the doctorate. That system offered me a chance of writing and publishing reviews and articles. Australian theology, both Catholic and Protestant, struck me as falling below the standard *both* of European and North American theology *and* of other disciplines in Australia. My criterion was harshly pragmatic. How often did international journals carry pieces by theologians working in my own country? By publishing articles in some of the main journals of theology, I hoped to do something for the general morale of the subject in Australia. Success in publication would also meet my pressing need to 'get runs on the board', and establish myself in a field that I was entering in my mid-thirties and so somewhat later than others. Although I chose Cambridge over Tübingen, I hoped to visit Tübingen during the summer months, and enjoy the best of both the British and the German theological worlds.

The permission to study in Cambridge came quickly from my Jesuit provincial in Australia. The Cambridge Board of Research Studies and Pembroke College accepted me. Finally, I received word in the spring of 1965 that I had won a University of Melbourne Travelling Scholarship. I was impressed by the large-minded generosity of my old university in agreeing to finance my research, even though there were no theological jobs for me to return to, either at the University of Melbourne or (in those years) at any other Australian university.

Out of all the letters prompted by my decision to apply for Cambridge, I kept only two: one from George Gellie and the other from uncle Jim. As acting head of the classics department at the University of Melbourne, George had strongly supported my scholarship application. His encouragement came across warmly: 'I am delighted for you and your family. I confidently expect you to set the Cam on fire and do yet another superb course.' Uncle Jim wrote in May 1965: 'Thanks for your welcome letter of 10 March. I am glad to know that you are finding everything so interesting, beneficial and pleasant. It is a great opportunity for a young Australian to have the experiences that are and will be yours. You will find out how much these experiences will mean to you all through life, as you direct and form the characters of all the young men who will come under your care.'

But to return to my life in the tertianship. From the end of October we resumed our daily routine of prayer, study, conferences, and house work. We rose at 5.30 a.m. and after an hour's meditation normally celebrated Mass by ourselves and in one of the small chapels situated in the basement of the new wing. Each morning a squadron of German altar-boys swept into the sacristy, shook hands all round, and one by one led us off to our separate altars. As far as I can recall, the first concelebration of my priestly life occurred on 2 February 1965, when I said Mass with a number of tertians in the main chapel and preached. For the occasion I translated into German a sermon by Ronald Knox on the feast of Candlemas.

In our conferences we discussed the constitutions of the order, leading retreats for various types of people, hearing confessions, and further pastoral activities. Many of us presented papers on essential themes of religious and Jesuit life. I offered a three thousand word essay on St Ignatius' contribution to the theory and practice of religious poverty—the longest piece of writing I have ever done in German.

Ludwig Bertsch and Norbert Lohfink came from Sankt Georgen to run a three-day course on the use of scripture in retreats and other ministries. Otto Semmelroth, a *peritus* or theological consultor at Vatican II, gave a lecture on *Lumen Gentium*, the dogmatic constitution on the Church promulgated in late 1964 at the third session of the Council. Johannes Hirschmann, another Jesuit *peritus* at the Council, spoke to us for three and a half hours on the progress made at the Council and the prospects for the coming General Congregation of the Society of Jesus. (In 1964 Fr John Baptist Janssens died after serving as superior general of the order since 1946. The thirty-first General Congregation convened in May 1965 and in July elected Fr Pedro Arrupe to be our next general.) Hirschmann's performance astonished me. I never imagined that someone could address me in a foreign language, continue for over three hours, and remain consistently eloquent and entertaining.

Another German Jesuit, Wilhelm Bertrams (who taught canon law at the Gregorian University), came from Rome to defend the official Catholic ban on artificial birth control. Along with nearly all the tertians I found his dry legalism unpersuasive. At that point, while continuing to hear them with respect, I ceased to accept the teaching of Pius XI and Pius XII against contraception. It was a matter of rational principles, not revealed truth. The arguments offered no longer seemed to compel assent to the negative conclusions.

During the ten months of tertianship, I became very familiar with Münster, a pretty city of about 200,000 inhabitants. Haus Sentmaring was about twenty minutes on foot from the centre of town. The sixteenth century had seen some outbursts of religious savagery in Münster. The tower of one church still carried the cages, in which the bodies of unfortunate Anabaptists had been displayed after execution. In the Rathaus one could inspect instruments with which Catholics had tortured 'heretics'. But by the mid-1960s the people seemed to earn the epithet given them by southern Germans, '*stur*', which I understood to be roughly synonymous with 'dour'. When I recall Münster, I think not of violence but of stout ladies in round, black hats scoffing cakes and tarts over their afternoon coffee. Very few hints of the Second World War remained, apart from the dredge that fished for unexploded bombs in the town lake, the Aasee. There were large barracks for the army of the Rhine nearby, but the British troops kept aloof from the life of Münster itself.

After the long retreat Myles Lovell and I began again to spend most weekends at the British school in Hamm. In November the Archbishop of Canterbury (Dr Michael Ramsey), his wife, and chaplain (John Andrew) visited Windsor Girls School in Hamm. This counterpart to the boys school was about a mile away, and had its own, permanent Catholic chaplain. Myles and I were invited across to a reception for the archbishop. We sat behind him on the stage, facing an audience of five hundred girls and most of the boys from our school. After speeches from the Anglican chaplain of the girls school, the headmistress, and the head girl (who happened to be a Catholic), the archbishop spoke and concluded by asking the boys and girls to repeat after him a prayer by a medieval saint, St Richard of Chichester. The choice of this lovely prayer was ecumenically perfect. Over afternoon tea I chatted with Dr Ramsey, his wife, and John Andrew. They were all to visit Australia the following March. I mentioned to the archbishop the sorry theological and ecumenical state of the Anglican archdiocese of Sydney. 'Could you as a visitor do something about it?', I asked. He smiled below his bushy, attractive eyebrows: 'Yes, yes, I know all about that.' In Sydney he gave a newspaper interview which called for big changes of attitude, but the local Anglicans shrugged it all off as 'misreporting'. I exchanged one or two letters with John Andrew, who wrote on their return to England:

'My dear Gerald, We had a most happy trip to Australia, marred only by the illness of Mrs Ramsey that became serious, necessitating surgery at the Mercy Hospital in Melbourne. Those religious were simply marvellous and no praise is too great for the way they looked after her. It was a religious experience to wait alongside them as Mrs Ramsey began to recover.' John added: 'I am curious to know if in fact you won a scholarship and have got a place at Cambridge, or what you intend to do. I should love to see you sometime.' By the time I reached Cambridge, however, I had become so compulsively engrossed in my research and other activities that I never visited Lambeth Palace.

Alongside the work at Hamm, I accepted pastoral work for German communities. By the time Christmas came around, I was ready to spend several days helping in a German parish. On 22 December I took a bus to Ennigerloh, where pretty Fräulein Müller, aged twenty-four and pastoral assistant in the parish, met me at the bus-stop. She balanced my suitcase on the back of her bike, while she conducted me to the parish house. I was a bit startled to be confronted by my first *Seelsorgehelferin*. To get the conversation going, I asked, 'What's the parish priest like?' '*Ständig unterwegs* (always on the move)', she replied. Since she was leaving that evening to spend Christmas at home, she could let me stay in her room. I took a quick cup of coffee, and dashed into the church to hear confessions until 8 p.m.—my first experience of hearing confessions in German. When I I walked back to the parish house, Pastor Niebrügge welcomed me for an evening meal prepared by his sister. Conversation at meals turned out to be slightly embarrassing. I could understand the pastor perfectly, but his sister's *Plattdeutsch* eluded me.

The next day I walked around Ennigerloh in the weak, wintry sunshine, and realized at once how the parish church matched the chief basis of the village's livelihood. It was built of concrete and looked across a slight dip to the cement and lime factory where hundreds of men worked. More confessions followed at 5 p.m. I celebrated Mass and preached at 7.30. On Christmas Eve I heard more confessions in the morning and again in the afternoon without a break from 2.55 to 6.10. A few stragglers drifted into the church, but by 7 p.m. the great confessional rush was over. A remarkable hush had fallen over the village. The night was very cold and very still.

At midnight people jammed the church for the Mass that their pastor sang. Five firs, three to five metres high, loomed fragrantly behind the altar. The seventeen servers dazzled me: four young men in white albs leading a column of boys in green and red soutanes. The carols, the crib, and the warmth of all those people made me feel at home and at peace. On Christmas Day I walked across to help distribute Holy Communion at the 7.30 Mass and bounced along with joy. It was beginning to snow and would continue to snow for several hours. My first white Christmas! At 8.30 I said Mass and preached, and at 10 sang a Mass and preached again. A huge dinner with the pastor and his sister followed.

After the 5 p.m. devotions the pastor suggested, 'Come out and meet some of the families.' We wandered through the village, popping into homes and drinking Schnapps, while children rushed in shrieking, 'Pastor! Pastor!' We had to get down on our hands and knees to try out trains, cars, telephones, and other gadgets that the Christ Child had brought them. Back at the parish house I shared a bottle of wine with the pastor, a well read man around fifty who obviously considered the official Catholic teaching on birth control impossible. I told him how happy this Christmas had been for me and asked, 'When was your most memorable Christmas?' 'During the war', he replied, 'with a small group in a railway truck in Russia. That was really Christmas.'

On Boxing Day I helped distribute Communion at the crowded 7.30 Mass. I sang the 10 o'clock Mass, enjoyed the choir that was on visit from a neighbouring parish, and returned to Münster.

Back at Haus Sentmaring Myles Lovell told me of the Christmas he had spent in a Schloss acting as chaplain to a German noble family. He had decided that these great landowners, despite their admirable record of resistance to the Nazi regime, needed to be reminded of Christian poverty. He was still chuckling over his sermon, which began with St Francis's vision of Assisi turned upside down and developed the theme: 'He has put down the mighty from their thrones and has exalted the lowly.' Myles, I felt, had nerves of steel.

For the whole of Lent all the tertians left Haus Sentmaring to work in various pastoral ministries. I jumped at the chance of being a junior curate at St Gangolf's church in Trier. The snow still lay thick on both sides of the track, when the train from Münster passed Cologne and cut through the forests of the Eifel. I thought of Hitler sending his tanks through those trees for the 1940 victory over France and his last despairing counter-offensive of December 1944. We crossed the Mosel and slid into Trier, Germany's oldest city and once a capital of the Roman Empire. I twisted around in the taxi to enjoy my first long look at the finest Roman gate in the world, the Porta Nigra, which still sets its dark, windowless face towards the turbulent Germanic tribes of the north.

I took an instant and lasting delight in Trier's buildings that record in stone its long history. The late Gothic church of St Gangolf leans over the market place, which huddles around a Celtic cross erected by Irish missionaries well over a thousand years ago. The cathedral stands about a hundred yards away, and combines Roman, Romanesque, Renaissance, and Rococo elements in a mish-mash of styles that I have not seen paralleled elsewhere. St Helena built the original cathedral, of which one wall survives. Her son, the Roman emperor Constantine, left the lofty red-brick basilica that came to serve as the main Protestant church in Trier. Karl Marx studied at the diocesan seminary in the day when it was a high school.

But my boss for Lent, Pastor Heinrich Schneider, quickly put the city into perspective. Almost his first words to me were: 'You have to realize, Herr O'Collins, that Catholics on the Mosel carry their rosary beads in one pocket and a cork-screw in the other.' And then to make me feel at home he added: 'Do you know that we have a kangaroo quarter in Trier? That's where the public servants live. They spring about a lot but they don't have any money in their pouches.' Short, plump, red-faced, and forever perspiring, Pastor Schneider drew his grey hair over this head. His large black hat bobbed along the streets, and stopped when he button-holed a parishioner to swop news and crack jokes.

Pastor Schneider gave me plenty of opportunities to preach, hear confessions, and visit the sick. At his church's thirteenth-century bronze font I performed my second baptism ever. Apart from the prayer of exorcism, the entire liturgy was now in German. 'Does the devil', I asked myself, 'still understand only Latin?' I celebrated my first requiem Mass, followed by the burial in the Trier cemetery. We prayed in the cemetery chapel before moving to a freshly dug grave. As we started our procession I suddenly noticed Roman tombs on the right hand side of the path. We were following death and interment from the age of Constantine right down to the twentieth century.

For the first time I officiated at weddings: one wedding between two Germans and the other between a German girl and an American serviceman. After the ceremony the first bridal party visited a new cemetery that clung to the hillside above the Mosel. The bridegroom's mother, killed in a traffic accident not quite two years before, lay buried there. The bride walked ahead to put her bouquet on the grave. I helped the bridegroom's father up the steps to the cemetery. He had been wounded in Russia and limped heavily, supporting himself on a stick. The rain lashed us. The other wedding seemed equally sombre, but for different reasons. The (Protestant) serviceman had lived with his blond, Catholic girl friend, and in a basket their baby was present at the wedding. I was surprised when the boldly beautiful girl wept in the sacristy after the ceremony (which I conducted in English and German). Shortly afterwards her husband was posted to Vietnam. Later I sometimes wondered what had happened to him, and whether I had been right to encourage them to marry.

My work in Trier climaxed with Holy Week, when I helped to run the ceremonies and heard hundreds of confessions. On most Saturdays many people, who had come from nearby villages to shop in Trier, dropped into St Gangolf's to pray and confess their sins. Easter was a particularly busy time. On at least two occasions I heard confessions non-stop for four hours. Although the effort to be concise, sensitive, and encouraging in a foreign language left me exhausted, those hours 'in the box' comforted me. It was always mysteriously possible that this priestly ministry would help some to a happier and more Christian way of living.

Back in Münster there were only two more months of tertianship to run. Some work with refugees and soldiers offered new pastoral experiences. I spent two weekends at a parish and 'Flüchtlingslager' in Stukenbrock, a village near Paderborn. About three thousand people, many of them elderly Germans from eastern Europe, lived in a refugee camp, where some of the buildings survived from a former prisoner of war camp. Sixty-five thousand Russians lay buried in the cemetery. A feeling of human suffering, past and present, appalled me in Stukenbrock. Two things softened that sense of misery, the devotion of the Caritas sisters (who staffed the camp hospital, cared for the old, and did the cooking), and the skill of a German gardener. He kept the cemetery in perfect order and grew banks of flowers around the graves. That spring the Russian authorities rewarded his untiring respect for their dead by giving him a holiday in Moscow.

Twice I went down to Trinity House near Cologne to lead retreats for groups of British and Canadian soldiers. Some of the men looked as if they had been sent by a despairing sergeant major, even bundled out of guard houses in the spirit of 'let's see if the padre can knock any sense into them'. But the group discussions, the sentimental hymns at benediction, Moody Institute films, individual chats, beer from the bar, talks (about God's love, the purpose of life, and some other basic items), daily Mass, and the easy atmosphere of that mansion on the banks of the Rhine resulted in a stream of the most rapid conversions I have ever experienced. The honest simplicity of the soldiers touched me, especially when without any fuss they would come to my room, sit down, and pour out their stories of sin and suffering.

The tertianship hurried to an end with a flurry of secular and sacred events. We took an all-day excursion to Wolfsburg, where we toured and lunched at the Volkswagen works, the largest automobile factory in Europe. In the afternoon we pushed on a few kilometers to inspect the East German border. Beyond the minefield a large notice announced that fifty-five million people had died in the Second World War, and called on West Germans to oppose atomic weapons being stationed in their country. A guard in a white building waved to us from the other side. Suddenly the solemn horror of dividing a nation with minefields and barbed wire seemed a little less intolerable. A few days later I walked out with a Portuguese Jesuit to Our Lady's shrine at Telgte, our personal pilgrimage to end the year. We all made an eight-day retreat, posed for group photographs, and enjoyed a farewell party (at which Myles Lovell delivered a witty speech of thanks to Fr Stein). On 30 June most of the tertians departed.

Tertianship did at least three things for me. It brought home the international character of the Jesuit order, offered an enriching variety of pastoral experiences, and introduced me to another tradition of Catholicism. The quality of architecture and music, concern for preaching, centres of pilgrimage, and massive theological strength of the German Church led me beyond the limitations of Catholic life in Australia. Yet at the end of the tertianship a sense of zest seemed to be lacking. During the closing eight-day retreat I noted: 'I should *feel* the tremendous importance of this retreat for myself, my fellow tertians, and all those whose salvation and sanctification depend on us. But I don't...At the beginning of my life in the Society there was *élan* without wisdom. Now there is wisdom without *élan*.' But Fr Stein's advice promised to remedy this: 'Keep close to young people. They have *élan* and are ready for change.'

Travels with Mother

On her first trip overseas since 1923, mother had travelled alone to Europe. When she moved north from Italy, I was to hire a car in Cologne and drive south to meet her in Heidelberg. Before she arrived, I felt so anxious to resume theological studies that I used some free days to write a 'note' for *Theological Studies* and to hear three lectures at Münster university: Anton Vögtle on 'Gospel and Tradition', J. B. Metz on 'Revelation and Faith', and a visitor from Hull on the Reformation. I have never heard a German produce longer or more complicated sentences than Vögtle. The students clapped him, when he achieved the seemingly impossible and got all the verbs correctly marshalled at the end of one gigantic period. The piece for *Theological Studies* sharply criticized the sloppy quality of an article that had just appeared in its June number, 'Anti-Semitism and the Gospel' by John Dominic Crossan, later to become famous (or notorious?) for his work in the Jesus Seminar. My tone reflected the impatience I felt to be away and into research at Cambridge.

I became, however, infected with some of mother's sheer delight at the beauty of Europe, which she had last visited over forty years earlier. We marvelled at the great Romanesque cathedral in Speyer, tracked down the original Liebfrauenmilch vineyard near Worms, admired Balthasar Neumann's altar in the Worms cathedral, paid our respects to the Luther monument, and explored Heidelberg thoroughly. I noted that the full title of the Catholic parish priest ran: Stadtpfarrer Monsignor Professor Doktor Richard Hauser! After I said a Sunday Mass and preached in Heideberg's Jesuitenkirche, an American nun came up to say: 'Father, I knew you weren't German, once I heard you reach the Latin part of the Mass.'

From Heidelberg we drove up the Neckar to Tübingen, where we stayed at the Hotel Lamm, right on the ancient market place. For me it was love at first sight, when I glimpsed the fifteenth-century townhall leaning over a fountain out of which Neptune rose, his trident festooned with flowers. I found in Tübingen what I had looked for in Heidelberg: the unspoiled beauty of a medieval, university town. At the Lamm a waitress suggested kangaroo-tail soup. When I chose something else, she smilingly agreed: 'Of course, no one takes his native dishes when he's abroad.' I did not have the heart to tell her that, unlike many Germans, I had never in my life tasted this soup.

We made a refreshing stop at the Benedictine monastery of Maria Laach. Mother did not know what to praise more highly: the beauty of the liturgy or the unsophisticated comfort of the hotel. As we left, she assured me, 'It's been a real cure for soul and body.' We crossed to England after a fortnight of constant travel that gratified mother and satisfied my academic hunger by visiting the universities of Heidelberg, Tübingen, Freiburg im Breisgau, Strasbourg, Cologne, and Louvain.

Like any good Jesuit visiting London for the first time, I stayed at Farm Street to meet Martin D'Arcy, James Brodrick, Archbishop Tom Roberts and other legendary Jesuits who lived in that West End residence. After dinner I explained over coffee that I was off to Cambridge to do research in theology. One of the fathers asked in surprise, 'Why do you want to go and study with those heretics?'

Archbishop Roberts, to my delight, exploded with laughter and saved me from trying to answer. On my first evening a Jesuit brother took me to Marble Arch, the site of Tyburn Hill to which many English martyrs had been dragged on hurdles for execution. We slipped across to Hyde Park corner to hear the speakers. A man carrying a board that proclaimed 'Jesus saves' caught sight of our clerical collars and shouted, 'Wolves in sheeps' clothing!' John Eddy, who already had a year's research behind him at Oxford, came down to welcome me. He introduced me to the British Museum, as well as passing on to me with a chuckle a mutual friend's comment: 'So, Gerald is off to Cambridge. I hope he doesn't run off with the vice-chancellor's daughter as another Jesuit did a few years ago.'

After five days in London I flew with my mother to Dublin, where I stayed at the Jesuit theological college, Milltown Park. Simply being in Ireland felt like coming home at last. Mother hired a car and we set off quickly to County Limerick, where grandmother Fitzgerald's relatives greeted us with enthusiastic affection. Sunlight poured down on the wide Shannon estuary. The hills of Clare beckoned from across those shining waters. The scenery and the living occasion fused inseparably to convey a sense of peace, deeper than I have found anywhere else in the world.

From Limerick we drove north to Gort, the town where my grandfather Glynn was born and grew up. It lies deep in the west of Ireland, about ten miles from Galway Bay. The Blackwater River, which flows through Gort, runs underground for much of its course and emerges here and there in holes, until it empties at last into Coole Lake. This is the river celebrated by W.B. Yeats in his poem 'Coole Park and Ballylee, 1931', written from his Norman tower near Gort more than fifty years after my grandfather left for Australia:

> Under my window-ledge the waters race,
>
> Otters below and moor hens on the top,

Run for a mile undimmed in Heaven's face

Then darkening through 'dark' Rafferty's 'cellar' drop,

Run underground, rise in a rocky place

In Coole demesne, and there to finish up

Spread to a lake and drop into a hole.

What's water but the generated soul?

The estates around Gort had been owned by hated landlords, like the Shaw-Taylors, or by the more congenial Goughs and Gregorys. The workhouse in George Street and the mass pauper graves in Bullies Acre contrasted with the serenity and wealth of the great houses, like the Gregorys' home, Coole Park, and with the comfortable prosperity of those town houses where merchants, like the Glynns, had lived for centuries. It was a countryside rich in the natural beauty of lake and mountain, and in the long, grim history of wars that had left ruined castles and towers in the fields.

We visited grandfather's house, his school, the church where he prayed, and the cemetery where his parents and ancestors lay buried. The parish priest, who had known uncle Jim and uncle Gerald during his studies in Rome, startled me by asking, 'Now, what's all this about the ecumenical movement?' Then I learned that his entire parish contained only one non-Catholic family. But the townspeople remembered with gratitude that during the 'Troubles' the Church of Ireland minister had rushed out to prevent British troops from carrying out their threat to burn Gort down. On the second day of our visit a cattle fair took place. Fine rain fell on the cows and heifers huddled behind temporary pens that lined the streets. A soft stench filled the air. Our hotel had laid covers over the carpets. The boots of the farmers left a trail of manure through the entrance, along the main passage, up the stairs, and into the dining room. But it was the beauty of Gort that stuck in my mind and haunts me still.

I left mother in Wexford with a cousin and hurried down to Cork, where I led an eight-day retreat for a group of nuns. During tertianship I had prepared my retreat lectures: an amalgam of biblical material, theological reflections, and anecdotes that followed the general outline of St Ignatius's Spiritual Exercises. The eight days went by smoothly, but I did little more than follow through a pre-arranged scheme of talks, prayers, and Masses. I failed to explore and be guided by the real needs of the sisters.

Next door to the convent were the remains of the old gaol. I remembered Terence MacSwiney, the major of Cork who died in 1920, as a result of a hunger strike undertaken in protest against the British occupation of his country. At that time many buildings of 'rebel Cork' had been burnt down or blown up. Nearly fifty years later the city still looked slightly ramshackle. A few people continued to speak of the British as 'the enemy'. I was beginning to notice the scars that centuries of occupation had left behind.

After the retreat I went over to Limerick to meet uncle Jim, then on his way to the fourth and final session of the Second Vatican Council. He had just attended the opening of the new Galway cathedral, a building for which he had literally given his blood more than fifty years earlier. Around 1910 two Irish priests had visited Australia to collect money for this cathedral. Uncle Jim's youth club arranged a boxing tournament as a way of raising a contribution. He fought his way into the final, in which he suffered a battered nose.

Mother had made her own way back to England. I rejoined her in Manchester where we hired our car and took our third trip together that summer, this time nine slow days wandering south to Wells, Glastonbury and, finally, Cheltenham (where I left mother with friends). I was moving into the beautiful world of English cathedrals: Chester, Worcester, Hereford, Gloucester, and Wells. In Wells cathedral a lamp burned in the chapel of St John the Evangelist and a notice read: 'The Blessed Sacrament is reserved for the comfort and help of the sick and dying.' I had been surprised and pleased to see the Eucharist reserved also in Chester Cathedral, Gloucester Cathedral, and Tewksbury Abbey, as well as find a notice about confession by appointment in Chester. Anglo-Catholic practices were familiar to me, but I had not expected to find lamps burning before the reserved Eucharist in Anglican cathedrals.

After almost two months on the road, it was a relief to spend four weeks at Heythrop College and Campion Hall, two Jesuit houses of study, the first some kilometers out of Oxford and the other right in the city itself. In mid-September mother left for Australia, and at the end of the month I went up to Cambridge. But before that the Third International Congress of New Testament Studies took place in Oxford. There I met some new groups, notably such scripture scholars from the United States as Krister Stendahl of Harvard Divinity School (who dominated the conference), Amos Wilder (a brother of the novelist Thornton Wilder), Raymond Brown, and George MacRae. A German academic delighted Amos by telling him: 'Herr Professor Wilder, I have found much theology in your brother's novels, but no fiction in your theology.' Lectures ranged from top class offerings by Stendahl, MacRae, and the Archbishop of Canterbury (who opened the congress) to quaint and erratic papers. One country vicar defended the thesis that on his missionary journeys St Peter carried around with him as an *aide-mémoire* the Gospel of Matthew. I puzzled over a short paper by John Bligh, a Jesuit New Testament lecturer at Heythrop College. St Paul recalled the enthusiastic welcome he had originally received from the Galatians and asked: 'What has become of the satisfaction you felt? For I bear witness that, if it had been possible, you would have plucked out your eyes and given them to me' (Galatians 4: 15). Bligh detected here one of the apostle's 'bloody witticisms'. Explaining 'eyes' to be a vulgar expression for testicles, he understood the passage to mean: 'You would have castrated yourselves, if I had asked you to do so.' This exegesis struck me as highly unlikely and slightly sick.

On 24 September I took the train from Oxford to Cambridge to begin three years of research at Pembroke College. My first great burst of journeying was over. It had led me to the Mediterranean sources of my western culture, to the Catholicism of northern Europe, and then on to England and Ireland. In England I found my mother-country, the source of those political and social institutions that have shaped the Australian way of life. In Ireland I made my way back to family origins in the town of Gort and on the banks of the Shannon. With scrubbing brush, washing soda, and a bucket of hot water, I had attacked the tombstones in Kilmacduagh cemetery outside Gort. The moss and lichen fell away to reveal the names of ancestors. I have never returned to Gort, and let nine years pass before visiting Limerick again. The summer of 1965 pacified some deep need to hunt down the traces of my forebears and settle my historical roots. Now my own place in the world was to be questioned. Deciding for Cambridge had already changed the pattern my Jesuit superiors and family anticipated for me—Rome and then home. Uncle Will muttered anxiously, 'I hope Gerald knows what he is doing.' By the summer of 1968 I was to begin asking myself, 'What is my Church doing, and what am I doing?'

7

Pembroke (1965-68)

The longest journey is the journey inwards

Dag Hammarskjöld

Pembroke College faced me with yet another forbidding situation, in which I had to make new friends and find my identity in a new community almost from scratch. I knew none of the fellows and students. James McCaughey had just taken his degree in divinity and left for Trinity College Dublin, to revive his classics after 'exorcising the theological demon', as he put it. But knowing James and his family helped me to establish friendship quickly with two of the fellows, Hugh Mellor and Meredith Dewey.

Hugh Mellor and Meredith Dewey

Dark-haired and middle-sized, Hugh thought and spoke with the enviable speed and precision of an adept philosopher. He enriched Pembroke life enormously by his interest in college societies and passion for acting. Under his direction a small theatre was beautifully (and economically!) equipped in the Old Reader, the ground floor of the college library building. A highlight of the Easter term was 'the Pembroke Smoker', in which Clive James (a postgraduate student at Pembroke), Germaine Greer (a research student at nearby Newnham College), and others tried out acts that they were to put on later for 'the Footlights' and other Cambridge reviews. Two memories of Germaine return: her success at singing 'Land of Hope and Glory' entirely off-key, and an act in which she played a nun stripping off her habit to go spear-fishing. Hugh's own standard of acting in plays like Max Frisch's *Count Oederland* and Eugene Ionesco's *The Lesson* astonished me.[1] During my three years in college, I never saw a play at the Arts Theatre or anywhere else in Cambridge. As in other ways, Pembroke proved sufficient for me.

Hugh involved me very quickly in the Matthew Wren Society and in the Thomas Gray Society. More than anything else membership in these two societies made me feel accepted and ready to make my contribution to college life. The Mathew Wren Society took its name from a seventeenth-century bishop of Ely and master of Pembroke, whose famous nephew, Christopher Wren, designed the college chapel. Paperbacks by Ninian Smart (about to move from Birmingham to become the founding professor of religious studies at Lancaster University) and Colin Williams (an Australian theologian who became dean of the Yale Divinity School) provided material for our discussions in the philosophy of religion. We marked the 299th anniversary of Matthew Wren's death by holding a formal dinner. Shortly after that the society became extinct.

The Thomas Gray Society enjoyed a large membership (including a number of fellows), met for long evenings over port and coffee in Hugh's spacious, Victorian sitting room, and discussed a wide variety of papers. Donald Broadbent reported the latest findings from his experiments on short-term memory. Ian Jack spoke on Thomas Gray himself, and I read a paper on the theology of hope. In March 1966 I was elected secretary for a term of office that ran to the following December. The 'Grays' met for two dinners each year, held in the Old Library. The toasts had to incorporate a phrase or two from the poet's 'Elegy Written in a Country Churchyard'. Then Gray's 'progression' from Peterhouse (his first college) to Pembroke was re-enacted. We

---

1 Max Frisch (1911-91) was a Swiss playwright and novelist; Eugene Ionesco (1912-94) helped found 'the theatre of the absurd'.

picked up some candles from the table and marched together to the Thomas Gray Room, his former set that then served as an extension of the Senior Parlour.

In the spring of 1968 a demonstration against Denis Healey (the Secretary of State for Defence who was in Cambridge to speak that evening) took place in Trumpington Street, right outside the Old Library. Formally dressed, we sat at a long table in the fourteenth-century room enjoying the wine and our right to use some pieces from Pembroke's rich collection of silver. When gusts of shouting drifted in, I stepped out to stand at the college's entrance and survey the scene. Surging knots of cheering students blocked the street, while they waited for Healey to appear. At my side the senior porter looked on and said disgustedly, 'And they call this education.'

Each year the 'Grays' formed a punt party in the first week of June. Those long evenings blended the magic beauty of early summer with loud hilarity. Cygnets and ducklings scudded by, when we poled our way up the Granta to spread rugs and wash down some cold chicken with college claret. The return to Scudamores boatyard became a wild race between punts. On one occasion I took fright when I knocked Hugh into the river. But all was well. He surfaced, flung an arm over the side of my punt, and seized a bottle of wine before swimming back to his own punt.

My debt to Hugh goes far beyond the way he drew me into Pembroke's cultural and social life. My research into modern interpretations of biblical revelation owed much to him. He encouraged me to expound Jürgen Moltmann's views on hope to the Gray Society, discussed at length articles I published on Ernst Fuchs and Wolfhart Pannnberg, and never tired of entering into theological debate with me. I doubt whether Donald MacKinnon, Dennis Nineham, John O'Neill, Maurice Wiles, or anyone else connected with the divinity faculty sparked more theology in me than Hugh Mellor, allegedly an ex-Anglican and non-believer.

Soon after I arrived at Pembroke, I called to pay my respects to Meredith Dewey, the Anglican priest who was dean of the college. He gave me a glass of sherry, sat me down, and asked. 'Who sent you?' I explained that Pembroke was my own choice, but felt his approach to be startling. Did he suspect a Jesuit plot against the college? But before long I learnt to look behind the abrupt, sometimes acerbic, and frequently amusing style of this balding, middle-aged celibate. He followed the best Anglo-Catholic tradition of a personal spiritual life built around regular prayer and reflective reading. No one could question his imperturbable devotion to the college and its members. His flashes of slightly caustic wit constantly amused me. When Robert Graves dined at high table one evening, the other fellows sat back to allow Meredith to spar with the poet, for whose view of life he showed little sympathy. Exasperated by his opponent's negative attitude, Graves finally asked, 'Aren't you being unnecessarily sceptical?' 'Oh, no', Meredith replied, 'it's just that I save my credulity for my religion.'

It took me over a year to overcome my Catholic uneasiness about attending college evensong, at least on Sundays. Then I realized what a treasure I had been missing in Meredith's thoughtful and provocative sermons. From 1967 I began to preach at college evensong. The Roman Catholic bishop of Northampton, whose diocese included Cambridge, gave permission to celebrate Mass in college chapels, provided college authorities allowed it. Several times I said Mass in the Pembroke chapel for the small group of Catholics who were members of the college. It delighted me to find that the silver cross on the altar commemorated a brother of Ronald Knox, Wilfrid Knox, who was a distinguished New Testament scholar and a fellow of Pembroke until his death.

In the spring of 1967, Meredith touchingly showed how far his regard went. He consulted me over some prayers he was to say at the launching of a Polaris submarine in Birkenhead. He knew that I would disapprove of this action, but he invited me and Owen Chadwick to comment on the service he had prepared. I suggested only that he should replace the opening lines of one prayer ('O almighty God, we thank you for the skill and labour of the men who built this ship') with the words, 'O almighty God, we pray for the men whose skill and labour built this ship.' The day Meredith went north to perform the ceremony an anonymous phone call warned that a bomb had been placed in the college chapel. The police came, searched the building, found a large tin placed against a wall, and called the bomb squad. After taking hours to arrive, they found that the tin contained nothing but a rude note and some candles tied up to look like sticks of gelignite.

If Hugh Mellor and Meredith Dewey helped me find my feet in Pembroke, the publication of *Patrick McMahon Glynn* brought some recognition from other fellows of the college. The July before I arrived in Cambridge, my sister Dympna arranged with my other sisters a book launch in Melbourne. Her cable announced: 'Author acclaimed. Epic launching. Literary social ecumenical spirits rampant. Encore. Sisters three.' A letter followed quickly: 'Friday was a huge success', 'easily *the* most delightful and/or successful launching imaginable'. She listed such guests as Sir Reginald Sholl (a judge of the Victorian Supreme Court), John La Nauze, Davis McCaughey, Sir George Paton (Vice-Chancellor of Melbourne University), Geoffrey Searle (a leading Australian historian), Sir John Barry, and 'Lady Curtis oozing charm in the most delightful way. She was marvellous. Dr McWhite, the Irish Ambassador, spoke at length & I am sending a copy of his speech to you tomorrow.' She added that she had given 'Peter Ryan [the publisher] a bottle of champagne as a thank you today...Four hundred copies of the book have been ordered by book sellers, he tells me, and have gone out...I am dropping one in to

Dame Mabel [Brookes] & to Lady Casey as gifts tomorrow.'[2] A week
later Dympna wrote again to report that '*the* book has been given to
the Knight of the Thistle [Sir Robert Menzies, who was still Prime
Minster of Australia] as a parting gift by Mother Philippa after his
Mercy Hospital sojourn. Sir George Paton said that the party was
the most delightful launching he had ever attended.' *Patrick McMahon
Glynn* received almost uniformly good reviews, but after the first burst
of sales sold badly, not much over one thousand copies out of the
two thousand printed. I consoled myself with what the Roman satirist
Juvenal remarked about virtue: '*laudatur et alget* (it receives praise but
is left out in the cold).'

In those days Cambridge University Press distributed Melbourne
University Press books in the United Kingdom and in the United
States. That brought me an invitation to a Cambridge University
Press party, held in January 1966 for their authors of the previous
year. At a bright luncheon, pretty secretaries vied with older editors
to make all manner of writers welcome. Tony Camps, a specialist in
the classics and later master of Pembroke, spotted me and asked with
cheerful surprise. 'What are you doing here, Gerald?' I explained that
my biography of Patrick McMahon Glynn entitled me to the same
invitation as his work on the Latin poet Propertius. Like a shaggy lion,
Sir Mortimer Wheeler, a famous archaeologist, stood in the middle of
the room surveying the crowd. One stranger introduced himself, and
told me that the topic for his book was 'locust control in Africa'. I
enjoyed a long chat with Father David Knowles, who subtly made me
feel that I was part of a significant and proper movement, the return of
Catholic clergy to the old universities of Oxford and Cambridge. He
had himself been Regius Professor of Modern History at Cambridge
(1954-63) and a fellow of Peterhouse.

---

2 Lady Elvie Curtis was the wife of Sir Leo Curtis, the Mayor of Melbourne; Baroness
Maie Casey was the wife of Lord Richard Casey, Governor General of Australia (1969-
74).

Dennis Nineham and the Divinity Faculty

When I reached Cambridge, my supervisor, Dennis Nineham, had been one year Regius Professor of Divinity and a fellow of Emmanuel College. As my reading took me through twentieth-century interpretations of revelation, I bombarded him with papers on the views of Gerald Downing, Wolfhart Pannenberg, Alan Richardson, Ernst Fuchs, and Jürgen Moltmann. All of these theologians were still very much alive in the 1960s. But, unlike some other famous institutions, Cambridge University did not exclude finding one's thesis topic in the thought of the living. I even heard of one young philosopher writing his dissertation on the thought of John Wisdom and under the supervision of John Wisdom. Dennis sent my paper on Downing off to Downing himself, who earlier had been his student at Oxford. This produced a lengthy, useful, and slightly peevish reply to my criticisms. I never met either Downing or Fuchs. During my three years of research, I had one long discussion with Pannenberg and many talks with Moltmann (who became a lifelong friend). In the end the thesis turned into a critical, comparative study of Downing, Fuchs, Pannenberg, and Moltmann, entitled *The Theology of Revelation in Some Recent Discussion.* Dennis played his role as supervisor in a negative but friendly fashion. At most points he questioned and challenged my argument. I felt sure that, wherever he had let my case stand, it would have little trouble from the examiners.

In my first year I treated Dennis with solemn and sometimes excessive deference. I always wore my university gown when I trotted off for supervisions in his rooms at Emmanuel, and addressed him, of course, as 'Professor Nineham'. He surprised me when he moved to first-names in the Michaelmas term of 1966. In the spring of 1967 I failed to appreciate what he was hinting at, when he talked about 'possibilities' at Emmanuel. A few weeks later he met me and asked, 'Why didn't you apply for that research fellowship here?' In the event

I was glad to have missed the implicit invitation. Shifting from one college to another always looked to me a little like an unpleasant divorce and re-marriage. In any case, shortly after Emmanuel chose their new fellows, Pembroke elected me to a research fellowship. About that time Dennis's wife underwent surgery in a London hospital. Ruth seemed to value greatly my visit, largely, I suppose, because so few bothered to travel down from Cambridge to see her. During my second and third year Dennis and Ruth dined with me several times at Pembroke. Increasingly I went to their home for a meal or for tea. In May 1968 Dennis suggested that I apply for an assistant lectureship in divinity. I suspect that my failure to do so contributed a little to his willingness the following year to accept an invitation to become Warden of Keble College, Oxford. He expressed his respect for my decision by asking with a smile, 'Was Cambridge worth a Mass?'

Dennis combined a strain of historical scepticism with High Church piety. At the end of one summer he showed me with glee a photograph of himself, Ruth, and their four children talking in Rome with Pope Paul VI, whom he called 'the Holy Father'. Dennis reacted coolly to my suggestion that bishops should be elected by some form of popular vote rather than appointed from above by the Vatican. 'I don't know about the Catholic Church', he commented. 'But in the Anglican Church the people would chose sportsmen.' On the one hand, I found his reluctance to place much historical trust in the Gospels a minimalizing position. On the other hand, I could not fully share his seemingly unqualified respect for church authority, papal or otherwise. But I became very fond of him, and idealized his role in my life as 'Doktorvater'. He and Ruth afforded me what I also received from John and Judy O'Neill, the chance of escaping sometimes from student life to an affectionate family home, where I could make friends with children and share a little in their growth towards maturity.

Apart from Dennis, there were three other professors on the

Cambridge Faculty of Divinity: Geoffrey Lampe, Donald MacKinnon, and Charlie Moule. While attending only occasionally MacKinnon's lectures in the philosophy of religion, I became a regular participant in his D Society, a seminar that met every fortnight in his home. A large, ungainly Scot with a wild stare, he had read extraordinarily widely in theology, philosophy, and literature, seemed to forget no detail of what he had read, and went out of his way to suggest lines of research which he hoped might be profitable. His knowledge of continental theologians, both Catholic and Protestant, seemed like a breath of fresh air, when I occasionally found the theological atmosphere in Cambridge dull and parochial. His forgetfulness and odd behaviour gave rise to many MacKinnon stories, some of which may have belonged originally to other Oxford eccentrics. Thus I wonder about the historical attribution of a story in which MacKinnon, when still in Oxford, seizes a sign from a pub, rushes through the streets with a crowd in pursuit, disappears into a building, and appears at an upper window to shout to the crowd below, 'An evil and adulterous generation seeketh a sign, but a sign shall be not be given.'

Let me record four stories for which I can personally vouch. I was walking one day down King's Parade, when MacKinnon beckoned me across the street. He proceeded to tell me that a student whom I had agreed to supervise for a graduate course was undergoing psychiatric treatment. He thought that, as his supervisor and a priest, I should know this. I thanked him for his kindness. The student's behaviour had been puzzling me. When I turned to go, MacKinnon asked, 'In what direction was I walking, Father O'Collins, when I stopped you?' I gestured towards Great St Mary's. 'Good', he exclaimed with relief, 'then I have had lunch.' On another occasion I arrived a little early for a session of the D Society to overhear MacKinnon saying over the phone to one of his students, 'Yes, we ALL sometimes feel like taking a train to nowhere and never coming back.' The student had just written to Buckingham Palace requesting the hand of Princess

Anne in marriage and naming MacKinnon as a referee. The palace authorities had alerted MacKinnon to the fact that one of his students seemed to be suffering from a breakdown.

Kenneth Woodward, then the religion editor of *Newsweek*, phoned me one day from London, where he had broken his flight from Rome to New York. He wanted to use the opportunity to write a piece on the current state of theology in Britain. He thought MacKinnon might be helpful, and spent the day in Cambridge. MacKinnon took us both to tea in Regent House. When Woodward mentioned his topic, MacKinnon assured him, 'You have to start with Kant's *Critique of Pure Reason.*' The American journalist sat in stunned silence, as MacKinnon proceeded to lead him into the nineteenth century and eventually reached John Henry Newman. But by that stage Woodward was beyond caring.

I regularly attended the New Testament seminar of Charlie Moule, a birdlike, learned and devout Anglican. One afternoon MacKinnon slipped in late and sat next to me at the end of a long table. After a while he muttered in my ear, 'Have you a knife?' I went through the motions of looking for one in my pockets, knowing full well that I had none. A girl sitting one up from me overheard his question, and leaned across me to hand him a pen knife out of her handbag. Bending down below the level of the table, MacKinnon got to work with the knife as he compulsively sharpened a pencil. A few moments later from the depths, MacKinnon interjected into the general discussion, 'It can never be a moral obligation to castrate yourself.' His remark made some oblique sense in the context of the context of an ethical theme which the seminar was debating. But for a mad moment I had the wild fancy that I might have to grab his hand, in case he tried to do himself some mischief.

Both to take a break from hours of reading in the university library and to fill out my theological education, I heard lectures by Moule (on eschatology) and Lampe (on Luke-Acts), took a course in Hebrew, and attended a short-lived seminar on issues of history and faith run by Dennis Nineham. I read papers at that seminar, the D Society, Moule's New Testament seminar, and a seminar on Christology conducted by Lampe and Maurice Wiles, then dean of Clare College. These groups provided forums, in which I tried out ideas that later made their way into my thesis. Articles that I was publishing in the *Heythrop Journal, Interpretation, Religious Studies*, the *Scottish Journal of Theology* and *Theological Studies* also helped to clarify my arguments, and brought useful criticisms from readers.

At a meeting of the Hort Society in the Michaelmas term of 1966 I gave some major themes of my thesis an early airing by reading a paper on 'the Idea of Revelation in Modern Theology'. That year I served as junior treasurer of this society, which allegedly catered for all theological students in Cambridge but was dominated by the research students. During my three years Charles Davis, R.P.C. Hanson, David Jenkins, Ninian Smart, and others visited Cambridge to address us. C.H. Dodd came out of retirement to speak on 'The Portrait of Jesus in John and the Synoptics'. The crowd proved so large that evening that we had to shift the meeting from the music room of Clare to the college chapel. A trim but deaf eighty-two-year old, Dodd was widely known for his work on John and the parables of Jesus, and as general director of the New English Bible project, 'the word of Dodd', as some jokingly called it. The president of the Hort Society, James Dunn, had to relay (and sometimes abbreviate) the questions by shouting them into the old professor's ear.

Apart from the Hort Society, the divinity faculty itself and other bodies provided occasions to hear visiting theologians like Günther Bornkamm, Paul van Buren, Piet Fransen, Robert Funk, and Ian Ramsey. In his debate with MacKinnon, van Buren insisted that an imaginary God who makes a difference is preferable to a real God who does not count. MacKinnon's deep concern about matters of truth and falsity could sometimes lead him to lapse into sarcastic and even bitter attacks. That evening, however, he showed himself remarkably sensitive and restrained in the face of his opponent's touchy agnosticism.

Others like Hugh Montefiore, Harry Williams, Willie Frend, George MacRae, and Herbert McCabe also helped to create the theological milieu into which I moved at Cambridge. Some critics spoke of 'Hugh Montefiasco', but the lively success of the services at Great St Mary's, where Hugh was vicar, gave the lie to that nickname. I found him consistently kind and concerned with people's needs. But his theological and biblical thinking could be shallow and sensational, as when he once went into print suggesting that Jesus was a homosexual. In the late 1960s Harry Williams was dean of Trinity College. I recall his contribution to a series ('The God I Want') as the most artistic lecture I heard in Cambridge.

Willie Frend sometimes ambushed me when I reached the narrow (King's Parade) end of Trinity Street, and rushed me into his rooms at Caius to give me one of his latest offprints. At that time the direct train to Oxford via Bletchley still ran. On the way to buy books at Blackwell's, George MacRae once found himself in the same compartment as Willie. When George asked what was taking him to Oxford, Willie explained that he was delivering the manuscript of *Early Christian Martyrdom* to his publishers, Blackwell's. 'Do you mind if I have a look at it?', George asked. Willie pulled the manuscript out of his satchel. George skimmed through the text and found a section that his own study of Gnosticism made him familiar with. 'There's nothing here on Antonio Orbe's work', he remarked. 'Never heard of him', Willie admitted. George mentioned one or two books (in Spanish) by Orbe, and explained where they could be found on Blackwell's shelves. When they reached the bookstore, Willie took down the volumes, added some footnotes, and delivered his manuscript to Sir Basil Blackwell.

A chunky Jesuit from New England, George had studied at Johns Hopkins with W. F. Albright and in Louvain before beginning his doctoral research at Cambridge. He was very self-possessed, had a brilliantly perceptive mind, and enjoyed the friendship of Raymond Brown, Joseph Fitzmyer, Robert Funk, James Robinson, Krister Stendahl, and other leading biblical scholars in the United States. When he finished at Cambridge in the spring of 1966, he quickly established a reputation for being a superb lecturer. George overlapped only with my first term in Cambridge, but both then and later I owed much to his encouraging regard for my ability He enlisted me in the work of summarizing articles for *New Testament Abstracts*, and persuaded Herbert McCabe to invite me to review books for *New Blackfriars*. The close study involved in making abstracts furthered my scriptural education. So many review copies flooded into Herbert's office at Blackfriars, the Dominican house in Cambridge, that he left me free to pick books that tied in with my own research. He proclaimed his solution for that glut of publications: 'contrascriptives' to be fitted onto the pens of theological writers.

Lodgings

During my three years in Cambridge, I lived first in a Pembroke College hostel in Clarendon Street, for a time in Fisher House (the Roman Catholic chaplaincy to the university), and for my last year in college itself. As far as I can recall, during 1965/66 James Burtchaell (an outgoing and articulate American in Gonville and Caius) and I were the only Catholic priests studying in Cambridge, who did not live in St Edmund's House. What had been a residence for priests doing undergraduate studies was at that time developing into a graduate college for all comers. I resented a little the way the master of St Edmund's and others there made me feel that I had done something suspect by deciding to live elsewhere. I had to resist some slight pressure to pack my bags and move up to St Edmund's. Apart

from George MacRae and Edmund Campion (a diocesan priest from
Sydney), much of the clerical company there made me uneasy. That
kind of over-concern with ecclesiastical affairs, which gatherings of
priests and ministers can generate, hung in the air. Only a handful of
laymen lived at St Edmund's, including Mr G.M. Fitzgerald, a trim
old gentleman with a Van Dyck beard. Born in 1883, he delighted
me with stories of holidays spent as a schoolboy in Bad Homburg.
In the closing years of the nineteenth century the aristocracy of
Europe thronged that spa town near Frankfurt. He recalled his father
gravely raising his hat, when they passed the Russian royal family.
Mr Fitzgerald's friendly courtesy conveyed a small but pleasing sense
of history repeating itself. His uncle Nick (the Honourable Nicholas
Fitzgerald) entertained Patrick McMahon Glynn, shortly after my
grandfather reached Melbourne in 1880.

A college porter, his wife, and little daughter occupied the hostel
in Clarendon Street, along with myself and three other postgraduate
students: an Indian, an American from William and Mary College,
and another American (from Princeton), Star Lawrence. As affiliated
students, all three took a two-year course which led to examinations
and a (second) B.A. degree that eventually turned into a M.A. Tall,
handsome, and dark-haired, Star amazed our landlady by occasionally
padding around the house in a red night-shirt. He spent his second
year at an elegant house in Newton Road, where an elderly lady
normally kept one Ivy League lodger. She charged next to nothing
and provided large teas on Sundays, at which she liked the guests to
stay long enough to see a hedgehog emerge onto the croquet lawn.
In the summer of 1968 I received an invitation to Star's wedding: 'Mr
and Mrs Marshall Hornblower request the pleasure of your company
at the marriage of their daughter Virginia to Mr Starling Ransome
Lawrence.' Sadly I could not attend and have never seen Star since our
days together in Cambridge.

During my year in Clarendon Street, I said Mass daily and helped at weekends in the nearby Catholic parish church, Our Lady and the English Martyrs, now often known as OLEM. The parish priest made me extraordinarily welcome. In Holy Week 1966 I preached at the main services, heard confessions, and led a special bible service on Palm Sunday. Some months before that, a change had taken place that would shift the centre of my pastoral ministry in Cambridge. Monsignor Alfred Gilbey left Fisher House after serving for exactly one hundred terms as Catholic chaplain. A gracious priest with private means (from trade in gin and sherry), he preferred public school boys at Fisher House and positively drove girls away. After World War II he had helped many ex-servicemen to make their way back to normal living, but by the mid-sixties his day was done. His successor, Richard Incledon, became one of my closest friends.

Three years older than me, Richard was the epitome of a charming English priest. He had a fund of stories, an astonishing memory for names and faces, and preached effective, personal homilies. He could reveal more of himself before a congregation than he did in private conversation. Since his childhood, Jesuits had been his teachers or near neighbours: as a boy at Beaumont College, during his undergraduate years at Trinity College, Oxford (when he lived for a time at Campion Hall), as a seminarian at the Venerable English College in Rome (where he studied under the Jesuits at the Gregorian University), and then as the assistant Catholic chaplain in Oxford (where he lived in the Old Palace under the shadow of Campion Hall). He laughed and told me: 'I had hoped that moving to Cambridge would finally let me escape from the Jesuits, but then I found you there.' Richard gave me a room at Fisher House for my second year, but insisted that I should not let creeping involvement with chaplaincy work interfere with my doctoral research. I said the early morning Mass, preached on Sundays, occasionally heard confessions, and ran a scripture study group. In my last year a research fellowship entitled me to rooms in college, but I continued to help at Fisher House, which in any case was only a few hundred yards from Pembroke.

The Society of Jesus had no house in Cambridge, but half a dozen American Jesuits studied at the university during my time, and most lived at St Edmund's. I sometimes took meals with one or other of these fellow-Jesuits, did not feel at home with most of them, and looked after one when he suffered a mild nervous breakdown. I failed to do what I was well placed to do—make a community out of these scattered individuals by gathering them together regularly for prayer and some form of celebration. When I was back at Pembroke in 1973-74, I brought the Jesuits studying in Cambridge together for an informal evening Mass and supper. Those gatherings could last until two in the morning. But in 1965-68 I kept my Jesuit identity alive by correspondence with superiors and others in Australia, and by frequent contacts with several Jesuit houses in England (Campion Hall, Farm Street, and Heythrop College) and in Ireland (Milltown Park).

Dublin, London and Oxford

In 1966 and 1967 I stayed at Milltown Park, the Jesuit theological college in a Dublin suburb. During the Easter vacation of 1968, I returned there to lead a triduum of prayer for the scholastics and to lecture on contemporary German theology. Those Irish Jesuits made me feel thoroughly welcome, and I enjoyed happy relations with several of them. At Easter 1968 Fr Aubrey Gwynn, a cultured historian and convert to Catholicism, told me how dearly he would like to visit Paris again, which he had last seen more than thirty years earlier. 'Take a flight from Dublin to Orly', I suggested. 'I will be there at the airport to meet you, and look after you in Paris for a week.' We had arranged our rendezvous, when the May revolution came like a bolt from the blue. Fr Gwynn wrote sadly to cancel his trip: 'I am a frightened old man, and couldn't face Paris in its present state.'

Those three trips to Dublin allowed me to meet Terence McCaughey (the youngest brother of Davis McCaughey) and Ernest Nicholson. Terence had been an undergraduate in Cambridge (naturally as a student at Pembroke), before studying theology in Edinburgh and taking up a post in Irish language and literature at Trinity College Dublin. I treasured and profited from a piece of advice he offered me. When I complained about the mass of theological books to be covered, he remarked: 'Read the big chaps and let the little chaps look after themselves.' Terence always struck me as a theologian manqué. When the Australian National University proposed to introduce religious studies, I thought of encouraging him to resume New Testament studies and come to Canberra. But that dream failed. Like his wife Ohna, a native Gaelic speaker, Terence was witty and the soul of kindness. For years he walked a hard road, as a Presbyterian minister from Belfast who was truly ecumenical, loudly critical of injustice on both sides of the border, and politically anti-Unionist.

Big, warm hearted Ernest also came from 'the North'. He taught Old Testament at Trinity College Dublin, until he took a lecturership in Cambridge. I found the uncomplicated goodness of Ernest and his wife Hazel compellingly attractive. During his first months in Cambridge he lived in University (later Wolfson) College, while Hazel and the three children remained in Ireland. I invited Ernest for meals at Pembroke, where Meredith Dewey encouraged him to be ordained, serve as college chaplain, and become his successor as dean. On his way to that position Ernest turned down an invitation to become dean of King's College. It made me happy that I played a small part in his finding a home at Pembroke.

The memory of Irish hospitality and charm floods back from my days in Dublin, when violence had not yet flung the whole country once again in turmoil. Almost the only irritant was a frequent disinclination to call me 'Gerald O'Collins'. Many Irish, including my publishers in Cork (Mercier Press), initially refused to admit 'O'Collins' as a proper Irish name. 'Gerard' (from the popular Redemptorist St Gerard Majella) was a proper Catholic name, while 'Gerald' was Protestant. I often had to protest against being called 'Gerard Collins'. But—not to end on a sour note—I still laugh over the remark of a Dublin taxi-driver, who quickly realized that I was Australian and had arrived from London. I mentioned the breathalyser test, which the British government had just introduced to curb drunken driving. He appealed to a viral disease for rabbits recently propagated in Australia with his comment: 'Sure, it's just like the myxomatosis. They'll build up resistance to it.'

On visits to London I took meals and occasionally stayed at Farm Street, the residence for the Jesuit provincial, the church staff, and some others. Once I was assigned Martin D'Arcy's room, when he was away lecturing in the United States. During his years as master of Campion Hall, he had gathered together for that Jesuit hall of residence in Oxford a remarkable collection of chalices, vestments, paintings, and pieces of sculpture—the 'objets D'Arcy', as some called them. (In 2011 later experts identified one crucifixion scene as a work by Michelangelo; the painting has now been moved to the Ashmolean.) It never occurred to me to check whether his bookshelves in Farm Street contained any autographed works by Evelyn Waugh, whom he had received into the Catholic Church. But he had the latest works by Marshall McLuhan, a Canadian philosopher and literary critic who coined such phrases as 'the global village' and 'the medium is the message'. My knowledge of McLuhan is confined to what I read during my days in Martin D'Arcy's room.

At Campion Hall, John Eddy never disappointed me by the warmth of his welcome. Now bald and a little portly, he exuded affectionate interest in what his friends were doing. His steady cheerfulness led someone to remark a little enviously, 'Jack lives in the best of all possible worlds.' When he took out his DPhil in the spring of 1968, it was inevitable that his 'big day' would draw together from various part of Europe the largest group of Australian Jesuits I have ever seen gathered overseas. In the early 1960s Campion Hall had suffered under a disastrous master, but from 1966 it moved through some golden years. About ten dedicated and attractive Jesuit priests lived there while studying at Oxford University. Half of them belonged to what was then still called the English (rather than the British) province. These included Michael Kyne, a man of radiant holiness who became the master of novices a few years later. I also found the resident, English scholastics outstanding persons and congenial companions. For three years (1965-67) I enjoyed spending Christmas with them and the rest of the community. An ex-chef from the Mitre Tavern in Oxford provided a feast that included a boar's head, which always set the old carol running through my mind: 'A boar's head in hand bear I.' On Boxing Day we entertained a laughing, noisy party of small children from poor families.

Among the younger priests on the permanent staff at Campion Hall, Ted Yarnold was still in his thirties. A quiet, sensible, and determined Yorshireman, Ted proved an effective master and a successful theologian. In 1974 he became the first Roman Catholic since the Reformation to earn his DD at Oxford. He invited me in 1966 to contribute a volume on revelation to a series of fifty paperbacks that he was to edit for the Mercier Press in Ireland and Fides Press in Indiana. I owe Ted much for that invitation, which made the publication of my first theological book a smooth and successful affair. *Theology and Revelation* sold over five thousand copies in the English original, as well as appearing in French, Italian, and Spanish translations.

From the summer of 1965 I was often out at Heythrop College, the theological college for English Jesuits that lay to the north-west of Oxford. The Heythrop Hounds hunted through the college's woods, fields, and nine-hole golf course. The central buildings huddled around a stately home, which had belonged to the family of Thomas Brassey, an international railway contractor in the nineteenth century. At various points along the lengthy drive from the main road, houses for members of other religious institutes had been built or were being

At Rock Lodge early 1969.

planned. Some Benedictines, de Montforts, Passionists, Salvatorians, and religious sisters already studied at Heythrop. The staff included a few non-Jesuits, among whom Charles Davis, the editor of the *Clergy Review*, was the most notable. The attempt to build up this 'pontifical athenaeum', a Catholic theological powerhouse out there in the Oxford countryside, came to an end in the late 1960s. It was too far away from the daily life of cities, universities, and churches. The Westminster Bank bought the estate for a training centre, and Heythrop College moved south to become a part of the University of London. Even in the summer of 1965 cracks were beginning to appear in the walls of that Heythrop attempt to maintain religious life and theological study remote from 'the world'. News came in that the American Jesuits were planning to move their theological colleges from rural settings to university campuses. The need for an ecumenical context for theological teaching forced itself on the attention of the communities at Heythrop. The golf course was now overgrown. Myles Lovell and his companions had been the last group of scholastics, who thought it worthwhile working long hours to keep Jesuits home and happy on their own private course.

At Heythrop I was glad to meet Bernard Leeming again, and assure him how affectionately Australians remembered his visit in 1961. I made new friends, notably Fr Bruno Brinkman. Genial, plump and supported by a superb secretary, Mrs Jeanette Scott (whom the scholastics nicknamed 'Brunette'), Bruno enlisted me quickly in the task of reviewing books for the *Heythrop Journal*, which he had founded in 1960 and continued to edit. I contributed an article on Wolfhart Pannenberg's theology of revelation, and a short piece on the non-historical nature of Christ's resurrection, which caused ripples of interest that I had in no way expected. After *Theology Digest* and a similar Spanish journal published summaries of it, reference to my piece popped up in bibliographies in the *Jerome Biblical Commentary*,

Sacramentum Mundi, and elsewhere. That minor success prompted me to do further work on the resurrection and produce (in 1973) *The Easter Jesus.*

Thus far I have concentrated on some of the headlines that record my three years in Cambridge. Let me turn now to the small print in the story of moving to the summer of 1968.

8

The Road to 1968

My three years at Cambridge were to end with questions that I had hoarded unheard suddenly emerging to throw my sense of myself, my church, and my world into some confusion. To indicate the road which led to that summer of sixty-eight, let me re-trace my steps from the autumn of 1965.

The First Cambridge Year

My diary ticked off the landmarks of that first Michaelmas term, the honeymoon months when I came to know and love Cambridge and my own college: a sherry party with Sir William Hodge, the Master of Pembroke; meeting Canon Hugh Montefiore and Fr Piet Fransen (visiting from Louvain); signing the college roll; passing the 'loving cup' at the freshmen's dinner (where one stood, bowed to those on either side, said '*Floreat Domus*', and took a sip from the cup); meeting other research students at a sherry party in the Divinity School; coffee with John and Judy O'Neill; settling down to a regular game of golf each week at the Gog Magog course with a maths undergraduate from King's College; welcoming John Eddy across for the annual Oxford-Cambridge Australian Rules football match; dining at Caius high table with Fr Jim Burtchaell; attending the Advent service in King's chapel and hoping my memory would steal the sound of those carols forever; sherry with the Master of Downing College, Professor W.K.C. Guthrie, with whom I had studied during his 1957 visit to the University of Melbourne; dinners with George MacRae at the Turk's

Head where we always ordered a bottle of Medoc; and the term ending with a theology conference at St Edmund's House. Herbert McCabe gave one of the main lectures. My Jesuit mind thought: 'Surely here is a Dominican who can deliver a lecture without feeling compelled to drag in Thomas Aquinas?' But I was wrong!

I spent most of the month-long Christmas vacation in Campion Hall, enjoying my first full chance to explore Oxford. An ageing attendant in the Divinity Schools delighted me when he pointed out the highlights of the stone ceiling created about 1430: an angel covered with feathers, two doctors engaged in debate, and 'the scholar and the ape'. A visitor had once asked to see 'the monk and the monkey'. I joined the gentle old man in admiring the lovely representation of Our Lady, and lamenting the fact that Oliver Cromwell's soldiers, when quartered in the Divinity Schools, had found it necessary to knock the head off a carving of St Peter.

The Lent term of 1966 had hardly begun, when my sister Maev and niece Marion Peters arrived in Cambridge on a whirlwind trip around the world. Outgoing, red-haired, and just out of high school, Marion revelled in the chance of meeting English undergraduates and other members of Pembroke. I enjoyed my role of introducing my sister and niece to Cambridge life. A review of *Patrick McMahon Glynn* had appeared in the *Irish Press*, which annoyed Maev and me by its antipathy to grandfather's views on home rule. We composed a letter to the paper, which appeared over Maev's name on 4 February:

> Having recently arrived from Australia, I have had my attention drawn to your review on 11 December of the biography of Patrick McMahon Glynn. As a granddaughter of Glynn I appreciate your interest in a man who helped to prepare the Australian Constitution and became a cabinet minister in three Commonwealth governments. Due to his efforts, the Australian Constitution, unlike the American, includes in the preamble a reference to reliance upon almighty God. Glynn's record, which

made him the most notable Irishman so far to sit in the Australian Parliament, should be a matter of pride, not only in Australia but also in the land of his birth and education. Your review, however, passed over this record in silence, possibly because Glynn, although a strong and consistent supporter of Home Rule, felt that it should be achieved by parliamentary methods.

He felt, too, that realistically Ireland needed to retain links with Britain in order to develop as a nation. Glynn held, similarly, that Australia should develop closer links with the countries of the Pacific unswayed by sentiment or antagonism. He would have approved as much of Australia, the land of his adoption, forgetting past enmities to make trade alliances with Japan, as he would have approved today Ireland, the land of his birth, having closer economic links with Britain. Men like Glynn helped to establish a strong Irish tradition in Australia, and today Ireland benefits from the image which they created. His Australian contemporaries considered Glynn an eloquent Irish scholar of great integrity, and it is a matter of regret that his sincere belief in the parliamentary method of achieving nationhood should lead to his worth as an Irishman in Australia being underestimated.

With that outburst of family pride behind us, I settled down to a busy term of reading and writing. My diary had already become pretty spare again. On 31 January it noted: 'Fr Charles Davis read a paper on "Nature and Supernature".' I did a little better on 17 February: 'Danilo Dolci spoke on his work in Sicily against the Mafia and in improvement of agriculture and education. When one student asked whether the Mafia were connected with the Vatican, he said, "Things aren't that bad yet."' But by 23 February the diary had lapsed back into brevity: 'Seminar on Tillich, followed by afternoon tea with D.E. Nineham in Regent House. E.M. Forster was dozing quietly on a sofa.' By and large my record covered only the barest details of dinners, teas, coffees, and lectures.

For much of the Easter break of 1966 I was back at Campion

Hall. A conference at Oriel College on John Henry Newman provided an extra attraction. In preparation I read his *Grammar of Assent*, a work that let my theological thinking leap ahead. More than anyone else Newman encouraged me to shun that terminal disease of theologians—arguing for what the state of affairs must be, rather than enquiring as to what in fact it is. Scholars like J.M. Cameron, Stephen Dessain, and Gordon Rupp created the atmosphere by their culture, learning, and kindness. The opening address was given by Archbishop Michael Ramsey, who wore a ring presented to him the previous week by Pope Paul VI. Those days at Oriel linger in my memory as the most pleasant conference I have ever attended: about fifty people drawn together not by the politics of academic advancement but simply through their affection for Newman himself.

A week in the west country rounded off that Easter break. John Eddy had invited me to join him, as well as Brian Conway, a Welsh Jesuit whom we connected with the head of the royal family of Connacht, 'the O'Conor Don', and nicknamed 'the O'Conway Don'. Bald, cheerful Brian had a knack for producing inadvertently some classic situations of popular comedy. In the middle of a film he suddenly wondered whether he would be late for dinner at Campion Hall, found he had forgotten to wear his watch, and approached an usherette to ask, 'Have you the time?' 'No, nor the inclination', she told him with angry disdain. On that spring trip we stopped the first night at Glastonbury to drink in its prayerful peace. Then we drove on to St Ives and Land's End, returning along the south coast of Cornwall. Names live on in memory and recall the rugged charm of those fishing villages: Mousehole, Penzance, Mevagissey, Fowey, Polperro, and Looe. We rushed home to Oxford via Dartmoor, Exeter, Winchester, Salisbury, and Stonehenge.

On 18 April I was back in Pembroke to begin the Easter term. It was my first spring in Cambridge, but I was too busy to spend time exploring and recording its beauty. 'May Week', which the colleges celebrate in early June, soon arrived. I went to a concert in King's chapel to see Benjamin Britten conduct his *Voices for Today*. Gustav Holst's daughter, Imogen Holst, came to hear her father's *The Hymn of Jesus*. Two days later I left to spend the heart of the summer studying and writing in Germany. The Divinity Faculty supplied £100 from the Bethune-Baker Fund towards those summer months in Tübingen. The following summer I received a similar grant from the Hort Memorial Fund.[1] It cheered me to think that good Anglican money should support a latter-day Jesuit in his theological research.

The Summer of 1966

On my way to Tübingen I stopped in Münster and Mainz. During my year at Haus Sentmaring I had met a Detroit Jesuit, Jared ('Jerry') Wicks, who had done his own tertianship there and remained in Münster to complete a doctorate on the young Luther's spirituality with Erwin Iserloh as his *Doktorvater*. I liked Jared from the start, and invited him to spend the Christmas of 1965 with me at Campion Hall. He brought with him a copy of Jürgen Moltmann's *Theologie der Hoffnung* and told me, 'This is the hottest thing in Germany at the moment. You may be interested in it.' Now in June 1966 he arranged for me to meet Johannes Metz, a Catholic theologian who had shifted from being Karl Rahner's *braver Schüler* to develop a 'political theology', closely allied with Moltmann's theology of hope. 'Very helpful discussion', I noted in my diary and pressed on to Mainz. Wicks has always embodied for me the natural ease with which Jesuits can help each other in their professional work. As much as anyone else he kept me informed about the publications, debates, and movements

1 J.F. Bethune-Baker (1861-1951) was a Lady Margaret Professor of Divinity at Cambridge and an expert on early Christianity. J.A. Hort (1828-92) held the Hulsean and the Lady Margaret professorships in Cambridge. With B.F. Westcott (a notable New Testament scholar who became Bishop of Durham), he produced a famous critical edition of the Greek New Testament.

that kept West Germany at the forefront of serious theology through the sixties into the seventies. The value of Wicks' help was to hit me smartly a Easter 1968. A reporter from *Time* magazine phoned me late one day, when he was trying to sample British views on the theology of hope. 'Thank God', he sighed, 'I've found one theologian in England who doesn't think I mean Bultmann, when I mention the name of Moltmann.'

I stayed three days in Mainz to discuss with Pannenberg his theology of revelation. With dramatic suddenness a hot spell of weather broke, just when we were speaking together in his office at the university. Outside dark clouds swirled across the sky to blot out the light. Stabs of lightning and crashes of thunder punctuated our conversation. By the end of the hour torrential rain lashed down outside. Pannenberg sat through the apocalyptic storm, refused to switch on the light to offset the gathering gloom, and continued to talk in calmly passionless tones. He disappointed me, because he seemed content to repeat what he had already written. Whether I put questions about the relation between human knowledge and divine revelation, the role of the Holy Spirit in our coming to faith, or the grounds for accepting the late-Jewish expectation of resurrection, Pannenberg simply summarized passages which were already familiar to me.

Other events made the stop in Mainz worthwhile: a visiting lecture by Rudolf Schnackenburg (on 'the Church and the World'), a rapidly delivered class on revelation by a Dr Schmitz (of whom the students said, '*Blitz wie Schmitz*'), a visit to a research institute devoted to the work of Nicholas of Cusa, a chat with Gustav Stählin ('a very charming friend of Professor Moule', I noted), and a lecture by Herbert Braun on the titles of Christ. Braun had won notoriety for views that seemed to reduce the reality of God and Christ's absolute value to little more than the human person's understanding of our common humanity. Seemingly, these views ruled out the possibility of being, respectively, either an atheist or a non-Christian. It amused me to find this *enfant terrible* of German Protestant theology to be a tubby, middle-aged man lecturing to a sleepy audience, while he stood there wearing an open shirt with his trousers held up by braces.

It is hard to write about my first summer in Tübingen without indulging nostalgia. There were only two minor drawbacks: accommodation and the hour of daily Mass. In those days the summer semester ran from 1 May until the end of July. I had arrived halfway through the semester in a small city that lacked rooms to cater for its student population of around fifteen thousand. I tried the Carl Sonnenschein Studentenwohnheim, a twelve-story hostel next to the French army barracks. A blind law student overheard me enquiring at the desk. 'You can take my room', he told me. 'I'm off for a long weekend.' A few days later I found accommodation with a family in the Galgenbergstrasse ('the street to gallows hill'). For a hundred marks a month I had a bedroom, the use of a small study, breakfast on Sunday mornings, and the opportunity to take a morning shower. Occasionally my landlady left bowls of fruit on my table. Almost her only house rule was that I should be home on Saturday afternoon. After she, her husband, and their daughter had taken a bath, she would knock on my door, hand me a towel of heroic size, and send me downstairs to the steaming bathroom. My daily showers did not count if I were to be truly clean each week.

The Catholic and Protestant faculties, university library, and *Neue Mensa* or students' cafeteria were all about forty minutes away on foot. Most mornings I broke my walk there to say Mass in German at six a.m. for a community of Italian nuns. They ran a kindergarten, where some working mothers left their children during the day. The sisters rewarded my willingness to rise so early by giving me breakfast. The Mass resembled a spiritual endurance test rather than any kind of joyful community celebration. Yet I never thought of suggesting to the sisters that we might postpone the Mass until the evening.

Immediately after my arrival in Tübingen, I rushed around sampling lectures by a range of Catholic and Protestant professors: Gerhard Ebeling, Ernst Käsemann, Hans Küng, K.H. Schelkle, and Max Seckler. I settled down to follow Käsemann's course on the Letter to the Romans. One could go no further in New Testament studies, I felt, than hearing a Lutheran who was among the world's top biblical scholars lecture on Paul's masterpiece. He mixed his exegesis with frequent flashes of polemic against ecclesiastical politicians and fundamentalist movements like *Kein Anderes Evangelium*, as well as with occasional glances over his shoulder at Heinrich Schlier, his former colleague from Marburg days who had become a Catholic in 1953. Käsemann agreed with Schlier that the central question posed by the New Testament was that of the church. Where Schlier had switched to a Catholic answer, he continued to give a Protestant reply.

Käsemann had recently returned from lecturing in the United States. He kept his contact with Americans alive through the *Ausländer Kolloquium*, which met fortnightly in Lustnau, a village on the edge of Tübingen. One could speak in either German or English. Visiting American professors like Robert Evans, Robert Funk, and James Smart attended, as well as a number of young German theologians, including Käsemann's severely beautiful assistant, Irmgard Kindt. Both at his lectures and in the seminar meetings Käsemann radiated intellectual power and passionate conviction. My admiration almost went to the point of idolizing him. He was the only one from the school of Rudolf Bultmann to have been gaoled under the Nazis, even if that imprisonment lasted only a few months and was mild enough to allow him to complete an early work on the Letter to the Hebrews. He broke decisively with Bultmann by maintaining three theses: the significance of the historical Jesus for Christian faith, the future-oriented quality of Paul's theology, and the error involved in taking John's Gospel as the guide to New Testament belief. Käseman fed my passion for St Paul, freed me to ask larger questions about the origins of Christianity, and fired my thinking with the kind of one-sided but brilliant remarks that he was to sprinkle through *Jesus Means Freedom* and *Perspectives on Paul:* 'The history of Pauline interpretation is the history of the apostle's ecclesiastical domestication'; 'unlike the usual sermon, the apostle is exceptionally unconcerned with our deficiencies; his attacks are directed against the strong.'

In 1971 I was to encourage one of my students to publish a two-part article on Käsemann's understanding of the church—as a tribute to him on his sixty-fifth birthday.

Not long after that I had my last conversation with him, when he had just finished writing his commentary on Romans. 'The prophet [Ezekiel 3:1-3; Revelation 10:10-11]', he remarked, 'only had to swallow a small scroll, while I have to gulp down tons of paper: commentaries and monographs by the dozen and articles by the hundreds.' I suggested that it would be a shame if he failed to write his autobiography. 'Not at all', he answered. 'I see the old Adam in the mirror every day. That's enough. Anyway, I would be shot four or five times over if I were to publish such a book.' When I handed him my copy of *Perspectives on Paul*, he signed it: '*Erinnerung an einen Ketzer* (In memory of a heretic)'. Then he dragged out of his drawer a reproduction of an eighth-century picture of Paul being lowered from the walls of Damascus (Acts 9:23-25; 2 Corinthians 11:32-33). Gripping the sides of the basket, the apostle looks down towards the ground with a quizzical expression on his face. 'That's me', said Käsemann. 'That's theological existence today—a little sceptical.'

I wish that I could remember Käsemann with unqualified admiration. But before retiring he dumped two doctoral students, including Irmgard Kindt, who transferred to Marburg and tried to 'promote' under the supervision of Ernst Fuchs. Eventually Gerhard Ebeling, who by that time had shifted back to Zürich, took her on. Years before he had known Irmgard's mother when they both

belonged to Dietrich Bonhoeffer's circle in Berlin. It hurt me to find
that Käsemann could display towards students an unconcern for their
welfare that still occasionally surfaces at universities around the world.

Besides Käsemann's *Kolloquium*, I attended in that summer of 1966
Hans Küng's *Sozietät*, a seminar which met in his ecumenical institute
and largely catered for his own doctoral students. I was naturally
curious to see how this super-star of Catholic theology came across.
He had shot to fame through his book on justification, his tracts on
church reform, and his gadfly role at the Second Vatican Council.
Still under forty years of age, he had held his chair at Tübingen since
1960. His significant work dedicated to Archbishop Michael Ramsey,
The Church, was to appear in 1967 and three years later his book on
infallibility. I found Küng a smiling, charming, well dressed man who
had an enviable grasp of English, French, Italian, and Spanish, not to
mention his native German. His teaching, writing, trips abroad, and
work for *Concilium* and other journals kept him frenetically busy, but
from time to time he managed to invite students to his home on the
banks of the Neckar. During my second summer in Tübingen I was
at his home when a pretty girl bustled in with the supper. For some
reason I imagined she was one of his several sisters, but later learned
that this was his secretary who shared the house with him.

From the start I struck up a warm friendship with one of Küng's
doctoral students, Josef Nolte. Affectionate and amusing, Josef
combined a professional stringency in theology with a love for
literature and the arts. Küng saw him as a pioneer in the movement
towards more lay theologians, used him as his assistant for four
years, and dropped him at the end of 1973. Against the opposition
of Professor Joseph Ratzinger, Küng had battled to persuade a bare
majority of the Catholic faculty in Tübingen to accept Josef's doctoral
dissertation (on the history and nature of dogma). Ratzinger rejected
the thesis as unorthodox, whereas Küng appealed to it with approval
in his own *Infallible? An Enquiry*.

Josef stood to the left of Küng both politically and theologically. He wanted to know why Küng refused to sign a petition (signed by many professors at German universities) requesting a fair trial for Angela Davis, and why he had not taken the opportunity of a 1971 trip to New York to visit Fr Daniel Berrigan in Danbury Federal Penitentiary. But how could a wealthy Swiss theologian have involved himself with a black American militant or an anti-war priest serving a term in gaol? Some critics showed themselves superficial by dismissing the section 'the Pope as he might be' (which rounds off *Infallible? An Enquiry*) as no more than 'Küng as Pope'. Yet it is impossible not to notice how he remained silent about the need for papal and Vatican poverty—a point made by Morris West in *The Shoes of the Fisherman*, Harvey Cox in *The Seduction of the Spirit*, and others. More and more Josef's thought displayed undercurrents of sympathy for Franz Overbeck and Friedrich Nietzsche. Küng had Josef's slim volume of reflections on *Antichrist* withdrawn from the *Theologische Meditationen* series, and discouraged the firm of Herder (which had published Josef's dissertation) from accepting anything further by him. Josef and Küng parted, the *Assistent* being sacked by his *Herr Professor* and the *Doktor* breaking with his *Doktorvater*. Küng, now long retired from teaching, continues to live in Tübingen. So too does Josef, also retired from teaching but from teaching in Hildesheim.

In that summer of 1966 my diary entries grew longer, and hoarded up the happiness of those golden weeks: Sunday trips alone to Bebenhausen and Rottenburg; a walk through the woods to Wurmlinger chapel; Josef Nolte's party in the cellar of the Stauffenberg *Verein* (a student fraternity called after the hero of the July 1944 plot against Hitler); the fresh flowers on the grave of the lyric poet Friedrich Hölderlin[2]; a visit to the grave of the theologian

---

2 When this nineteenth century poet became irremediably but harmlessly insane, he spent his last years living in a tower hidden among the willows on the banks of the Neckar.

Karl Adam; four hours with Irmgard Kindt discussing an article I had written (and would publish) on Ernst Fuchs; Dr Bergmann defending the fundamentalist *Bekenntnisbewegung* at the Schlatter Haus (the centre for Protestant students); Joseph Ratzinger delivering a lecture there on the Eucharist as meal and sacrifice; lively debates at the Erasmus Haus (the centre for Catholic students); attending but not communicating at a Protestant Eucharist at the Schlatter Haus; reading prayers at an ecumenical service in the Evangelische Stift; an engagement party in a nurses home; and nearly every Saturday evening the chance of hearing Bach's motets in the fifteenth-century, Gothic *Stiftskirche*. Those sacred Saturday evenings never failed to convey a rich sense of peace. I sat in one of the medieval stalls, feasted on the beauty of Bach, heard a passage of scripture, joined in the closing hymn and Lord's Prayer, and slipped out to drink some wine with friends, including a devout, elderly German lady who had numbered among her student lodgers such future stars as the Old Testament scholar Gerhard von Rad.

On 5 August I left Tübingen to spend the next two months in prayer and travel, before returning for the Michaelmas term and my second year in Cambridge. I began by heading south to Beuron and making my annual eight-day retreat at an eleventh-century abbey. Benedictine peace wrapped around me. I could walk from my ground-floor room across the terrace, through an orchard, and down the sloping meadows to the dancing waters of the upper Danube. In the evening and early morning one of the brothers sometimes walked past my room to the far end of the terrace, played his alpine horn, and drew echoes from the cliffs across the river. After the Second World War, Gerhard Kittel, a Tübingen scripture scholar who had collaborated with the Nazis, took refuge in the abbey to continue his work on the monumental *Theological Dictionary of the New Testament* (ten volumes). He expressed his thanks to the monks for their hospitality by insisting that two grandchildren born during that period should be called Benedict and Scholastica (the sister of Benedict). I brought with me a paperback edition of the sixteen documents from Vatican II, which had closed the previous December. During the retreat I spent some time slowly reading these texts. Through prayer and reflection I wanted these conciliar documents to guide my thinking and living. Most days I concelebrated at the main community Mass and joined the Benedictines in some parts of the divine office. At meals one monk chanted the reading. We were listening to the life of a German Catholic who represented the Kaiser in Rome soon after the First World War had broken out. As part of an effort to win Italy over to their side, the Allied Powers spread the story that 'when the German Protestant soldiers marched into Belgium, they raped a thousand nuns.' That sounded startling enough being chanted in monotone across rows of monks at refectory tables. But the author pressed on to inform us that his hero felt unwilling to deny this report without instructions from Berlin.

From Beuron I took the train to Salzburg, where Nick Fassnidge, an undergraduate from Pembroke, was waiting for me at the railway station. We found rooms at the local seminary, were entertained by the Kirchtag family (acquaintances of mine who ran an umbrella shop in the Getreidegasse), and plunged into four days at the festival. We began by seeing Hugo von Hofmannsthal's *Everyman* performed in front of the cathedral, and ended by hearing the Vienna Philharmonic Orchestra play Beethoven's seventh symphony. That performance won Claudio Abbado a prize for the best piece of conducting at the Salzburg Festival. When we left the large Festspielhaus, it was still raining softly and banks of mist partly obscured the illuminations, lending a ghostly look to the great fortress above the city. We walked home utterly entranced. During our visit torrential rain deluged Salzburg, the Kirchtags broke their old record by selling 190 umbrellas in a single day, but I have never known four such days of aesthetic experience. The period of solitude and intense prayer with the Benedictines gave my senses a heightened awareness for Mozart's Mass in C Minor (which we heard in the cathedral), Manzù's exhibition (where I gazed in horrified silence at his violent representations of Christ's crucifixion), Hermann Prey's *Lieder* recital with its four encores, a choral concert of Slavic music, and the struggle for Everyman's soul before he finally made his way into heaven, represented by the vast Salzburg cathedral.

Nick travelled on with me to Vienna, where we stayed four days at the Jesuit residence in the Dr Ignaz-Seipel Platz. We made the usual tourist round. *The Tower of Babel, The Peasant's Wedding,* and other paintings by Peter Brueghel the elder alone made my trip to Vienna worthwhile. We remembered Graham Greene's *The Third Man* (the book of the film that starred Orson Welles as Harry Lime), slipped down to look at the huge Ferris wheel in the Volksprater, and were amused to notice in the Taubstummengasse a health institute which advertised 'penicillin inhalations'. Shades of Harry Lime and the adulterated penicillin that he sold! On Sunday I celebrated Mass and preached in the chapel of St Stanislaus Kostka, a Polish teenager who lived in Vienna exactly four hundred years before and ran away to join the Jesuits. His room had been turned into a baroque chapel, while the building itself served as a home for elderly ladies. Some of them startled me at the end of my sermon (on Christ's resurrection) by crying out, 'Vergelt's Gott (God bless you)!' The custom was new to me. After Mass we tramped off to look at the house in the Berggasse where Sigmund Freud had lived for forty years. In Vienna a standard sign (three small Austrian flags and a white tablet) marked places of special interest. I was surprised to find that Freud's house was not marked in that way. One inside wall carried a tablet erected in 1953 by the World Federation of Mental Health. I asked an Austrian, 'Aren't you proud of Freud?' I have forgotten his precise answer, but it failed to satisfy me. Nick, being an Anglican, went off to Mass at an Old Catholic church, while I filled in the time by visiting a treasury and gaping at some astonishing relics: St John the Baptist's tooth, a tooth of St Peter, and several relics of Christ himself—a large fragment of his crib, a table cloth he had used, and a phial claiming to contain some of his blood! An afternoon in the city park completed our Sunday. At one end a band played the waltzes of Johann Strauss. At the other end Mormons canvassed for new adherents, and a Salvation Army band was in action.

On 29 August the annual conference of the Studiorum Novi Testamenti Societas was to open in Cambridge. The organizing committee had asked me and several other research students to help with the arrangements. From Vienna I took a week on the return journey to allow stops in Passau, Nuremberg, Bamberg, and Trier. I picked up a heavy cold, staggered off the boat in Dover, and felt utterly exhausted by the time the train reached Victoria Station around seven o'clock in the morning. A diminutive sailor appeared next to me on the platform, grabbed my heaviest suitcase, and insisted on taking the underground with me to Liverpool Street, where he put me on the train for Cambridge. I spent most of the conference in bed, getting up to chat with George MacRae (who had come across from Boston) and to hear Ray Brown lecture on 'The Paraclete'.

Ted Yarnold had asked me to lead an eight-day retreat for the Campion Hall scholastics at a house in a Birmingham suburb. This was due to start on 27 September. September is a dead month in Cambridge: college kitchens remain closed, the library shuts for a fortnight, and tourists rather than members of the university fill the town. But my unexpressed reason for spending most of that month in Ireland was that I desperately wanted some affectionate but 'safe' female company. When I had been writing *Patrick McMahon Glynn*, I corresponded with Marie O'Connor, the eldest child of my grandfather's favourite brother. After her mother died, she had been brought up by my great-grandmother in Gort. Marie gave me the sense that through her I could touch the origins of my mother's family. In person this grey-haired widow in her seventies turned out to correspond nicely to the impression her letters had given me: a delicious blend of kindness, quiet honesty, and mischievous wit. I never met her husband, a dentist who died before I first visited Ireland. But her clutch of married daughters seemed uncannily prepared for the role of my newly-found sisters: Eleanor Harbison (in Dublin), Pat Hayes (in Ardee, a town north of Dublin), Mary O'Connor (who had married a lawyer of the same name in Dublin), Monica Ellison (in Paris), and Bobby Corcoran (who lived with her mother, husband, and children in Wexford).

In the early part of September I stayed in Wexford with Marie and the rest of her household. Monica happened to be across from Paris with the younger of her four daughters, Emma and Charlotte. Wriggling organisms infested the tap-water. It seemed to cause no one any harm, but I thought the water tasted strangely. 'A donkey died in the reservoir', Monica assured me, and plied me with bottles of Harp lager. She epitomized some strains of Irish beauty: blond, blue-eyed, fair complexion and, altogether, seriously lovely. Unlike any of her sisters, she had married an Englishman, John Ellison, and gone to live abroad: first, in London and then in Paris, where John was posted as the European correspondent for the *Daily Express*. Perhaps our common readiness to break old patterns partly explained why we both felt instantly and easily at home with each other.

From Wexford I pushed north to Dublin, where I stayed at Milltown Park, talked endlessly with the Irish Jesuits there, visited my relatives, and prepared the retreat in Birmingham. That proved to be hard work as I moved through eight days of lectures, Masses, services of the word, benedictions, confessions, and hours of private interviews. Despite the fact that I offered a pre-arranged structure, the retreat seemed to meet some real needs. It helped greatly that I already knew a number of the scholastics quite well from regular visits to Campion Hall.

The Second Cambridge Year

In October 1966 my second year at research began without the slightest hint of the storms that were to break around Christmas. I had my room at Fisher House. Richard Incledon now had two terms behind him at Cambridge, and was established as chaplain to Catholic members of the university. Jerry Golden, an Australian Jesuit who had been a chaplain at the University of Melbourne for many years, came on a sabbatical to stay with us for the Michaelmas term. To celebrate my return, Richard invited Germaine Greer to dine at Fisher House. She had known Jerry at Melbourne University, where I had been her contemporary but had never met her. That evening a story about designing bottomless dresses and the rest of her vulgar hilarity encouraged us to face the year with laughter. An amusing letter from Peter Kelly, one of the Australian delegates to the Jesuit general congregation in Rome, provided a cheerful boost to my resumption of work in Cambridge:

> Dear Gerald, Pax Christi. I thought you might like to know that history was made today. At this session of the congregation, they have decided to have refectory reading in the vernacular: two days English, two French, two Spanish, two Italian, then English again, and so on. Today, for the first time since 1540 to the best of anyone's belief here, English was heard in the refectory at the Curia. There is to be one fixed, permanent reader for each language, and the English reader is I. The voice was the voice of Kelly, but the words were the words of O'Collins. For upon the fascinated, attentively listening ears of the General Congregation fell the opening words, 'Divine Revelation: An Article from *The Month* by Gerald O'Collins, s.j.' I hasten to say that I didn't chose it. I would have been too afraid of being accused of nationalism. It was selected by Tom Byrne, who is a sort of prefect of reading for English.
>
>   'Who is this Collins?', an Austrian, Coreth, rector of Innsbruck,

asked me afterwards—proof that I hadn't distinctly enunciated
that 'O'. 'I've never heard of him', he added. 'I asked several others
who he was, and none of them had heard of him.' 'So, you hardly
would yet', I replied. 'A good article', he said. And so said many.
Now, what better way can a man pick to get known in the Society
than to have his article read to the General Congregation? You
can let your friends know that, for a generous consideration, I am
prepared to read their articles during these next two months. This
extraordinary event, the first English for four hundred years being
an Australian writer and an Australian reader, is regarded here as
being very significant. Some even consider it meaningful.

At Pembroke I felt very much at home with the graduate students
and other members of the college. As junior treasurer of the Hort
Society I had worked with Jimmy Dunn (who was to be become a
world famous New Testament scholar) to arrange speakers for the
coming year. Work on my thesis was pushing ahead well. In Tübingen
I had completed a section on Moltmann's theology of hope, which
Interpretation accepted for publication and which I delivered as a
paper to various audiences during Michaelmas term. Several people
arrived from Australia to enlarge my circle of friends in Cambridge:
in particular, the Carnleys and the McCaugheys.

Peter and Ann Carnley had not long been married, were very much
in love, and instantly brightened the ranks of research students in
theology. A tall, dark-haired Anglican priest, Peter combined dashing
good looks, an unassuming charm, and a sharp theological mind. His
gentle and lovely wife resumed school teaching, supported Peter in his
many activities, and worked hard to ensure the success of parties held
by the Divinity Faculty. Peter and Ann had both studied at Melbourne
University. They became the only close and lasting friends among all
the other Australians I first met in Cambridge.

Davis McCaughey came from Ormond College to spend a
sabbatical year as a visiting fellow of Pembroke. He brought his wife

Jean and the two teenage daughters, Mary and Brigid. His youngest son, John, also stayed for a time. I had met the McCaugheys in Australia, but during that year I grew to feel myself accepted as part of their family. On various occasions they all dined in Pembroke as my guests. It was almost the only return I could make for the Irish love and hospitality they shared so easily. Davis regularly took meals with the other fellows, but in those days the college had not yet permitted ladies to dine once a week at high table. As a research student I could invite him and Jean to dine in the Old Library, or I could bring Mary and Brigid to Friday dinner in hall. Davis was a tireless ecumenist, showed himself an excellent New Testament lecturer and scholar, preached sermons that applied the scriptures to life, and liked to bring people together when he anticipated that good things could come from such meetings. I loved that many-sided man, not least for the small but striking touches of courtesy that seemed second nature to him. In May 1967 he sent me a slip of paper on which two Latin formulas were written: '*Ego nomino magistrum O'Collins in socium ex fundatione dominae; ego eligo Magistrum O'Collins in socium ex fundatione dominae.*' A covering note from Davis explained his gift: 'I thought your mother might be amused to see this. It is the slip of paper which the Master gave me so that I might have the honour of proposing, and then electing you to a fellowship at Pembroke. A lot of pleasing things have happened to me this year; I certainly count this among them.'

But back to the Michaelmas term of 1966. It raced by with a flurry of reading and writing, rounds of teas and dinners, and the Cambridge habit of sherrying others and being sherried. Visitors arrived to be shown the sights: two friends from Tübingen and several Australian Jesuits. I found a learned and lively theologian with whom to spend hours in discussion, Hans Frei, an inspiring personality who was taking a sabbatical from Yale University. Doing pastoral ministry for the chaplaincy combined naturally with my own life as a research student. After a year in a college hostel I was glad to live with two other priests in Fisher House, where I could slip out of my room to pray in the upstairs chapel.

When the Christmas vacation arrived, Jerry Golden left to visit other chaplaincies in England; Richard Incledon lent me his car and went into hospital for an operation on his varicose veins; and I drove across to Heythrop College to offer nine lectures on contemporary theologies of revelation. As the Heythrop Christmas break was shorter than Cambridge's, I could deliver half the lectures in December and half in early January, without taking any time off from the end of the Michaelmas term or the start of the Lent term in Cambridge. Besides giving much of my thesis material another airing before a critical and intelligent audience, this mini-course yielded my first and only Roman Catholic degree in theology, an STL (licentiate in sacred theology).

The Vatican had not empowered Canisius College, where I had studied for four years, to confer the licentiate or any other degree in theology. The dean at Heythrop, Bruno Brinkman, agreed that I could apply for a STL, provided I supplied a transcript of my examination results from Canisius. Several faculty members attended my lectures, asked questions during the discussion period, and treated the occasion as an extended oral examination. I hoped that my STL would satisfy Peter Kelly. He had secured my provincial's permission to study in Cambridge, but on the condition that I somehow acquire a Catholic doctorate in theology as well. On 23 January 1967 Peter wrote to me: 'Although I have no great esteem for most ecclesiastical degrees, and although I also understand very well and sympathise with your desire not to do any more degree-style study after your time in Cambridge, still one other thing has to be considered. The number of ecclesiastical degrees available may be of importance in any setting up of a faculty in Australia.' Peter added: 'I discussed this matter at length with Dezza.[3] What he says comes to this. In the present state of things (which, he stressed, cannot be assumed to be permanent), the ecclesiastical doctorate is desirable.'

I registered a doctoral topic at the Gregorian University, Pannenberg's theology of revelation. However, the decision to shift the staff and students of Canisius College from Sydney down to Melbourne and work with the Protestant/Anglican United Faculty of Theology at the University of Melbourne meant that I never had to pursue the doctorate at the Gregorian. The Australian Jesuits abandoned any attempt to create their own ecclesiastical faculty with authorization from the Vatican to grant church degrees.

But to return to my Christmas lectures at Heythrop. I had begun the series when my Australian friend from Westminster College, John O'Neill, arrived from Cambridge to stay overnight, meet some of the faculty, and visit the library. I introduced him to Bruno Brinkman, the philosopher Freddie Copleston, and other Jesuits. In the evening I gathered a small party for a drink with John in a snug, little parlour. Bernard Leeming, Robert Murray, the grandson of James Murray (the editor of the *Oxford English Dictionary*), and others came. The following morning we visited Charles Davis, found him packing, and stopped for only a brief chat. I put John on a train back to Cambridge, continued my lectures, and came out of the final, pre-Christmas one to hear that the rector had summoned everyone, Jesuit and non-Jesuit alike, to a meeting in the largest hall. To a stunned audience, he broke the news: 'Charles Davis has left the Church, and is getting married.' He refrained from making even implicit criticisms of Charles, warned us that there would be heavy newspaper coverage, and urged us to put the affair in perspective by recalling how history could offer many previous examples of such departures.

---

3 Fr Paolo Dezza was one of the four special advisors to Fr Pedro Arrupe, the superior general of the Jesuits, as well as being confessor to Pope Paul VI and Pope John Paul I. Later, when Arrupe suffered a debilitating stroke, Pope John Paul II nominated Dezza as interim head of the order and then created him a cardinal.

Most of us had looked on Charles as the leading Catholic theologian in England, even if we knew him to be frankly derivative rather than an original thinker. Some newspapers indulged in silly exaggeration by going back to 1845 and suggesting that English Christianity had not lived through an event of such magnitude since John Henry Newman's passage to Catholicism. I knew Charles slightly, felt grateful for his high appreciation of my theological talent, and found his conversation pleasant but restricted in range. He seemed to have little middle ground between empty joking and serious-minded talk about theology. The *Sunday Observer* carried a long article by him giving the reasons for his rejection of Catholicism. Jared Wicks, who arrived from Münster to spend part of his Christmas break with me in Oxford, nodded approvingly when he returned the article to me: 'There's a lot to be said for his stand.' For once, I found myself on the 'conservative' side in a discussion with Jared. I dismissed Charles' self-justification as non-biblical and too rational. He turned religion into a matter of the head rather an affair of the heart. He replaced love with truth. My conscious mind put up a good fight. I desperately tried to close the gash that Charles had made in my understanding of church authority. He felt angered that Pope Paul VI had 'lied' about the issue of birth control when in October 1966, nearly two years before issuing his encyclical *Humanae Vitae* (upholding the rejection of 'artificial' birth control), he had affirmed the traditional teaching even though he knew that a solid majority on the official commission had already reported in favour of change. Unconsciously I was taking some tiny steps towards asking myself: how far do compromises, bland assurances, and even suppression of the truth shape some of the official teaching of the Roman Catholic Church?

The day Charles publicly announced his departure from the Catholic Church, I drove in the afternoon from Heythrop to Oxford. Once again I was to spend Christmas at Campion Hall. My diary noted the time of arrival, when I learnt the frightening news: '6.10.

Heard that Richard Incledon has suffered a near fatal embolism.'
Eleven days before I had visited him in a hospital outside London.
The operation seemed a routine affair. He intended to recuperate
with his sister who lived in Holland. We wished each other a happy
Christmas, and looked forward to beginning again at Fisher House
early in January. But an unforeseen death had almost taken him away.
I suddenly realized how much I had come to love him, and rely on
him as a pillar of my Cambridge life. I dashed down to his hospital in
Cheam, found him weak but recovering, and some weeks later drove
him to his mother's house in Dartmouth. Obviously there was need
for a locum tenens to run Fisher House, at least for the Lent term
of 1967. It struck me that Jerry Golden, who was free and already
knew some of the students and teachers in Cambridge, might be the
happy answer. As arrangements for Catholic chaplaincies in England
then went, Archbishop George Patrick Dwyer of Birmingham took
responsibility for finding at short notice a replacement. I was on the
point of phoning him and suggesting that he invite Jerry, when one
of the priests at Campion Hall gave me the thoroughly bad advice,
'Don't get involved.' Joe, a Jesuit from the English province, was
appointed.

When I arrived back at Fisher House on 14 January, the
housekeeper had distressing news to give me. A group of Catholic
students, who felt aggrieved that they had not been consulted about
Richard's temporary replacement, was waiting to confront Joe in the
sitting room. He was upstairs in bed—drunk. I told them that he
was indisposed, and finally prevailed on them to go by mustering up
the courage to act with a little aggression. 'Has there been a death?',
I asked. 'You all look as solemn as undertakers.' They showed no
concern that Richard had almost died. Their grievance was absurd.
Even if Archbishop Dwyer had wanted to canvass the views of
Catholic students at Cambridge about a locum tenens, he could not
have done so. He needed to find a replacement fast, and the students

were away on vacation. This little group of dissidents continued to prove mildly bothersome, but their stolid self-righteousness had an enormous advantage. They were incapable of recognizing that Joe had a drinking problem.

I felt utterly dispirited and helpless. Richard's brush with death and my lecturing programme over the vacation had left me tired out. As an Australian lodger with no authority in the chaplaincy, I was bewildered about handling a senior priest whom I had never met before. In the 1950s I had heard of Joe as a flamboyant and effective speaker, who ranged from preaching popular retreats to representing Catholic causes in the Oxford Union. Now I felt angry at this outsider who threatened to damage my friend's ministry in Cambridge. Intellectually I could see what had happened. It had been unbearably alarming and lonely for Joe to walk into this strange situation. My commitment to complete the series of lectures at Heythrop meant that I had been unable to reach Fisher House first and give him a friendly welcome when he arrived.

I had set aside Lent term to write my volume on revelation for the *Theology Today* series, having promised Ted Yarnold that I would deliver the manuscript to him by Easter. Since I had already gathered my material, all that remained was to put it together in elegant English. But for several days I sat in the university library paralysed by my misery over the situation in the chaplaincy. Jerry Golden offered a straw of hope. He had disappeared in his travels around England, but was due to return to pick up some luggage. Never in my life have I been so relieved to see another Jesuit as when Jerry walked into the sitting room at Fisher House. After ten minutes of conversation, he told me what I had been desperately hoping that my account of the situation would elicit from him: 'I can't possibly leave now.'

Joe suddenly seemed less threatening. He welcomed Jerry's presence. His old-style theology quickly attracted a following among conservative students. His Scottish warmth made him effective with those who suffered a death in their families or some other deep and sudden grief. He seemed to enjoy meals with me at Pembroke, and responded by inviting me to dine with him in the Cambridge Union before he took part in a debate on the proposed abortion bill. The other speakers included Ann Mallalieu (who was to become the first woman president of the union and in later years a QC and a life peer), Professor Glanville Williams (who had drafted the bill), and David Steel (the MP who proposed the bill in the House of Commons). The pro-abortionists won the debate, the only one I ever attended in the union. Dinner with the speakers and the debate itself proved pleasant, not least because the president, David Horowitz, was not only with me at Pembroke but also a fellow member of the Thomas Gray Society. That evening I realized what Joe reminded me of. This tubby, red-faced priest wore his black frock-coat, talked the language of dated apologetics, produced gestures out of old manuals of oratory, and, altogether, suggested a friendly but ageing member of a provincial repertory company.

Through that Lent term I remained haunted by the fear that Joe would clash spectacularly with some Catholic students, either with those who were left-wing politically or with those whose theology was less conservative than his. Instead he had a row with a fellow Jesuit, Archbishop Tom Roberts, who came to speak one evening at Fisher House. The archbishop criticized authoritarianism in the Catholic Church, supported responsible birth control, and expressed other 'liberal' views for which he was already widely known. Joe walked into the meeting, and cut the question period short: 'This man is talking heresy. This cannot take place in my house.' Joe had drunk too much. Even so, I doubt if he would have stopped proceedings and made his charge, if Jerry Golden had not encouraged him to do so. I confronted Jerry about this afterwards. He alleged that he could 'smell evil that night', and defiantly published a letter in *The Times* defending

Joe's stand. The *Daily Express* and other papers headlined the clash between the archbishop and the chaplain. But the BBC came to the rescue by inviting the two of them to resolve their differences in a television discussion. Before millions of viewers Joe humbly withdrew his charge of heresy. A pleasantly sentimental scene of reconciliation took place between the two men, who had lived together for years in the same Jesuit community of Farm Street.

Other storms shook my teacup that Lent term of 1967, notably Herbert McCabe's removal from the Cambridge scene. Herbert had responded to the departure of Charles Davis by a frank and sympathetic editorial in *New Blackfriars*. He agreed with Charles that the Catholic Church was 'plainly corrupt'. Faceless church authorities promptly removed Herbert from his post as editor, and even 'suspended' him from his priestly functions. He went off to Dublin to lick his wounds. The extreme reaction to his editorial caused a howl of outrage. The 'suspension' was quickly lifted, and three years later he took over *New Blackfriars* again. His first editorial began: 'As I was saying before I was so oddly interrupted, ecclesiastical authorities can behave in some fairly bizarre ways.' In early 1967 I winced at the stupid punishment imposed on Herbert, but failed to register my protest in any way. Charles Davis's coming to Cambridge did, however, induce me to take one public stand.

Clare College gave Charles a visiting fellowship, and Pembroke provided a house in a village outside Cambridge. After marrying Florence Henderson, he settled down to write his apologia, *A Question of Conscience*. Hugh Mellor smelt an evening's fun for the Thomas Gray Society, and wanted to arrange a debate between Charles and myself. Charles begged off, explaining that he wanted to devote all the time available to the task of completing his manuscript. However, he did give a long interview to the weekly paper for Cambridge students, *Varsity*. The interview prompted me to set aside my usual timidity and publish a letter in reply on 11 March. As the text of this letter will be more vivid than any summary, let me quote it in full:

> Your interview with Charles Davis increased my appreciation of his sincere convictions and deep personal integrity. Yet when reading the interview the question came to me: what would Karl Barth, the leading Protestant theologian of this century think, if this number of *Varsity* should fall into his hands? For here was an account of the Roman Catholic Church and of one man's reasons for disassociating himself from its organization in which God and Christ were never mentioned—or at least only by very occasional implication. In our day no one has insisted more than Barth that our theological criteria must be genuinely theological, i.e. taken not from man but from God revealed to us in Christ.
>
> The points raised in the interview are constantly human. We read of people being perverted in outlook by handing themselves over to the system, overemphasis on the role of authority in the Church, the Pope telling a lie in his October statement on birth control, the evil of the 'idea that truth can only be found in the statements of bishops and popes', the episcopacy and papacy 'being largely irrelevant' to many Catholics, etc. etc. One reaction to this catalogue of complaints would be to argue the tedious details. For instance, who in fact holds the proposition 'that truth an only be found in the statements of bishopsc and popes'? But this method of argument would not merely be tiresome; it simply doesn't reach the heart of the matter. Barth's objection would be that Charles Davis's arguments as presented seem merely human.
>
> Surely we must look first towards God? How did God reveal himself in Christ? What are the permanent structures which he gave the Church through Christ and the apostles? What is the will of God now for the Church? We must concern ourselves first with such questions rather than begin by asking, for example, what contemporary science would suggest to us. Charles Davis puts before us the model of the international scientific community,

instead of asking us to examine first what permanent shape the
new people of God received in Christ. Karl Barth's view of the
Church differs from that of Roman Catholicism. But I would
feel at one with him in insisting that in trying to understand the
Church, we must begin, not with criteria drawn from human ideals,
but with God made known to us in Christ.

In retrospect it seems surprising that I managed to complete
the manuscript of *Theology and Revelation*. I dedicated it to my niece,
Marion Peters, and to Jerry Golden, without whom I would not have
survived the term. His part in the clash with Archbishop Roberts
hardly bothered me. That was a seven-day wonder, notable both for
the English restraint that stopped anyone from saying publicly that
Joe had been in his cups and for the silliness of those students who
had originally protested over the manner of his appointment. They
now tried to win support for a move to have Joe sacked or at least
forced to resign. Their efforts came to nothing, since the term had
almost finished and Joe was about to leave anyway within a fortnight.
By that time I felt bruised and exhausted from the last three months.
There had been extra commitments to carry, some pleasant and
others burdensome. When Ernest Nicholson arrived in March from
Dublin, I brought him at once to dine at Pembroke and tried to play
some part in making him feel at home in Cambridge. A friend come
from Tübingen on a quick visit. I put him in touch with students
during research in his area, modernism and, in particular, the work
of George Tyrrell. At least every month I visited a forlorn group
of nuns in Bury St Edmunds, and tried to support them by giving
talks on aspects of the spiritual life, leading discussions, hearing their
confessions, meeting with individuals, and holding services in their
chapel. In mid- March I ran for cover and a rest with my Irish relatives.

I divided my three-week stay in Ireland between Tom and Pat
Hayes in Ardee, Jock and Eleanor Harbison in Blackrock, and the
Jesuits in Milltown Park. The affectionate hospitality of my two

cousins, their husbands, and children drained away all the tension of Cambridge life. Soft peace filled those days, except for a chilling visit to 'the North'. The border roused that sense of a violated people, which I had felt two years earlier when viewing the zone between the two Germanys near Wolfsburg. On the south side a little green, white and orange flag marked the grave of a republican, killed in an incident near the customs station. After B specials had poked submachine guns through the windows of our car at the border, we drove into Newry and my first sight of British police carrying guns and going on patrol in pairs. It was Easter Sunday morning.

Back in Cambridge the Easter term drifted by blithely and completed my recovery from the trauma of the winter and early spring. Pembroke College elected me to a research fellowship. Ted Yarnold accepted my work for publication among the first volumes of the *Theology Today* series, and Bob Murray (to whom Ted had sent the manuscript for an opinion) wrote encouragingly from Heythrop: 'Ever since reading your book on revelation I've been meaning to write & congratulate you it, and now I hear there's something else to congratulate you on, your fellowship. I'm not a bit surprised at the latter! I think the book is absolutely splendid.'

I was deeply grateful to see Richard home again and back at his priestly work in Fisher House. One evening he invited Charles and Florence Davis to a dinner party there. The conversation ran along in animated style between the groups of guests, until most of them suddenly and simultaneously paused. Into the abrupt silence I could hear Charles saying to Dennis Nineham, 'What we are *really* looking for is...' Every ear pricked up at that. Would the great Catholic dissident inform the Regius Professor of Divinity that he was searching for a new doctrine of the Church or some other theological prize? To our disappointment the sentence ended, '...an electric carving knife'. A few weeks later the Davises invited Richard and me to a party at their home. It was one of those perfect summer evenings, when light and warmth linger on and the fields smell agreeably from fresh cut hay. I wondered how to interpret Charles's renunciation of Catholicism. Most of the guests turned out to be Catholics, both priests and lay people.

During the Easter terms encouraging letters poured in from my family in Australia. At the end of April my brother Jim married Rosemary ('Posey') Calder and gave me a loving, lifelong friend in his bride. Maev had been accepted to begin graduate work at Columbia University in New York, and mother was coming back to Europe.

June arrived and I left for Tübingen. On the way I made a detour to spend four days in and around Copenhagen with my mother, who had just arrived via Italy and the Soviet Union. She was to travel on as far as Iceland, before turning back to meet Maev and me in Paris on 15 August. In 1965 I had worried about mother's long journeys alone. But by 1967 she had established herself as a determined and successful traveller. Copenhagen was celebrating its foundation eight hundred years earlier. We watched a Danish princess and her French husband ride through the city in a horse-drawn carriage after their wedding. The city offered a festive stopping place before I moved south for a summer's study in Germany.

The Carl Sonnenschein Studentenwohnheim provided me with a room to be shared with a stolid student of classics, whose former room-companion had gone away for psychiatric treatment. I felt instantly and agreeably at home back in Tübingen. Many German and American friends were still studying there. I helped again in the parish of St Michael's; fortunately the Italian nuns no longer wanted Mass at 6 a.m. The Jesuit population had risen to its highest point in living memory, sixteen priests and scholastics. A Californian Jesuit played the role of host with cheerful perfection. One calm evening he led all sixteen of us in a convoy of Volkswagens out to dine at Schloss Weitenburg. The hills and the Neckar valley hung suspended in light and loveliness.

That summer I often spent evenings with John Dwyer, a Jesuit from the New York province, at the Berghaus Hügel, a residence for student priests that stood close to the banks of the Neckar and later became a monastery for Carmelite sisters. Brush-haired and big-bodied, John spoke fluent German and never wavered in his kindness and hospitality towards me. We frequently fell into exhilarating debates over such topics as prayer, resurrection, and church authority. The others present drank their beer and ate sausage meat, while John and I slugged it out. The others included Ray, an affable American, who had been a Protestant minister, entered the Catholic Church with his wife and brood of brilliant children, and began a doctorate under the supervision of Küng. Ray was ordained to the priesthood by the bishop of Rottenburg and given a small parish on the outskirts of Tübingen. Not much more than a year had passed after his ordination before he ran away with an Italian girl, a graduate of the Biblical Institute in Rome who had come to Germany for pastoral work among the Italian migrant workers.

Tübingen reached its theological best for me in the summer of sixty-seven. Heiko Oberman had arrived from Harvard to direct an institute for Reformation and pre-Reformation history. I spent one confused evening with a couple of his children, who spoke a mixture of English, German, and their native Dutch. I was showing them how to throw a boomerang. As our missiles whistled near power lines, I feared for one crazy moment that we might cause a blackout in that part of Württemberg. The Catholic faculty had acquired Joseph Ratzinger, who delivered for 'hearers of all faculties' a marvellous series of lectures on the Apostles' Creed, later published as *Introduction to Christianity*. One Sunday I went with him and his sister to hear a perfect performance of Mozart's Mass in C minor in a baroque church at Zwiefalten. I tried to make conversation with Ratzinger's sister, who acted as his housekeeper: 'That was an excellent book on revelation and tradition that your brother wrote with Karl Rahner.'

A Midlife Journey

'Never heard of it', she admitted cheerfully.

I took part again in Küng's doctoral seminar. He was glad to receive first-hand news of Charles Davis, although he annoyed me by brushing aside my personal reflections on Charles's situation. But Küng lacked those prejudices which, both then and later, allowed some Catholics to put some shameful questions to me: 'Isn't it true that Charles Davis has had a nervous breakdown and is in mental home? Hasn't his marriage collapsed?' That summer I took a little malicious pleasure in replying: 'Well, if that has happened, it could only have been during the last month. Everything seemed happy and normal, when I joined a party at his home a few weeks ago.' The worst piece of such nasty gossip I heard from a Catholic acquaintance in Oxford. He assured me: 'They can't have any children, as Florence has undergone a hysterectomy.' When I heard she was pregnant, I wanted to phone this person, tell him the news, and add, 'It must have been a very small hysterectomy.'

As far as I was concerned, Jürgen Moltmann's presence in Tübingen made the most significant change from the previous year. He had come from Bonn, and was to make his first visit to the United States in late 1967. I went to hear him lecture (on hope) to major audiences in the Auditorium Maximum, introduced myself to him, and was flattered to become quickly part of his circle. My enthusiasm for his theology doubtless helped, as well as the fact that the previous winter I had persuaded Alan Webster (the warden of Lincoln Theological College) to invite him for a lecture tour. That was to be Moltmann's first visit to England since his three years there as a very young prisoner of war. From the outset I liked his easy, boyish charm that set him apart from the lordly grandeur of the typical Herr Professor. He remains the only German professor I have ever come to address with the familiar 'du'. That summer I translated into English a paper he was to read at a conference in Chicago. He arranged for me to meet Ernst Bloch, an old, existentialist-style Marxist philosopher who played the role of grey eminence for the theologians of hope.

Bloch and his wife welcomed me for an afternoon in their home on the banks of the Neckar. A thatch of white hair, the thick-lensed glasses, and his lined face gave him the look of a latter-day prophet. He feared that theologians were taming his views, 'spreading hotel sauce over everything', as he put it. He recalled the anti-revolutionary German president, Friedrich Ebert, who 'said something a Jesuit could have said'. With a smile Bloch added, 'an earlier Jesuit of the seventeenth century', and went on to quote the words of Ebert: 'I place myself at the head of the movement, in order to break off the head of the movement.' Bloch's wife cut in, 'You have to realize, Herr O'Collins, that my husband is an atheist.' Bloch smiled: 'Yes, an atheist for the sake of God.' At that time he was writing *Atheismus und Christentum*. I expressed regret that none of his works had so far been translated in English, and went away to write an article on Bloch's influence in contemporary theology, 'The Principle and Theology of Hope'. It appeared a year later in the *Scottish Journal of Theology*. In the winter of 1967/68 Justus George Lawler wrote out the blue to invite me to translate (for Herder and Herder) Bloch's *Das Prinzip Hoffnung*. I enthusiastically endorsed the project, declined to undertake it myself (mainly because of the sheer size of Bloch's great work), and offered to write a book on the theology of hope. The result was *Man and His New Hopes*, which I was to finish writing in November 1968 and which appeared the following year.

A seminar on Christ's resurrection conducted by Gerhard Ebeling provided a further theological treat in the summer of 1967. For years I kept expecting that the thought of this highly dignified and very Lutheran theologian would enrich my own theology immensely. But, in fact, I learnt more from his sensitive evaluation of what others had written on the resurrection: from Thomas Aquinas, through Barth and Bultmann, down to Pannenberg and Moltmann. I marvelled at

Ebeling's capacity to keep lively and productive discussion going with sixty or seventy students. Of course, they were serious, prepared, and enthusiastic. One evening after a session of his seminar, I passed a couple walking home hand in hand down the Wilhelmstrasse. 'What we really need', the German boy was explaining to his girlfriend, 'is a theology of the empty tomb.'

Two marriages helped to fill my closing week in Tübingen with dinners, parties, and concerts. I joined Josef and Ingrid Nolte in celebrating their civil wedding, before they went off to a church service elsewhere. A British couple I knew arrived on their honeymoon. I joined them for a party at the Evangelische Stift, where one of the tutors or 'Repetenten' whisked me off to see the records in the library. I laughed over a report on the young Georg Friedrich Wilhelm Hegel which noted that he had 'neglected the study of philosophy'. He was to become the most famous nineteenth-century philosopher in Europe and beyond.

I left on a midday train for Frankfurt on 28 July, but managed to fit in two engagements that morning: an hour's discussion with Ebeling and a visit to Käsemann. At a huge conference in Hanover, Käsemann had delivered an address on 'the Presence of the Crucified One', in which his brilliant polemics had angered both the fundamentalists and church authorities. 'The Church', he declared, 'needs more guerilla fighters and fewer managers.' He returned to Tübingen to face prolonged treatment for tuberculosis of the bone. A sheet spotted with fresh blood stretched across him, as he lay huddled up like a lion at bay. He appeared pleased to see me, but a little distracted—not, I suspect, by any physical pain. The vehement response to his critics, *Ruf der Freiheit*, was already gathering in his mind.

I stopped in Frankfurt to do two things: attend the ordination of several Jesuit friends and make my annual eight-day retreat. To my surprise a letter arrived from the Australian provincial notifying me that I could take my final vows in Paris on 15 August. Some months before I had been in contact with him about this, but after hearing nothing further I imagined that I would have to wait another year. Most of the eight Jesuits who took their final vows with me made a special trip to Paris, so that they could do so in the chapel at Montmartre, where St Ignatius and his first companions took their vows together on 15 August 1534. The simplicity of the occasion struck me, as with no solemn or nervous fuss we vowed ourselves one after another to remain Jesuits for life. The superior of the Rue de Grenelle residence where I stayed was chief celebrant at the Mass. He impressed me by his courtesy in speaking as slowly and clearly as possible, for the sake of those, like me, whose French was weak.

Mother and Maev arrived in Paris later that day. We spent a cheerful evening with Monica Ellison, her husband, and four daughters, hired a car, and set off for eleven days that took us north through Verdun to Trier, then south through Colmar to Provence, and than back to Paris by way of the Loire valley and Chartres. It was a particularly happy holiday together. Mother loved 'la belle France', as she like to call the country; Maev was glad to be free at last to begin graduate studies in New York; and I felt gently flung about in my emotional reactions to what we saw. A cemetery where 130,000 French soldiers lie buried and other signs of carnage at Verdun stirred deep feelings of horror at war. The crucifixion scene on Grünewald's Isenheimer altar hit me hard. The next hall in the museum at Colmar contained an exhibition of recent Picassos that revealed a frantic obsession with human heads and genitals. The sunlight blazing down on vineyards and broken columns made Provence sheer joy. Out of nostalgic respect for the church councils held there, I suggested Orange as our base. We almost died on the deserted 'autoroute' when driving at nearly ninety miles an hour. A Chevrolet overtook us, pulled fifty yards clear, and blew a front tire. Somehow the Dutch driver kept his twisting, spinning car on the road, while Maev managed to slide our Peugeot past.

I spent September working on my thesis at Campion Hall, and hearing one or two lectures at an international conference on the early Fathers of the church. Mother and Maev took me to a bloodthirsty and memorable performance of *Macbeth* starring Paul Scofield. Maev and I learnt our lesson that evening. We had joked about mother's habit of falling into conversation with strangers, kept our distance when she looked as if she were about to pounce, and made up a description that we suggested should be circulated to the European police: 'Grey-haired lady, age sixty-seven, height five feet four inches, will talk on sight.' That evening she rejoined us after the interval to report with glee a long conversation with a descendant of Mrs Sarah Siddons (1755-1831), a famous actress known for playing Lady Macbeth. A few days later I caught a bus across to Cambridge and began my third and final year of research.

The Third Cambridge Year

Admission to my fellowship at Pembroke took place in the college chapel. I knelt before the master, placed my hands in his, and recited a Latin formula affirming my loyalty to the college. He also used a Latin formula to admit me, concluding with an invocation of the Trinity, '*in nomine Patris, et Filii, et Spiritus Sancti*'. I decided not to point out to the other fellows that it was 10 October, the feast of St Francis Borgia, a Jesuit saint whose family name inevitably conjures up poisonings and a range of other crimes and vices. My college duties, if slight, all seemed linked with drink. Once a fortnight I acted as host at wine parties held for junior members of Pembroke. My position as one of the junior fellows meant that most evenings I took the port, madeira, and claret around the senior parlour after dinner. Some of the senior fellows felt a little self-satisfaction as having elected the first Jesuit and (after David Knowles and James Burtchaell) the third Roman Catholic priest to hold a fellowship at any Cambridge college since the sixteenth-century Reformation. I welcomed the chance of coming to know many of them better. They ranged from the gentle, cultivated Basil Willey to the impossibly conservative Vernon Pennell, a retired surgeon who had become a fellow in 1914. I asked him once about Jawaharlal Nehru who had been at Harrow with him. 'Nehru', he said. 'I used to kick him in the arse at school. Then he went out east and caused trouble.'

Being a fellow allowed me to hold small dinner parties in my rooms, an elegant second-storey set (in a seventeenth-century building) which one of the other fellows asked me to occupy while he was away on work in Hawaii. His library included all the novels of Iris Murdoch. I heard her lecture (on the supremacy of the good) to a crowded audience in the Senate House, admired her language, and enjoyed the way she ran her fingers through her hair like one or two male conductors I had seen. By the summer of 1968 I had read most of her novels. It intrigued me to find how vividly she could evoke the mysteriousness of decisions that shape human lives forever.

During Michaelmas term, John O'Neill agreed to supervise me, since Dennis Nineham was on sabbatical leave. John encouraged me to battle against some sloppiness of style into which I had drifted. His criticisms gave the thesis itself a much better shape. It became an attempt to answer the question: what happened to the theology of revelation after Barth and Bultmann?

Twelve lectures for a branch of the University of Leicester at Northampton offered an agreeable safeguard against the disease that can afflict some research students in the last stage of their work: endless and obsessive preoccupation with minor details in their theses. About fifteen clergymen, mainly Anglican priests, took my course on twentieth-century theology. After my mini-course at Heythrop College the year before, this mature and friendly group formed a second stage in my learning to lecture in theology. One of the Anglicans, a vicar from Rutland, invited me to preach at matins during the church unity week and announced in his parish news letter: 'For the first time since the Counter-Reformation a Catholic of the Roman Obedience will preach in Uppingham Church. The sneer used to be made that differing Christians spend their time in fighting with each other. This is as out of date as the long skirt.' I took special pleasure in preaching from the pulpit Jeremy Taylor had filled for six years. My name suffered slightly in the news letter, appearing as 'G.O. Collins'. However, it suffered a more spectacular change in Trinity Hall, Cambridge, where I preached the same day (and used the same sermon) at evensong. The chapel card listed me as 'The Revd. G.O'Higgins'.

Two American friends who lived in Hampstead offered another remedy against any tension building up as my thesis fell into final shape. We saw a number of shows together in London: Sir John Vanbrugh's *The Relapse*, Peggy Ashcroft in Ibsen's *Ghosts*, Sir Laurence Olivier in Strindberg's *Dance of Death*, and Tito Gobbi with James McCracken in Verdi's *Otello* at Covent Garden. This hospitality was a pleasing prelude to the warm-hearted welcome I would meet later in the United States.

By the winter of 1967/68 I had decided to do some teaching in the United States on my way home to Australia. The residential requirement for a Cambridge PhD obliged me to stay there until June 1968. It made little sense to rush back to Australia to teach in the dying months of the academic year. Besides, if my thesis had to be revised and re-submitted, a temporary post in the USA would allow me to do this, without incurring the extra expense of returning all the way from Australia. George MacRae had written in May 1967 and sown the thought: 'If you'd like to dally in the US for a year on the way back home, just let me know. Theologians are in short supply, and good ones are more than welcome.' With the approval of my provincial in Australia, I contracted to stop in

Boston for the fall semester of 1968 and would teach two courses at George's theological school, Weston College.

Maev's presence in New York gave me another strong reason for wanting to visit the United States. We kept up our regular correspondence with each other. She bombarded me with her early impressions of American politics, education, and religion. The readings for her various courses uncovered such odd jargon as 'the status of the reduced process is that of an epiphenomenal by-product with no causal reference'. 'I don't know what it means', she added, 'but it sounds so wonderful that I intend to use it in some assignment.' Some language she found 'unfortunate' and 'grim', like the articles entitled 'The War on Unmarried Mothers' and 'The War on Unwanted Children'. She laughed over a notion from a seventh-century Abbot Kaioumos (the souls of immoral but humane people finish up in limbo) that I had heard at the Oxford patristics conference and passed on to her: 'Freud would have been very pleased with the idea of being "immoral but humane"—no harsh, oppressive superego to worry about. When I finally depart, I feel it would be a nice inscription on the headstone: Here lies Maev O'Collins, immoral but humane social worker, presumed to be in limbo.' 'Re-write your thesis', she urged, 'and give old Kaioumos his due.'

A discussion weekend at a farmhouse fifty miles out of New York startled Maev. At the liturgy, in which the priests wore 'check shirts and grey trousers', the 'brown bread we used for meals was broken in pieces', 'most of the prayers' were omitted, and the service ended with 'a spirited version of "Hello Christians" to the tune of "Hello Dolly"'. She admitted: 'I had some doubts at first as to whether it really was a Mass but finally decided that, whether or not, it was best to be as enthusiastic as possible for the spirit, which certainly was love of Christ, even if a bit consciously searching for new spiritual experiences. She continued:

With Maev in Boston, 1970.

Only two or three out of sixteen seemed to have some certainty and not to be tortured by tremendous doubts. Motivations were being questioned all the time. I tried to talk about the idea of Christian hope as I recalled you describing it, and a somewhat emotional Austrian flung his arms around me and shouted, 'Zat ees the most beautiful idea!' Everyone talked about searching for God. They seemed a little cross with him that he made it so difficult to find him. Hell seemed to be other people in New York, and I wondered why existentialism wasn't founded here instead of France. I struck a weak blow, with a wary eye on the Austrian, for the idea that other people must have a chance of seeing Christ in us. Apparently we must all have our own liturgical procedures. It was very good for me. I feel as if thrown into a cold pond. This is probably old hat to you, but as my first encounter it was a startling one.

All this was not in fact 'old hat' to me. At Fisher House in Cambridge we stuck pretty rigidly to the official directives, as the whole Mass gradually moved into English. In Germany church services differed from those I experienced in England, not by their unauthorised innovations but through the excellent singing, modern vestments, quality of altar furnishings, and sense of liturgical style. In Tübingen some Catholics took the consecrated host in their hands at Holy Communion. I once heard a warm and effective sermon on foreign missions by a Benedictine nun, who had served for some years in Africa. But that was all. Nevertheless, I showed annoyance at a friend who visited Cambridge on his way back to Australia after teaching at university in the United States. 'At Communion the students', he told me, 'grab at the host.' 'You mean', I suggested, 'they receive Communion in the hand.'

Christmas at Campion Hall brought 1967 to a happy close. In the last days of December I led a triduum of prayer for the nuns in an Ilford convent. One senior sister came to me for a long chat. Her good sense and intelligence were impressive. I had no answer to her disturbing question: 'What is the point of being a teaching nun? A dedicated lay woman can have just as much influence for good on her students.' The flattering attention of John Bowden, the managing director and editor of SCM Press, soon distracted me from my puzzlement. He took me to lunch on 2 January as part of his campaign to encourage me to write for him an introduction to Roman Catholic theology. It was the first time I had been wooed by a publisher. He gave me a proof copy of the English translation of Moltmann's *Theology of Hope*, asked me whether Carl Braaten's *The Future of God* deserved publication in England, rejected my thesis for publication, and left me alone for a little while. In 1977 he was to publish my *The Calvary Christ*, and organized with great efficiency the 1983 *A New Dictionary of Christian Theology*, to which I contributed eleven entries.

One German made the Lent term of 1968 notable for me: Gerd Theissen. In some ways Gerd was a walking parody of the 'mythical' German: tall, blond, forceful to the point of arrogance, fluent in English, and possessed of a mind that was fearsomely powerful. When we first met in 1966, he took a great liking to me. I was intrigued by the challenging, leftwing theological and political talk that poured out of him. He was simultaneously working on two doctorates, one under Ebeling in Tübingen and the other under Isaiah Berlin in Oxford. Gerd took me to hear Berlin lecture in Cambridge on 'Our Russian Heritage'. We stood near the front of a packed theatre to greet him before he spoke. 'Good luck', Gerd said, as if there was the slightest possibility of something going wrong for that fluent polymath who constantly had audiences hanging on every word he spoke. It was like wishing God good luck. In early March, Gerd came to my rooms in Pembroke to say goodbye, before he returned to Germany. He flooded me with useful suggestions about the title, order, and content of the book I had begun to write on hope. A thread of silent sadness ran through our afternoon together. I suspected that I would never see him again. He had received treatment for cancer and spoke of his condition with terrifying detachment: 'I can never become the father of a child.' He died in June on the day I flew to Germany. I tried to handle my sense of loss by visiting Ebeling, his 'Doktorvater'. 'Gerd', I said, 'wanted to do so much.' He was not yet thirty. He had swept into my life and disappeared like a sudden tornado.

Gerd had encouraged me to read Marx, Mao Tse-Tung, and a study on Marx by Ralf Dahrendorf (who was to become rector of the London School of Economics). My previous study of Ernst Bloch had already led me in that direction, as well as a meeting with the French Marxist, Roger Garaudy. A friend invited me to Jesus College for that occasion, the most memorable luncheon in my three years at Cambridge. A cultivated and gracious scholar, Garaudy looked pleased when my bad pronunciation made him think my thesis concerned revolution. I had to disabuse him: 'révélation et non pas révolution'. With other guests I sat enthralled by the discussion on China and Pierre Teilhard de Chardin, a French Jesuit paleontologist, which developed between Garaudy and Joseph Needham, the Master of Caius and a world expert on the history of Chinese science.

In mid-March I was to fly over to Dublin to lead a triduum of prayer for the Jesuit scholastics at Milltown Park. The Divinity Faculty in Cambridge had advertised an assistant lectureship. The notion of applying attracted me. In a tentative letter I put the possibility of applying to Peter Kelly, who had just taken over as Australian provincial. When I hurried back from Dublin on 25 March, I felt relieved to pick up an answer from him and find that he had decided against my applying. He pointed out how much I was needed for theological education in Australia.

Peter Carnley rushed me off to Oxford for the annual conference of the Society for the Study of Theology. The presidential address by Tom Torrance struck me as 'a model of orthodoxy' but—as my diary continues— 'in desperately irrelevant language'. John McIntyre (also from Edinburgh) engaged in several tussles with Torrance. Once he wanted to know in precise terms what St Athanasius meant by 'no *physis* except in the *hypostasis*'. Twice Torrance offered a paragraph of explanation. When McIntyre kept insisting on an exact paraphrase, Torrance suggested: 'Nothing emerges into reality unless it is real.' Most of the audience laughed at this, because—whatever Athanasius intended—it was obviously not just a tautology. I was sitting next to Patrick Rodger, whom I had met four years earlier at the World Council of Churches headquarters in Geneva and who was now a canon in Edinburgh. I pushed a note in front of him: 'If I stay here and listen to Torrance much longer, I will become an atheist.' We crept out for a beer in a nearby pub. Years later I came to appreciate greatly what Torrance wrote on the Eucharist and the priesthood of Christ.[4]

When the conference ended, I went out to Heythrop to hear an Australian Jesuit, John Wilcken, defend his doctoral thesis on Dietrich Bonhoeffer's ecclesiology. There were two internal examiners, Bernard Leeming and Robert Murray, as well as an external examiner, John Marsh from Mansfield College. Before proceedings closed, members of the audience could pose questions or make comments. John Bligh brought up an issue, and produced a general gasp of astonishment by his bland presupposition: 'The role of the Church is to safeguard the faith of its members.' I wondered to myself, 'How on earth then could the Church have ever started?'

In those days Bligh used to worry me not so much by the derisive unfairness of some reviews he wrote for *Heythrop Journal*—especially reviews of books in German—but more by the way he seemed to refuse to face difficult questions about the birth of Christianity. He pursued to excess a suggestion from a notable Anglican scholar,

4 G. O'Collins and M.K. Jones, *Jesus Our Priest: A Christian Approach to the Priesthood of Christ* (Oxford: Oxford University Press, 2010), 224-29.

Austin Farrer, and detected chiastic patterns from one end of the New Testament to the other. He even alleged that Farrer's action in reminding experts about chiasms might prove as important for biblical scholarship as the discovery of the Dead Sea Scrolls. John also championed the existence of some primitive Aramaic gospel, which lay behind all four gospels. Rightly or wrongly, this appeared to me as an attempt to establish a false security in the face of threatening historical questions, just as the concern for chiasms looked like a silly but dangerous diversion of interest.

The 1968 Easter issue of the London *Tablet* carried an article by me on Christ's resurrection, which drew a counter-article from Bligh. He hammered me for suggesting that some aspects of John's narrative could be 'an early Christian creation' and not literally historical. He maintained that my view made it impossible to 'trust' any of the gospel writers. I decided not to reply to his criticisms. The problem seemed personal rather than scriptural and theological. Bligh was a man of rare and high intelligence, who had won a double first in Greats at Oxford. I expected that he would eventually suffer a nervous breakdown. Instead he left the Jesuit order, married, and taught English at a Canadian university. He published a 'goodbye to all that' article in the *Heythrop Journal* for October 1970. No article in the history of that quarterly ever provoked from its readers such a response, including the cancellation of his subscription by an angry bishop. The editor invited me to write a reply to Bligh, but I declined. I did not care to shout answers after a man who had just left the field of theology. In any case it made me glad to see Bligh finally facing squarely such basic questions about the birth of Christianity as the shift from Jesus to Paul and the somewhat creative freedom that the Holy Spirit inspired in New Testament authors.

On 29 March I took a bus back to Cambridge through an afternoon of raging sunshine. A few days later one of the other junior fellows invited me to join a dinner party in his rooms. Margaret, an American graduate student, was there. I knew her as an affiliated student preparing for the English tripos. She was gentle, very pretty, and had been dated by one of my Pembroke friends. When I rose to leave at the end of the meal, she lifted her face, smiled at me, and said: 'Do come with us, Gerald, to the Arts Cinema.' I joined the group for a James Bond film, sat beside her, and knew that her smile across the room had touched me in an unexpected way. A couple of weeks later she came to dinner in my rooms with a married couple and an affiliated student from Pembroke. I refused to admit even to myself my new feelings about her, and tried to cover things up by being the odd man out. She sat among us, her hair piled up and a new dress flowing around her. She looked regal and mysterious.

At the end of April I hired a car and drove north for five days. Three lectures at Lincoln Theological College and two for the department of religious studies at Lancaster University paid for the trip. My time in England was running out, and I wanted to cram in a visit to the cathedrals of Lincoln, York, Durham, and Coventry. Spring in Cambridge seemed particularly lovely that year. I stood transfixed one day by the sight of a drive that ran through the 'backs' to a bridge over the Cam and on into the New Court of Trinity. Red tulips shone everywhere beneath two inner rows of fresh young elms and two outer rows of cherry trees in full white splendour. Now the radiant fields of tulips flanking the road to Lincoln, the affectionate welcome of Alan and Margaret Webster in Lincoln, the warm hospitality of friends in Lancaster, and the sacred beauty of the cathedrals stirred up a painful awareness of what I was leaving.

Back in Cambridge I went round to lunch one day with Margaret in the house in Chaucer Road that she shared with a visiting American professor and his wife. She padded around the kitchen in bare feet. We said very little. It was a peaceful hour or so, like the eye of a storm. Through May she kept to herself preparing for the finals. I gathered fresh material for a book on hope, and started writing the first draft.

On 21 May I faced the viva for my PhD. A few days earlier I had climbed the narrow stairs inside the gate-tower of Trinity College to visit Kitson Clark, an amusing and kindly historian. When I declined to drink some whisky with him, he ended the visit quickly but not before giving me some advice: 'When you go for your viva, O'Collins, you should fling the door open, look at the two examiners, and say to yourself, "God, what a pair!"' When I opened the door on 21 May, only the external examiner, Ronald Gregor Smith from Glasgow, was there. The internal examiner, Donald MacKinnon, arrived fifteen minutes late, full of apologies and explaining that he had been on the phone to a former student who was now living in Zürich. "He's been caught by rising prices', he added, 'and you *both* know how prices can rise in Zürich.' I caught Gregor Smith's eye. The wild fancy swept through my mind that we had just returned together from investigating the rate of inflation in all major European cities. Dennis Nineham had told me beforehand that both examiners were satisfied with my thesis. That news took away any real worry, and left me looking forward to a lively discussion with these highly gifted theologians. But I had picked up a heavy cold. MacKinnon rambled on, and gave Gregor Smith little opportunity to develop any debate with me. In any case I was feeling deeply shaken and confused by a proposal made to me the day before. The Divinity Faculty had postponed its decision to appoint any of the applicants for the assistant lectureship that had been advertised. Dennis invited me to let my name come up.

It struck me as important, both for the Roman Catholic Church and for relations between Christian churches, that a Catholic priest should hold a post on the Cambridge Divinity Faculty. But I doubted my staying power. A vague sense pursued me that the pleasant life as a don was beginning to corrupt me. Even before I took up my fellowship, I noted during my retreat in August 1967 my 'tired dullness' and need for 'courage': 'Where is the Holy Spirit crying out in my heart, "Abba, Father"? All I feel is that Jesus lives. To give up, get

married, and take a theological position, that would be putting myself
at the centre of my life, not the people of God and still less God
himself.' The specific concern had grown that I could not sustain my
Jesuit life in Cambridge but would leave the order and marry.

Unwittingly Fr David Knowles, the emeritus Regius Professor of
Modern History, pushed me towards requesting official permission
to apply for the post. The night before my viva, Knowles dined as my
guest in Pembroke. His learned charm reminded me vividly of how
much he had done for the morale of Catholic scholarship throughout
the English-speaking world. I wrote to Peter Kelly and asked Dennis
to write as well, putting reasons for my taking the Cambridge job.
A flurry of letters followed; at the end, when I had already reached
Tübingen for the summer, I had to withdraw my name. The chairman
of the Divinity Faculty replied briefly: 'I am sorry you had to
withdraw. Doubtless, however, Australia will benefit.' Dennis wrote
affectionately: 'Your telegram did arrive well in time and I need hardly
say saddened us all, though we had of course half expected it. It's
idle to speculate, but I think you might well have been the successful
candidate had you been able to stand. We shall miss you terribly in
Cambridge next year, not least the Nineham family.'

Before leaving Cambridge I tried to deal with my confusion over
the lectureship and Margaret, by making a pilgrimage to the shrine of
Our Lady at Walsingham. Peter Carnley came with me. Heavy rain had
just stopped, but depressing clouds hung over our heads as we drove
across the flat fens. On the return journey we met police roadblocks;
here and there patrol cars sped by. They were hunting for an escaped
convict. Back in Cambridge we learnt that Robert Kennedy had been
assassinated.

After the Tet offensive in Vietnam, the murder of Martin Luther
King, President Lyndon Johnson's decision not to run for re-election,
and the Paris revolution, the assassination of another Kennedy made

the political world of 1968 even more incoherent and fearful. In New York, Maev had become increasingly involved with the black community, African students, and the Poor People's Campaign—the 'last hurrah for non-violence', as she called it. On 3 February she warned me: 'They are all set for a summer of riots.' By May, her Columbia University School of Social Work was on strike 'to get various quite reasonable things like minority group and poverty group emphasis into the curriculum'. She added: 'The big trouble for me is that that School is so ghastly old-fashioned that I am in sympathy with the efforts to smarten it up, but I cannot get with the leading lights in the strike committee. I wish they were a little more courteous in their demands. The perfectly malevolent picket line captain and chief demagogue has been disclosed as "a Roman Catholic priest from Massachusetts".'

Between Cambridge and Tübingen I stopped two nights in Hampstead with American friends, who took me out to a round of rapid entertainment: an opera at Glyndebourne, the ballet *Une Fille Mal Gardée* at Covent Garden, *Hadrian VII* at the Mermaid Theatre, and an Elizabethan dinner at a hotel in Queen's Gate. The audience jumped with fear, when a visitor drew a pistol and shot Pope Hadrian. The scene recalled too vividly the death of Robert Kennedy three days earlier. But those two days in London eased the strain enough to let me face the summer in Germany. I had set myself the task of completing as much of my book on hope as I could.

During my 1967 stay in Tübingen I had met 'Mac', a handsome Methodist minister from Atlanta, Georgia. Behind his southern charm and passion for skiing lay an intense love for Christ and generous affection for his friends. When I arrived back in early June 1968, I stayed the first night above a noisy Gaststätte, appropriately named 'Hades'. Next morning I attended an early Mass, went for breakfast to the university's club house, and pondered the problem of finding some lodgings in a small city crammed with students. I caught sight of Mac sipping his coffee out in the courtyard. Within an hour he had picked up my luggage, lent me a typewriter, and driven me to a new house on the outskirts of Tübingen. My room was large and pleasant. The other lodger turned out to be an Austrian graduate Klaus, who specialized in such fatalistic sayings as '*es wird kommen was kommen muss* (what must come will come).' The landlady wasted no time in telling me about the hotshot on the block, Professor Joseph Ratzinger, who lived next door with his sister Maria, who was his housekeeper.

My landlady, Viktoria Freifrau von Gillhausen, was bulky, divorced, engaged with doctoral studies at the university, and surrounded by her three children, one foster-son, and a fleet of dachshunds, which Mac and I called the 'Freihünde'. She smoked incessantly, cared little about her appearance, and radiated a zest for learning. Our conversations ran from German logic and Jesus Christ to her family history. In the cellar she had hung the helmet of an ancestor who fought against Napoleon at the battle of Jena. Before the First World War her grandfather, a general in the German army, had married a young American girl. In her own youth Freifrau von Gillhausen had trained to throw the javelin at the 1940 Olympic Games that were cancelled when war broke out. I thought she was going to kick me out after only a week. Klaus joined me in holding a party, to which Mac brought his guitar and several Irishmen, including Enda McDonagh. About midnight Freifrau von Gillhausen burst into the room and angrily asked, 'Do you call yourselves adults?' When I apologized next morning for the noise, she assured me, 'Don't take it too tragically, Herr O'Collins.' She worried about disturbing the neighbours, especially Professor Ratzinger. The partition walls between the houses were not too thick, and he retired to bed about 9 p.m. and rose about 4 a.m. to pursue his theological research.

Soon after I moved in, I met Ratzinger on the street. As had happened the summer before, he was friendly—he asked about my work. I asked about his. After that we continued to chat and I got the impression he was a shy character. There was always an air of formality about the way he looked. You would not see him in jeans and a T-shirt; he would often wear a dark suit and a dark tie. Unlike some of the local professors, he never seemed too big for his boots. He did not have a great sense of humour, but he was witty. If I got a word wrong in my imperfect German, he might tease me for it.

His sister Maria was always very pleasant, and seemed unperturbed by her brother's formidable intellectual reputation. But she did know, and was a big fan, of his best-selling *Introduction to Christianity*. The royalties were rolling in, and Herr Professor and Maria were hoping to get a house in Bavaria on the proceeds, as they later did.

His work was very important to him; even his social circle consisted mostly of PhD students. His favourite restaurant was 'the Museum' on the Wilhelmstrasse, where you could eat well on Wiener schnitzel and dumplings, washed down with Bavarian beer and local wine. Ratzinger had long lunches there with his students, deliberating over theological matters.

We had different academic interests; so I went to only one or two of his lectures, but they were a revelation in terms of his character. When I met him on the street, he was consistently quiet, but on the podium he was transformed: sure of his ground, able to beef up his arguments and deliver his words with authority. In Cambridge, there had been a lot of sitting on the fence intellectually, but here was a man not at all afraid to nail his colours to the mast.

I never imagined then that he would one day become Pope, but I did think he would make it to be a bishop. There was a tradition in Germany of appointing academics who had done very well, very fast. I was still teaching in Rome when he was elected, and when he came out on the balcony above St Peter's Square that day in 2005, I could not help but think back to our times together in Tübingen. His sister Maria, sadly, did not live to see him become Pope. But the two of them helped make the summer of 1968 for me.

Over that summer I celebrated Mass regularly with Enda McDonagh in the Erasmus Haus, where he was spending a sabbatical year with an American scripture scholar, Bruce Vawter. Enda taught moral theology at St Patrick's College, Maynooth (Kildare). I enjoyed the contrast between the two of them. Bruce's conversation moved at a snail's pace compared with Enda's Irish speed. One evening the three of us saw Ingar Bergman's *The Hour of the Wolf*, a film in which obsessive fantasies with sex and violence oppressed the student audience into horrified silence. As we streamed out aghast, I tried to start a conversation by remarking to Bruce, 'Well, that's put me off sex for life.' Instantly Enda cut in, 'No hasty decisions.'

On 26 July I left Tübingen for Frankfurt to make my annual retreat and attend the ordination of some young Jesuits. After the ceremony in the cathedral, I went back to Sankt Georgen, found an American priest I knew, and spilled out all the pain and questioning of the last few months. Thin, shrewd, and immensely kind, Jack seemed the obvious person to confide in. We talked for hours. Eventually I met with him in a crowded restaurant to make a general confession of my last four years, the period of my stay in Europe. When I finished and we began our meal, I asked: 'Do any of these students understand English? Some of them must have heard me.' 'Don't worry about that', Jack assured me cheerfully. 'They'll never see us again.'

Meanwhile Mac turned up to stay for two days at Sankt Georgen. When we went out to eat in Sachsenhausen, a newspaper boy walked into the restaurant; I shrank back from the headlines: '*Der Papst sagt nein zur Pille* (the Pope says no to the pill).' The encyclical *Humanae Vitae* had just been published to re-affirm the official Catholic prohibition on 'artificial' birth-control. Next morning over breakfast I asked the professor who was supervising Jack's doctoral dissertation what he thought of the encyclical. He dismissed it as '*simpliciter falsch*' and added: 'The one word I would love to hear on papal lips is *erravimus* (we have made a mistake).' Within a day or two of the encyclical's appearance, I saw Cardinal Julius Döpfner and other leaders of the Catholic Church in West Germany arrive at Sankt Georgen. It was obvious that the German bishops would not simply reject the papal teaching. But, while respectfully hearing it, they would, like the bishops of other countries, introduce mitigating nuances into a flat rejection of contraception and not follow absolutely what Pope Paul VI had declared: 'each and every marriage act' must be open to the transmission of life (no. 11).

The months that followed the appearance of *Humanae Vitae* tested the ways Catholics around the world understood and applied its teaching on sexual morality and in many cases changed their views of church authority. Nearly ten years later I read what Cardinal Albino Luciani of Venice (to become Pope John Paul I in 1978) and the archbishops and bishops of fourteen neighbouring dioceses in northern Italy proposed as an examination of conscience for married people before approaching the sacrament of reconciliation: 'In agreement with my spouse, have I given a clear and conscientious answer to the problem of birth control? Have I prevented a conception for egotistical motives? Have I brought a life into the world without a sense of responsibility?' These questions tested the heart of the matter: the loving and responsible decision of two spouses. Nothing was asked about the methods used to prevent what they would judge together to be an 'irresponsible' pregnancy. But it was only in the late seventies that I read what Patriarch Luciani and these other Italian bishops proposed. In 1968 I had to cope with the turmoil Paul VI's encyclical had unleashed for myself and those around me.

Throughout the retreat I made in Frankfurt it troubled me that my prayers for direction remained unanswered. God was vividly present, but like a kindly old uncle who said nothing. 'It seems', I reflected, 'almost as if my decision gives value to the side I decide for, as if I create value by that act. This can't be so. I feel as if God won't answer my prayer and that I will feel justified before him whichever way I decide.' A reflection I had heard during my tertianship in Münster kept coming into my mind: 'In the evening of life there is no greater joy than to have loved Jesus Christ.' But what precisely did loving Jesus Christ mean for me?

Mother had come from Australia and Maev from New York. Before joining them in England, I visited the Ellisons in Paris and found John away in England with his parents. I stayed up half the night with Monica, talking about the decision not to take the job in Cambridge, about *Humanae Vitae* and, inevitably, about falling for Margaret. Monica's detached amusement ('Has she got big boobs?') startled me but was probably what I needed to hear. She put a puzzling question to me: 'Do you want to stick with what is old and dying in the Church, or become part of the new?' Yet how could I identify securely those new developments to which the Holy Spirit was truly leading Christians? Monica's affectionate but hardnosed sympathy touched me. She drove me out to the airport with her lovely clutch of four little daughters. When I moved through passport control, I turned to wave goodbye. Her golden hair streaming behind her, six-year-old Emma ran after me and gave me a final hug. I have never been so moved by the affection of a child.

I had a little over a week in Cambridge to pack and say goodbye to Peter and Ann Carnley, Richard Incledon, Meredith Dewey, Ernest and Hazel Nicholson, Dennis and Ruth Nineham, John and Judy O'Neill, and other friends. One evening I had a drink in a pub with a young couple who brought their tiny baby with them. They were uncomplicated Catholics. Making love, finding enough money to live on, regular attendance in church, and sharing an easy friendship with others defined life for them. Before they arrived, I wandered over to a middle-aged man, who had drunk too much and seemed very troubled. He told me of his terrible grief at the recent death of his wife with whom he had always been deeply in love. They had no children and he was left desperately alone. These were my people—Bill and Susan, their baby, and the lonely drunk. I could not leave them. All my well argued criticisms of the Catholic Church in its calamitous state finally failed to blind me to one insight. If I left the ministry and married, I would probably not care as much about the needs of others.

Mother, Maev and I flew out of London on 1 September for a fortnight's holiday in Spain. I still felt torn to pieces and half wished the plane would crash to end the pain of it all. Spain revived me: the paintings by Velasquez in the Prado, the sweeping view from the walls of Avila, the royal tombs in Granada and, above all, the city of Toledo, which I persuaded mother and Maev to visit twice. I wanted my memory to steal away forever the other-worldly beauty of El Greco's paintings. The monogram on an altar frontal in Toledo caught my eye and stayed with me: '*Amor sacerdos immolat* (love the priest offers the sacrifice).'

We flew from Madrid to New York. Maev stayed there to resume work at Columbia University. Mother and I flew at once to Washington, DC. The weather had turned mild and sunny. I saw cricketers playing on the banks of the Potomac. My sister Dympna and her husband were there to welcome us. Kevin was reading a paper on licensing laws at an international conference on alcoholic drink. After two days I took a plane to Boston where George MacRae met me at the airport. It felt as though I had been flung up on the shores of America—fragile, precarious, and anxious to find a fresh identity in the new world. Everywhere I was to go, the affection of friends, relatives, and Jesuits kept pace with me, and helped me to make sense of the road I had chosen.

9
Boston and Melbourne (1968-70)

Clov: 'What is there to keep me here?'
Hamm: 'The dialogue. I've got on with my story
I've got on with it well.
Ask me where I've got to.'
Samuel Beckett, *Endgame.*

When I reached Boston to teach for Weston College, the seven leading theological schools in the area had just founded the Boston Theological Institute. Students at one school could take courses at any of the others, even though they were to receive their degrees from their own school. The inauguration of the BTI involved Weston College moving from the town of Weston nearly twelve miles into Cambridge. There we used the lecture theatres, seminar rooms, chapel, cafeteria, library, and other facilities of the Episcopal Theological School, and enjoyed very close relations with ETS and Harvard Divinity School. Until Weston College bought houses and leased apartments in Cambridge, nearly all the Jesuit faculty and students continued to live in the old building out in the town of Weston. We travelled in each day by car or in a yellow bus that announced in large letters along its side 'School Bus'.

Weston College

'Mother Weston' or 'Weston-in-the-woods', as the Jesuits called their college, was a vast, red-brick building situated a mile or so out of town.

White houses were dotted here and there among the trees. Henry
Wadsworth Longfellow IV lived a hundred yards from our entrance.
Along the twisting road that led past the college the men of Weston
had marched to the battle of Concord in 1775. I delighted in the
many places and buildings which conjured up the Puritan origins of
New England, the War of Independence, and the rich literary history
of the Boston area. During my five semesters of teaching for Weston
College, I never tired of visiting the House of Seven Gables in Salem,
or wandering through the fishing village of Rockport to look across
the water to Dry Salvages, a reef made famous by T.S. Eliot's *Four
Quartets*. The house where George Washington stayed during the
siege of Boston lay just off the ETS campus. Soon after I arrived in
September 1968, the New England woods began to blaze with red
and gold colours. Phil Donnelly, one of the older priests at Weston,
took me north to Dartmouth College and across to Williamstown in
western Massachusetts. It was what he called 'the Annual Donnelly
Foliage-fahrt'. Few aesthetic experiences have ever matched for me
the hour we spent in the Clark Institute in Williamstown. My eyes
drifted from the French Impressionists to gaze through the windows
at the radiant loveliness of the maples that shone in the sunshine
outside.

Amusing stories, expert mimicry, and affectionate encouragement
flooded out of Phil. An uncle of his had died in Colonel Custer's last
stand. Phil himself had been through endless and frequently comic
adventures in his theological career. He had taught at centres across
the United States from San Francisco to Boston, opposed Leonard
Feeney's fanatical insistence that 'there is no salvation outside the
Church', been a visiting professor at Heythrop College, and served
on the faculty of the 'Papal Mausoleum', as he called the Pontifical
Gregorian University in Rome. I grew to love this overweight,
reformed alcoholic, who radiated a compassionate and priestly love
for all human beings, and sometimes made faces at people in the

subway if they looked too sad or serious. Weston College owed a great deal to Phil for the strength he communicated in the late sixties, those difficult years of transition.

A liberating, somewhat iconoclastic, spirit hung in the air. Many scholastics avoided the large, traditional chapel and attended evening Mass in a converted classroom, 'the Son of Man Chapel'. Priests used experimental liturgies, new hymns accompanied by guitars were popular, and much anxiety was reflected in shared homilies and the spontaneous petitions included in the prayers of the faithful. Theological education alongside students who belonged to other Christian denominations delighted many. But it seemed unsettling and threatening to a few. Some faculty members had opposed entering the BTI: 'The scholastics will all want to rush off to the Protestant professors.' In fact a few Weston teachers, like George MacRae, drew many students from the other schools of the BTI, while the Jesuit scholastics often seemed slow to exploit the opportunity of studying with the best available professors in various branches of theology. For years the imbalance between cross-registrations *into* rather than *out of* Weston College proved flattering and even embarrassing. The new setting meant that most scholastics and many priests dropped clerical dress as their daily attire. I followed their example in ransacking a second-hand shop in Weston, where our wealthy neighbours sold for charity their discarded suits, jackets, and ties.

The aftermath of *Humanae Vitae* affected us directly in Weston. John Ford, a senior moral theologian who had strongly endorsed the stand that Pius XI and Pius XII had taken against 'artificial' birth control, played some role in the publication of Pope Paul VI's encyclical. He was still living in the college when I arrived. In the autumn of 1968 he supported Cardinal Patrick Aloysius O'Boyle, Archbishop of Washington (1948-73), who 'suspended' from their pastoral duties a large group of priests (including his own confessor) who publicly disagreed with *Humanae Vitae*. One or two mornings

I had to hurry away from the telephone box, when Fr Ford's voice echoed down the corridor as he spoke with 'Your Eminence'. Despite Ford's opposition, most of the Weston faculty, myself included, signed a letter which went out to all the American bishops. We politely protested against the summary unfairness of the penalty inflicted upon the Washington dissidents, and asked the bishops to ensure that Cardinal O'Boyle observed 'due process' in dealing with these priests. As I recall, we received no answers and only one or two acknowledgements.

During my three months at Weston College I worked hard on my two courses: a lecture course on the theology of hope and a seminar on St Paul that concentrated on his letter to the Galatians. That set the pattern for my subsequent four semesters as a visiting professor at Weston. In 1969 I lectured on Christ's death and resurrection, in 1970 on 'the theology of hope revisited', in 1971 on Christ's death and resurrection again, and in 1972 on 'salvation through Christ'. In the seminars which continued each year I covered the texts of Paul's major letters, as well as central themes of his theology. In both courses and seminars, the students produced class papers, took part in general discussions, and usually decided to be graded on the basis of a long essay. In my first semester, I drew about forty students to the theology of hope and twelve to the seminar on Paul. But numbers for the seminar grew later to forty or fifty, while my course in systematic theology came to attract only an average of twenty-five. In the confused situation of church life, many students preferred to return to the New Testament for solutions to their theological bewilderments. I found it both attractive and complicated dealing with scripture. I was continually looking over my shoulder at Käsemann and other scholars. I felt uneasy interpreting St Paul, without first noting how their views supported, opposed, or qualified my own approach. My seniors in New Testament studies struck me as a crowd of brilliant and dauntingly learned men. Library shelves bulged with the results of their meticulous labours.

One of the Weston faculty remarked a little enviously, 'Gerry, you put down roots fast.' Friendships grew easily with many of the Jesuit scholastics, especially a group of Californians and with colleagues like Dick McBrien and Avery Dulles. A diocesan priest, Dick taught then at the John XXIII seminary for delayed vocations, and published popular pieces on theology in Catholic papers across the United States. Some months prior to my arrival he had cited and supported my thesis that we should not classify Christ's resurrection as an 'historical' event or event within history. That article in the *Boston Pilot* drew sharp criticism from a lawyer employed by the Kennedy family. He felt it a shame that 'someone with a fine Irish name like "O'Collins" should hold such views'.

A convert to Catholicism and the leading Jesuit theologian in the United States, Dulles preached at the Mass of the Holy Spirit with which Weston College began its academic year in 1968. During the concelebrated Eucharistic prayer it happened that Avery said the prayer for the dead. When he paused for a few moments of silence, I knew he was praying for his father, John Foster Dulles, the Secretary of State whose high-minded but rigid policies it had become popular to deride. Avery once told me of a dinner that his father gave for Charles Lindbergh in the hope of finding out whether the famous aviator really was a fascist. But right from our first meal together at the Midget, a Cambridge restaurant commemorated in Eric Segal's *Love Story*, we mostly talked shop. Avery put matters flatteringly, 'I want to milk you for your theological ideas.' Just forty years later, in December 2008, I was to write Avery's obituary in the London *Tablet*.

Other new friends included Paul and Heidrun Rotterdam. A Viennese Catholic, Paul taught at the Carpenter Center for fine arts in Harvard, but eventually gave up that post to live in New York and concentrate on his own painting. Heidrun was a German Protestant and worked as a pathologist in a Boston hospital. When I baptized their daughter, I used German for the ceremony. They seemed touched by that, and we remained friends.

An Australian woman doctor introduced me to the Rotterdams and gently encouraged them not to delay further the baptism of their baby, who was already several months old. The Australian wanted to visit Cardinal Richard Cushing, the old Archbishop of Boston and friend of the Kennedy family. He had strongly defended Jacqueline Kennedy when she married Aristotle Onassis, but refused to tell reporters what had been said when he met Jacqueline shortly before the wedding. I phoned the cardinal's secretary, who assured me at once: 'The Australian doctor is very welcome, and come round yourself.' The cardinal looked tired and ill, lamented the number of highly educated nuns who were leaving their congregations, listened patiently when the doctor suggested ways to improve the training of nurses in Boston, and ended by asking us, 'Well, can I do anything for either of you?' We assured him that there was nothing we wanted. Afterwards we laughed and admitted to each other that one question had instantly come to mind: 'What did you and Jackie Kennedy talk about?'

The months in Boston rushed by in a flurry of work and other engagements. Hans Frei arranged a visit to Yale, where I presented a paper for those in religious studies, gave a lecture, and preached at More House, the Catholic chaplaincy. At Thanksgiving, Ed and Jane Kirby invited me to join their family in New Jersey. During the Second World War, Ed had visited my home in Australia as a young officer in the First Marine Division. Thanksgiving dinner with the Kirbys became a fixed engagement during the five years I spent a semester as visiting professor at Weston College.

From Boston I looked back longingly to Cambridge and England. In September Meredith Dewey wrote comfortingly from Pembroke:

'I shall miss you sadly next term. In fact the prospect fills me with gloom. But you *will* come back, won't you, for your third year? I value your support so much. It's so refreshing to find someone steadfast and not a crumbler. My love & take care of yourself, & don't let that German theology go to your head.' Instead of resigning my research fellowship at once, I had taken leave of absence for my second year. If everything failed me elsewhere, at least I could go back to Pembroke. Another cheering letter came from England—from the Warden of Lincoln Theological College, Alan Webster, who was to become Dean of Norwich (1970-78) and Dean of St Paul's (1978-87). When he told me of his plans to invite a German theologian for a short visit and an English Jesuit to teach for a term, I had suggested Jürgen Moltmann and Robert Butterworth. Now I learnt how both suggestions had turned out:

> I know you will be delighted that Moltmann's visit was a very great success. He did relatively simple papers on the theology of revelation, and did them very well indeed. We liked particularly his constant reiteration that one can face the future either with anxiety or hope, and most of us waver between these two. I liked him personally, especially as he had joined in one of those marches in London and had been very amused to walk down Whitehall shouting, 'We are all foreign scum.' He thought this particularly quaint for someone who was taken prisoner by the English at the age of seventeen.

> As you may have heard, we have been able to persuade Father Butterworth from Heythrop to come and spend a whole term with us. He's going to lecture in doctrine and the New Testament, and also give some popular lectures on Roman Catholicism. This is the first time an Anglican college has ever had a Jesuit full-time on the staff for a term, and it ought to be very exciting. It's in part due to the fact that we already have a Methodist on the staff. It is such a mistake to think that it is either Rome or Protestantism for the Church of England. It must be a growing openness all around.

If I felt nostalgia for England and Cambridge, my impending return to Melbourne frightened me. Would I be buried there forever? Were the Australian bishops demanding assent to *Humanae Vitae* before priests could receive 'faculties' to preach and celebrate the sacraments? Home after his Harvard studies, Greg Dening was engaged in chaplaincy work at the University of Queensland. He explained to the Catholic archbishop of Brisbane his difficulties with Pope Paul's ban on 'artificial' birth control, the archbishop reacted by making it, in effect, impossible for Greg to continue: 'I'm not suspending you, but I do not want you to preach and hear confessions.' Greg retired to Sydney, 'licking his wounds after his bad experience', as John Eddy put it in a letter to me.

Then the rector of Weston College stepped in to make my return to Australia less fearful. He invited me to come back and teach again. On 6 November I wrote to Peter Kelly seeking permission to accept: 'My first act of the Nixon-Agnew era is to put a request to you, the result of an invitation to teach for Weston in the fall semester of 1969. I am asking to teach in Australia during the first two terms of 1969 and then be free from mid-August until February 1970. Weston would, of course, finance the matter, so that there would be no financial burden on the Australian Province. The Weston dean will write to you, so that you can hear the request from their side.' I also wrote to Bill Daniel, dean of studies and professor of moral theology at Canisius College. He encouraged Peter Kelly to grant my request, and was mildly reassuring about the pressure to uphold *Humanae Vitae* in Australia. 'I don't know if they have gone as far as to require a profession of loyalty to the encyclical for the giving of faculties in Melbourne, but I have heard that the hard line is very much in the ascendancy. I am not letting that worry me too much, however. Time is on our side. The cumulative reaction of the more sensible hierarchies must work towards a relaxation of bigotry.'

Meanwhile something had happened to trouble my attempt to

make a fresh start in my life as a Jesuit and a priest. In November, Margaret arrived in Boston. At first I could hardly bear to look at her. 'Gerald', she said, 'you are as jumpy as a witch.' One afternoon she took me to meet her eighty-nine-year-old grandmother. The widow of a Harvard Divinity School professor, she was confined to bed, welcomed me affectionately, presided serenely over tea, and sang for us 'Over the Sea to Skye'. The courageous charm of the old lady touched me. Of course, I was dishonest and cruel in seeing Margaret. She loved me and hoped I would marry her. She seemed so tenderly beautiful that I shrank from leaving her finally. She came to the last meeting of my seminar. There was irony in the topic for discussion, St Paul's theology of the cross. We took coffee together in the basement of the ETS cafeteria, with the Beatles' song 'Yesterday' being played again and again in the background. Several Jesuits had invited me to dine with them in Concord, before I flew out of Boston the following morning en route for Melbourne. I kissed Margaret goodbye, walked across the ETS campus and joined the scholastics in the evening trip home to Weston. As the yellow bus whisked me off, I twisted around in my seat to see Margaret walking alone down Brattle Street as she went home to her grandmother.

I never saw her again and we never corresponded. I tried to make the break complete by refusing to find out where she went to live and what became of her. But I kept the copy she gave me of *Anna Karenina*, read it as soon as I reached Australia, and identified with Konstantin Levin's resolution: 'He decided that from that day on he would stop looking for any extraordinary happiness such as marriage was to have given him, and that consequently he would no longer think little of what he possessed at present.' Like Levin I wanted to hear the voice which said: 'One must not submit to the past and one can make what one likes of oneself.' But, as Anna told Vronsky, I thought 'always of the same thing'. For over three years few days seemed to pass without Margaret's name rising to my lips or her face coming before my eyes.

Return to Melbourne

The trip back to Australia began with a snowstorm in New York, and ended with an Australian doctor next to me on the flight out of San Francisco swallowing a whole handful of sleeping tablets. He was rushed to emergency services in Honolulu, pumped out, and put back on our flight several hours later. 'The saga of your journey home', Maev commented, 'sounds like par for the course. I think we have a fatal fascination for those crazier than ourselves. Why else would so many would-be suicides, desperadoes, and demented liberals attach themselves to paths we traverse?'

John Eddy, Bill Daniel, and my aunts gave me an affectionate welcome in Sydney. Davis McCaughey had an offprint waiting for me; it was an article ('Current Theology: Australia') he had published in an American journal. His opening sentence was sombre: 'Australia lacks many of the obvious signs of theological activity.' But his note was encouraging: 'Gerald, not to depress you, but to indicate how much we need you in Australia.'

My mother, sister Dympna, and eleven nieces and nephews met me at Melbourne airport to carry me off to spend Christmas at Rock Lodge, the first Christmas I had spent there with my family since 1949. I had been overseas for four and a half years. My married brothers and sisters all had new babies to show me; I baptized Glynn's fourth child, Philippa Mary. I met for the first time Jim's lovely and lively wife, Posey, who had worked for the Australian Security and Intelligence Organization before her marriage. The three of us went one evening to a performance by a visiting company of Russian ballet dancers. Posey laughed afterwards over the number of Australian intelligence agents she had spotted in the audience.

The love that all my family lavished on me kept me going from the end of the sixties and into the seventies. I often had meals with them, played golf with Jim, Glynn, my nephew Stewart, and other relatives, and regularly celebrated a Sunday Mass for those who came to Rock Lodge at the weekend. In Melbourne, along with my family, the McCaugheys and my Jesuit friends met my need for affection and support.

My academic life in Australia settled into a pattern that continued for five years: teaching fundamental theology in the first term (March to May) at the Jesuit Theological College (Parkville), and in the second term (June to August) at Corpus Christi (Glen Waverley), which changed its name and location in 1973 to become Catholic Theological College (CTC) in Clayton. With its soaring brick tower, Corpus Christi topped the highest hill near Melbourne. In the 1950s uncle Jim had taken charge of the building operation for the board of Victorian and Tasmanian bishops. He wanted a building of Roman

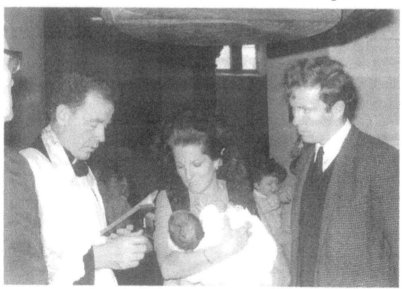

At family christening in 1969 with sister-in-law Posey and nephew Stewart.

grandeur that would last for at least a century. The seminarians left there at the end of 1972, and the Victorian government turned it into a police training college. In my courses I covered themes like God's self-revelation, human faith, tradition, and theological method. After 1970 I was to increase the amount of material drawn from the New Testament and spend time, in particular, on the death and resurrection of Jesus. My early book, *Foundations of Theology*, represented much of the content of my courses in 1969 and 1970.

The Jesuit community in Parkville occupied a row of ten terrace houses, which were built around 1880 and looked out on the elms and traffic of Royal Parade. We lived where a line drawn from the Melbourne zoo to the University of Melbourne intersected with a line drawn the Royal Melbourne Hospital to the Melbourne General Cemetery. We held classes across Royal Parade in the theological hall of Ormond College, where our library was housed, and we shared other facilities with the Congregationalist, Methodist, and Presbyterian students and staff in the United Faculty of Theology (UFT). Eventually the Jesuit Theological College (JTC) formally joined the UFT, as did the Anglican group from Trinity College. In 1973, I taught fundamental theology to a class of fifty, which included Anglican, Catholic, Methodist, and Presbyterian students, as well as a Coptic priest, a Greek Orthodox priest, and a Norwegian Lutheran. I valued the ecumenical setting of the theological teaching in Parkville. Both there and at Corpus Christi, the Jesuit staff were all pleasant colleagues, and some of them close friends. The large group of young Jesuits who took my course in the first term of 1969 included some of the most remarkable students I have been fortunate enough to teach anywhere in the world. I enjoyed the challenge of teaching, tried to practise a method of Socratic questioning, and proved less successful with the weaker students. From 1969 I began to help such excellent students in Melbourne as Brendan Byrne, Mark Coleridge, Peter Elliott, and Marc Playoust and their counterparts in Boston, like Dan Harrington, George Hunsinger, Michael McNulty, and Bill Reiser, publish articles in a variety of journals: the *Australasian Catholic Record, Colloquium, Compass, Heythrop Journal,* and the *Scottish Journal of Theology.*

Outside engagements offered a variety of audiences in Melbourne: Methodist and Presbyterian parishes on some Sundays; university students on holiday camps; Loreto 'Old Girls' on retreat; Council of Adult Education groups; conferences of catechists; articles for the Melbourne *Age*; radio talks for the Australian Broadcasting Commission; and public lectures at Melbourne and Monash universities. This recognition encouraged me, and somewhat offset the feeling of being a second-class academic in my own country. In England, West Germany, and the United States, the presence of departments and faculties of theology and religious studies at both old and new universities made my subject 'respectable'. Theologians and other church leaders had helped found Cambridge, Harvard, Oxford, Tübingen, and other ancient universities that I knew at first-hand. But the Australian universities still refused to accept my field as a legitimate academic discipline. In the theological hall at Ormond College we belonged at but not to the University of Melbourne. However, it seemed that better days were coming.

In September 1968 John Eddy, now with the Institute of Advanced Studies at the Australian National University (ANU), wrote to tell me that religion was one of 'the projected new Arts Faculty departments. The recent faculty meeting unanimously gave the project full support.' 'In a few years time', he added, 'someone will surely be needed to become a professor of religion or a reader here. Who knows, it might be right down your street by then?' With John Nurser, the Warden of St Mark's Library (an Anglican theological centre in Canberra), John started the Canberra Society for the Study of Religion and Theology. In May 1969 I read a paper on the theology of hope at the inaugural meeting to which about forty academics came. The two Johns publicized me at ANU, and pressed me to plan my theological future at Canberra. I discussed the whole matter with Davis McCaughey, suggested that he should apply if a chair was advertised, and told him how happy I would be to work in a department under him. But he shrank from leaving his two youngest children behind in Melbourne, urged me to become a candidate, and assured me of his fullest support. In mid-1969 I wrote to Peter Kelly seeking his permission to apply, if and when a post came up at ANU. My long letter ended somewhat pretentiously:

> What I am asking for is the chance, in fact the only real chance to do theology in Australia alongside university faculty members of other fields and to try to make my work match their degree of excellence. It means professing to be a Christian theologian right out in the open academic world, and trying by one's standards of excellence there to spread the Gospel as well as to help one's fellow Catholics and Christians. I make this request because I have answered in those terms the following questions: what context for applying my talents will be of most value to the Church in Australia as a whole? If I am to become a theologian of influence and standing in the English- speaking world, where else in Australia can I do that except in Canberra? That this aim is not deluded or absurd for me is suggested by what I have already achieved.

Somewhat to my surprise, Peter approved my request. John Eddy continued to keep my interest alive while the planning moved along at a snail's pace. In November 1969 he wrote to tell me that he had been appointed to serve on the Vice-Chancellor's committee 'to make firm plans to introduce the teaching of Religious Studies in the University. The basis of planning is that at least one full-time appointment will be made and that other members of the University will assist in offering courses.' The following month he reported that the first meeting of the committee was 'very interesting and satisfactory'. 'They will need and want a theologian, with recognizable status, degrees, publications etc., used to a secular set-up, able to teach undergraduates, form the nucleus of a department, co-operate with other scholars on the spot etc. It might suit you very well?'

Eventually ANU advertised a chair. I applied and was short-listed, but endless delays followed. In August 1972 I was interviewed in Canberra, just as I was leaving Australia for the United States. But weeks later a letter reached me in Boston to say that I had not been appointed. For a variety of reasons the disappointment hurt. I was not used to competing and losing. Friends had encouraged me into thinking that I stood an extremely good chance. I had set my heart on the opportunity to create my own department at the ANU, which was initiating other new fields of study and developing into Australia's leading university. John La Nauze, John Mulvaney, and others I had known at Melbourne University had shifted to the ANU. I welcomed the thought of becoming their colleague and settling down with John Eddy in the small Jesuit community in Canberra. It all looked like the happy and logical end to my journeying. Besides, I had watched acquaintances and friends successfully launch the department of religious studies at the University of Lancaster, and had a sense of what might be done in that area.

It was, of course, expecting a great deal from the members of the ANU committee that they would select a Jesuit for the very first chair in religious studies at any Australian university. I hoped that someone would be appointed quickly and set the programme going. Then I could apply for one of the several lectureships that would have to be created, and in that way find in Canberra the peaceful conclusion to my travels. But the years slipped by without any appointment being made. As John Eddy put matters in late 1972, 'I suppose you might have to continue your journeys until country and calling meld more neatly than at present.' My own inner and outer life moved on. I came to feel some gratitude towards ANU for having dangled that bait before me.

The possibility of teaching religious studies at an Australian university pushed me into clarifying my personal hopes and goals.

To resume my story from Christmas 1968. When I arrived back in Melbourne, Greg Dening had just published an article in *The Australian*, arguing that many Catholics did not really believe in the humanity of Jesus. At points Greg's language was harsh, and he introduced an unfair anecdote about an old nun who had prepared him for First Communion. Yet his central thesis was not only true but had also been developed by various contemporary theologians. Many Catholics and other Christians continued to accept vigorously the divinity of Jesus but to play down, at least in their spiritual practice, the genuine humanity of Jesus. Greg stirred up a storm of criticism. *News Weekly* published a dreary letter that attacked Greg both for attributing such an error to Catholics and also for insisting that Jesus was a man! The paper inserted on the same page a reproduction of a picture showing Judas kissing Christ. I wrote a letter to *News Weekly* defending Greg, and was attacked in my turn. Greg had agreed to lecture on church authority at a refresher course in theology for Jesuits working in schools and parishes, but now pulled out to leave the job to me. The audience of thirty or forty priests pleasantly surprised me by mostly agreeing with my paper, which drew heavily on Paul's letter to the Galatians and in which I developed three rules of thumb. (1) *Who* is teaching this? For instance, a limited group of bishops? All the world's bishops meeting in a council with the Pope? The Pope alone? (2) What *degree of authority* is being invoked? (3) What is the *source* of this teaching? Is it drawn from the divine revelation communicated through Jesus Christ? Or has it been developed on the basis of human reasoning? In 1981 I was to publish various themes from this paper in *Fundamental Theology* (Paulist Press, pp. 180-86).

Some months later I read the same paper to a group of Catholic married couples, who had been meeting regularly for discussions with

Greg. They alarmed me with their despairing anger against church leaders. Greg spoke of a parish Mass he had attended where the parish priest had denounced birth control as indulging selfish and impure pleasure: 'A young, pregnant woman sat near me weeping.' It was on the tip of my tongue to ask him, 'Did you speak to her and try to help her afterwards?' I could not join Greg and his friends in abusing bishops and priests. Yet I was distressed over the failures of some or even many in leadership roles. While preparing my paper on authority, I looked up various issues of the weekly, English edition of the Vatican's *L'Osservatore Romano*. Apropos of the encyclical *Humanae Vitae* and the qualifications that conferences of bishops introduced into its teaching, some contributors like Cardinal Pericle Felici showed a disregard for truth. I stopped reading the journal as a threat to my vocation and faith.

Before I returned to North America in August 1969, I often took meals with Greg who lived at La Trobe University where he had been appointed to a lectureship. One painful evening Jim and Posey invited him to dinner. A fierce argument developed between Greg and Jim, while my sister-in-law and I sat there silent and helpless. Jim had worked in a civilian hospital in the Vietnamese countryside; he still supported the American attempts to win the war. Greg astonished me with one of his main points: 'In Vietnamese villages the Catholic priests get the profits from the power plants.' If the crucified people of Vietnam suffered only from a clerical monopoly on electricity, I was willing to settle for that. The Catholic Church had come to look like a madhouse or prison to Greg. In 1970 he left the Jesuit order, was appointed to a chair of history at the University of Melbourne, and married an ex-nun whom he had met during his studies in the United States. Their baby died shortly after birth in 1973. Greg did not answer my letter of sympathy. His midlife journey took him away from me. As a boy and a Jesuit, I had cherished his friendship too much not to feel sad.

Returning to Boston

An American friend once complimented me on making 'another successful cultural adjustment. Your resiliency in changing from environment to environment amazes me.' From August 1969 I locked myself into certain fixed habits, which provided a framework for four years of incessant travel and made it easier to settle down quickly to work. At her home in Melbourne, Moira gave me a farewell or 'welcome home' party. Dympna drove me to the airport with two bottles of Australian wine in my suitcase, a present from my brother Glynn to American friends. In Sydney, aunt Mary, other relatives and friends saw me off or welcomed me back. From 1969 to 1972 I spent the fall semester in Cambridge, Massachusetts with many of the same Jesuits; from 1970 to 1972 I lived in the same house in Lexington Avenue. In ETS I had the same library carrel during my five semesters of teaching for Weston College. From 1969 to 1971, I would go down to Boston to visit Maev at Columbia University often several times during the semester. For five years I always went to the Kirby family in New Jersey for Thanksgiving. When I left Boston in mid-December I always stayed for a few days with Eleanor and Jock Harbison in Blackrock, Dublin. Invariably my Sunday homily included a story about a boy and a girl, whom I named Tony and Naomi after the youngest of the four Harbison children. From 1969 to 1972 I stopped each Christmas in England to visit friends in Cambridge, Oxford, and at Heythrop College. For three years I saw in the New Year with John and Monica Ellison in Paris. I devoted January and part of February to reading and writing, either in Tübingen (1970 and 1972) or in Rome (1971 and 1973). Home in Australia I occupied the same room in the Jesuit Theological College during the five years I taught there.

From 1969 to 1971 I broke the journey from Melbourne to Boston by spending several days with Laurie Drake in the San Francisco Bay area. We had been fellow boarders at Xavier College, entered the Society of Jesus within a year of each other, and remained friends ever since. Through the late sixties Laurie worked relentlessly towards his doctorate in seismology at Berkeley, where he showed uncomplicated kindness to the white American, black American, Mexican, Filipino, and Chinese people of the parish where he lived, and remained unashamedly conservative in his politics. In May 1969 he wrote to tell me of the situation on his campus: 'Last week we had more National Guard here than trees. It is incredible what 1000 trucks and troops look like in a city street. I think most of the students asked for what they got, though most students would not agree with me about this. They are against firmness, on account of the war.' Three months later I was with him and noted in my diary: 'I am staying with Laurie in St Anthony's parish, Oakland. When I was here last December, the young owner of a nearby corner store had recently shot dead a bandit who tried to rob the store. Since then she has shot dead another bandit and wounded one of his colleagues; this happened in an attempted hold-up by three men.' Before I left St Anthony's in August 1969, several teenagers robbed the cook on her way home from the parish rectory. It was all Laurie could do to stop her large sons from hunting down and battering the two boys who had stolen sixty dollars from their mother.

On my way to Boston that year I attended a colloquium on theological method in Montreal. Bernard Lonergan, Schubert Ogden, and Gustaf Wingren read papers to an audience of three hundred. Karl Rahner and Jürgen Moltmann prepared their long papers, but could not attend when they both fell ill. I read Moltmann's paper for him, defended his viewpoint as best I could, and found it an unnerving experience. His text, which reached me only the night before I was to present it, lacked footnotes (to explain the references and quotations), and confronted me with something quite unexpected: Moltmann's early reflections on the theology of the cross that would be developed into *The Crucified God* (German original, 1972). A revolution-oriented, Australian Dominican I knew tried to turn the colloquium into a series of discussion groups, but Lonergan and the audience refused to budge. One morning we sipped coffee outside the main hall, while over the loudspeaker system we could hear Lonergan and my friend still arguing fiercely on the otherwise deserted platform. 'Well', growled Lonergan, 'if you are lacking in all decency and courtesy, yes.' His *Method in Theology* was then moving into its final shape for publication. But what he said seemed so abstract and so controlled by his theory of knowledge that I decided not to study his views further. When someone asked Lonergan what he understood by 'objectivity', he replied, 'authentic subjectivity'. I felt a little like the professor from the University of Notre Dame who was sitting behind me. He belched perceptibly and muttered, '[Expletive], I could live with that.' Forty years later I read some more of Lonergan, and introduced a little of his theological method into *Rethinking Fundamental Theology* (Oxford University Press, 2011).

Back in New England I found that Weston College had bought or leased apartments and houses around Cambridge for almost all its faculty and sixty-five Jesuit scholastics. Fifty non-Jesuit faculty and students also lived nearby. I shared apartments with the rector and eight Jesuit scholastics on Concord Avenue, right opposite the Students International Meditation Society and just a stone's throw from the Cambridge Common. A sense of liberation at being back in the United States released the energy for a semester of furious activity. Besides my course and seminar for Weston College, I went once a week to a pastoral institute of the Boston Archdiocese. I remember those sessions of nearly two hours on Christ's resurrection to an average group of thirty-five priests as a wonderful initiation into fruitful work with diocesan clergy. Each week I also drove an hour up the Massachusetts Turnpike to Worcester to teach a course on the resurrection for an ecumenical institute at Assumption College.

As a result of the extra teaching, there was a surplus of a thousand dollars to cover part of the travel expenses for a visiting professor at the Jesuit Theological College (Parkville) in 1970. On behalf of the JTC dean I invited a colleague to fly out to Australia and teach a term-long course on the theology of the sacraments. I was glad to provide the man and some of the money for that visit. I wanted to prove to myself and others my genuine concern to help the Australian Jesuit province.

In the middle of that fall semester at Weston, Jim Burtchaell, the chairman of the theology department at the University of Notre Dame, invited me to give a lecture and consider an appointment there: 'We are seriously looking for someone in New Testament studies and, although our department is considering several scholars for the vacancy, I have strong professional and personal reasons for wanting to be able to consider you for such an appointment.' He added: 'Our theological enterprise is growing, and I have every intention of making it grow much more.' In November, I flew out for a weekend in South Bend, lectured on the resurrection, drank Jim's 1938 port, and declined to apply. Years later I would start visiting Notre Dame to teach three-week courses on the doctrine of Christ and the Trinity for their summer programme.

My diary ticked off other landmarks in that tumultuous semester: preaching (on 'watching our language in the presence of God') at the Mass of the Holy Spirit that began the academic year; taking part with Max Stackhouse and George Ernest Wright in a symposium on prophecy; sampling a talk by Michael Novak (which I dismissed for not being 'a professional account of the consciousness of American college students'); chatting happily with Mary Daly (who was to become an extreme feminist theologian) after her defensive and tentative paper on 'Catholicism. Death or Rebirth?'; praying at a candlelight rally on Cambridge Common as part of a Moratorium Day in protest against American military involvement in Vietnam; an evening's discussion with 'John Galvani (one of the Boston Eight) and Ann Walsh (one of the New York Four) about their activities in burning selective service records'; joining Harry Wolfson (a world expert on the ancient writer Philo of Alexandria) for a day in western Massachusetts; and launching my *Man and His New Hopes* in front of the cameras of West Germany television.

Wolfson had been an undergraduate at Harvard with T.S. Eliot and Joseph Kennedy, and took a year in Berlin where he studied with such legendary figures in classical scholarship as Ulrich Wilamowitz-Moellendorf, Adolf von Harnack, and Hermann Diehl. He returned to the United States, and became Professor of Hebrew Literature and Philosophy at the Harvard Divinity School. It delighted me to get to know this old scholar, the last of a generation of giants that included Werner Jaeger and Arthur Darby Nock. 'Harnack', he told me, 'was no aristocrat like Wilamowitz-Moellendorf. But he knew where the toilets were in the Potsdam palace.' I failed to ask Wolfson what he thought of Harnack and Wilamowitz-Moellendorf for strongly supporting Germany's entrance into the First World War. Even in retirement Wolfson seemed to work in his office at the Widener Library more than 360 days in the year. Once a year he visited an old colleague called William Thomson, who had been Jewett Professor of Arabic at Harvard Divinity School. I marvelled at the way these old colleagues still called each other by their surnames. As we left, Thomson said in all seriousness, 'Wolfson, beware of the mob at Harvard.' 'Don't forget', his guest replied, 'that Aristotle distinguished between the *dēmos* and the *ochlos*.'

Harvey Cox, George MacRae, and Max Stackhouse shared in a symposium at ETS to celebrate the publication of my book on hope. At the last minute a German television team turned up to film part of the evening for a programme on Christian theology in the United States. Cox contrasted my 'Protestant' book with his own 'Catholic book', *Feast of Fools*, which was to be published in 1970. One hundred and forty people attended, compliments flew around, and we enjoyed some hard discussion on New Testament views of the future, Christ's resurrection, and the dangerous implications of a theologian's self-interest. 'All of us', Cox remarked, 'take Caesar's penny.' I went home immensely encouraged, if haunted by one question. A girl left the auditorium, loudly demanding, 'What the hell does the resurrection have to do with life anyway?'

When the three thousand copies of *Man and His New Hopes* sold out in less than a year, Herder and Herder declined to order a second printing. They also failed to do anything about publishing or distributing the book in Britain. They turned down my *Foundations of Theology*, which Loyola University Press (Chicago) brought out in 1971. They accepted my resurrection book, and then pulled out, leaving it to be published by Darton, Longman & Todd (as *The Easter Jesus*) in England and the Judson Press (as *The Resurrection of Jesus Christ*) in the United States. But I remained grateful to Herder and Herder both for commissioning my book on hope and for, unintentionally, giving me a useful introduction into the hard habits of some publishers.

My family scarcely noticed my first theology book, perhaps because it was a slim paperback. But *Man and His New Hopes* delighted them. They sent me a joint letter from Ballarat, where 'the clan' had gathered for one of uncle Jim's feasts. My younger brother-in-law added his teasing note: 'Thanks for the book. The first twelve pages are magnificent. I got through them in five days. Kevin.' Maev wrote from New York, pleased to find that the book was dedicated to her (and my other brothers and sisters) and giving me news of a Harlem family she taught once a week:

> Yesterday THE BOOK arrived. It looks absolutely terrific, and I was most impressed with the careful arrangement of brothers and sisters that put me at the end as the baby of the family. On Monday I had my usual tutoring session with the Joyner family. In the midst of it their welfare investigator arrived, the most terrible,

thin, acidulated, stereotyped, white power structure emissary you could imagine. She put us through a sort of third degree, as I stood humbly in her presence, hoping that what I was saying was not in some way an indictment of the family. Then to my horror I discovered that Mrs J. had let drop that I was a student at Columbia, and she asked me what I did. It turns out that SHE has a M.S. in social work, and she got very unctuous and told me how good and kind I was—all that in their presence, so that I wanted to 'kick her teeth in', to use the rhetoric and verbal overkill of my frequent militant associates. Instead I oiled back at her, hoping that this would hasten the special arch-supported shoes, glasses, and other goodies she has in her power to authorize for the underprivileged, more-or-less deserving poor.

On re-reading this, it sounds a bit nasty, which is the way I felt but may not fit in with *Man and His New Hopes*. Or maybe it is the Christian revolutionary in me getting the upper hand.

That fall semester of 1969 I revelled in my work, often sat up into the night drinking Black Label beer with several scholastics, and enjoyed the passing parade of visitors to Harvard. Pyotr Kapitsa, a seventy-year-old Russian physicist who had studied with Ernest Rutherford at Cambridge University, lectured to enthusiastic audiences. They tried to refrain from smiling, when he insisted that older scientists should have 'frequent intercourse' with younger scientists. When John L. McKenzie, the doyen of older Catholic scripture scholars in the United States, came to dinner one evening, I served him some white burgundy I had carried from Melbourne. When I congratulated him on his anonymous contribution to *The Experience of Priesthood* (a book edited by Brian Passman), he expressed surprise: 'How did you know it was me?' How indeed? His chapter was crammed with such typical McKenzie remarks as 'I have dealt with ecclesiastical superiors for over thirty years, and over thirty years I have been knee-deep in pygmies.' When we met for dinner, he had just written an article for *The Critic*, in which he had sharply criticized Pope Paul VI and for which he was rebuked by the Jesuit superior general. This led McKenzie to leave the Jesuit order but not the priesthood.

From mid-1969, all around me priests, both Jesuit and non-Jesuit, seemed to be leaving the ministry and marrying. Some, like a nephew of the remarkable Bishop Helder Camara, wanted Jim Burtchaell to find them a teaching position at Notre Dame or elsewhere. With cynical relief Jim remarked about one Dutch priest: 'He made the supreme sacrifice. He not only left his order and the priesthood, but he also gave up theology.' Both inside and outside the Catholic Church I ran into painful tension. The Vietnam War had steadily poisoned the public atmosphere in the United States and beyond. Louis Bouyer's *The Decomposition of the Church* and Jacques Maritain's *Peasant of the Garonne* revealed how developments in Roman Catholicism had deeply upset the old and the conservatives. But was it true that departures from the priesthood mainly took place among the younger 'liberals'?

Reasons for leaving the ministry varied from priest to priest. No one ought to imagine that I can come up with some standard explanation. Yet a few generalizations can be risked. Two words gather together some of what can be said: expectations and change. The Second Vatican Council and other events built up expectations that remained partially unfulfilled. Rome continued to insist on the centralized control of liturgical changes. Optional celibacy did not come. The Catholic Church hardly shifted towards any general participation in the election of bishops and parish priests. Theologically Pope Paul VI often appeared fearful that he would betray the past. Nevertheless, from the late 1950s vast changes did occur at three levels: in the relations between Christian churches, within the Catholic Church, and in both the theory and practice of priestly and religious life. Catholics had sometimes refused to recite even the Lord's Prayer with others, but now joint services had arrived. The ministry of married men and women in other churches challenged the ways in which Catholic priests had defined their identity. Members of religious orders and congregations began to wear lay dress, move into small communities in ordinary houses and apartments, and question the 'sacred' separation that had characterized their lives.

Somewhat ludicrously one ex-priest expressed his disappointment to me: 'The Church simply has to accept a new understanding of ministry. When it does, it will find me waiting there.' I suspect that such rigid inability to cope *either* with frustrated expectations *or* with change lay behind many departures from the active priesthood, irrespective of whether the ex-priests appeared to have belonged to the liberal left or the conservative right. What else could they do but flee the pain, bed down with a wife, and hope to find love in their ruined world?

Back to Tübingen

When I reached Tübingen early in January 1970, I began but quickly dropped an attempt to write an autobiographical sketch, 'On the Way to the Parousia'. My self-image of a midlife journey was beginning to take shape, even though I continued to picture myself as an organism that shifted restlessly to escape pain. Instead of pursuing the autobiography, I finished *Foundations of Theology*, immersed myself in the New Testament, and wrote pages of reflections on my ministry as a priest.

In the preface to *Foundations* I recalled the lovely Tübingen summer of 1967, 'when painful theological problems still seemed no larger than a tiny cloud above the Black Forest. This book and other studies form an attempt to explain to myself and others why Christian revelation and life still make sense.' Shortly before writing the preface, I had been shaken by the film *Elvira Madigan*. When gently challenged to return to the norms of conventional morality, the hero replied: 'The old words have lost their power for me.' Haunted by this statement, I made some notes about my own condition and ministry:

Is it true that only 'romantic', mystifying images are capable of keeping me where I am? I am thinking of the inscription on the antipendium of the high altar in the Toledo cathedral that I saw in September 1968: '*Amor sacerdos immolat* (love the priest offers).' Or think of the various arguments one hears for the present (celibate) structure of the western priesthood: e.g. 'availability for other people'. Do any of these slogans prove convincing when one reflects on the concrete situation? For a time I find comfort in some phrases and words: '*amor sacerdos immolat*', 'building community', 'building the Kingdom', and 'facing the emergency demands that a crisis-situation imposes'. But can such words give me the vision and courage to carry on? I put it to myself: 'Do I carry on out of fear? Fear of hurting my family, fear of the difficulties involved in starting again in mid-life? Is there some true and supremely valuable vision which can (& does) carry many through a lifetime of service in religious life, but which is ultimately not capable of *clear* and *convincing* statement?'

Questions hammered me about the nature of Christian faith, the theology of the cross, and my own role as a religious priest. Käsemann's *Perspectives on Paul* pushed the problem at me: 'What is genuine faith, a life of genuine faith for me?' Perhaps my decision to teach in *both* Melbourne *and* Boston represented an attempt 'to pile too much on my plate'? Was that it—a simple case of 'overweening desires' that would lead to my 'destruction'? I feared that I had already become greedy, trying to force more out of life than it naturally contained.

One evening I attended a lecture by Dorothea Sölle ('short, lively, attractive person') at the Evangelische Stift. A few months earlier this divorcée with three daughters had married Edmund Steffensky, an ex-Benedictine later to become a Protestant pastor. She spoke for an hour on the need to construct an 'inductive' theology, 'based on experience'. We must not use God as an 'alibi'. 'The other world', she continued, 'makes no difference' when we try to solve our problems. Throughout she stressed 'our needs and wishes' as the appropriate basis for decision-making. The first question from the audience boldly and bluntly put the case of a wife whose husband fails to respond with love. Sölle pointed quickly to divorce as the solution. Käsemann cut in at once to remind her that 'very often, both in this situation and others, our love will not be returned. It is no solution to say that we simply ought to remove ourselves from the situation.' She agreed, but insisted that the wife's 'Ich' must be strengthened by the experience. The Käsemann-Sölle duel continued through much of the ninety minutes of discussion. She dismissed his theme of Jesus' lordship as 'a medieval, feudal notion'. Then he made a comment that hit me hard: 'Jesus promised the cross to his own followers, not to others.'

The following day the debate kept going but now in my own mind. 'What of Jesus' insistence that we must be ready to lose our lives for the sake of the Gospel? He did not talk of fulfilling our needs and wishes, strengthening our "Ich", finding our identity etc., but of our readiness to leave all things.' St Paul reassured me that this discipleship should not mean terrifying loneliness: 'Personal friendship and the preservation of excellent relations between Paul and the community were of acute importance.' The love of John Eddy, Bill Daniel, and other friends in the Society of Jesus promised the support I needed.

And yet the questions would not cease. On the one hand, I recognized that I held a 'position of power' to help others. 'To live in a tradition (official Catholicism) and a group (Society of Jesus) spreads out one's life into the past & future, and gives one a sense of being in a very great clan.' On the other hand, I asked: 'Are we standing at a time when the Church is undergoing some of the greatest changes ever? Will I wake up in a radically changed Church in ten or twenty years' time?' Whether I looked at the past or the future, reflection hardly blunted the central question: 'Do I keep going, because I refuse to look at the issues', and because 'I enjoy success, trips, and friends?'

Tensions in the local church exacerbated my struggle for answers.

When Steffensky married Sölle, Cardinal Joseph Höffner of Cologne was angered by the departure of this Benedictine and struck out wildly: 'It's untrue that Catholic priests are not married. Many are married to a thousand things—from good food and drink, through many other things, even to self-abuse, a girl friend, and homosexuality.' The rector of the Freiburg seminary committed suicide, a fifty-eight-year-old Catholic prelate in Essen turned Protestant, and the number of Catholic seminarians in West Germany dropped by twenty-five per cent that year. The Vatican wanted priests to reaffirm their acceptance of celibacy by taking an oath at the Holy Thursday liturgy. In February 1970 the German bishops met in Essen, supported Pope Paul VI's stand in retaining the obligation of celibacy. Through Cardinal Julius Döpfner they declared: 'The German bishops are determined to continue calling priests from the ranks of those who for the sake of the kingdom of heaven accept the grace of celibacy.' Was this simply putting on a bold and loyal front? Would there be any candidates to call? In Cardinal Döpfner's own diocese of Munich only six out of twenty seminarians had returned for their year of diaconate.

Although the seven weeks back in Tübingen let a host of obsessive questions rise to the surface of my mind, friends like John Dwyer, Freifrau von Gillhausen, Irmgard Kindt, 'Mac' McCullough, and Josef and Ingrid Nolte were still there. I moved onto first name terms with Jürgen Moltmann. In the Berghaus Hügel, where I stayed, I noticed that two large clocks had stopped. No one seemed concerned to set them going again. A large clock also stood still in the von Gillhausen household. A letter from Maev urged me to 'take care in the academic hurricane'. But those silent clocks conveyed a feeling of friendly timelessness, or at least a sense that the eye of the hurricane was large enough to allow questions to be put on hold.

On the eve of leaving for Melbourne, I preached (in English) at the Disciples Institute in Tübingen. Many of my American and German friends came to the ecumenical service that evening. I took

the parable of the prodigal son for my text, and reflected on the lonely
decision which he had to reach before returning to his father's home.
Afterwards one German asked me with a smile: 'Who is this young
man coming to himself among the foreign swine?' But this friend had
failed to notice my own identification with the elder son. I had begun
by quoting some lines from T.S. Eliot's *Burnt Norton*:

> *Footfalls echo in the memory*
> *Down the passage which we did not take*
> *Towards the door we never opened*
> *Into the rose-garden.*

Then I asked: 'How much did we lose by not taking that passage,
by never opening that door, by not walking into that rose-garden?
Memory can hurt or even torture us by reminding us of all that we
have lost.' I had preached on the younger, prodigal son. But there was
much of the elder brother in me. I had stayed to carry out my duties,
but had not yet found peace. The words addressed to the elder son
reproached my bewildered self-questioning: 'My child, you have been
with me always, and everything I have is yours' (Luke 15: 31). Why
was I missing the whole point and failing to enjoy my life with God?

Through those troubled months in early 1970, Maev plied me with
some of her liveliest stories. A letter of 6 January reflected that 'life is
certainly full of strange events':

> Take last Saturday. I was on my way to see *Jacques Brel is Alive and
> Well* at the Village Gate in Greenwich Village, when one of my
> company ran into an old friend and the following Noel Cowardish
> conversation took place. 'How is our sister?' 'My God! Haven't you
> heard?' 'Heard what?' 'She has abandoned being a vegetarian and
> wants to become a ROMAN CATHOLIC!' 'Good grief! Whatever
> for?' 'Who can say what goes on in the sewers of her mind?' Well,
> *Jacques Brel* was a little dull after that.

Back to Parkville

When I arrived back in Parkville to begin my next round of teaching fundamental theology for Jesuit Theological College, Maev wrote to tell me of a 'very amusing encounter with *Man and His New Hopes*':

> At the Center for Urban Education, a very elaborately and luxuriously furnished establishment on Madison Avenue, I was walking along a corridor to the seminar room where we discuss 'Urbanism and Education', when I saw through the open door of room 618 a familiar, brilliant cover resting on a table. Further investigation revealed that my suspicions were correct. *Man and His New Hopes* has infiltrated the Center for Urban Education. It is rather hilarious to think that probably Federal funds, or at least staff time which is paid for by Federal funds, is being used to digest your brain child. I shall investigate further and try to locate the owner. I had the class in hysterics by shrieking, 'That's my brother's book.'

A follow-up letter carried suggestions for my next book: 'I have decided that you might look at the Theology of Alienation or, alternatively, the Theology of Apathy, also known as the Theology of Moderation—fairly rich, unworked fields.'

The five months in Australia whizzed past until August 1970, when I flew back to Boston for my third semester of teaching for Weston College. Three pages of my diary listed the fierce round of engagements that had made it difficult to write or even reflect during those five months: teaching in Parkville and Glen Waverley; lecturing to a Council of Adult Education class on 'The Future of Christianity'; giving lunch-hour talks at the University of Melbourne (on 'Infallibility and Collegiality' and 'Salvation'); suffering a severe attack of haemorrhoids during the three-day congregation of the Australian Jesuit province; flying to Adelaide to speak to the Christian Education Association; addressing the Faithful Companions of Jesus on community life; winning a golf competition with my brother Glynn; leading a retreat for fourteen deacons just before their ordination to the priesthood; and much else besides. I found the retreat peculiarly satisfying. All of the deacons had belonged to my spiritual semester group at Werribee in 1964. Whatever my uncertainties about the future shape of the Church and the priesthood, I was glad to have been with them both at the beginning and at the end of their training.

The Fall of 1970

In the fall semester of 1970 Maev successfully passed her comprehensives at Columbia University, and now tackled her last two objectives before leaving New York: completing her doctoral dissertation and finding an academic post. She began to share my experience of being unwanted at Australian universities but wanted overseas. 'The brain drain', she told me in July, 'becomes much clearer to understand when, even without looking, I have been offered several jobs here, and I am selling myself at home to little avail.' From September she began to teach part time at Hunter College to support herself while she worked on her thesis.

During that semester I visited Maev five times in New York. She ran a round of parties, including one for five Australian aborigines. After attending a conference, they stayed on to visit the United Nations, speak at several universities, and draw support from American blacks. I flew down from Boston for Maev's 'Reception in honour of the Australian Delegation to the Congress of African People'. An American lady annoyingly lectured me on the need for 'more righteousness in Australia towards the aborigines'. Why did she think I had come down from Boston, if not to welcome the delegation and help raise money towards their fares? But it was a joy to notice how disconcerted one waiter in a New York restaurant was to hear a strong Australian accent emerging from what he had taken to be a normal black American face.

Two conventions also drew me to New York during the semester: a special colloquium at Union Theological Seminary on Karl Barth's contribution to theology in North America, and the combined meeting of the American Academy of Religion and the Society of Biblical Literature at the Hotel New Yorker. That meeting made it thoroughly clear to me what power George MacRae and Jim Burtchaell exercised in the AAR and SBL. For years George tugged me towards concentration on New Testament studies. It was at his suggestion that I read a paper on a passage from Paul's Second Letter to the Corinthians at a third conference which I attended that semester, the Catholic Biblical Association meeting in Albany, New York. That paper, which later appeared in the *Catholic Biblical Quarterly*, marked the end of any ambition to become simply a scripture scholar. Probably my early interest in philosophy meant that I felt more and more at ease specializing in fundamental and systematic theology.

In November a group of Jesuit philosophers invited me as a 'tame' theologian to St Louis for the annual meeting of their North American Council on Belief and Unbelief—my fourth conference for the semester and the most dramatic one I have ever attended. I joined Edward MacKinnon, a Jesuit friend from Boston College, for the flight out and back between Boston and St Louis. In 1969 he had agreed to prepare the main position paper for the next meeting. In the course of the year he ceased to believe in God. His paper movingly put the case for his own unbelief. Ed's announcement startled and saddened the other Jesuits, but no one tried to wheedle, let alone bully, him back into belief. Nevertheless, many of us challenged the way Ed decided the issue of belief and unbelief in terms of 'the internal logic of arguments'. To say the least, this approach bypassed the element of free decision that affects the whole life (and not merely the arguments) of anyone who asks: does God exist? On the flight back to Boston a strong tail-wind boosted the speed of our almost empty aircraft to seven hundred miles an hour—the fastest

I have ever flown. Ed plied me with bourbon and asked: 'Why do you believe in God?' All I could say was: 'God seems as real to me as someone sitting down the aisle from us.' Ed left the Jesuit order, married, and taught philosophy for the University of California. I will always remember his question, and still cannot truly answer it in any other way.

Despite all the work, turmoil, and travel which had filled the semester, I felt sad to leave Boston in December 1970 for six weeks of reading and writing in Rome. I drew strength from the affectionate friendship of the Jesuit scholastics and other students I taught. Yet during those years I still felt filled with an aching hollowness, wanting to escape loneliness and find someone to share my daily life with. It was an unspecified longing, not a desire to marry some particular woman or search belatedly for Margaret. One day I stood transfixed, when I glimpsed a poster carrying an observation from Henry David Thoreau: 'The mass of men live lives of quiet desperation.' That described my state. It reinforced a judgement on my ceaseless travelling that persistently came to mind: 'An organism in pain keeps moving.'

Had I chosen my own nightmare? Or was I following some dim but God-inspired dream? One day I told a friend how I had left Cambridge University and broken with Margaret. The comment burst from deep inside me: 'It hasn't worked.' Some weeks later he sent me these lines by Dag Hammarskjöld:

The road / You shall follow it.
The fun / You shall forget it.
The cup / You shall empty it.
The pain / You shall conceal it.
The truth / You shall be told it.
The end / You shall endure it.

The poem comforted me, and I kept in on my desk for months. I hoped somehow to break through the pattern of bewilderment and be told the truth. I felt ready to go down in an air crash and endure my end. It would be all over then, that long struggle to accept the decision I made in the summer of 1968. But I never really believed that death would catch me unawares, flow over me like lava, and fix me fast before I had reached the end of my struggle.

I continued to alternate between Australia, the United States, and Europe in a state of suspended being like a ghost from an unquiet grave. It remained unclear exactly what I was waiting for or how I should interpret my present existence. Phrases like 'it's better to be part of the solution than part of the problem' came easily. My mind employed such clichés without much criticism. They helped a little. I yearned for something that might give me a feeling of total consecration, something that I could commit myself to completely. I looked for a great challenge, even a global human catastrophe, anything that could give my life the sharp focus of generous dedication. Underneath all this lay a forlorn quest for innocence, a yearning to make my way back to some naïve commitment in a much simpler world where everything would be perfectly clear. I half suspected what I was after, and sometimes repeated to myself the title of Thomas Wolfe's novel *You Can't Go Home Again*.

Through all those years I remained deeply aware of how privileged I was in being, even uneasily, still a Jesuit. At the very least the Society of Jesus not only made it possible for me to teach each year in both hemispheres, but also offered me a chain of friends and companions around the world. Several old Jesuits in Australia and the United States persistently reminded me of that quotation from Jacques Maritain which had stayed with me from tertianship: 'In the evening of life there is no greater joy than to have loved Jesus Christ.' In their different ways they told me this with the flat superiority of old campaigners. I drank in their wisdom slowly, feeling a little of their warm happiness spread through my tired, limp spirit.

An American friend once troubled me more than I cared to admit by remarking, 'Gerry, you are a real jet-Jesuit, a Madison Avenue Jesuit.' His comment stirred me to question myself: 'Have I remained in the Society of Jesus for what I can get out of it or for what I can put into it?' Stung by the sense that I was no more than a worldly sham, I flung myself more and more into study, lecturing, and writing. External results would prove that I was successfully furthering the mission of my order. Some Australian Jesuits interpreted my annual six months away from the country as 'catching up' on the latest developments overseas. This cultural cringe annoyed me, and provided a further spur to action. My teaching and publishing would show them that an Australian could contribute as well as receive in the field of world theology.

My inner life of prayer had become little more than spasmodic. I had left tertianship in 1965 with high intentions of continuing daily meditation, recitation of the breviary, and other prayers. But regular practice faded by the time I left Cambridge University. During my annual eight-day retreat in 1969 and again in 1970 I resolved to resume a serious programme of prayer. But I corrupted easily. The resolutions dribbled away. On good days I might give thirty minutes to prayer, on bad days only a few moments. Praying privately became little more than a desultory holding operation in my life. What kept the rumour of prayer alive in my life were the psalms and the Eucharist.

I never spent a better three shillings and sixpence than when I bought the Grail translation of the psalms in 1967. Other forms of prayer could fail, but the slow recitation of one or two psalms from that paperback repeatedly created a life-giving sense of communion with God. Nor did the Mass ever fail me. Someone asked me once: 'When you celebrate the Eucharist, do you think that as a priest you are joining with Christ in offering his sacrifice to God the Father?' I could only explain that, for better or worse, I never thought that way. The Mass brought an intense feeling of the Risen Christ's presence, as well as a prayerful companionship with others. The Jesuits I lived with in Boston freed me to celebrate the Mass informally, when the occasion made that appropriate. We sat around a table, used a wide variety of Eucharistic prayers, and blended spontaneous praying with the set formulas. Both for these and for more formal Masses I would prepare a brief homily or a longer sermon, as well as select or write some prayers to give each celebration some cohesion and freshness. Sheer gratitude for the life that flowed to me from the Eucharist made it easy to be conscientious about these preparations.

For nearly three years I found no fresh clues in my external pattern of travel as I oscillated between Boston and Melbourne—teaching, writing, and studying. It was not clear where it would all lead me in the end. I was often so busy that I had no real time to think or feel. Some friends expressed concern at my mode of existence. In September 1971 Bill Daniel wrote to say: 'My main wish for you now is that you should find some post that suits you and be able to settle down into it. I cannot believe that your present Wandering Scholar status is a very satisfactory one for you. But this may just be the prejudice of my own domesticity.' Two months earlier Dennis Nineham admitted in a letter: 'I just don't know how you manage to survive all that endless journeying about! Don't you sometimes feel almost envious of medieval demands of *stabilitas*?' Yet I clung to my beaten track, the road which my Jesuit superiors had at least allowed me to take. But in the early months of 1971 the sense of inner stalemate started to lose its grip. I began to move again in that journey whose destination was self-knowledge.

10
The Last Lap (1971-74)

Do not plan long journeys, because whatever you believe in you have already seen. When a thing is everywhere, then the way to find it is not to travel but to love.

St Augustine of Hippo

Maev's first letter to me in 1971 announced: 'I have a great feeling that 1971 is a good year. Why don't you start writing something on humans for a change? Hope in Australian historical thought? Hope in a founding father's ethos?' She was right about the year and the need for change. Relationships with others began to offer more hope and make fresh sense out of my world. I started to reach out in new ways to fellow Jesuits and my students. All of this began to unify and integrate diverse strands in my life.

Exploring Rome

I spent January and most of February 1971 in Rome at the Bellarmino, a college where about one hundred young Jesuit priests lived while studying for graduate degrees at the Gregorian University, the Biblical Institute, or elsewhere. A couple of hours after my arrival on 6 January, three Colombian Jesuits arrived at my door like latter-day magi. They swept me off to celebrate the Epiphany in the Piazza Navona. Children surged everywhere, balloons flew away into the air, and those three laughing men from South America shared with me a happiness that set the tone for the weeks to come. Before reaching Rome I had known very few of the Jesuits at the Bellarmino, but felt quickly at home with them all. There was no struggle for recognition or need to identity myself. A wave of joyful energy allowed me to read a mass of theological books, begin writing a work on Christ's resurrection, and systematically explore Rome. I took tea at Babington's on the Spanish Steps, heard an American defend his doctoral thesis at the Gregorian, lectured on the resurrection at Propaganda College, lunched at the Jesuit curia or headquarters, prayed at Pope John's tomb, and wandered one afternoon through the damp and deserted Roman Forum while blackbirds sang away cheerfully on the slopes of the Palatine.

It was my first real taste of Rome, and Jesuits seemed to conspire to make me warmly welcome. A Spaniard, who had worked as a missionary in Tokyo, was writing a doctoral dissertation at the Gregorian, and in 2008 would become the superior general of the Jesuits, Fr Adolfo Nicolás, arranged for me to share an enchanting day with his Japanese friends. I described it in a letter to my mother:

> Last Sunday I went to Civitavecchia for a High Mass celebrating twenty-six martyrs crucified in Nagasaki in the early seventeenth century. About one hundred Japanese came for the service in a Franciscan church dedicated to these martyrs, some of whom were Franciscans. The Japanese ambassador to the Vatican attended. I went down with the first secretary and a Japanese girl who sings opera, in the main cities of Japan but on the provincial circuit in Italy. The prior spotted her, removed her from the congregation, and added her to the choir (who stood at the back of the altar). She treated us to Gounod's *Panis Angelicus* after Communion. The Spanish ambassador to the Vatican also attended, a tall Castilian nobleman with eight children, three of them nuns. He is caught in the crossfire over the new concordat between Spain [still ruled by General Franco] and the Holy See; the planned changes please neither the conservatives nor the liberals. 'It's like being a bad bull-fighter', he explained. 'Opinions are divided; some curse his father and some his mother.'

One evening an Indian Jesuit took me off to dine on the Aventine with the Mennini family. On a wall of the sitting-room, one photograph showed the parents with their fourteen children flanking Pope Pius XII. A second photograph, in which they stood around Pope Paul VI, recalled another visit to the papal villa in Castel Gandolfo. We rushed through the family rosary in Latin, before eating in what resembled the refectory of a small monastery. 'Is this the family', I asked in my diary, 'that Paul VI had in mind when he wrote *Humanae Vitae*?' As a director of the Vatican Bank, Signor Mennini had accompanied cardinals and bishops to the translation of the relics of St Nicholas of Bari and to other special church functions. In many snaps taken on those occasions he stood there in his business suit and tooth-brush moustache, looking, I thought, like the only honest man among a bunch of ecclesiastical rogues. One son had become a surgeon, a daughter was completing medical studies, two or three daughters were married, one or two sons had gone into banking, some of the children

At Rome airport January 1971 with Luigi Mennini and one of his sons.

were still at school, and one boy had become a Jesuit missionary in India. I almost felt that I could close my fist on the warm threads of love that united the whole family.[1]

Return to India

When the Mennini parents heard that I was to break my journey between Rome and Melbourne, spend a week in India, and give some lectures at St Mary's College, Kurseong (a hill station near Darjeeling), they asked me to take 'a few things' out to Pier Giorgio. He was now studying theology at that college. The 'few things' turned out to be packets of Italian pasta, a stack of medals and holy pictures, and two dozen pairs of football socks. In India, Pier Giorgio trained a soccer team that wore the colours of the Roman club. At the customs in Calcutta (now Kolkata) a thick-set lady rushed through a series of questions about cigarettes, liquor, and transistors. I could answer every question with a truthful 'no'. 'Move on please', she said, before I could ask in embarrassment about importing Italian foodstuffs and football gear.

The Indian customs treated me well, but not the local airline. When I checked at the national terminal for my flight up to a small airport at the foot of the Himalayas, I found that I had been bumped off. In the middle of a crowd of school children heading back to their boarding schools in Darjeeling, I noticed a Sikh officer and approached him: 'I'm sorry to bother you. I had a reserved seat on the next flight to Bagdogra but I've been bumped. What should I do?' He looked at me for a moment and then said: 'Please give me your ticket and passport.' A few minutes later he returned with my boarding pass: 'You are sitting next to my daughter on the flight. You will look after her, won't you?' Seven years earlier a Sikh had taken very good care

---

1 In 2010 one of the sons, now Archbishop Antonio Mennini, was appointed the apostolic nuncio to the United Kingdom.

of me in Calcutta, and now a Sikh had turned up trumps for me at the same airport.

St Mary's College turned out to be a kind of Shangri-La, with astounding views across rich forests and tea plantations to the majesty of Kanchenjunga rising to 28,000 feet. I gave the ninety students five lectures on the theology of hope, held two seminars to discuss other movements in contemporary theology, and drew deep peace from their company. On the second day there I decided to explore thoroughly the grounds of St Mary's. I stepped out of the grey, stone seminary built by Belgian missionaries ninety years earlier. Sunlight came through the tree tops, and was warm on my face and arms. I lifted my eyes beyond the gaping valleys, the forests, and the tea plantations to the mists that still shrouded the huge mountains. I sensed how far my inner journey had taken me since I first visited India. The very bedroom they gave me at the college thrust that reflection on me. I was in 'the bishop's room', where Thomas Merton stayed in late 1968. He had come to northern India to immerse himself in Buddhism and prepare for a conference with eastern monks. A few days after leaving St Mary's College, he met his death by an accident in Bangkok. But I felt sure that there were still 'miles to go' before I slept.

One of the professors at St Mary's was the Belgian Jacques Dupuis, with whom I grew closer after he transferred to Rome and the Gregorian University in 1984. Besides his work as a theological teacher and writer, 'Jim', as he was called, helped Tibetan and other refugees along the frontier of India. A luminous intelligence shone through the glasses perched on his oval face. Wiry and tireless, despite bouts of bad health, he was most energetically hospitable. On our free day (Thursday), he took me to a Buddhist monastery in Ghoom (at the elevation of 8,000 feet) and to a Tibetan self-help refugee camp run by the Dalai Lama's sister-in-law. We pushed on to meet some other people, including the Sherpa Tensing, who shared in

1953 with the New Zealander Edmund Hillary the first proven ascent
of Everest; in the early seventies Tensing headed a mountaineering
school. As Jim raced his Yugoslavian motorcycle along the narrow
roads of the Himalayan foothills, I clung to him for dear life, and
prayed not to fall down the sheer precipices so close to our wheels.
When later that year the staff and students of St Mary's left their
mountain peace and shifted to New Delhi, Jim rode his motorcycle
right across India to his new home.

Change beckoned to me both in Kurseong itself and in Calcutta
where I stopped for a couple of days. Ian Travers-Ball (who had been
a fellow novice in Australia twenty years earlier) took me to see his
ministry among the derelicts, the dying, and the poor. As an ordained
priest he had ceased to be a Jesuit, so that as Brother Andrew he could
create a congregation of men to work alongside Mother Teresa's nuns.
In founding her own congregation, she had left the Loreto sisters.
Both she and Ian had followed a call that took them away from their
settled place in the world to accept the risks involved in such new
enterprises. About two dozen people lived in the small house that
served as Ian's headquarters. I came away from there, boosted by the
gentle happiness with which they shared all things and thinking to
myself: 'This is what the early Christians were like.'

Back to Melbourne

Back in Melbourne in February 1971, the usual round of teaching
began again quickly, but there was one decisive difference—a
remarkable group of twelve Jesuit novices. During the second year
of their novitiate they took my course in fundamental theology, as
others did before and after them. But this group stood out by their
united zest for theological study. Enthusiasm supplied for what they
lacked in academic background. Subsequently I encouraged three of
them to write a collection of prayers, *Three Days* (1974). I was helping

to communicate theological understanding, or at least allowing such understanding to grow. That brought a cheering sense of fulfillment.

Apart from the change of accent, were there any differences between teaching in Boston and Melbourne? On balance I found the American students a shade more active in the class room. In both places the best students produced essays that were excellent in kind and quality. Both situations threw up some unusual people. In Boston my classes included a fifty-year-old woman psychiatrist (who appears in Sylvia Plath's *The Bell Jar*) and an American investor who had been active in Zaire. Over his expensive business suit he continued to wear a tooth and a whistle, symbols of an African tribe that had adopted him. One Jesuit in Boston painted five studies of Christ's resurrection in lieu of an essay. We spent an afternoon discussing and interpreting these large canvases. In Melbourne a beautiful Norwegian, the wife of an exiled Czech musician, topped the class in 1973. Six months earlier another brilliant student, Marc Playoust, died in a car smash just a few days before he was to be ordained a priest. At the age of thirty-five he had left his post in the medical faculty of Sydney University to enter the Society of Jesus. He planned to study for a doctorate at Harvard Divinity School. I had supported his application and found a supervisor for him. When I received news of Marc's death, I phoned the registrar at HDS and explained that there was now no point in handling his application. Few phone calls have ever been so painful. The registrar impressed me when he wrote later to sympathize over the sharp loss that he guessed I had felt.

From 1968 to 1973, I taught over twenty different groups in Boston and Melbourne. In size these classes ranged from fifty-five to a dozen students. Their moods, needs, abilities, and limitations varied greatly. I recall with gratitude the way they always challenged me to put aside preconceptions, scrutinize each group for its special qualities, and work together in that precious student-teacher relationship.

From 1969 a close friendship developed with George Hunsinger, a student from HDS who took two of my courses. I introduced him to Jürgen Moltmann, supported his applications (when he won a grant to study with Moltmann for a year and then was accepted for doctoral studies at Yale), and encouraged the editor of *Heythrop Journal* to accept two articles George wrote. From the outset I admired the way he combined social responsibility with theological study. After his undergraduate years at Stanford University, he spent some time teaching underprivileged children in New York before beginning at HDS. I was delighted at his progress that eventually brought him to occupy a chair at Princeton Theological Seminary, as well as to lead Christians and others in opposition to government toleration of torture.

But to return to my 1971 stay in Australia. Those six months took me past some family milestones. In April, my eldest sister, Moira, celebrated her twenty-fifth wedding anniversary. In June I turned forty. My diary listed the range of engagements that ate up much free time: speaking at La Trobe University on the current state of Christian theology; incorporating green balloons and a liturgical dance into a service for students on Easter as 'the Greening of Christianity'; flying north to Bathurst to give eight lectures at an autumn conference; delivering a paper on contemporary theology at Monash University and Melbourne University; lecturing to two hundred nuns on faith and hope; describing for some university chaplains my experience of chaplaincies overseas; taking part in a panel discussion on my newly published *Foundations of Theology*; and helping to entertain Hans Küng when he visited Australia.

When Küng arrived at Melbourne airport, I walked out onto the tarmac to welcome him off the plane. None of his Anglican hosts at Trinity had ever met him before. I was relieved when he recognized and greeted me, as the Australian Broadcasting Commission's cameras were already whirring and our handshake was to open a film,

Meet Hans Küng. As a friendly gesture on the part of Catholics in Melbourne, I encouraged my sister Moira to hold a cocktail party in his honour. Archbishop James Knox pleaded a previous engagement and did not attend. But he did invite Küng to meet him a few days later. They exchanged gifts: Knox gave his visitor a book on Mother Teresa of Calcutta and received from him a copy of *Infallible?* The Catholic Archbishop of Melbourne was not intent on simply snubbing the *enfant terrible* of Catholic theologians, who had chosen to mark the centenary of the First Vatican Council by challenging papal infallibility. Up to a thousand people came each evening to hear Küng's five lectures at Melbourne University. When he spoke on infallibility, he frustrated many in the audience. He never thrilled the liberals or horrified the conservatives by actually saying, 'The Pope is not infallible.'

In the second volume of his autobiography, when Küng tells the story of his Melbourne visit, he changes my surname to 'O'Connor'. He also moves the reception I arranged from my sister's home in the city to our 'family estate'. He says nothing about his friendly meeting with Archbishop Knox.[2]

A week later at a meeting of the Australian and New Zealand Society for Theological Studies staged in Sydney University, I took as my subject Küng's anti-infallibility book and the 'Honest to Infallibility' debate that it prompted. I drew attention to two lines of criticism. First, he exaggerated the status that some conservative Catholic theologians attributed to the papal rejection of 'artificial' birth control. It became easier to reject their arguments, once he had maximized their claims. Paul VI himself had gone out of his way, at the publication of *Humanae Vitae*, to indicate that he made no claim to be teaching infallibly. Second, some ambiguities and confusion drifted through Küng's own account of religious truth and error. He responded to my paper in his cheerful and self-assured

---

2 *Disputed Truth: Memoirs*, trans. J. Bowden (London: Continuum, 2008), 199.

way. He correctly noted that my observations largely coincided with criticisms others had made, reiterated his position, and pressed on. In the subsequent stages of the infallibility debate he continued to insist that no one had shown that his challenge to infallibility needed any real correction, revision, or serious clarification. All the same, I was grateful to him that he pushed me into reflecting further on the Church and my responsibility towards its life and growth. He championed the cause of freedom within the Church. But the last few months of 1971 forced on my attention the sufferings of a wider world, which had already confronted me earlier that year in Calcutta.

Suffering and Joy

Shortly after I reached Boston to begin my semester's teaching for Weston College, United States marshals ended a riot at Attica prison by shooting dozens of black convicts and at the same time killing some guards who had been held hostage. The senseless massacre outraged me, and I joined a demonstration outside the federal penitentiary in Danbury, Connecticut. During the march past the gaol a middle-aged driver spotted my clerical collar, stopped his large car, and roared angrily at me: 'What the hell do you think you are doing, Father? Are you a proper priest, who would get up and give me the last sacraments at three in the morning?' I hesitated to reply, since he would have been even further enraged if he heard my Australian accent and realized that I was not even an American. Behind me there was a quiet Jesuit from western Massachusetts, who had decided to remain incognito by wearing an open-necked shirt. He dropped his normal reticence and shouted at the motorist: 'Why don't you sell your Cadillac and give the money to the poor?'

A week later I went to New York for a weekend conference on hope and the future of humanity. More than eight hundred theologians, seminarians, teachers, and students attended to hear lectures from representatives of three currents of thought: the theologians of hope, process theologians, and the exponents of Pierre Teilhard de Chardin's evolutionary optimism. Moltmann came to present one of the main papers. He pointed out sharply that the invited participants included no women, no poor people, no one from the third world, and only one black theologian, James Cone. 'What on earth am I doing', I asked myself, 'flying down from Boston to share in this gathering of affluent white theologians?' The world was not waiting breathlessly to hear what we would decide about humanity's future. The protest at Danbury the previous Saturday probably altered nothing, but at least the speakers looked more convincing: the mother of a black prisoner awaiting trial for murder, a bishop in exile, a conscientious objector who had been gaoled during the Second World War, and a priest charged with conspiring to kidnap Henry Kissinger.

Scenes and images of suffering kept sweeping down on me during that semester. At a symposium on prisons a man who had served a fifteen-year sentence sweated and shook in front of me. When I went down to Philadelphia to lecture on Christ's resurrection, some friends took me to dine in a restaurant. At the next table a man walked out on his woman companion, who drank herself unconscious and was carried out by the cook. When we finished our meal, we strolled down a street crowded with young people wandering around in a drugged stupor. Just before the semester ended, I crashed into Daniel Ellsberg at the Harvard Faculty Club. He looked anxious and harried, waiting to go on trial for having threatened American interests in Vietnam by releasing to the press 'the Pentagon Papers'. One of my students took me to an early performance of *Godspell*. For days the song from the crucified Jesus ('Oh God, I'm dying') kept running through my head.

Even after I left Boston, suffering caught up with me during a brief stopover in Dublin. I attended the funeral of General Richard Mulcahy, an Irish revolutionary who fought in the 1916 rising, served as Chief of Staff of the Irish Republican Army during the war of independence (1919-21), was a close associate of Michael Collins, and survived (despite the posters which announced 'Wanted Collins and Mulcahy: Dead or Alive') to become head of the army in the Irish Republic. Under a grey sky I watched the mourners file out of the church: Eamon de Valera, T.F. O'Higgins (the nephew of Kevin O'Higgins, an assassinated minister of justice), Erskine Childers (whose father had been executed on orders from Kevin O'Higgins), Jack Lynch (still Taoiseach or Prime Minister of the Irish Republic), and eight veterans of 1916 who formed a guard of honour. I thought of the violence that had in 1969 exploded once again in the north, little guessing that it would engulf the south and spread across the sea to England.

In retrospect the Mulcahy funeral looks like a hinge-point, after which I was swept through various episodes of enriching joy. My Dublin cousins entertained me at a dinner that saw the conversation fluttering from one brilliant moment to another. During four days in London I twice visited the Hogarth and Blake exhibitions at the Tate Gallery, sat entranced through two plays in which Jill Bennett, Sir Alec Guinness, and Ralph Richardson starred, and felt warmed by the hospitality the Jesuit faculty gave me at Heythrop College, now situated in Cavendish Square. We talked theology until midnight, while the professor of liturgy danced away in the background to the music of *Godspell*. Richard Incledon invited me home to Cambridge for Christmas. Contrasting poems about Christ's birth enthralled me at the prayer service that preceded Midnight Mass. On Christmas afternoon the choir boys threw their stove-pipe hats into the air when they streamed out of evensong, ran across the lawns of King's College, and left for their vacation. I went back to Fisher House, where we sat down at half past six and rose from the table after midnight—to end the little eternity of a perfect Christmas dinner in England.

Paris was the last stop before I paused in Tübingen for seven weeks of research and writing. Cheering sunlight streamed down on

New Year's Eve as I hurried along the boulevards to visit a Van Gogh exhibition and then exult over sixty-five paintings by Monet in the Musée Marmotan. His son's death had released them to the public view. That evening John and Monica Ellison took me to a dinner party in the Latin Quarter. No one seemed to resent my halting French or the fact that I made the thirteenth at the table. I felt free enough to get up and dance in the New Year with my cousin—the first time I had danced for more than twenty years.

At Stuttgart airport I fell into the arms of George Hunsinger and his wife Susan, who drove me south to Tübingen. German friends welcomed me back, my work on *The Easter Jesus* rushed ahead happily, and I delighted in introducing George to Ernst Käsemann, Karl Rahner, and other veteran scholars. With what I hoped was innocent pride I showed off my first real disciple.

Through those six months from September 1971 until February 1972, I could trace a pattern in images of suffering and episodes of joy. For the most part I merely witnessed the suffering, but experienced the joy. These fugitive events nourished a growing sense that my life must somehow mirror more clearly Christ's dying and rising. They played a part in preparing me for the last struggle on my midlife journey.

Deciding

For eighteen months decisions repeatedly arose about jobs in the United States, Australia, New Zealand, England, and Rome. I came to loathe the procedures involved in reaching those decisions. Yet they forced me to face two questions. What did I really want to do with my life? And where?

The sequence began easily in late 1971. A friend persuaded his college in California to offer me the chairmanship of the theology department at any salary I cared to nominate. It was flattering, but I turned down the invitation without the slightest hesitation. Retiring to the beautiful campus of a small, liberal arts college made little sense. The only appeal was utterly marginal, the whimsical desire to collaborate in a plan to build something unique in the United States, a department staffed largely by theologians who had studied in Tübingen.

Then just before I left Boston in December 1971, Weston College invited me to take up a full time appointment. The offer promised both to end my journeying and to provide a peaceful home in a vigorous theological environment. From his perch at the Australian National University, John Eddy proved mildly encouraging, when I wrote seeking his advice:

> About the Weston appointment, I am not surprised and really cannot advise you not to pitch your tent among the New Englanders. It is a first rate set-up, academically, ecumenically, socially etc. I was hoping, through ANU, to help reconcile country and calling for you; and indeed there will be good opportunities opening up. But in the meantime life is running out with uncomfortable rapidity. So, my support for whatever you decide. All is vanity. Love for Christmas.

Without thinking matters through in prayerful depth, I asked the Australian provincial, still Peter Kelly, to approve my accepting the invitation from Weston College:

> I would very much like to take up this offer, above all for the chance it offers to do my theological work more effectively and for a wider audience. I hesitate to say what 'good' my teaching and writing of theology does for people training for the ministry, for the Catholic Church, and for a wider public. But I am sure of the demanding stimulus, which I have received during four fall semesters (1968-71), from students and faculty members of

the Boston Theological Institute. Through the BTI with its more than 1,200 students, members of my classes come from Boston University, Harvard Divinity School, and other schools, as well as from Weston College itself. The book I am completing on Christ's resurrection, articles in *Theological Studies* (September 1970), the *Catholic Biblical Quarterly* (October 1971), and the *Scottish Journal of Theology* (to appear) were all generated by work at Weston. I have certainly not rushed into this request. Between 1969 and 1971 I turned down two firm offers and two tentative offers from other theology departments in the USA, without bothering to raise the matter with you. It is not that I am anxious to live in America. In a sense it would have been easier to have turned down Weston's offer, continued to teach there merely in the fall, and returned to Melbourne for the March-August period each year. But if I am to 'do' theology for the rest of my working life, I would like to do it as well as possible, for the largest number of people, and as effectively 'outside' the Church as well as within it.

Peter Kelly reluctantly agreed to my request, but, from the point of view of the Australian Jesuit Province made his own misgivings clear: 'I do not think that highly qualified men from the province, trained by the province, should accept long term appointments elsewhere, unless their doing so is manifestly for the greater service of God. I am not convinced that your accepting the Weston offer is manifestly for this greater service.' He went on to raise questions about my motives: 'I am not sure, I simply do not know, whether the reason really behind your desire is truly the greater service of God, or whether it comes from more personal ambition. I do not like putting this in writing, but would like to discuss it with you face to face. Since, however, you require an answer before the end of the month [February 1972], I feel I must say so.' Peter ended his long letter gently: 'All the implicit judgements made about you in this letter may, so far as they seem to be unfavourable, be quite wrong. So I what I put before you I put rather as matter that you should think on, and if possible discuss with someone truly spiritual and yet close enough for you to talk easily to.'

My provincial's letter shook me. Quite apart from any particular points, it made me admit to myself that I had failed to reflect deeply on the responsibilities and opportunities facing me. Just before his letter arrived, another invitation abruptly changed the situation. Fr René Latourelle, the dean of the Theology Faculty at the Gregorian University in Rome, asked me to take a teaching post there. At that time about a thousand students from seventy-five countries studied theology at the Gregorian, which badly needed more English-speaking professors and a large injection of younger staff. Its theological faculty had been remarkably stable for years. But Juan Alfaro, Zoltan Alszeghy, Maurizio Flick, and others who had helped to 'liberalize' the Roman scene were moving towards retirement. The Gregorian offer attracted me, made all my self-questioning about ultimate goals suddenly flare up again, and quenched my desire to accept the Weston College invitation. If I were to live outside the Australian Jesuit Province, Rome appeared to have a stronger claim than Boston.

I returned to Melbourne, turned down the offer from Weston College, and decided to spend an eight-day retreat praying and reflecting on my future. Back in Australia I heard that Sydney University and some other universities (besides the ANU) seemed poised to introduce religious studies. A position was vacant in that field at the University of Canterbury in Christchurch, New Zealand. The hunger for a fixed home became stronger than ever. My mind fluttered uneasily from one possibility to another: Rome, the Jesuit Theological College in Parkville, or the post in Christchurch. The last choice would not involve living outside the Australian Jesuit Province, which included New Zealand. On the eve of starting my retreat, I wrote to Peter Kelly on 22 May:

> It seems that three 'areas' need to be considered: the Gregorian; the
> Australian Province and, in particular, the JTC; and myself. (1) The

Gregorian: that university needs young, effective, English-speaking theologians. It offers the chance of having a wide effect in Catholic theology, especially as most of those in graduate studies become seminary professors. (2) The JTC: I will in any case (i.e. if the Gregorian invitation were accepted) be teaching there in the first term of 1973. Fr Jim Lyons would be back from Oxford in March 1974, and is willing to take on teaching fundamental theology.[3] (3) Myself: I would deeply welcome the chance and stimulus that the Gregorian would offer. But I have been through all that with you before. I can think of many objections against granting the permission to accept the invitation: (1) If I don't go to the Gregorian, Latourelle could pick up substitutes elsewhere. (2) If I were permitted to leave the province (for a 3-5 year period at the Gregorian), what if others receive similar invitations? Where would it all stop? With numbers of teachers in theology so limited, how could the JTC survive? (3) The needs of the Australian Province are obvious; the needs of the wider Church are vaguer, and the role I could play in meeting them less clear. (4) I am succumbing to sheer personal ambition. Talk about helping Church theology is a mere cloak for ladder-climbing. (5) I ought not leave this province unless it is manifestly for the greater glory of God. And this is hardly the case. I really don't know what to say in my own mind, let alone to others, about these and similar objections. Take no (4). Anyone who decides to move from a 'smaller operation' to a 'larger operation' is open to that objection. What one man calls initiative another would call ambition. Or take no (5). I really don't know how that condition could ever be fulfilled—in my case or anyone else's. The future is so obscure. I don't know how my theology will develop here or elsewhere, or how it will help others. Nor is it clear what will help me to grow as a man of faith and a Jesuit priest.

The other thing that has come up is a post in Christchurch. Very briefly, I see this post as a chance of reaching a post in religious

---

3 Sadly Jim Lyons died of a melanoma before returning to Australia; in Oxford he was awarded the DPhil posthumously.

studies back in Australia in a few years time, not just a chance but in the circumstances a necessary condition. The way to Sydney University or the ANU might have to lead via Christchurch. All that I have said and written to you before about teaching religion on a secular campus is still there affecting my 'feelings'. It is something that I would very happily do.

My retreat ended with the decision to apply for the lectureship in Christchurch. Yet another letter to Peter Kelly set out my main reasons.

(1) If Australian Jesuits are to work anywhere as teachers on the university faculties, it should be in programmes and departments of religious studies. (2) For some years (at least since 1967) I have experienced a deep desire and steady call to teach within a university context. This call and desire to teach on a university campus led, as you know, to my request to accept a lectureship at Cambridge University and again in 1969 to apply for the chair of religious studies at the ANU. (3) The post in Christchurch is a highly desirable and perhaps even necessary step, if I seriously plan to teach religious studies at the ANU or elsewhere in Australia. (4) In Christchurch and after that back in Australia, I would not be off the scene for the Australian Province, as a Gregorian appointment would involve.

My retreat notes recorded the jumble of obscure motives that rose within me. Did Rome look attractive partly because I found European life pleasant? The Gregorian offered long summer vacations which I could spend studying and writing in Tübingen. But I wondered whether teaching in Italian would prove tolerable. Was the supply of theological students at the Gregorian going to dry up? [In fact, enrolment grew after I arrived full time at the Gregorian.] That Roman university still looked too much like a male 'clerical ghetto'. Comparatively few lay people, women, and non-Catholics studied there. Nevertheless, wherever it was to be, I longed 'to find and settle down in some work to which I could devote myself wholeheartedly'. The question prodded me: 'Why give up on the Australian scene now, just when so many things are about to happen?' During the retreat three issues threw some light on the road ahead: the needs of the Christian Church both in Australia and overseas, the apostolic work proper to Jesuits, and the problem of my own spiritual growth. The 'call to teach within a university context', which I had consistently experienced, pointed towards Christchurch.

In reaching that decision my confessor and spiritual director, Patrick O'Sullivan, helped greatly. Through the early seventies we met every month when I was in Australia. He listened to the interminable story of my confusion, absolved me from my sins, and gently led me to reflect prayerfully on what I finally wanted from life. Our routine followed a set pattern. We poured a drink, before sitting down in front of a small electric radiator. I looked across at my large, prematurely white-haired friend, and talked incessantly, while he sucked a pipe and sipped his drink. Patrick's sheer presence exuded the feeling that he cared deeply that I should find stronger faith and lasting peace. After one meeting I noted: 'It is remarkable how liberated and calm I feel after having got it all out in the open with Patrick.' The reflections I jotted down after those ninety minute sessions show how I groped my way towards the goal of my journey:

> (1) Is it more important to identify myself as priest, Jesuit etc. through what I am than through what I *do*? (2) Does my faith in Christ coincide with my present situation? Or do I remain a Jesuit-priest, because of the opportunities for good influence it affords, because I wish to stick to my word, because I love the men I have come to know in the order etc, BUT NOT precisely because of my faith in Christ? (3) Is remaining where I am tantamount to choosing death over life, the past over the future? (4) What texts from Jesus do I find life-giving for me? The text about 'eunuchs for the kingdom of heaven', 'carrying one's cross', or 'I have come

that they may have life and have it more abundantly'? (5) What
does my hope for the resurrection mean for me in the concrete?

During that time of deciding in 1972, I looked for help also from
the work of an American Jesuit, John Futrell, on Ignatian spirituality,
Making an Apostolic Community of Love. Clear assurance had been
eluding me. To my surprise, Futrell spoke to my muddled state when
he noted how St Ignatius Loyola appreciated 'the extreme difficulty of
arriving at complete certitude about the will of God, especially in the
sometimes baffling complexity of concrete circumstances' (p. 107).
This book forced me to acknowledge that fixing some permanent
place of ministry must also mean discovering and asserting my
personal identity. 'All the factors of one's past and present self-
awareness', Futrell wrote, find 'their coherence in the commitment of
oneself to a certain life-form' (pp. 179-80).

The decision to decline the Gregorian's invitation and apply for the
Christchurch post involved a mass of practical details. With the dean
of the JTC and others, I began working out tentative arrangements
for someone to take over my lectures there in 1973. I wrote to Dennis
Nineham and others, asking them to support my application. In
such cases I normally wrote again to thank them for agreeing, and
then a third time to let them know the outcome. The University of
Canterbury in Christchurch sent the relevant forms, required a medical
examination, and then eliminated my name without shortlisting me.
Some weeks later several friends in Cambridge suggested that I
apply for an assistant lectureship that had become available in the
Divinity Faculty. I applied, still hoping to find my journey's end on
a secular campus. There was another flurry of correspondence with
my provincial, several referees, and the faculty. Again I was eliminated
without being shortlisted.

It left me stunned to be set aside so quickly both in Christchurch and Cambridge. A couple of years later someone from Christchurch told me that, although the vice-chancellor had received my application with delight, the department had really wanted someone in comparative religion, even if their advertisement had not said so. I stared back blankly when the man from Christchurch asked, 'Didn't you know that?' In late 1972 I had received only a brief and unexplained note of rejection. I knew that only one or two members of the department in Christchurch matched my own qualifications. The outcome seemed an absurd anticlimax, after I had taken such elaborate pains before reaching a conscientious decision to apply.

Coming so soon after my unsuccessful application for Christchurch, my rapid elimination from the Cambridge list induced a sharp bout of self-doubt. Four years earlier, some members of the Divinity Faculty had wanted me to stay in Cambridge. Now I did not even reach the shortlist for the very position I had let go in 1968. Did my former teachers believe that my theological promise had dribbled away into a soup of mediocre books and articles? Ironically the only publications (that I knew of) by the successful candidate, several reviews, included an enthusiastic welcome to my *Foundations of Theology*.

A sense of meaninglessness flared up again. My mind tried to cope with the failure to find a permanent home in Canberra, Christchurch, or Cambridge by falling back on an empty cliché: 'Life must be teaching me something.' But suddenly a destination came in sight, and I found myself on the last lap of my journey.

Choosing Rome

When I declined Latourelle's invitation to teach permanently at the Gregorian, I agreed to offer a three-week course in January 1973. I would then be on my way home to Melbourne after a fifth and final semester of teaching in Boston, and could stop in Rome as happily as anywhere else. A manuscript that I was completing would easily provide the material for a seminar (in English) on the theology of secularity. During my five weeks in Rome, Latourelle for the second time offered me a chair in fundamental theology. Once again I could appreciate the arguments favouring acceptance. The Gregorian needed younger, English-speaking theologians. It provided the chance of promoting healthier trends in the Catholic Church. Many of its graduates taught in seminaries around the world. About a quarter of all Catholic bishops and even more cardinals had studied at the Gregorian. But once again I could acknowledge good reasons for turning down Latourelle's invitation. How far would teaching half my courses in a foreign language (Italian) inhibit theological expression and discussion? I feared that church politics still choked true freedom at Roman universities. I refused to rush to a decision, talked the matter over with friends, and then found myself encouraged to accept by three events: the Díez-Alegría affair, a visit to Cardinal John Wright, and a High Mass at St Peter's Basilica.

Fr José Maria Díez-Alegría was a smiling, sickly Spaniard, who taught sociology at the Gregorian until he published a book against the wishes of the Jesuit superior general. *I Believe in Hope* argued that Marxism included some points of value, that the Vatican's wealth could hardly be reconciled with Christ's good news to the poor, and that the Catholic Church should stop imposing compulsory celibacy on priests of the Western rite—something that has never been the case with priests of the Eastern rites. None of this was new. But now it came from a Jesuit teaching at a papal university in Rome, whose brother, an army general, headed the liberal group within the Spanish military. Newspapers in Italy and elsewhere blew the story up. The Vatican put pressure on both the Jesuit order and the Gregorian University to penalize Díez-Alegría. His support of the Italian divorce law had already made him a marked man.

An American priest, who was also a visiting professor at the Gregorian, joined me in writing a letter to the rector and asking for an interview. We admitted that we lacked accurate information about what had transpired between Díez-Alegría and his religious superiors. But we defended his right to retain his professorial position, whatever problems he might face within the Jesuit order. If he lost his place on the faculty, this would seem 'but another case of proper academic and Christian freedom being denied in Rome'. Poor Díez-Alegría went back to Spain. But I was glad to have made my protest, found to my surprise that the Gregorian did not withdraw its invitation to me, and no longer felt so ill at ease about any nasty side of ecclesiastical studies in Rome. At least the university knew where I stood on such issues.

One morning an American friend took me off to visit Cardinal Wright, the former Archbishop of Pittsburgh who now served as prefect of the Vatican's Congregation for the Clergy. It scandalized me to meet a man like that holding such a position of authority. The anger breaks through the entry in my diary:

> We arrived at Wright's office at eleven. After a brief wait the Cardinal dashed into the room to greet me: 'I believe you're an Australian, a Jesuit and a theologian, three things I don't like.' After this preliminary jollification, away he went on various topics: Leonard Feeney (who had been his confessor), Pius XII (whom he had visited apropos of the Feeney affair), Pierre Teilhard de Chardin (with whom he spoke in New York a few days before his death in 1955), the Díez-Alegría affair, and the state of the American clergy about which we disagreed. (He tried to play down the crisis.) He told me that when he was in Boston three years ago, he took a cab over to watch the police break up a demonstration by Harvard students. He was standing looking over a fence next to the wife of Arthur Schlesinger.[4] 'Did you see that?', he asked her. 'The police brutality?' 'No', he replied, 'the police finesse.' (A

---

4 An American historian and social critic, Arthur Schlesinger Jr (1917-2007) was a special assistant during the Kennedy administration.

policeman had just clubbed four students to the ground with four strokes of his 'billy', without needing to move a step). 'Pusey will pay for this', she said. (A short time later Nathan Pusey announced his resignation as Harvard's President. It was he who had called the police in.)

When I was there in Wright's office, Mrs Golda Meir drove by to visit Pope Paul VI. 'The first leading lady from that part of the world to visit a pope since St Helena', the cardinal quipped; 'and this one is not bringing relics.' Wright talked too about ex-bishop James Shannon and their recent correspondence. Shannon had remarked wistfully: 'Sometimes I wonder whether you or I have done more harm to the Church.'[5]

If the Gregorian's toleration of my 'intervention' in the Díez-Alegría affair had banished a reason against settling in Rome, meeting Cardinal Wright provided strong motivation for accepting the university's invitation. During my long conversation with him my mind darted back to an evening spent in New York just two months earlier. As usual, I had come down from Boston for Thanksgiving weekend. I decided to see a production of *Much Ado About Nothing,* and found myself a few rows from Richard Nixon, his family, and a sinister friend, the Florida banker Bebe Rebozo (1912-98). Earlier in the month Nixon had annihilated George McGovern in the 1972 presidential elections. He had also just ordered American planes out over North Vietnam to club his opponents into signing an agreement to end the war. When the presidential party rushed out of the theatre at the end of the play, some people clapped, others hissed, but most of us stood silent. On the other side of the world people were dying that night on Nixon's orders.

For me, Cardinal Wright recalled insistently the corrupt and

---

5 James Patrick Shannon (1921-2003), who had been an auxiliary bishop in Minneapolis and prominent in social justice issues, resigned his ministry in protest against *Humanae Vitae* and married a divorced woman.

murderous insolence of his president. At least, for better or worse, that is how I put it to myself. It amazed me that the cardinal could talk in such a self-incriminating way with a total stranger. My distaste for his attitudes reached its peak when he blandly dismissed all the priests who had left the ministry: 'They made two mistakes—getting ordained and marrying the women they did.' I thought sadly of one ex-priest who had taken two courses with me in Boston. He remained unmarried and continued his pastoral ministry by working part time for a Protestant minister. 'My bishop', he told me, 'was John Wright, and I found him a pig.'

My angry disgust at Cardinal Wright unfairly ignored his liberal past and permanently good qualities. But that disgust helped create a perspective that organized my future. During my five weeks in Rome I dined at one college after another and talked with students from every continent. 'Hungry sheep', I thought to myself. I could at least try to offer them both personal concern and theological instruction, as well as support attitudes different from those represented by the cardinal.

When reflecting back on one's life, it is, of course, only too easy to impose patterns rather than take time to find them. But in early 1973 several reflections broke through to give order to much of my experience. My mind could no longer be satisfied with such appeals to life as one drawn from St Irenaeus of Lyons that was much in vogue then: 'The glory of God is man fully alive.' The glory of God, I recognized, had once been a wounded Man who stumbled, fell, and became fully dead. I jotted down the thoughts that came to mind: 'The man who dreams to nourish himself only with the positive dimension of his experience will never live fully and responsibly. I must accept the losses, the broken dreams, hostility, and pain. We have to accept both life *and* death.' Ordinary as they were, such thoughts drained away my sense of quiet desperation. The feeling of hollow meaninglessness faded.

It now looked as if my desire to teach on a secular campus sprang, at least partly, from a deep reluctance to commit myself fully and finally to the life and ministry of celibate priesthood in the Society of Jesus. A well paid job at the ANU or elsewhere would have insured my future, if ever I were to retract my decision of 1968. Perhaps Canberra was really a foiled escape route. At any rate, my vocation survived in the end, when I accepted the broken hopes and let some things die. The decision to teach at the Gregorian came with inevitable ease.

On Sunday morning I went to a High Mass at St Peter's and heard a voice within me saying quietly, 'Come to Rome.' One can and perhaps should offer a natural explanation of this 'voice'. But from that moment feelings of confusion about my future faded away for good. I stepped out into the wintry sunshine to wait for the Pope's midday address. Some of the crowd smiled at a man who wandered around holding up a large sign: 'Don't believe the priests. Keep your money for yourselves.' From his window the Pope welcomed the armistice in Vietnam, which came into effect that day. Then he mentioned the thirty cardinals he had just created: 'They show the catholicity of the Church.' I chuckled to myself: 'Come, come—eight Italians out of thirty! Surely a bit unbalanced?' Through the flood of sunshine I crossed the Tiber, passed some Jesus people singing, laughing, and playing their guitars, threaded my way through children in the Piazza Navona, and went home in peace for lunch at the Gregorian.

Leaving Australia

Five days later I flew home to Melbourne for my final stay in Australia (February-September 1973). Work for the renewal for church life engaged me at once. The Fortieth International Eucharistic Congress took place. I had helped to plan an ecumenical conference as part of the proceedings. My committee had to cope with a vicar-general of the archdiocese, who seemed to dislike or even fear ecumenical leaders from overseas. Fortunately study leave at Oxford took him away during our planning period. When he rose to leave early from his last appearance at the committee meetings, he offered a final comment on the suggested list of participants: 'There are too many foreign names.' In my new mood, however, such criticism gave me fresh determination to work towards the goal: a truly international conference which might encourage the Christian churches in Australia to seek unity more effectively. I invited Jürgen Moltmann to come and stay with me at the Jesuit Theological College. One evening in the Melbourne Town Hall, he joined Mother Teresa of Calcutta and spoke to three thousand people on the Christian vocation to spread peace. He teased me afterwards: 'Is that what you wanted to do at the Eucharistic Congress? Make a team out of a Catholic saint and a leading Protestant theologian?'

During the congress I made my second appearance on television. The Australian Broadcasting Commission produced a forty-five-minute documentary on inter-church relations and Christian issues. I felt quite at ease in stating my views: 'Yes, I do want to live my Christian life with and under a pope. But I hope to see power decentralized in the Catholic Church. Yes, I do expect inter-communion in the coming years, and before too long optional celibacy for Catholic priests in the western rite.'

During the congress I went to the opening of a seminary at which Cardinal Wright spoke. His message mitigated the negative view of him that I had carried back from Rome. He contrasted a Greek maxim ('know yourself') and a central theme from the best of the Romans ('control yourself') with what Christian love required: 'Give yourself.'

After the congress I joined a group of Christian theologians in contributing to a world-wide study initiated by the Faith and Order Commission in Geneva. The theme ('Giving an Account of the Hope that is within us') amounted to a question: how should one express

Christian faith and hope in terms appropriate to our time and country? I wrote an Australian Creed. The full text was published in various places, including the final pages of my *Faith Under Fire* (Polding Press, 1974). Let me quote the final three verses:

> I believe in our hopes for a great human family as Christ wishes it;
> in hopes fostered by memories
> and banishing from the land of the Holy Spirit the stupor of despair.
> I believe in myself,
> in the mobility that God has bestowed on me to experience the greatest of all joys,
> to give myself on my road to Emmaus and Jericho.
> And I hope for living waters to flow from the dead heart of Christ
> to transform our heart of death into the image of the risen God.

I wrote this prayer as part of my ecumenical commitment, a contribution to the Faith and Order group in Melbourne. But it was also a way of trying to make peace with my native country.

At a farewell party a lecturer from Monash University stirred my dormant anger by remarking, 'Australia has let you down.' A woman broadcaster asked me to give a radio interview before I left. She asked about my future work and stirred old frustrations by her exorbitant comment, 'It's the usual story. A prophet has no honour in his own country.' My feelings rallied their forces to make a final campaign of resentment against Australian universities for disdaining so far religious studies. But I determined to say a grateful goodbye. My last engagement was at an inter-church conference, where I explained my creed and argued that our prayers should include such national imagery as 'the land of the Holy Spirit' and 'the dead heart'.

The Australian Creed also expressed a farewell to my fellow Jesuits and family. For five years I had taught for the Jesuit Theological College. At times I missed the spontaneous affection and easy companionship which the American priests and scholastics offered.

In Boston I had shared a house with seven or eight other Jesuits. It was easy to relate personally to them. But at the JTC my emotions and concerns seemed split between the smaller 'group' and the larger 'community'. The ten of us who lived in two terrace houses made up the group. We took meals together at weekends, prayed together most days, and shared one or two Masses together each week. The twenty or thirty other Jesuits in the adjacent houses made up one community with its chapel, dining room, and frequent activities in common. My loyalties remained divided until the last year. The group claimed me then. Decades earlier the fireplace in our sitting room had been sealed up. We tore it open, rebuilt it, and made trips into the countryside to collect wood. I covered the walls with a print of Tübingen, a small carpet from the Tibetan self-help refugee camp in the foothills of the Himalayas, an old print of the city of Trier, and other spoils from my journeys. For the first time since my childhood at Rock Lodge I spent hours sitting with others before a fragrant fire—grateful that I could 'kind love both give and get'.

Shortly before I left Melbourne, Polding Press agreed to publish two books of mine: a large edition of my grandfather's letters and a slim volume of theological essays, *Faith Under Fire*. I dedicated the former to my group and the latter to the whole JTC community. That preference indicated the happy peace I felt with those nine Jesuits at 159/161 Royal Parade.

In mid-1973 my brother Jim and his wife Posey rebuilt Rock Lodge. They farewelled me at an elegant dinner party for my closest friends in our renovated family home. The great mahogany table was gleaming and glorious, comforting love surrounded me, but I felt a little relieved to be moving away from Melbourne. My mother, four married brothers and sisters, their spouses, nineteen nephews and nieces, as well as uncles, aunts and cousins, made my family seem omnipresent. I delighted in their company, took pride in their achievements, but came to find the close presence of the whole team

somewhat constricting and consuming. In any case, each year two
or three of them were sure to visit Europe, attending conferences,
studying, or simply taking a trip. On my side I looked forward to
seeing them in Australia through my being asked to return for speaking
engagements. The link of deep love remained. But my journey had
called me to move abroad, and no longer live at close quarters with
such a united and affectionate family.

Pembroke College offered me a peaceful stopping place for a
sabbatical year as a honoured visitor (1973/74), the final stage of my
path to Rome. The Ninehams had returned to Oxford; the Carnleys
had gone home to Australia. But other friends welcomed me back to
Cambridge. The old bedmaker for my rooms in the Orchard Building
stood by my desk one morning in late November and informed me:
'They usually get married out of this set. I've had three fellows in this
set and they all got married.' I laughed politely at this piece of news
from a lively great-grandmother. But the mournful brightness of
memory recalled Margaret lifting her head and smiling at me across
that very room. In the afternoon, as the sun slanted across the college
garden, I wrote to Maev, who was now teaching at the University of
Papua New Guinea:

> It's a strange feeling being back in Cambridge, once again in an
> institutional style of living that takes away the strain, knowing
> myself to be much more of a piece, at the end of a mid-point
> journey, with—surprise, surprise—Rome as journey's end. All the
> *outer* journeys of the last few years have fallen into place, because I
> have started to be able to see the *inner* journey that has happened.
> Those words from Robert Frost ('The woods are lovely, dark and
> deep, but I have promises to keep and miles to go before I sleep'),
> which you wrote out for me in 1968 and which I have carried with
> me ever since, suddenly got illuminated in a new way, as the image
> of the journey came home to me. I miss you and all the family
> greatly, but in a bitter-sweet way, a kind of warm and loving way
> that is not hurtful.

Around that time I began writing this autobiography—to tell my story and complete the process of finding myself.

One last journey helped in its own special way to make sense of the road I had taken. Dr Lukas Vischer invited me to attend the Faith and Order Commission meeting at the University of Ghana before I took up residence in Rome. During those two weeks (22 July-5 August 1974), the theological arm of the World Council of Churches revised its consensus statements on baptism, Eucharist, and the ordained ministry. It selected topics for new studies, discussed future steps towards church unity, and drew together a study made by Christians all over the world on 'Giving an Account of the Hope that it is within us'. I enjoyed working with two hundred theologians from nearly fifty countries, wrote reports for journals in Australia, England, Ireland, Italy, New Zealand, and the United States, and found that two experiences in particular threw light on my own hopes.

With some members of the commission I visited the dungeons of Cape Coast Castle to the west of Accra. Bats darted over our heads, as the guide took us through vaulted caverns. In past centuries up to a thousand slaves were held there, before being hurried through three outlets to the beach and the waiting ships. Archaeologists had unearthed beads, pipes, and human bones in the mud-encrusted floor. From one section of the dungeons slaves could hear Christians praying and singing in the chapel directly above them. I climbed up to the main courtyard of the castle, silent and appalled. All those slaves crammed together in stench, darkness, and misery seemed to cry out to me, as they waited to walk their way of the cross. I strolled around the castle wall, looked down into a small courtyard, and noticed three prison officers pacing up and down among groups of convicts. From a wall high above, seven vultures scanned the scene. A prisoner glanced up at me and put two fingers in front of his mouth. I understood his gesture but had no cigarettes to throw down to him. That visit to Cape Coast Castle pushed the question at me: how far was I willing to commit myself in trying to bring peace to suffering men and women?

One Sunday I went with Jürgen Moltmann to a Presbyterian service in Accra. The African congregation thundered out their hymns in the Twi language. From either side we could hear the beat of drums from two 'spiritual' churches, where the Christians sang, clapped their hands, and danced. In our service drums were used only at the offering; the whole service was more sedate, but warm happiness hung in the air. My eye drifted beyond the brightly dressed ladies to the back of the congregation. A giant Ghanaian in a vivid green shirt took off his dark glasses and smiled at me. I felt at home with my brothers and sisters. The joyfulness of their faith cried out the message: 'Keep spreading the good news of Jesus Christ.'

It was just ten years since I first left Australia and visited the Faith and Order secretariat in Geneva. Back in 1964, Lukas Vischer had encouraged my plan to write a doctorate in Rome on some theological issues connected with church union. Instead I had gone to Cambridge, studied in another field, came close to giving up my Jesuit vocation, travelled incessantly, and yearned to keep clear of the institutional churches by teaching religious studies at a secular university in Australia. By bringing me to Accra, Vischer did more for me than simply mark the beginning and end of that decade which made up my mid-point journey. He confronted me with the suffering and vitality of Africans and African Christianity. That encounter injected joy into my determination to accept my place and work in Christ's Church. I would do my best to serve suffering humanity and let Christ's love shine in my world. When we flew from Accra to Rome, however, my mind flicked back to pre-Christian days. I pictured myself as a latter-day Aeneas, washed up on the banks of the Tiber and facing a new destiny ten years after I had left my original home. The decade of 1964 to 1974 fell into shape as kind of minor *Aeneid*.

The travelling was finished. I had found another home. Writing this book both saw me through the last few miles to Rome, and formed the final stage of the journey to myself. Looking back at it all, I did not wish to complain about things or disown any part of the story, as if it belonged to someone else. I wanted only to pass on what I had learnt, without any apology and without too much explanation. Telling the whole tale disarmed the painful elements, gave sense to my world, and made it possible to start again. I now hoped to find not a slow decline into the evening twilight but the dawn of a fresh day. Thanks to the grace of God and the loving support of friends, relatives, and others, I had found my journey's end.

[*Coda.* It was in 1974 that I wrote the above story, drawing on letters, notes, and a diary that went back many years and even decades. Re-reading the manuscript nearly forty years later, I recognize how some of the views expressed are naïve, brash, or even worse, and how thirty-two years of teaching in Rome changed me. But, apart from correcting some factual errors, dropping some paragraphs that seemed tedious, and adding a few notes to identify people, I have left the text more or less as it was. Honesty prevents me from producing a bland and sanitized narrative that would cover up how I experienced life *then*. I prefer to let the story stand, without excusing or apologizing for what I thought and did. Some of my former students and colleagues at the Gregorian may be interested in learning how I came to teach there, and why I found the experience so enriching. They provided a project that gripped me for thirty-two years, the great challenge that I had yearned for.]

Index of Names

434 A Midlife Journey

Rotterdam, Heidrun 357–58
Rotterdam, Paul 357–58
Runyan, Damon 97
Rupp, Gordon 300
Rush, Archbishop Frank 207
Rutherford, Ernest 376
Ryan, Austin 156–57
Ryan, Noel 154–56, 161, 164
Ryan, Peter 228–29
Rynne, Xavier (F. X. Murphy) 223

Salvado, Bishop Rosendo 181
Santamaria, Bob 79–80, 157–60, 183
Schelkle, K. H. 304
Schillebeeckx, Edward 221, 232
Schlesinger, Arthur 413
Schlier, Heinrich 304
Schnackenburg, Rudolf 302
Schneider, Heinrich 265
Schroen, Marie Louise 238
Scofield, Paul 332
Scott, Sir Walter 30
Scullion, John 187, 252, 257
Searle, Geoffrey 279
Seckler, Max 304
Semmelroth, Otto 260
Sempill, Baron William Formes- 50
Shannon, Bishop James Patrick 414
Sheed, Frank 193
Sheen, Bishop Fulton 102
Shepherd, Brigadier-General Lemuel 66
Sheppard, Sir John 170
Shirach, Baldur von 240
Siddons, Sarah 332
Simonds, Archbishop Justin 206, 209
Smart, James 304

Smart, Ninian 276, 285
Smith, George 161
Smith, Ronald Gregor 343
Smyth, John 23
Sobers, Gary 195
Sölle, Dorothea 379–81
Southwell, St Robert 146
Speaight, Robert 195
Spellman, Cardinal Francis 102
Stackhouse, Max 373–74
Stählin, Gustav 302
Stanislaus Kostka, St 310
Steel, David 321
Steffensky, Edmund 379, 381
Stein, Alois 252–54, 267–68
Steinbeck, John 150
Stendahl, Krister 273, 287
Stephenson, Paddy 72, 78–79
Stewart, Douglas 150
Sullivan, John 119
Swain, John 183
Symons, Bill 28–29

Tagore, Rabindrinath 34
Taille, Maurice de la 144
Talbot, Matt 43
Tanquerey, Adolf Alfred 223
Taylor, Bishop Jeremy 72, 334
Taylor, Vincent 187
Teilhard de Chardin, Pierre 190, 339, 401, 413
Tensing (sherpa) 395–96
Teresa of Avila, St 163
Teresa of Calcutta, Blessed Mother 396, 399, 417
Theissen, Gerd 338–39

Thomas à Kempis 123–24, 255
Thomas Aquinas, St 145, 147, 298, 329
Thompson, Francis 104
Thoreau, Henry David 386
Tillich, Paul 187
Torrance, Tom 339–40
Travers-Ball, Ian 396
Triado, Ray 97–98
Tyrrell, George 324

Utzon, Jorn 237

Vawter, Bruce 193, 348
Victoria, Tomás Luis de 151
Vischer, Lukas 238, 421–22
Vögtle, Anton 268

Walsh, Ann 374
Watson, Ken 196
Waugh, Evelyn 97, 145, 185–86, 292
Webster, Alan 328, 342, 359
Webster, Margaret 342
Welles, Orson 310
Werfel, Franz 108
West, D. J. 167–68
West, Morris 307
Westcott, Bishop W. F. 301
Wheeler, Sir Mortimer 280
Wicks, Jared 301–02, 318
Wilamowitz-Moellendorf, Ulrich 374

Wilcken, John 231, 234–40, 247, 340
Wilder, Amos 273
Wilder, Thornton 273
Wilding, Tony 44
Wiles, Maurice 277, 285
Willey, Basil 333
Williams, Bernard 171–72
Williams, Colin 276
Williams, Glanville 321
Williams, Harry 286
Wingren, Gustaf 371
Wisdom, John 281
Witte, Jan 228
Wolfe, Thomas 387
Wolfson, Harry 374
Woodfull, Bill 20–21
Woods, Archbishop Sir Frank 212
Woodward, Kenneth 284
Wren, Christopher 276
Wren, Matthew 276
Wright, Frank Lloyd 110
Wright, George Ernest 373
Wright, Cardinal John 413–15, 417
Wynyard, Diana 181

Yarnold, Ted 293, 311, 320, 325
Yeats, W. B. 270
Young, Archbishop Guilford 207

Zerafa, Andy 128–29

Family Trees

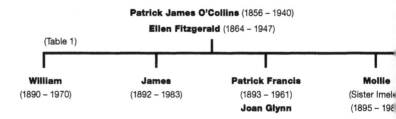

Patrick James O'Collins (1856 – 1940)
Ellen Fitzgerald (1864 – 1947)

(Table 1)

William	James	Patrick Francis	Mollie
(1890 – 1970)	(1892 – 1983)	(1893 – 1961)	(Sister Imel
		Joan Glynn	(1895 – 198

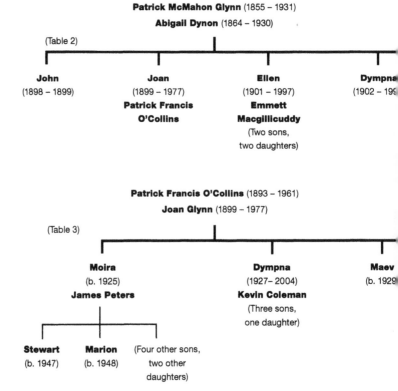

Patrick McMahon Glynn (1855 – 1931)
Abigail Dynon (1864 – 1930)

(Table 2)

John	Joan	Ellen	Dympn
(1898 – 1899)	(1899 – 1977)	(1901 – 1997)	(1902 – 199
	Patrick Francis	Emmett	
	O'Collins	Macgillicuddy	
		(Two sons,	
		two daughters)	

Patrick Francis O'Collins (1893 – 1961)
Joan Glynn (1899 – 1977)

(Table 3)

Moira	Dympna	Maev
(b. 1925)	(1927– 2004)	(b. 1929
James Peters	Kevin Coleman	
	(Three sons,	
	one daughter)	

Stewart	Marion	(Four other sons,
(b. 1947)	(b. 1948)	two other
		daughters)

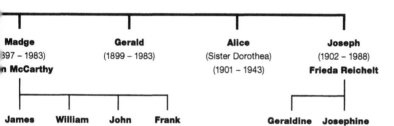

Madge (897 – 1983) n McCarthy | Gerald (1899 – 1983) | Alice (Sister Dorothea) (1901 – 1943) | Joseph (1902 – 1988) Frieda Reichelt

James William John Frank

Geraldine Josephine

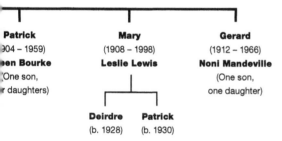

Patrick (904 – 1959) en Bourke (One son, r daughters) | Mary (1908 – 1998) Leslie Lewis | Gerard (1912 – 1966) Noni Mandeville (One son, one daughter)

Deirdre (b. 1928) Patrick (b. 1930)

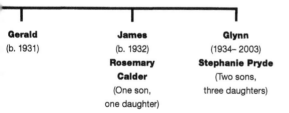

Gerald (b. 1931) | James (b. 1932) Rosemary Calder (One son, one daughter) | Glynn (1934– 2003) Stephanie Pryde (Two sons, three daughters)

Lightning Source UK Ltd.
Milton Keynes UK
UKHW010629261021
392864UK00001B/183

9 780852 448038